REHABILITATE MARX!

RUSSIAN AND EAST EUROPEAN STUDIES
JONATHAN HARRIS, EDITOR

REHABILITATE MARX!

THE CZECHOSLOVAK PARTY INTELLIGENTSIA AND POST-STALINIST MODERNITY

JAN MERVART AND **JIŘÍ RŮŽIČKA**
TRANSLATED FROM THE CZECH BY MELINDA REIDINGER

UNIVERSITY OF PITTSBURGH PRESS

This book is the result of research carried out at the Institute of Philosophy of the Czech Academy of Sciences.

Published by the University of Pittsburgh Press, Pittsburgh, Pa., 15260
Copyright © 2025, University of Pittsburgh Press
All rights reserved
Manufactured in the United States of America
Printed on acid-free paper
10 9 8 7 6 5 4 3 2 1

Cataloging-in-Publication data is available from the Library of Congress

ISBN 13: 978-0-8229-6774-3
ISBN 10: 0-8229-6774-X

This book is a revised and expanded English translation of "Rehabilitovat Marxe!": Československá stranická inteligence a myšlení poststalinské modernity, © Nakladatelství Lidové noviny, 2020.

Cover design by Melissa Dias-Mandoly

Publisher: University of Pittsburgh Press, 7500 Thomas Blvd., 4th floor, Pittsburgh, PA 15260, United States, www.upittpress.org
EU Authorized Representative: Easy Access System Europe, Mustamäe tee 50, 10621 Tallinn, Estonia, gpsr.requests@easproject.com

To our family members and pub buddies, who often become participants in our endeavors against their wills.

It is the responsibility of Czechoslovak Marxists to fully utilize Marx's dialectical conception of nascent, contradictory social tendencies and to create philosophical starting points in advance to allow the innovative theoretical involvement of new moments in the development of socialist society. Bold social experiments—that is the proper home of Marx's revolutionary-critical work.

**—JOSEF CIBULKA, "REHABILITOVAT MARXE!"
[REHABILITATE MARX!]**

The criticalness of thinking is always a mere accompanying phenomenon of the critical work of reality itself. Critical thinking could not appear as a real force, dogmatism could not be experienced so painfully by the broad cross-section as something harmful, if the true movement of reality did not condemn dogmatism to be an obstacle to its own development.

**—KAREL KOSÍK, "PŘELUDY A SOCIALISMUS"
[SPECTERS AND SOCIALISM]**

While Marx's criticism of capitalism was directed first and foremost at the relations of production, it was never limited to this aspect; on the contrary, the entire system of industrial civilization as shaped by capitalism came in for critical analysis, penetrating to the roots of the civilization process, embracing the way in which nature and its social relationships have hitherto been appropriated and the mode of man's self-realization within the confines set by capitalist property. The supercession of this stage was conceived as a revolution in the relations and forces of production, anticipating the laying of a new foundation for civilization—and including what we term today the scientific and technological revolution—as an integral component of future communist reconstruction.

**—RADOVAN RICHTA, *CIVILIZATION AT THE CROSSROADS*
[CIVILIZACE NA ROZCESTÍ]**

CONTENTS

PREFACE

XI

AUTHORS' NOTES

XIII

CHAPTER 1.
CZECHOSLOVAK POST-STALINISM: A DISTINCTIVE SPACE FOR SOCIALIST VISIONS

3

CHAPTER 2.
REAL STRUCTURE

48

CHAPTER 3.
SEEKING A NEW SUBJECTIVITY

106

CHAPTER 4.
BETWEEN FOLKNESS AND THE NATION
158

CHAPTER 5.
THINKING REVOLUTION
184

CHAPTER 6.
BEYOND THE HORIZONS OF POST-STALINISM
226

NOTES
273

BIBLIOGRAPHY
343

INDEX
379

PREFACE

The book you are holding in your hand was begun in 2016; the Czech manuscript took until 2020 to complete. It is the fruit of a project funded by the Czech Science Foundation (GAČR) titled "Visions of Post-Stalinist Czechoslovakia: Variations of State-Socialist Modernity," which we worked on at the Institute of Philosophy of the Czech Academy of Sciences between 2016 and 2018. Our team originally consisted of five members, and besides the authors of this publication it also included Petr Kužel, Roman Kanda, and Šimon Svěrák. The plan had been that three of us were going to write the book, the third author was to be the first person named in the previous sentence. However, a grant proposal (possibility) and its realization (reality), despite the convictions of the responsible official bodies, are two different things. Only after some time had passed did we realize that the indisputable advantage of an authorial trio was in the extent of research material it would allow to be covered, but that this would evidently come at the price of losing a shared analytical and interpretive key. Thus, instead of following through with the original conception of bringing chapters written by different authors into one monographic whole, we preferred to approach the work as coauthors. In other words, instead of taking the proven approach of "mapping the territory," we chose a riskier and more demanding path, attempting at the beginning and end to provide clear and concise conceptual framework. The present form of the book gradually took shape based on debates about Czechoslovak post-Stalinism and Stalinism that had been conducted earlier within the original authorial collective. We therefore owe sincere thanks to Petr Kužel, without whose polemical input this work could hardly have been created.

Thanks are also due to all the participants in the workshops and presentations that we organized at the Institute of Philosophy and Institute of Contemporary History at the Czech Academy of Sciences during the time we were working on the book, as well as to participants in the relevant panels at the annual conventions of the Association of Slavic, East European, and Eurasian Studies in Washington, DC, and Boston. Specifically, we want to thank Milena Bartlová, Miloš Havelka, Juraj Halas, Jiří Hoppe, Roman Kanda, Nikolay Karkov, Jiří Křesťan, Michal Kopeček, Ivan Landa, Zsófia Lóránd, Ying Quian, Jakub Rákosník, James M. Robertson, Vítězslav Sommer, Matěj Spurný, Zhivka Valiavicharska, Piotr Wciślik, and Jan Wollner, as well as many others.

The concluding chapter originated within the framework of Jan Mervart's scholarly sojourn at Imre Kertész Kolleg at the University of Jena. This project, which eventually grew into an entire book, was first presented at the institute's regular seminar (July 2018) whereas the main thesis of this chapter was developed somewhat later (November 2019). Thanks are also due here to all the participants in seminars and to the Institute of Philosophy, Czech Academy of Sciences itself for providing support for the necessary finalization of the manuscript. Decisive financial support, which enabled the revision, enlargement, and translation of the whole manuscript, was provided by the Czech Academy of Sciences program Strategy AV21, "Europe and the State: Between Barbarism and Civilisation."

Various parts of the manuscript were read by Richard Cisler, Milan Ducháček, Josef Fulka, Adam Hudek, Jiří Křesťan, Ivan Landa, Dana Musilová, Denisa Nečasová, and Marianna Placáková. We are more than grateful for their friendly criticisms and assistance. Special thanks are due to Joseph Grim Feinberg, who provided us with detailed comments throughout the whole Czech manuscript. Thanks are also owed to the reviewers of the original Czech (Kristina Andělová and Jiří Janáč) as well as the revised and enlarged English version of the book, which significantly contributed to the development and internal consistency of the final version of the manuscript. We have tried to accommodate the critical commentary of all reviewers but responsibility for the book's final form naturally rests with the authors. Finally, we would like to thank the translator of the final manuscript, Melinda Reidinger, whose help has been invaluable. She has been more than patient with our writing as well as with all the nuanced shades of Marxist jargon.

AUTHORS' NOTES

NOTE ON TRANSLATIONS

While preparing the English manuscript we sought to use existing translations of the source texts. However, after comparing these cases with their Czech originals we have found in some cases that the published translations were not entirely accurate. This especially pertains to passages by Karel Kosík from *Dialectics of the Concrete* and *The Crisis of Modernity*, as well as Vítězslav Gardavský's book *God Is Not Yet Dead*, which was apparently compiled from German translations. Thus, some of these passages were newly translated or adapted by Melinda Reidinger. The same applies to the epigraphs introducing this book.

NOTE ON GENDERED LANGUAGE

In many direct citations as well as in some parts of our own text that paraphrase statements made by period authors, we use the original masculine singular "man"/"Man" to preserve historical accuracy instead of anachronistically projecting contemporary concerns about gender representation onto previous generations.

REHABILITATE MARX!

CHAPTER 1
CZECHOSLOVAK POST-STALINISM

A DISTINCTIVE SPACE FOR SOCIALIST VISIONS

> The ideology of renewal was not liberalism in the sense of mere modifications to an old structure, nor in the sense of a creeping transition to western conceptions [. . .] but increasingly aimed toward finding a Marxist solution for the new problems of modern society in the spirit and in favor of a socialist alternative.
>
> **–LUBOMÍR NOVÝ**

This book examines the ways that new forms of socialist modernity were conceptualized during the post-Stalinist era—in the second half of the 1950s and in the 1960s. After the demise of Stalinism, Czechoslovak intellectuals within the Communist Party realized that the primary challenge they were facing was not merely the further development of socialism, which would lead to communism, but a need to reformulate the entire socialist project. Thus, post-Stalinist intellectuals gradually abandoned the Marxist orthodoxy and began searching for new interpretations of classic Marxist works that would provide an adequate conceptual framework for solving contemporary problems. While other research has focused on the history of communist reformism with its culmination in 1968, and therefore more or less subsumed intellectual activities into political developments (H. Gordon Skilling, Galia Golan, Vladimir V. Kusin), our book presents post-Stalinist thought as an autonomous sphere. In our analysis, the post-Stalinist intelligentsia's thought, with all its richness and diversity, emerges as a world of varying socialist visions.

The period between Stalin's death and 1968 was long considered a transitional era wedged in between the "heroic" Stalinist period of building socialism and the exhausted, empty form that arrived in the 1970s and 1980s under the name of "actually existing socialism." Only recently have we encountered approaches that attempt to capture the autonomous nature of post-Stalinist thought, and our book builds upon this trend. However, in contrast to other researchers, we do not see the dominant trait of post-Stalinism as a turn to subjectivity (Anatoly Pinski), or as indecision based in a tension between the legacy of the past and the advent of a new socialist future (Pavel Kolář); rather, we see its projective character. Thinkers of the time engaged in critical analysis of the present in an effort to help society achieve a socialist future. Therefore, we do not understand post-Stalinism primarily as an era of "thawing" (Denis Kozlov and Eleonory Gilburd) or as a mere rejection of the past (de-Stalinization), but as a search for new paths and possibilities that aspired to direct socialism onto a new developmental trajectory.

We derive the interpretation we arrive at in this book from the crisis of Stalinism as a particular variety of socialist modernity. As readers will see in this chapter, we therefore follow the line of research exemplified by Stephen Kotkin, which understands the perspective of modernization and modernity as central for interpreting Stalinist socialist projects. As a theoretical innovation, we draw upon the periodization of modernity introduced by Peter Wagner, whose approach to Stalinism as a form of organized modernity allows us to identify specific problems that the post-Stalinists encountered in the second half of the 1950s and throughout the 1960s. In our understanding of the crisis of Stalinism in the 1950s, we interpret it as a reevaluation of the Stalinist forms of organized modernity that manifested in the Eastern bloc countries not only at the economic and social levels, but even in Marxist thought. Although it has been widely recognized that Stalinism was an ideology of modernization (and Kotkin as well as Wagner have promoted this view), the details and intellectual ramifications of this identification have not been studied in depth in a Central and East European context.[1]

An emphasis on the intellectual essence of Stalinism allows us to understand the richness of post-Stalinist intellectual efforts applied to overcoming Stalinism and using a better, more appropriate Marxist theory. It is crucial that the post-Stalinists criticized not only the "dogmatism" of Stalinist Marxism-Leninism but also the entire Marxist orthodoxy in the form that had crystallized after the Second International. The post-Stalinists reproached Marxist orthodoxy for having intellectually stagnated within the confines of industrial civilization, for having upheld scientific objectivism, or, sometimes, for having an utterly erroneous conception of dialectics.

In our view, post-Stalinism was also characterized by a special dualism. Although post-Stalinist Marxist reflection did overcome

Stalinist thinking and create a distinctive field of thought, its relationship to modernity was not so transgressive. Thus, in our estimation, the post-Stalinist intellectuals' critical approach had its limits, and rather than overcoming organized modernity, post-Stalinism represented its consummation. In other words, our book demonstrates that post-Stalinist intellectuals were not concerned with rejecting the socialist modernizing product, but with a critical reevaluation of its Stalinist type, and they sought new points of departure for a new post-Stalinist modernity.

Our analysis is based on a qualitative reading that allows us to conceptualize the Czechoslovak case, which we also consider unique in its way. While other researchers have focused on individual figures (Satterwhite) or dedicated their investigations to a certain area of the period's intellectual spectrum (James H. Satterwhite, Vítězslav Sommer, and Egle Rindzeviciute), we distinguish three general intellectual trends that determined the distinctive nature of Czechoslovak post-Stalinism. The first is Marxist humanism, which oriented its inquiries toward the problem of human praxis.[2] Next, we introduce the trend that we term "techno-optimism." As the name suggests, its proponents place science and technology at the center of their reflections. Finally, we identify a very distinct current that has been nearly forgotten in Central and Eastern Europe, which we call "dialectical determinism" because its advocates attempted to dialectically reconceptualize social and historical laws.

While some researchers have set the period Marxist humanists and expert techno-optimist intellectuals into opposition (Satterwhite, Sommer), we demonstrate that despite their partial differences and emphases in distinct areas, both of these currents were concerned with developing a concept for a new socialist modernity, and that despite their dissimilarities (focusing on art vs. technology), they both arose from the same intellectual substrate. The uniqueness of the Czechoslovak case was determined by the coexistence of these three contending yet intertwined intellectual groups. In Poland, Yugoslavia, Hungary, East Germany, and even in the Soviet Union, we can find the presence of these trends to varying degrees (for instance, humanists in Poland, Hungary, and Yugoslavia; determinists in the Soviet Union, and techno-optimists across the entire region); however, we believe that there was no state in the Eastern bloc where these three groups were all as fully developed as and coexisted in the same way as in former Czechoslovakia.

In our view, using the Czechoslovak example allows us not only to demonstrate how post-Stalinism followed upon the previous era and how it reckoned with the past but also—and primarily—what kind of original visions it gave shape to. We defined the main actors in our treatise as members of the party intelligentsia (i.e., experts who held party membership cards). Our interpretation is based mainly on the production of intellectuals who were oriented toward the humanities and social sciences: in particular, philosophy, history, sociology, and sometimes aesthetics. Others were active in period cultural and political journalism, that is, these thinkers came from the part of the party spectrum that was trying to analytically grasp the Stalinist past and their contemporary post-Stalinist present, on the basis of which they were modeling visions of a socialist future.

At the same time, we do not intend for this book to serve only as an analysis of the singular Czechoslovak case, but also as a testimony of post-Stalinist thought in general. We start with the assumption that despite the partial differences, and in view of certain limitations, the model of post-Stalinist thought presented here can be considered paradigmatic for the other states of the Eastern bloc as well. Although the post-Stalinist thought of the party intelligentsia had a different temporality and historical specifics in Central and Eastern Europe, we are still convinced that it can be defined using the same parameters.[3]

THE CONTINUITY OF STALINIST MODERNITY

Many interpreters claim that Stalinist modernization represents a deliberate strategy by which backward countries could attempt to catch up with and, in exceptional cases, even overtake the most developed countries. Moreover, this form of "progressive modernization" contains a key ambition that distinguishes it from nonprogressive modernizations—the attempt to build just and egalitarian societies.[4] We agree with these researchers on two points: first, that strong tendencies to centralization and bureaucratization can be understood as a necessary operational mechanism without which the Stalinist modernization project would have been impossible to implement; and second, that the analysis should not be focused on Stalin as a personality, but on the operational and often radically violent processes that the Soviet form of modernization initiated. This model has been expressed by Domenico Losurdo as a "developmentalist dictatorship."[5]

The term "dictatorship" itself is often overused, and the phrase "socialist dictatorship" refers to the stable socialist regimes of the Eastern bloc. In our usage, "dictatorship" does not label any kind of "autonomous" type of regime with a regular political-legal structure, but a specific set of conditions within the framework of this structure itself, which always has a transitional character. Although the Soviet Union was not a regime of this type at the political and legal level in the 1930s, it is certainly possible to talk about a great deal of instability and movement at the social and economic levels. For this reason, Sheila Fitzpatrick and her protégés speak of a "Stalinist revolution," which in and of itself asserts a transitional state. By contrast, we use the phrase "state socialism" when referring to regimes in the Eastern bloc, which, except for the events of 1956 and 1968 and the establishment of Stalinism at the end of the 1940s and beginning of the 1950s, displayed a great degree of stability.

We thus arrive at a certain pitfall in defining post-Stalinism, which is the uncritical extrapolation of the scholarly literature about Soviet Stalinism to the other states of Central and Eastern Europe. While from the perspective of the history of the Soviet Union, the period at the end of the 1940s and beginning of the 1950s can accurately be termed "late Stalinism," in Central and Eastern Europe this was actually a period of revolutionary Stalinism in the sense of the concept of a "dictatorship" as sketched out above. In the first case, it is possible to describe a post-Stalinist stabilization that followed the revolutionary upheavals of the Stalinist dictatorship, and in the second, it is possible to speak about a stabilized society that flowed smoothly into post-Stalinism.[6] Furthermore, if the concept of "thawing" is apt for the Soviet Union because it corresponds to a certain loosening of already-established institutional-political frameworks that can be traced back to 1952 at the latest, in Eastern Europe the era of post-Stalinism is connected far more frequently with the previous period in the sense of an incompleteness, or rather the culmination of processes that had been initiated earlier.[7] The different dynamics of social development in the Soviet Union and in Central and Eastern Europe can be traced through the institutional and social changes that accompany the transition from a people's democratic stage in socialist-type regimes: for example, the completion of transformations in the areas of collectivization of agriculture and the establishment of forms of socialist ownership took place in Czechoslovakia in the second half of the 1950s, whereas in the USSR, these changes had already taken place twenty years earlier.[8]

At the same time, in the context of the different forms of development in the Soviet Union and the Eastern bloc, we also have to emphasize that after World War II it was precisely the Soviet version of modernity that became for communists the model of progress.[9] However, in some cases, the reason was not only the drive to catch up economically and remedy "backwardness," but also devotion to the USSR as a model for the level of political and state institutions, educational system, solutions for what were referred to as "ethnic questions," and so on.[10] Therefore, at the end of the 1940s and beginning of the 1950s, even in states of the Czechoslovak type, where the industrial sector represented a significant percent of the country's overall production, we can trace the way Moscow was admired as a natural center of civilization from which progress spread to the peripheries. The legitimacy of this solution was also derived from the stability of the Stalinist regime in this period—it had proved able to overcome both inner turmoil (through the Stalinist lens of the political trials of the 1930s) and the external threat represented by the German invasion. The slogan "The Soviet Union—Our Model" was thus not necessarily understood only as the compulsory adoption of externally coerced norms, but also as a nod to the legitimacy and hierarchical primacy of the Soviet variant of modernity.[11] Even though regional specifics were ultimately repressed, it does not mean that this form of modernity was in all regards imposed from above (i.e., under the direct tutelage of Moscow). External pressure for Sovietization was combined with a multilevel mobilization of local societies.[12] We believe that this perspective will help us better understand the essence and historical progression of post-Stalinist thinking, as well as the way it worked to overcome Stalinism in the Eastern bloc—and especially in Czechoslovakia. Stalinism as a particular version of modernity became its paradigmatic application in these regions.

For our treatise it is important that the Stalinist version of modernity began to be thematized by communist intellectuals who had often taken part in the previous Stalinist revolution. If it is possible to speak about some kind of "sobering up," it consists precisely in understanding the end of Stalinism as a viable, progressive, and modernist project. The economic, political, and ideological crisis in the countries of the Eastern bloc during the 1950s clearly illustrates that the Stalinist variation of modernization was losing steam and becoming unsustainable. We can interpret the so-called critical or reform discourses in Czechoslovakia in the 1960s that were reacting to this crisis as a symptom of it, but at the same time also as an attempt to find a new progressive starting point.

Naturally, we are not claiming that in comparison with Stalinism, post-Stalinism represented as a dissimilar alternative as Nazism and Stalinism versus liberalism; nevertheless, since the very beginning, post-Stalinism has been framed by multileveled criticism of the previous era. Yet, at the same time, it is generally true—or it was at least in the beginning—that the criticism of Stalinist modernity was not conceived of as a refusal of it,[13] but as an attempt to overcome it dialectically. Stalinism was going to be subjected to investigation at the level of naming and locating its errors, after which the creation of a qualitatively new form of post-Stalinist modernity would follow.[14] In 1956 the philosopher Radovan Richta proclaimed that "the main goal is not to clarify all the mistakes of the past, it is primarily about the approach and especially about the future."[15]

In many regards, we thus find inspiration in the words of Marshall Berman, who, in connection with Karl Marx, spoke about hopes that the "scars caused by modernity" were to be "healed by means of a more complete and rigorous modernity."[16] For our treatise, we slightly paraphrase this proposition and we argue that post-Stalinism was attempting to "heal the scars of Stalinist modernity through a more complete and consistent socialist modernity." At the same time, we agree with the sociologist of modernity Peter Wagner, who says no ideal form of modernity exists, nor does it have one correct historical implementation—there are only various interpretations that have been implemented in history. More specifically: capitalism, parliamentary democracy, and state socialism are just interpretations of modernity, and do not represent the only possible and ultimate solution.[17]

It is Wagner's periodization of modernity that allows us to refer to the individual stages in the historical formation of modern society. The crisis of the "restricted" liberal model, which was created as a reaction to the great political revolutions of the emerging modern era (especially the French Revolution), represented the first of them. Its essential characteristic was that although it preserved many of the (bourgeois) freedoms and ideals that had been fought for, at the same time it also denied them because it excluded certain groups: first, the lower social classes, women, and mentally ill people, then, as the era progressed, the limitations were spread further on the basis of national, ethnic, and cultural criteria. The demise of the liberal model was primarily caused by these limiting measures that left entire groups of citizens at the margins of society, so it was unable to fulfill its own promises of universal freedom, social harmony, and a more democratic form of government. The general instability of (post)liberal regimes inspired the rise of new types of political, economic, and ideological practice, which, instead of the liberal emphasis on free associations among individuals (let us add, among those who enjoyed a privileged class position), emphasized controlling and organizing people into larger bodies, whether corporations, oligarchies, mass-based political parties, or trade unions. This is what provided the basis for what Wagner termed "organized modernity." In the context of this problem, it is important that Wagner understands Stalinism (or, in his own term, "Soviet socialism") as an accelerated, condensed form of organized modernity, or—more precisely cited—a form that is "more organized" than its Western counterpart.[18] In Wagner's view, the difference between them is not essential in nature; it is a matter of their degree of organization.

However, we do not consider the period after Stalin's death as a kind of fading phase of organized modernity, which after a sobering up from Stalinism would gradually disappear entirely, as the term "thawing" semantically implies. On the contrary, we perceive a twofold relationship to Stalinism as organized modernity: we claim that in post-Stalinism there was both a criticism of this Stalinist type of organized modernity and a process of its reorganization that refrained from repudiating "organizing" in the sense of strong institutional frameworks that were determined by the Communist Party and state. On the contrary, organization was to be achieved (by the proclamation of socialism) and preserved, even though it changed through various reform discourses. It is precisely this moment that establishes the distinctive nature of the post-Stalinist era.

Post-Stalinism as an independent phenomenon was defined recently by Pavel Kolář in a book published in German: *Der Poststalinismus: Ideologie und Utopie einer Epoche* (Post-Stalinism: The Ideology and Utopia of an Epoch). In his work, Kolář speaks of this era as an intermediate phase (*Zwichenphase*) between Stalinism and late socialism, which is torn between the unpleasant legacy of the past and the alluring promise of the future.[19] In his view, this position "in between" is the cause of post-Stalinist vacillation, indecisiveness, half-measure solutions, and the like. Although Kolář's approach is innovative in many ways, here it indirectly endorses the historiography that describes this period as naive and internally conflicted.[20] In contrast, our approach is based on different inspirations from the social sciences. Johann P. Árnason, referring to Max Weber, and even more to works by Cornelius Castoriadis and Alain Touraine, draws attention to the tension in modern societies caused by an "absolutizing demand for rational mastery" on the one hand, and individual or collective direction toward autonomy and creativity on the other.[21] We believe that in a figurative sense this tension can be considered a typical feature of the post-Stalinist period, when the Stalinist type of rationality is not replaced by a refusal of rationality as a principle, but themes of various forms of creativity and creative acts, whether in the spheres of science, art, or philosophy, come to the fore. While Kolář attributes indecision to post-Stalinist thinking, a projective visionary wager placed on another, albeit problematic, continuation of the socialist project is the dominant common theme in our conception.

At the same time, we claim that respect for rational organizing in Czechoslovakia, similarly to that in Western Europe, began being called into question only at the end of the post-Stalinist era, when the legitimacy of state-socialist organized modernity dissolved in the events of 1968 and various forms of autonomy were articulated (here we mean both radical leftist and liberal intellectual alternatives). We assign the end of post-Stalinism to this turning point, which in our estimation, at least in Czechoslovakia, ended hand in hand with the crisis of organized modernity in 1968. Despite the numerous ways in which the "order" after 1968 evinces continuities with the previous period, for example, in the techno-optimist approach to socialism,[22] in many regards its basic settings did in fact change. However, the "actually existing socialism" of the 1970s, and 1980s was lacking one of the defining traits of post-Stalinism, which was a critical approach to its own establishment and momentary political and social practice.

POST-STALINIST REFLEXIVITY

In his treatise about the relationship of state socialism and modernity, Johann P. Árnason argues that the all-embracing and all-enlightening ideology "limited the role of reflexivity in social life: the ability to confront problematic aspects and consequences of modernizing processes was undermined by a priori restrictions."[23] Although elsewhere he speaks about the Czechoslovak case and the reform process of the 1960s as an attempt to escape this rule, he does not further elaborate on the topic, and he concludes with a remark about the inevitability of the end of such an experiment.[24] Similarly, when Peter Wagner defines organized modernity, he describes one of its key characteristics with the concept of "conventionalization," which corresponds to ideas of legibility, manageability, and classification of the social world. When this principle is implemented from above, which is important for our analysis, the system's ability to react to processual problems is overshadowed by themes of governance and control. Wagner adds that after some time, when conventionalization has been achieved, the socially conditioned character vanishes from the thoughts of the social actors, and everything is "representing some natural order of reality," leading, in his opinion, to the reification and naturalization of social phenomena.[25]

In our understanding of post-Stalinism, we follow Árnason and agree with the way he attributes a key role to reflexivity in modern society; however, we disagree with his evaluation of state socialism as a monolithic period, and we claim that one of the most important aspects of post-Stalinism was its ability to be self-reflexive.[26] To Wagner's description of organized modernity we add that even if the process of conventionalization in Central and Eastern Europe was pushed from above through party and state interventions, the post-Stalinist era is characterized by questioning the function, meaning, and goals of individual constituent aspects of the social world as well as the system itself.[27] Even the achievement of conventionalization in itself in Central and East European states (for instance, if we admit that the official proclamation of socialism in Czechoslovakia in 1960 meant a truly institutional and legislative framing for a system of organized modernity) was accompanied by a certain degree of reflexivity. This trend gained momentum during the 1960s and culminated in 1968. In other words, we claim that post-Stalinism, in contrast to the previous era and the period of "actually existing socialism" that began after 1968, displayed a marked capability for (self-)reflection, which was manifested primarily at the level of various intellectual and artistic activities among the ranks of party intellectuals.[28]

The question naturally remains as to where this reflexivity came from. In his work analyzing modern society and seeking its revolutionary subject at the end of the 1960s, the sociologist Alain Touraine used the concept of "historicity." This term expresses the internal capability of a given society for understanding knowledge (in the broader sense) as the main production factor or "as the force directly transforming the state of nature" of the social world.[29] Touraine's concept can be summed up as a society's awareness of its own history and willingness alongside the intellectual and technical capability of entering into this process. Stated in his words, Touraine says the historicity of human society is linked to a "a symbolic capacity that enables it to construct the system of knowledge together with technical tools which it can use to intervene in its own functioning."[30]

In his analysis of modern society, Touraine applied a basic premise that was also articulated in Central and Eastern Europe in various formulations after Stalin's death: human society is not formed and does not endure only on the basis of adaptations to an environment, for the sake of its own reproduction, or because of the functioning of iron laws of history; instead, this happens because it has the ability to "work on itself"—the society produces itself.[31] Touraine claims that it is necessary to distinguish the adaptation, functioning, and reproduction of society from its production.[32] We could even say that it is exactly in the moment

1.1. Robert Kalivoda holding a banner (Cabinet of Philosophy, Czechoslovak Academy of Sciences) at a May Day parade, sometime between 1954 and 1957. Copyright Eva Kalivodová.

when historicity is identified with its own organization and functioning (in our case, by the Communist Party and state) that the society finds itself in a crisis. This gives rise to initiatives to overcome this condition, including mobilizing all the various resources and capacities needed—thereby also creating new forms of historicity (new models of knowledge and of accumulation and utilization of resources). This perspective enables us to grasp the extent to which various intellectual, scientific, or organizational initiatives and proposals are not simply another element of the functioning of society, but at the same time they are also not located outside of it in the position of a distant observer or reformer. Quite the contrary; historicity is inherent to a certain type of conflict (conflicts of classes, groups, or interests) within society.[33] We assume that the crisis situation described above corresponds to the condition in which state socialism found itself after 1953, and in our conception post-Stalinism is an example of a new form of historicity.

Touraine's emphasis on society and its material structure and productive mechanisms is crucial for our treatise on the history of state socialism. For it is no coincidence that the most elaborated deliberations that reflect on the past, present, and especially the future of state socialism have arisen from institutions that were originally founded by Stalinist revolutions; in our case, the Czechoslovak Academy of Sciences (extant since 1952/1953) and the individual artistic associations that brought together party intellectuals and artists.[34] Let us add to Touraine's discussion of socialism as a combination of radical accumulation of the means of production and control that this process led to the creation of an institutional basis, which later—at the latest after the Twentieth Congress of the Communist Party of the USSR—enabled self-reflexivity with a capability for social self-production (i.e., historicity).[35]

If we are to answer the question of the origin of post-Stalinist reflexivity, we cannot avoid the period shifts in the approach to knowledge in the process. As David G. Rowley aptly remarks, in the era of establishing Bolshevist doctrine, epistemology was not actually a "mere" philosophical discipline but primarily a question from which political action was derived.[36] Stalinism was consistently based on the Leninist idea of the party as the avant-garde of the working class, which was supposed to have exclusive access to knowledge and therefore had the prerogative to change reality as soon as it recognized something that needed changing, by means of political action. Already for Lenin, as Daniela Steila has noted, "only a leadership that firmly possessed the unique authentic truth could lead the masses to 'victory.'"[37]

Whether we consider Stalin himself or the closest circle of party leadership to be the main epistemological actor within the framework of Stalinism,[38] what is certain is that it was the originally Leninist idea of the immediate connection between knowledge and politics that dominated during the Stalinist era. Naturally, this does not mean that post-Stalinism had no need for scientific knowledge as a basis for making political decisions. Quite the contrary, as indicated by the formation of teams of experts at the end of the 1950s and beginning of the 1960s. It was a new relationship between knowledge and politics, and a way in which decision makers could gain knowledge about the society and then apply it. Whereas Stalinism implicitly assumed an immediate connection between knowledge (the dialectical laws of history) and its own politics, in post-Stalinism this relationship acquired a mediated nature, which guaranteed a certain autonomy for both spheres.

In this regard, Tom Rockmore remarks that for Lenin the question of knowledge was based on "the Cartesian search for a universal method to secure certain knowledge," and he claims that philosophy was abandoned in favor of a strongly scientific standpoint.[39] For Rowley as well, the elevation of Marxism, or rather the party's position on science, was vital for the revolutionary movement, because the "objectivity" of cognized reality guaranteed that politics itself (revolutionary actions) would not be seen as "subjective-idealist" decisions; moreover, this scientism relieved actors of any individual moral responsibility.[40] We add that the Stalinists' conception, which placed party resolutions on a par with science, had to adhere to Lenin's theory of knowledge.[41]

In his study of Aleksandr Tvardovskii's thought, Anatoly Pinsky considers "epistemological autonomy"—which he says arose based on a new reflection on "the source of truth"—as a distinction between post-Stalinism and Stalinism. Here, this means a shift from a privileged access to the truth for party bosses to the individualization of this category. Now it was no longer just the party or its leadership, but also the "I" as a knowing subject that can look at reality.[42]

In accordance with these conclusions, we consider the change of the epistemological subject to be pivotal. However, at the same time, we postulate that this movement led to the creation of the inner richness of post-Stalinist thought. The dominant position of the party as the main center of thought was simply weakened by the proliferation of thinking subjects.[43]

In his study, Pinsky uses the apt metaphor of a "sea of uncertainty" in which the political headquarters remained the flagship, but the smaller vessels were sailed by intellectuals who "claimed the same right of discovery."⁴⁴ We would like to clarify that a typical feature of post-Stalinism was that besides members of the party apparatus, scientists, experts, intellectuals, and artists also demanded an epistemological approach to reality and claimed the right to express themselves (first on the party's turf, but later also in public) about the current state of socialism and its further transformations. Most of them continued to consider themselves Leninists and did not question the party's leading role in politics.⁴⁵ Nevertheless, many of them still considered party avant-gardism as historically outdated (in the spirit of revolutions of transformed social conditions) and they articulated an idea that was typical in a post-Stalinist context: that ordinary party members, and not only the party leadership, had something to say about matters of socialism.⁴⁶ This was not a radical change of position or a step outside the system, but the previously sacrosanct truths mediated by the party leadership no longer bore the seal of incontestable objectivity.

In this context, Pinsky argues that "for Tvardovskii and other writers and critics, an allegiance to the party elite remained, only now they did not conceptualize that elite as epistemologically unique."⁴⁷ In other words, scientists, experts, intellectuals, and artists declared that their standpoints were in conformity with the official party line ("the question of whose side to stand on is fundamentally not a question, I have been satisfied with the party since the beginning of my activities").⁴⁸ Hand in hand with this, they also naturally refused categorical submission to official resolutions.⁴⁹

The watering down of universally binding, imperative truths mediated by the party leadership began in Central and Eastern Europe after Stalin's death. This trend is illustrated very well in a wide range of debates that took place at that time about the relationships between science and art, and between politics and ideology. At the same time, there was also much talk about cognitive abilities, political insubordination, and even a certain degree of autonomy for science and art.

INTERNAL PLURALITY

This proliferation of epistemological subjects and the resulting capability for reflection derived from it influenced the nature of the post-Stalinist intellectual world. The difference between Stalinism and post-Stalinism naturally manifested in the different nature of the regime itself—the weakening of centralism, the possibility of using violence, inspections, and so on; however, for the purposes of our treatise we are more interested in changes at the level of the party's theoretical approach (i.e., official Marxist-Leninist thought). While Stalinism—in the spirit of the above-mentioned approach to knowledge—was characterized by a unified and generally imperative theory subsumed in a condensed form in Stalin's theoretical works (primarily *Questions of Leninism* and *Economic Problems of Socialism in the USSR*), we can trace at least some indications back to 1953 and then the deterioration of the universal binding obligatory force of the official Marxist-Leninist theory began in 1956. At the same time, this was not an eclipse of the doctrine, but its transformation into a kind of theoretical tiltyard. The obligatory force of Stalinism gave way to a relative plurality of interpretations, which of course did not batter at the foundations of either Marxism-Leninism or the political system. Among the subjects on which theoreticians were engaging in lively discussions at the time were the relationship between materialism and idealism, principles of dialectics, questions of inherent historical laws, and the role of personality in history. On the other hand, a gradual transformation of several basic concepts in Marxist-Leninist philosophy also took place, especially dialectics and dialectical laws, and practice. Based on these intellectual shifts, Stalinism then began to be reproached as nondialectical, nonmaterialist, and thus as de facto idealist or even implicitly revisionist.

Along with the nature of Marxist philosophy, the way of thinking about socialism and where it was heading also changed. In other words, the Stalinist vision of achieving socialism also made space for a multiplication of views like the one that took place in the theory of knowledge. Acceptance of the Soviet example as the main frame of reference for modernity and progress had previously been typical for Central and East European Stalinism, but this was when a search for each country's own roots and the rediscovery of "national paths" to socialism based on particular circumstances in their historical development took place, and claims of the impossibility of generalizing were frequent.

In contrast to post-Stalinism, it may seem that Stalinism was characterized by having one hegemonic model for achieving historical progress in the form of building socialism. However, we are not claiming that the latter represented an absolute type of intellectual sterility and ossification;[50] rather, it is a question of how this singular "hegemonic model" was put into operation. Assuredly, even in Stalinist regimes internal differences of opinion arose concerning the formulation of individual policies and the further development of socialist regimes.[51] Nevertheless, there were also authorities (Stalin, the Politburo), whose final resolutions were understood as obligatory, valid, and, if necessary, also enforceable for everyone involved in the dispute.

By contrast, in the post-Stalinist era we can trace the formation of various approaches that were initiated by the party itself, which over time came to assume a growing degree of autonomy and freedom of expression—and not only within the framework of the Communist Party, but also externally.[52] By contrast with Stalinism, post-Stalinism was distinguished by other forms of differentiation in its ideas and projects, precisely with regard to the further development of socialist modernity. Thus, it cannot be put so bluntly as to state that Stalinism was lacking internal diversity, and diverse factions were only beginning to coalesce in the post-Stalinist era. Naturally, what matters most is the way they were formed and sanctioned, and how the party's role changed during this internal pluralization.

Therefore, in this case, we are speaking about a field of differentiation that is specific to Stalinism and post-Stalinism. In Stalinism this field was sanctioned by the party's governing bodies, and binding unity and obedience to the final resolution were understood as necessary by all participants of any conflicts that arose. It is precisely this unity and obedience that was shattered in post-Stalinism. Not because the party ceased to demand them, but because the very mode of control over this new field of differentiation—which it had itself brought into life—was transformed. As it turned out, with the passing years and the internal crises within the Czechoslovak regime, which mirrored similar situations across the Eastern bloc, this control proved to be increasingly less effective. Thus, this new field of differentiation did not represent a mere empirical multiplication of various forms of Marxism-Leninism, but a transformation in the entire epistemological groundwork in which the Stalinist version of the doctrine was becoming increasingly marginalized. It is possible to say that a certain form of dialectical movement was even taking place, where an instance of Touraine's historicity (artists' associations, scientific or pedagogical institutions that originated within the regime) then, thanks to certain "subjective" impulses, achieved independence and gained its own "objective" dynamic, which gradually slipped away from the control of its originators.

We would like to introduce the term "internal plurality" to describe the post-Stalinist differentiation in thinking among party intellectuals. Although it was not a case of a hermetically closed field, but of a set with a certain range of external inputs and outputs (an example pars pro toto is the Marxist-Christian dialogue that was conducted in the 1960s).[53] Here, the adjective "internal" indicates that this pluralization took place in a fairly clearly circumscribed space based on a Marxist understanding of the world. The pivotal and defining role in its formation was played by the party intelligentsia, who took key positions in organizations such

1.2. Arnošt Kolman, head of the Institute of Philosophy in the first post-Stalinist years. Copyright Masaryk Institute and Archives of the Czech Academy of Sciences.

as the Czechoslovak Academy of Sciences and artistic associations. In accordance with the previous interpretation, the intelligentsia, moreover, refused to continue fulfilling the function of gearshift levers between the party and the society and it began to formulate its own standpoints, while still getting extensive use out of the facilities at institutions built by Stalinism.[54]

The creation of internal plurality was connected both with maintaining the progressive nature of the socialist project and with renewing the legitimacy that Stalinism had definitively lost after Nikita Khruschchev's famous revelations in the "Secret Speech."[55] A new legitimacy was to be achieved by squaring with the past (in the period lexicon it would have been through means of criticism of the "cult of personality," "bureaucratization," "deformation," and "dogmatism") as well as through a new modeling of socialism that accompanied these two interlinked processes. Naturally, what the course of these developments would look like was neither predetermined given nor entirely predictable, either within the framework of the Soviet Union or in the states of Central and Eastern Europe.

A situation that allowed for many different development scenarios was favorable for the creation of various visions that overlapped to a certain extent, but at the same time they often emerged as distinct alternatives. Yet, regardless of their differing emphases and main themes, it is still clear that all the models of socialist modernity were still moving within the framework of Marxism (and sometimes also Leninism), which of course was gradually transformed into divergent epistemic fields (which in many regards were even created). After Stalin's banishment, authors usually based their work on the classics: Marx, Engels, and Lenin. The influences of Marxist and non-Marxist intellectual traditions, both domestic and foreign, penetrated Czechoslovak debates later, roughly at the turn of the 1950s and 1960s. However, quite often, non-Marxist traditions, such as phenomenology, existentialism, and structuralism, catalyzed new interpretations and revealed new levels in the classic Marxist texts, which then retroactively functioned as criticisms of these traditions, and thus confirmed the epistemic supremacy of Marxism (and Leninism) once again.[56] The individual people involved in the different currents within this plurality did not necessarily overlap with the party's most influential groups, and they often arose throughout the hierarchical structure of the Communist Party and its apparatus, as well as in state, educational, and professional institutions.

At the same time, official discourse also played a specific role: it opened space for criticism of the cult of personality and with calls for a renaissance of Leninism that enabled the development of this new field of differentiation or internal plurality. However, the party leadership wanted to keep the situation constantly under their control and they attempted to act from the position of an authoritative body that regulates metadiscourse. Thus, a permanent tension prevailed between the post-Stalinist party leadership and representatives of the critical party intelligentsia. Regardless of their affinity for any particular notion of socialism, the latter group therefore found itself in the position of loyal party opposition, which—just as H. Gordon Skilling had so trenchantly observed nearly fifty years earlier—"[seeks] to change or influence public policy by criticizing established policies, offering different measures to those proposed, or suggesting future courses of action."[57] But significantly, all the participants in the ideological controversies (that is, the highest representatives of the party apparatus, as well as scientists, experts, intellectuals, and artists) nevertheless considered their opinions and views on the development of post-Stalinist society to be a relevant continuation of the revolutionary path.

Accusations of revisionism, as well as defenses against them, were formulated using Leninist terminology. Or at least they invoked Lenin's name and his authority. The basic arguments in the 1957–1958 campaign against revisionism that was waged in the wake of the events in Hungary in 1956 also appeared in later ideological campaigns of many different types: "revisionism" mainly served in the practical function of a general and only vaguely defined concept that was used to distinguish something from the official discourse. However, it is necessary to state the following: notwithstanding that many party ideologues would have liked the party's ideology to continue to exercise the same binding and obligatory force, due to the post-Stalinist proliferation of intellectual currents, even the *official* ideology in the post-Stalinist era never again enjoyed the power it had in the context of Stalinist ideology. At the same time, the relationship between the official and alternative discourse was never unidirectional in an either/or sense. Czechoslovakia in the 1960s provides a good example of the mutual diffusion of the rhetoric of the party leadership with alternative views on post-Stalinist development, which culminated in "socialism with a human face" of 1968.

TIME LIMITATIONS

Even though we delimit the period of post-Stalinism with two turning points (Stalin's death and 1968) and we define it based on reflexivity, internal plurality, and its ability to generate its own intellectual productions, we do not consider this period to be hermetically sealed. If we were to say that these three attributes were only formed after 1953 and that they ceased to operate after the establishment of the "new order" at the beginning of the 1970s, it does not mean that we attribute any absolute exceptionality to post-Stalinism (i.e., that we would refuse to acknowledge overlaps of some of its features or emphases or the questions it raised with either the period of Stalinism that preceded it or the "actually existing socialism" that came after).

Moreover, we will indicate the interfaces with Stalinism in the entire exploration that follows, and attempt to overcome Marxist orthodoxy in areas ranging from questions of human subjectivity to the dialectical laws of history to the reinterpretation of revolution, as well as in the use of the Marxist-Leninist conceptual apparatus. We particularly attribute accumulation in the form of the nationalization of the means of production and the partial takeover and completion of institutional frameworks for knowledge (such as universities and the Czechoslovak Academy of Sciences) to Stalinism, and these policies unintentionally created the conditions for the later post-Stalinist reflexivity and intellectual production (historicity). At the same time, it is necessary to point out that these conditions also acted in the opposite direction, by enabling the production of Stalinist thought to continue. This perspective contrasts not only with the texts we analyze here but also with the period degree of official de-Stalinization. To wit: post-Stalinism is best distinguished from the revolutionary era of Stalinism by changes in thinking, or sometimes in minor changes in the social structure, rather than in sweeping personnel changes or purges that were undertaken to establish a new social order after 1968.

The fact that, with only the minor exceptions of a few journal contributions, no truly noteworthy philosophical work of a Stalinist character was created in the years between 1948 and 1953 can be interpreted as one of the conditions that gave rise to the post-Stalinist diversity we describe. However, at the same time, it also played a role in the continuity of Stalinist intellectual production. In principle, we can also apply Vít Schmarc's evaluation of the project of socialist-realist literary production, which he considers to be ultimately unsuccessful: in Czechoslovakia no literary work was created that was the equal of the Soviets' model socialist-realist novels.[58] The time span for Czechoslovak Stalinism was too brief for such an undertaking. If we consider that during the five-year period in which the country experienced Stalinism, the institutional framework for Stalinist knowledge was still under construction in the first two to three years and it was only completed at the very end of this period (the Czechoslovak Academy of Sciences, as well as *Filozo-*

ficky časopis [the Philosophical Journal] were only launched in 1953), the Stalinist overlaps are not so surprising.[59]

Although in the changed post-Stalinist conditions scholarly works do not contain direct references to Stalin, there are examples when the conceptual apparatus of the authors, the meanings of the categories they use, and the subjects themselves are in conformity with Stalinist conceptions to such an extent that these works can be used as sources for the intellectual history of Stalinism. At the same time, these authors did not necessarily adhere to the Stalinist paradigm throughout their careers. Erika Kadlecová's monograph *Socialistické vlastenectví* (Socialist Patriotism) (1957) and Jiří Cvekl's book *Lid a osobnost v dějinách* (People and Personality in History) from 1961 are examples of these types. While the first title essentially presents the Stalinist conception of the "national question"—including the emphasis on the class struggle—the second one is based in the orthodox Marxist conception of collective and individual subjectivity.[60] The debate over historical materialism in the second half of the 1950s also bears similar features (e.g., Jindřich Zelený, Jaroslav Klofáč, Vojtěch Tlustý, and Miloš Svoboda), though here the authors were further developing orthodoxy rather than overcoming it (see the section "Dialectical Laws" in chapter 2).

If we take into account findings by Vítězslav Sommer (in the area of party historiography) and Roman Kanda (literary studies), it seems that a full-fledged development of the scientific Stalinist paradigm had not taken place in the social sciences in Czechoslovakia in the years 1948–1953.[61] Seen from this angle, it was paradoxically only in post-Stalinism that institutional processes (the process of conventionalization that culminated in the proclamation of the achievement of socialism in 1960) that had been initiated earlier as well as the delayed stabilization of individual disciplines of Stalinist sciences were actually seen to their completion.[62] Whereas intellectual production had previously been limited mostly to articles and studies, which mainly accommodated the Stalinist demand that they be up to date, in the post-Stalinist period monographs were published that treated their subjects in more subtle manners than just as fodder for agitprop, while still playing in the appropriate key of orthodox Marxism.[63]

Naturally, there were also certain overlaps between post-Stalinism and the period after the suppression of the political and social movement in Czechoslovakia in 1968. The establishers of the "actually existing socialism" in the early 1970s were aware of potential continuities in the production of "revisionist tendencies," and academic and university workplaces (along with publishing houses and other media) were subjected to immediate purges including changes made to the contents of research plans. However, forms of technocratic thinking, without regard for the normalized techno-optimistic revolutionary ideas that were accepted within the framework of Czechoslovak "normalization" carried over into the 1970s.[64] Similarly, we can also track the development of the concept of the "national question," the understanding of the state as an important institutional framework of socialism, and to a certain extent also the concept of law in the spirit of a socialist understanding of legality and find practically no changes.[65]

Besides the overlaps of certain forms of thinking, this also relates to the production mechanisms themselves. Vítězslav Sommer's interpretation of normalization-era forecasting (*prognostika*) reveals the structural similarity between post-Stalinism and "actually existing socialism." If we conceive of the creation of post-Stalinist reflexivity as an unintentional result of Stalinist accumulation, the specialized discipline of forecasting that was separated during the normalization era from the "centralized system of making predictions, with the goal of enhancing the effectiveness of the economic administration" had transformed itself by the end of the 1980s into a focal point for criticism of the period's socialist order.[66] This chain of developments is unlikely to be unique, and it leads us to formulate the following hypotheses intended to guide further research: while post-Stalinist reflexivity ends in Czechoslovakia with the suppression of the reform communist movement of 1968, the normalization of the institutional framework for knowledge, which was in fact intended to prevent further spread of the original "revisionism"—in a manner similar to Stalinism—unintentionally creates the conditions for the subsequent type of late socialist reflexivity. The difference is that whereas Stalinism, along with providing the conditions for the next movement, also enabled the foundation for historicity—that is, for further social production—nothing like this was taking place in late socialism. The result of this reflexivity was not the emergence of another stage of state socialism, but the disintegration of the social and economic formation as a whole. This may be attributed to the fact that, while the era of "actually existing socialism" sought to maintain a techno-optimistic drive, it simultaneously aimed to prevent any changes to its political structure—let alone its chain of command with the old guard of the party functionaries at the top. Such a contradiction proved increasingly erosive, ultimately working against the regime's primary goal: the consolidation of sociopolitical conditions.

At the same time, post-Stalinism cannot be perceived as a homogeneous era. We are aware that because of the thematic division we have imposed here, in which our interpretations are more oriented toward the contents of individual problems than to their development over time, it may paradoxically seem that this period was marked by a certain inflexibility. But nevertheless, any impression of fixity within the post-Stalinist internal diversity, which the same achievement of conventionalization in the post-Stalinist era can evoke, would be a misunderstanding. As Kristina Andělová aptly points out with reference to Quentin Skinner in her analysis of the political thinking in communist reformism, nothing is farther away from the essence of this thinking than some kind of immutability. And, like Andělová, who sees the fundamental turning point as 1968—or more precisely, the military invasion—for the development of reformism,[67] we also believe that the development of the party intelligentsia's thinking during the post-Stalinist period was significantly influenced by events in political history: the Twentieth Congress of the Communist Party of the USSR and the proclamation of the Constitution of the Czechoslovak Socialist Republic in 1960.

An inexhaustible literature has been written about the impacts of the Soviet party congress and the events of 1956 on the societies of the Eastern bloc. Here, we agree with Pavel Kolář's interpretation, which highlights the activation of the Communist Party as the producer of history.[68] Even though we argue with this author elsewhere, we consider Nikita Khrushchev's principle of the party as a collective actor—which he emphasizes—to be one of the important influences on the formation of internal plurality within the post-Stalinist party intelligentsia.

However, Communist intellectuals did not wait for the results of the official de-Stalinization campaign, which was quite tepid in Czechoslovakia, before spontaneously starting to discuss Stalinism. That is to say, they acted not just on directives from governing institutions at specially convened emergency party meetings.[69] Only in the Cabinet for Philosophy of the Czechoslovak Academy of Sciences (which since 1957 has been called the Institute of Philosophy) were there several meetings convened after the Twentieth Congress, at which members discussed the ramifications of the "cult of personality" in philosophy and the form that de-Stalinization would officially take.[70] For instance, one year previously there had been discussions at this workplace about "the free exchange of opinions" and "liberation from dogmatism."[71] In April 1956, discussions also took place about the possibility of "sharply critiquing" the party press.[72] The academic disciplines that inherently belonged to the arsenal of orthodox Marxism, such as historical and dialectical materialism of the Soviet type, demonstrate that from the beginning, post-Stalinism was, at the very least, more than just an idea of "de-Stalinization" as a strict rejection of Stalinism founded on efforts to overcome that way of thinking. It was only *through* Stalinism itself and, moreover, upon the institutional and disciplinary bases it had founded, that an opening of new topics and questions as well as the later enrichment of established Marxist terminology came about.

An example of a paradigmatic nature is the analysis that bears the title "On Manifestations of the 'Cult of Personality' in Philosophy and How to Overcome It" by Ivan Sviták.[73] Even though it dates to the beginning of the 1960s, it is possible to consider this as a manifestation of a debate that began with the Twentieth Congress. The author had submitted it for discussion at the Communist Party of Czechoslovakia (KSČ) unit within the Institute of Philosophy, and it had already been debated beforehand within party groups in the departments of dialectical materialism, the history of philosophy, historical materialism, scientific communism, and scientific atheism. In principle, these engagements by the party with Sviták's polemic confirm Kolář's thesis about the post-Stalinist activized party that takes history into its own hands.[74]

In his analysis, Sviták names the main principles of Stalinism in the individual Marxist disciplines as they existed at that time. Thus, he claims that dialectical materialism was reduced to a vulgar and mechanical materialism distinguished by "torpor and inflexibility of thought" in the form of repeated phrases and the creation of a hierarchy of classics with Stalin in pride of place at the top. In a similar manner, a simplification of the conceptions of idealism and materialism in relation to the history of philosophy, as well as an utter flattening of historical materialism into inevitable evolutionary laws, had taken place. At the same time, Sviták also lists the (partial) positive outcomes of the Stalinist revolution: one was its propaganda ("they managed to instill some of the basic philosophical principles of Marxism-Leninism into the consciousness of hundreds of thousands and millions of people"), and another was atheist education, where "the spirit of Marxism was not overlooked, as well as its own means of persuasion." Sviták drew attention to the fact that in most disciplines, efforts to reckon with the "deformations of the cult of personality" had already appeared before 1956. Among the text's aims were a legible attempt to make "revelations" for the purpose of preventing the same things from repeating, and Sviták's explicit attempt to "overcome the method of the cult of personality in philosophy," which would mean a thorough and truly critical development of Marxist philosophy in all the disciplines analyzed.[75]

That fact that in 1963 Sviták already considered the post-Stalinist motifs that we discuss, such as questions of the human being in modern society and the scientific-technical revolution, as crucial issues vividly illustrates the impact of the Twentieth Congress on thinking among the party intelligentsia. Naturally, we do not want to propose a monocausal connection between the debate that followed Khrushchev's speech, and the subjects analyzed in this treatise, but it is clear that the degree of party activation is significantly different in the period before and after the Twentieth Congress. If we remain with the example of the Institute of Philosophy, the negative reactions by the local party organizations to the campaign against revisionism in the second half of the 1950s and to Ivan Sviták's later dismissal and expulsion from the party (1964) only confirm this trend.

We have designated the proclamation of the socialist constitution in 1960 as the second milestone. Although there is often discussion of the Twelfth Congress of the Communist Party of Czechoslovakia (December 1962), which called upon members to uphold Leninist principles in their party work (activation), the event's outcomes were not merely a reproduction of established doctrines. It also introduced an open cultural and ideological line of thought and opened the way for the party to rehabilitate victims of the Stalinist political trials; we work under the assumption that the new constitution played a no less crucial role in the party intelligentsia's thinking as such. This is because, despite its internal plurality, in the post-Stalinist period the party's intelligentsia all had one thing in common: even if after 1960 party members may have been dissatisfied with the quality of the present state of the socialism they were living in (whether their concerns were over economy, the forces of production in the form of science, or cultural policies), they could not dispute that this level of historical development had indeed been achieved.

With the proclamation of socialism in 1960, the conceptual map and even the Marxist vocabulary underwent sweeping changes. Class struggle was replaced by "interest," classes with "social groups," struggle with "dialogue," "antagonism" with "convergences," and so on. The social-institutional structure was completed, radical transformations at the level of Stalinist accumulation were accepted, and the methods of the cult of personality were denounced and overcome through further development and reforms. At the same time, most party intellectuals definitively abandoned the confines of the original disciplines of orthodox Marxism, especially historical and dialectical materialism. For example, the philosopher Lubomír Nový wrote in 1964 that the very term "historical materialism" is imprecise, because it could evoke "the necessary division of the unity of dialectics, history, and the human being" and reduce dialectical materialism to a mere dialectics of nature.[76]

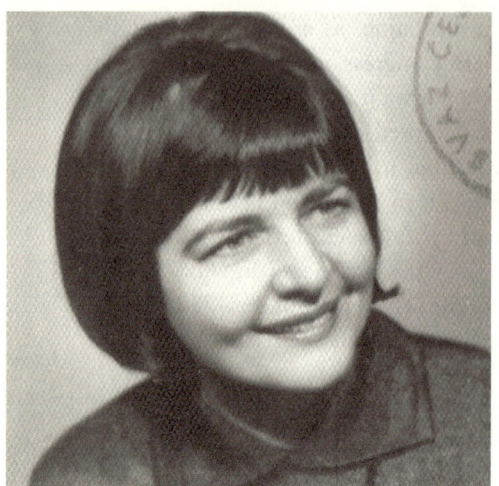

1.3. The sociologist Irena Dubská. Picture from the membership card of the Czechoslovak Writers' Union, 1970. Copyright National Archive, Prague.

Debates about historical laws and the movements of social-economic formations were then replaced with discussions about participation by socialist citizens in the development of society and legislation and about the freedom of the human individual. Simultaneously with the establishment of socialism, new academic fields arose, while others were rehabilitated and tasked with serving the interests of socialist development in the changed conditions. For example, sociology split from historical materialism, and the sociology of religion hived off from scientific atheism. A good example of an academic whose career followed these trends is the sociologist Irena Dubská, whose dissertation for the Candidate of Sciences degree on the classic Leninist subject of the relationship between party partisanship and scholarship was published in 1960. Three years later, she published a book about Auguste Comte and the founding of scientific sociology, and finally in 1964, she wrote a monograph titled *Objevování Ameriky* (Discovering America), which approaches contemporary American sociology positively, and—despite some criticism—operates with the unifying and positively construed concepts of "modernity" and "rationality."[77]

The development and instability of the Stalinist and early post-Stalinist periods, in the sense of incompleteness and makeshift arrangements in a people's democracy, were replaced by stability derived from the existence of socialism—starting with ownership and laws and ending with the state and a classless structure for society. Here, we repeat one of the defining theses according to which the conventionalization of the socialist model of organized modernity in the form of the proclamation of socialism afforded a sufficient foundation for thinking of various visions of socialist development: when socialism "had their backs," thinkers could model humanist or techno-optimistic versions of it much more easily than they could in times when they were aware of its incompleteness and instability.

CZECHOSLOVAKIA BETWEEN TECHNO-OPTIMISM AND HUMANISM?

As is clear from many of the references in the previous parts of this chapter, our understanding of post-Stalinism is exclusively based in analyses of the opinions of party intellectuals, whose participation in shaping the internal plurality of post-Stalinist thought was decisive. We are thus presenting the results of a probe into the period thinking; we do not want to generalize the conclusions and carry them over to other sections of the population or to other groups with different opinions or intellectual orientations that also existed in Czechoslovak society at that time. We are aware that if we proceeded in the way Anna Krylova suggests, which is through the examination of individual discourses, or if we included representatives of the church or other non-Marxist intellectual groups, we would arrive at a much more diverse picture of post-Stalinist plurality, and this would likely exceed the proposed singular episteme based on respecting the Marxist approach right from the starting point.[78]

However, our choice is not accidental, because, as Neil Harding has observed, "Of all modern ideologies, Leninism, more than any other, gives far more credence and authority to the role of intellectuals."[79] It is also important to mention that we do not look at the communist intelligentsia through the lens of moral, scholarly, personal (etc.) failure, but as an integral part of the system it grew out of and which at the same time, in Touraine's sense (historicity), it also produced. For the same reason, we relinquish the common interpretive key that perceives the difference between Stalinism and post-Stalinism as a shift away from Stalinist self-delusion to self-reflection and a critical approach to reality. We reiterate that we do not perceive post-Stalinism as a refusal and repudiation of Stalinism, but as a period that followed upon the previous era in many regards, while attempting to overcome it in others. In the era after Stalin's death, a search for new theoretical and practical starting points was typical among the party intelligentsia—and not only in Czechoslovakia.

Even though television gradually became prominent as a mass medium in the 1960s, the influence of the printed word (which was not produced only by the party intelligentsia) still certainly prevailed at that time. This was a general phenomenon across modern industrial civilizations, but for state socialist countries the emphasis on the written word was amplified by theories derived from the tradition of the classic texts. In the Czechoslovak case, Klement Gottwald was the last leader of the

KSČ whose personal papers were published and who was regarded as a significant theorist of the socialist movement. Post-Stalinist ideology was no longer derived from the authority of a political leader and main thinker (such as Stalin or Gottwald), but from suprapersonal socialist mechanisms based on Leninist principles. The published output of Antonín Novotný and Gustáv Husák, as well as Nikita Sergeyevich Khrushchev and Leonid Ilyich Brezhnev, consisted only of volumes titled *Speeches and Articles*.

The authoritativeness of speeches in the formation of ideology was naturally indispensable.[80] However, the generality and the possibility of interpretations according to present political lines was incomparable with the previous era, when the obligatory force of a sole theory was enforced. In other words, it was never necessary again in the history of state socialism to refer to the legacy of a given state functionary to the general theory of Marxism-Leninism as a guarantee of truth (Stalin's contribution to linguistics is well-known in this regard). However, this fact did nothing to change the primacy of the written word. These varied from articles in the daily and periodical press through scholarly and popular articles to party experts' analyses and materials prepared for party congresses (in the case of the KSČ, these were published in 1958, 1962, 1966, and 1968).

We consider members of party apparatuses as well as experts with party membership cards to be members of the party intelligentsia. Often in the Czechoslovak milieu—as with party historians or the lawyer Zdeněk Mlynář—one individual fulfilled both criteria. At the same time, the party intelligentsia occupied a specific position as a social class within the framework of the state socialist society.[81] Moreover, its role was enhanced by a particular aspect of the original creation of the modern Czech national identity in the nineteenth century, when intellectuals such as writers, university professors, lawyers, and the like were among the pillars of modern Czech society.[82] Even Stalinism did not disrupt the social standing of the intelligentsia, and it naturally continued even into the post-Stalinist period. This sector of society's approaches to modernity varied in different periods, but the intelligentsia's self-image as the bearers of progress who have a decisive influence on the resulting form of the national body endured.

From the perspective of intellectual history, the material benefits enjoyed by the party intelligentsia were not as important as their symbolic capital, especially their privileged access to sources of information and channels of publication. Both provided members with a good measure of social esteem and authority, which was additionally supported by their criticism of the past and the present—and this inspired their efforts in seeking post-Stalinist alternatives. In the eyes of the public, the party intelligentsia thus often became a guarantee that the process called "de-Stalinization" and the relaxing of conditions could continue.

In any case, because the party intelligentsia was considered a particularly important constituent element that helped form the ideological hegemony of the Stalinist system, this is the social group that gave shape to the distinct and specific feature of post-Stalinism—its internal plurality. Various visions of socialist modernity were conceptualized and formulated through the mediation of the party intelligentsia, which, although it was only one slice out of the entire society, had never ceased to occupy a privileged social position.

The Czechoslovak context provides a very suitable example demonstrating the internal richness of the post-Stalinist intellectual world. Within this milieu we can observe the creation of two distinctive and, at first glance, seemingly divergent intellectual trends within the party intelligentsia—humanism and techno-optimism—which both played an integral part in the development of internal plurality since the end of the 1950s and beginning of the 1960s. The former took shape around questions of the human individual and its full self-realization in a "truly" democratic socialist society, and the latter focused on science and technology as the determining productive force for the development of socialism. Interest in effective planning, expert analyses, and the integration of qualified productive forces in socialist management were also typical for techno-optimists.[83]

In its way, Marxist humanism was reacting to questions associated with both modern civilization and the possibility of its self-destruction as well as to experience with the Stalinist civilizational project and its emphasis on iron laws of history. As the humanists saw it, these concepts left no place for human individuals, or, by extension, their subjectivity. For the humanists, the nationalization of the means of production after the "Victorious February" turnover of political power (1948) represented a necessary condition along the way to the longed-for ideal of a Marxist "realm of freedom."[84] They believed that the new socialist relations would also create needful transformations in social relations as an intermediate stage.[85]

In its texts, Marxist humanism developed themes through which they addressed the deficits of Stalinist modernity: questions included the alienation of human individual in modern society; modern art and its role in socialism; ideology and its criticism; the relationship of Marxism to Christianity; and a models of a self-governing society.[86] As in Poland,

1.4. The most famous proponent of Marxist humanism and the author of *Dialectics of the Concrete*, Karel Kosík, in his office, 1968. Copyright Profimedia, photograph ČTK, Josef Nosek.

experience with working on materials drawn from the history of philosophy helped many Czech humanists (for example, Robert Kalivoda, Milan Machovec, Ivan Sviták, and Josef Zumr) define their own perspectives. Working with original texts by Karl Marx (*Economic and Philosophic Manuscripts*; *Theses on Feuerbach*; *The German Ideology*; *Grundrisse Notebooks*) and Friedrich Engels (*The Peasant War in Germany*), as well with others in the broader Marxist (Antonio Gramsci, György Lukács, and Karl Korsch) or European (Holbach, Hegel, and Montaigne) philosophical traditions as well as modern non-Marxist theories (anthropologism, existentialism, and personalism) also had a key influence on these circles. Personal relationships with representatives of the Polish school of the history of ideas, and, beginning in the 1960s, also with representatives of the Yugoslav group Praxis (for instance, Czech philosophers took part in summer school sessions with them on the island of Korčula), as well as with representatives of Western Marxism, such as Ernst Fischer, Erich Fromm, and Roger Garaudy, were also consequential.

Another of the important aspects of Marxist humanism was the critical development of the concept of "folkness" as it was introduced by the Czech doyen of Stalinist humanities studies, Zdeněk Nejedlý.[87] Folkness was considered one of the characteristics of the modern Czech identity, culture, and intellectual tradition. It had not been exhausted in Stalinism, and it was also to have its place in the post-Stalinist period, which the Marxist humanists believed was heading toward a truly democratic socialism. And by contrast with the strictly progressive concept of folkness (i.e., the cultural canon incorporated into the conception of Czech socialist realism), here was a democratic folkness that was to represent a regulating influence on intellectual elitism in the artistic sense and in 1968 also in the political sense (see chapter 4).

Naturally, culture played an utterly crucial role for Marxist humanists in modern socialist society.[88] At that time, the reception of art by the party intelligentsia (though not only by them) was one of the common matters of concern to which the authors of the time ascribed special importance. But in the eyes of the Marxist humanists, modern art, especially in the sense of literature, film, the fine arts, and so on, primarily represented a social practice with an extremely subversive character. After the downfall of Stalinism, or rather the exhaustion of the Leninist concept founded upon the proletariat and the party's role as its political avant-garde, it was culture and critical intellectual activity (philosophy) that were expected to replace the emancipatory function originally assigned to the party and in its own way also to the missing revolutionary subject.[89] According to the Marxist humanists, it was neither workers nor the party, but intellectuals and artists who were going to transform post-Stalinist socialism into a truly democratic socialism through their production (philosophy and art). This projection consisted in a shift for culture and art from servitude (a concept in the period interpretations of Stalinism) to independence from outer economic and political pressures. After satisfying both these conditions, culture could then fulfill its mission and humanize, that is, revolutionize, the reality of post-Stalinist socialism (see chapter 5).

In seeming contrast to the humanists, techno-optimistic thought, as its name suggests, primarily emphasizes the truly revolutionary role of technology and science in the development of modern society.[90] It did not understand the deficits or deformations of Stalinist modernity in terms of a superabundance of technology or even as the desubjectivization and alienation associated with the advent of technological civilization. Instead, the techno-optimists found fault in the period form of technology as well as in what they believed were some altogether misconceived ideas about technique and technology. This naturally did not mean advocating blind faith in the power of technology or science: the techno-optimists were well aware of the reality that these spheres of human activity could acquire emancipatory potential, particularly within the framework of socialist social relations.[91] However, their understanding of science as a specific modern force of production that replaces crafts and trades and Fordist organization in industry makes it quite clear that this is the determining factor for the future they are advocating, and not just in its technical aspects but also at the level of its overall development.[92] At the same time, the techno-optimists were drawing upon Marx's *Grundrisse*, Norbert Wiener's cybernetics, and John D. Bernal's concept of the scientific-technical revolution in creating their conception of the forces of production. In this regard, they either agreed with or drew inspiration from parallel Western and Soviet debates.[93]

For the techno-optimists, the scientific-technical revolution not only represented a further transformation within the framework of the evolution of the forces of production but also was an entirely unique form of revolution, which would move humanity into a new level of civilization. From this perspective, even the older revolution that was called "industrial" had not brought any fundamental historical turning point, because it was still part of the same developmental timeline as the development of craft production. This is another reason that the February Victory in 1948 and the subsequent industrialization and social transformation (the collectivization of agriculture and the formation of a new type of social or socialist state) were understood merely as a seizure of political power and the culmination of the previous stage of modernization, and not as a revolution in the strong sense of the word, or even as the revolution that was supposed to represent the true goal of socialism or communism. The society-wide significance of the scientific-technical revolution is betokened by the fact that it was formulated as radically "democratic" or "egalitarian." The term "scientist" was no longer to be a designation limited to a narrow professional or social group: in the future society, everyone would become at least to a certain extent a scientist. "Once we have the opportunity to cultivate them consistently, there will be no more obstacles to the steady growth, and finally universal validity of science as

1.5. Radovan Richta, the main representative of Czechoslovak techno-optimism and author of the concept of the scientific-technical revolution. Source: From the front page of *Památce Radovana Richty (1924–1983)* (Prague: Ústav pro filozofii a sociologii ČSAV, 1983).

human activity."[94] A demand for the "universalization of science," which was not dissimilar to the avant-garde approach to art, was conveyed here with an ethos of humanization and the progress of modern civilization.

It is indisputable that techno-optimistic discourse placed a much stronger emphasis on the development of technology, and especially of science in its heralding of a new era. Science became the driving force for the revolution that was going to shift post-Stalinist society to an entirely new level. However, for the humanists, creative work (or "praxis" per the period term) was determinative, because it transcended the narrow conventions of science and technology (see chapter 5). On the other hand, even for the humanists, the tool (i.e., technology) represented the determining moment in praxis.[95] Thus, they could not be considered supportive of a recursive return to a romanticized premodern condition in any way. For Karel Kosík, humanist philosophy absolutely did not mean a manner of thought that prioritized one aspect of human life (morality or subjectivity) over another (labor or science); it was an overall comprehension of human beings and the world in the totality of their relations.[96] On the other hand, the techno-optimists not only viewed the scientific-technical revolution through the lens of science and technology but also contextualized it into a social framework. This was expected to, and in fact had to enable the creative evolution of human powers and activities. Human creativity represented the crucial point from which both paths emerged. The techno-optimists considered the relationship of labor time to leisure time to be of key importance. However, in the type of scientific development they envisioned it was their explicit intention not to draw an opposition between time spent in leisure and laboring; instead, there would be an extension or perhaps a diffusion of one sphere into the other. Leisure time was thus not supposed to function only as a respite from labor, because in this way it would merely serve to reproduce labor within the complementary sphere of relaxation (work as the simple obverse side of relaxation); rather, it was a part of the continual evolution of the human being because the activities in both spheres directly and mutually enhance one another. The case was similar with the category of labor, for the humanists overshadowed by the theme of creativity, which they understood as a spontaneous expression of human praxis in the form of art and thinking.

For both intellectual currents, it is true that the greatest challenge was fundamentally revising what dialectics had meant for Marxism until that time (particularly regarding the legacy of the Second International and Stalinism). The question of the human being's position in nature and in society was to be posed anew precisely through a fundamental reconceptualization of this intellectual approach, achieved through new readings of Hegel and selected texts by Marx (*Foundations of a Critique of Political Economy, Economic and Philosophic Manuscripts from 1844, Theses on Feuerbach*, and the third part of *Capital*).[97] For the humanists and the techno-optimists alike, the human being was both the starting point and the vanishing point of their theories. This is exemplified in a quote by the economist and journalist Radoslav Selucký, who often took on the role of a kind of bridge between the techno-optimists and humanists. He summarized the endeavors of both streams of thought as aiming to achieve civilizational changes that would not just develop science, technology, and art for their own sakes, but also so that "any individual could fully develop all of his abilities in order to become a creator in this or that field, in order to become Man."[98]

There is also another area where the techno-optimists and humanists agreed. They did not understand either science and technology or thought and culture according to the Leninist conception based on the existence of two disparate national cultures (or bourgeois and socialist milieux), which were continuously clashing in an ideological struggle. Quite the contrary, they perceived the problems of culture, science, and technology in accordance with the period theory of convergence (i.e., as something common to both West and East). Regardless, they still considered socialism at the level of social-productive relations and Marxism at the level of theory as the only forms that could enable the full liberation and development of creative potential of the human being and society.

1.6. The Slovak philosopher Miroslav Kusý, Department of Philosophy at Comenius University in Bratislava, early 1960s. Copyright Dagmar Kusá.

In the historiography produced to date, the theme of post-Stalinist modernity is usually connected with techno-optimistic thought, or perhaps with the project of what was called the "scientific-technical revolution," which was led and exemplified by Radovan Richta.[99] However, the idea of technocratic socialism is now being traced by scholars from a long-term, transnational perspective as an inherent part of European modernity and even as a contribution toward global governmentality (in theory and potential practice).[100] By contrast with this, Marxist humanism, even when it is conceived in a global perspective as an answer to modern civilization in the sense of a *Zivilisationskritik* of Western Marxism, was soon to be perceived as a fundamentally different intellectual trend.[101] From its perspective, the techno-optimistic ideas were considered a new and more manipulative mode of alienation that was going to create a new type of post-Stalinist dictatorship: in other words, they are an obstacle along the way to the full liberation of the human individual and the development of all his potentials.[102] In this spirit, we attempt to show that both intellectual currents are part of the general post-Stalinist development. While the philosopher Erazim Kohák evaluated the Czechoslovak Spring of 1968 as an internal conflict of the modern era, based in the irreconcilability of the "self-propulsion of technology" and the realization of "humanistic ideals," we perceive techno-optimism and Marxist humanism as two sides of the same coin.[103]

However, our goal is not to limit Czechoslovak post-Stalinism to just a confrontation between the motifs of the Marxist humanists and the techno-optimists. We attempt to show that a multilayered intellectual space was created, where all the outgrowths shared a common foundation.

CZECHOSLOVAK POST-STALINISM

1.7. Proponents of dialectical determinism (from the left) Zdeněk Javůrek, Jindřich Zelený, one unidentified person, Vladimír Ruml, and Radovan Richta at the head of the table, 1978. Copyright Masaryk Institute and Archives of the Czech Academy of Sciences.

In our interpretation, we understand post-Stalinism as a unified epistemic field within which there was a reinterpretation of classical Marxist concepts, such as dialectics, historical laws, practice, and the forces of production, and additionally there was a new understanding of the categories of the people and the nation. The entire post-Stalinist epistemic field, whose contours we sketch out here, exceeds the framework of the above-mentioned intellectual movements. Furthermore, belonging to a specific movement as a collection of ideas, theories, or theses is not ultimately the determining factor for us: we are primarily interested in capturing the manner in which Stalinism was problematized, which these two intellectual movements (and perhaps others as well) had in common, and which made them possible. We then understand this field as (potentially) unlimited in its differentiations. Besides humanism and techno-optimism, we also speak about dialectical determinism, whose representatives include Josef Cibulka, Jindřich Zelený, Václav Černík, and Zdeněk Javůrek. In addition, we analyze texts by Zdeněk Mlynář, František Šamalík, Michal Lakatoš, and Miroslav Kusý, whom we categorize as legal philosophers, and there are also many others. In other words, the selection of intellectual production from the party intelligentsia does not depend on a person belonging to a given movement, but on the way they have problematized issues and posed questions.

The pluralization of intellectual trends did not simply mean an empirical multiplication in which the old Stalinist approaches were simply one variation that was just as real as the others. These old approaches, of course, could persist at various levels of the party, though naturally the "spirit" (to phrase it romantically) of post-Stalinist thought was already elsewhere. Although the critical confrontation with other Marxist and non-Marxist traditions did not put a dent in the hegemony of Marxism and Leninism, it still opened it up to new ways of interpreting classic texts and uncovering new facets, which provided original ways to prove their epistemic superiority.

METHODOLOGICAL-CRITICAL PERSPECTIVES

Above, we have elaborated what we consider the theoretical underpinnings of our work. "Theory" here primarily means the perspective from which we approach the historical material. Thus, we are concerned with capturing the essential characteristic traits of the objects of study. This requires us to clarify the methodological means of our approach (i.e., not the conceptualization of a historically unique object, but the manner of processing it). The methodology refers to a set of conceptual instruments that can mutatis mutandis also be used on other subjects of research. This is only a slight difference, and in many regards both forms of activity coincide. Nevertheless, we still want to make a distinction between them, so, simply put, theory answers the question of "what," and methodology answers the question of "how."

We do not want to swear by big names and impressive concepts, but at the same time it is necessary to clarify several perspectives to avoid potential misunderstandings and unfulfilled expectations regarding what this treatise is and is not about. Our book aims to be a contribution to a discipline that can best be described as the history of thought. However, this is neither the history of philosophy nor the history of ideas. Our goal is not to trace individual intellectual (Marxist or other) traditions and follow the ways in which they are projected into post-Stalinist thought. Nor do we want to demonstrate the extent to which the thinkers we track have elaborated on earlier Marxist impulses in original ways, or, on the contrary, the extent to which they distorted or misunderstood them, or, from the perspective of a greater distance, where they were clearly wrong. The oppositions of original and banal, true and false play no role for us. Therefore, it will not interest us whether, for example, Kosík interpreted Heidegger adequately, or whether the dialectical determinists truly did justice to the essence of dialectics, whether their criticism of structuralism, existentialism, and phenomenology was justified, or even to what extent their thinking was dependent upon these influences. We are also not interested in whether and to what extent Czechoslovak thought in the 1960s proved its originality in comparison with other related intellectual activities in the Eastern bloc during the period investigated, let alone whether they enriched—as a great many period actors believed—the "treasure-house of European civilization." Naturally, we consider all of these to be relevant research questions, but we have chosen to direct our attention along another pathway.

We understand individual conceptions, theoretical statements, and scholarly, artistic, and political concepts produced by the thinking of a particular period more in the sense of specific events—i.e., not as references to traditions, influences, the spirit of an age, or contexts that explain them, but as the results of relatively autonomous responses to historically situated challenges of the day.[104] To put it more concretely, particular challenges to the communist parties include Stalin's death in 1953, the Twentieth Congress of the Communist Party of the USSR, the official proclamation of socialism in Czechoslovakia in 1960, and the economic crisis in the Czechoslovak Socialist Republic at the end of 1962 and beginning of 1963.

However, we certainly do not want to say that these events and challenges represented some type of sobering up, or impetus toward it for the former Stalinists, who would then be transformed into reformers whose fate and creative peak would be the Czechoslovak Spring of 1968. This narrative is not convincing for us, precisely because it is a *Bildungsroman* type of story, or even a legend, embellished with a strong moment of catharsis. We are not about to write the history of individual stories based on the path away from Stalinist intoxication toward seeing the light, after which our actors would then behave as autonomous thinkers. We do not deny the legitimacy of this type of approach, especially regarding the history of philosophy, but instead of dealing with the thinking of individual thinkers in the classical philosophical sense our goal is to capture post-Stalinist thought at a paradigmatic level. Moreover, the religious conception mentioned above additionally presupposes the figure of the ignorant Stalinist, who in confrontation with "hard" facts gradually converts to the "correct" way.[105]

Despite its sophisticated and inspiring character, the perspective of "sobering up" is also projected to a certain extent into approaches that work with the conception of a generation as a unifying moment with visible internal coherence within post-Stalinist thought.[106] According to this formula, the post-Stalinists were a generation born in the 1920s, for whom the Great Depression, the demise of the First Republic, and living in the Protectorate of Bohemia and Moravia were defining experiences (Alena Wagnerová speaks of a "vanguard" generation).[107] The decisive formative moment for this generation was, in fact, its involvement in Stalinist building process. Their participation in shaping the reform project of the 1960s is deduced from this, or from the reevaluation of their own Stalinist past after the Twentieth Congress of the Communist Party of the USSR. Michael Voříšek, for example, speaks of the main "driving force" of reformist thought.[108] In addition to the previously mentioned problem with the "sobering up" trope, we believe that the sociologically defined generations allow for a portrait of the cohesiveness of the reform movement and its social impact instead of describing the actual contents of the period's intellectual production.

The second significant research perspective applied in the examination of the intellectual history of Czechoslovak reformism consists of research on expert groups.[109] This approach allows the capture of solutions to questions associated with the challenges of modernity and modernization over a longer period. At the same time, the relationship to the concept of modernity enables us to go beyond the geographical limitation of the Eastern bloc, or the Second World, and to examine this subject field in connection with the First World, thus transcending the dichotomy of West versus East. Yet, no matter how inspiring similar research projects have been for us (especially those relating to the project of modernity), we consider their circumscription to individual groups of actors as limiting. In the *longue durée* perspective and in the global view, the specific nature of post-Stalinism as a closed period of time and an epistemic field are lost to a certain extent.

While we operate with the term "post-Stalinism" exclusively in the Czechoslovak case, when we analyze Stalinism, we have often availed ourselves of primary and secondary texts of Soviet provenance. We do not want to claim in this way that Stalinism lacked a specific Czechoslovak version, and Czechoslovaks were only passively recipients of Soviet models; however, from our perspective, these differences are minimal. In our view, it is possible to construct a homogeneous Stalinist (and simultaneously also orthodox in many regards) model of Marxism that, despite local historical, personnel, and institutional differences, was applied across the entire Eastern bloc during the "Sovietization" process. This interpretation is borne out both by the brief duration of Stalinism in Central and Eastern Europe as well as by the "impossibility" of developing a domestic version, and additionally by Stalinism's own demand that there be obligatory force behind the application of its own theory.[110] The only significant exception is found in Czechoslovak scholarship in the figure of Zdeněk Nejedlý, who founded his own paradigm of "domestic revolutionary traditions."

We mentioned above that the late Stalinist regime was unwittingly creating both the tendencies and the capacity for its own self-restructuring, which we described using Touraine's concept of historicity. We therefore do not want to take these events and challenges as crude incursions of absolutely external factors into the stagnant "mud" of Stalinism, but as catalysts that sped up the transformation of thought and thereby initiated or even unknowingly produced tendencies whose directions and impacts were incalculable.

We thus grant a certain independence to thought. For us, it is not merely an expression of social and economic relations, even if these factors undoubtedly constitute their external and necessary conditions. Likewise, we suppose that we are in no way contradicting the part of the Marxist tradition that never considered thought to be a mere appendage of the material situation of the society. On the other hand, we also do not ignore the institutional, political, and social grounding of the authors on whose work we base our analysis. Elucidation of their situatedness allows us to sufficiently justify our selection of texts; however, at the same time, we clearly limit the scope of this type of analysis. We thus do not claim to capture the period's Zeitgeist, the world of meaning (*Sinnwelt*), or a mentality, which are supposed to be common throughout the population without differences. In our research, we are looking at a quantitatively insignificant slice of the society, albeit a slice that we consider to be significant because it had the disposition and a sufficiently powerful capacity to speak out in ways that affected events.

Because our analysis does not attempt to systematically reconstruct "post-Stalinist" thought in its entirety, it does not offer detailed expositions on individual intellectual trends. This is also why we refused to divide individual chapters according to disciplines, or intellectual currents.[111] We also did not divide chapters based on types of discourse (philosophy, economics, art history, social science, etc.).[112] Classification of the material using these artificial categories would also be confounded by the permeability of the categories and their transgression by various individuals. For instance, we can consider Radovan Richta as a symbolic representative of techno-optimism, and Karel Kosík as a representative of Marxist humanism. However, things become more complicated with the likes of Milan Průcha, Radoslav Selucký, and Dragoslav Slejška. Průcha promoted humanism in the early 1960s, then later he criticized its insufficient ontology and worked closely with Richta's team; Selucký spoke positively about the humanists, and vice versa; and Slejška, as a sociologist of industry, was close in his way to the determinists and the techno-optimists, but in his advocacy for the self-governance of employees' councils at the end of the 1960s he draws closer to the humanists. For the same reason, the antithesis between the "technocratic" and "radically democratic" visions of socialism discussed by Johann P. Árnason, Erazim Kohák, Karel Kovanda, and more recently by Ivan Landa is not determinative for us.[113]

This also is not a story about reform or reformism as a type of thought, because instead we are endeavoring to capture the conceptualizations of post-Stalinist modernity.[114] We have therefore focused on specific thematic clusters that either do or potentially could intersect with all the social science disciplines (the question of "real structure," the new subjectivity, the people, the nation, and revolution). At the same time, as stated above, we proceed from a certain epistemic field that we believe was common to various intellectual orientations that might seem entirely disparate. Naturally, for the above-mentioned reasons, it is also clear that mapping out this epistemic unity cannot be done based on individual more or less "finished" doctrines and theories but should instead be performed on the basis of a common form of (post-Stalinist) problematization.[115]

What do we have in mind with the term "problematization"? What creates its unity? Even though we do not deny that various intellectual trends could share concepts with approximately the same content, such as, for example, the "totality," we take it for granted that we cannot use ready-made terms or concepts that became flagships for individual intellectual currents—for example, "dialectical laws" with the determinists, "praxis" with the humanists, or the "scientific-technical revolution" with the techno-optimists—as a basis for our thinking about post-Stalinism. Nor can Marxism, Leninism, or Marxism-Leninism serve in this function, even though these are intellectual traditions and legacies that all thinkers, without exception, explicitly profess. For example, we cannot get very far with Marxism, because its very content is precisely the subject of controversy. Nominally, from the position of the unbiased observer, everyone is therefore a Marxist, both in relationship to one another and in relation to what they primarily aimed to distinguish themselves from: Stalinism as one of the variants of Marxism.

The case of "Marxist revisionism" is similar—it has undergone complicated development from the perspective of historical semantics. This is because the term "revisionism" has primarily been used in contrast with orthodoxy (i.e., as a symptomatic expression with negative connotations). Thus, for example, Karl Kautsky labeled Eduard Bernstein's departure from the still revolutionary Marxism of the Second International as revisionism, but then Lenin called Kautsky a revisionist for his tacit support of the war and criticism of the revolutionary movement in Russia and Germany, and György Lukács's and Karl Korsch's Hegelian Marxism was called revisionist even though they had supported the revolution. However, Lukács understood himself explicitly as an orthodox Marxist! The Soviet leadership was then branded as revisionist by China for its criticism of Stalinism; similarly, party intellectuals in Central and Eastern Europe who "contaminated" Marxism were so branded by the Soviets. The history of revisionism thus represents the history of deviating from a norm that is in itself a fluid and slippery phenomenon whose form depends on the current distribution of power and the forces that control ideology. Barring the possible exception of certain Polish anti-Stalinist Marxists in the 1950s and 1960s, no Marxists would have consciously called themselves revisionists in a positive sense. For many who were pigeonholed in this way, whether in defamatory speeches by party elites or in serious scholarly treatises, there was no "revision" in this sense of the word. Instead, they understood their interpretation of Marx's intellectual heritage as a return to the "real" and "undistorted" Marxism. Therefore, unlike many previous researchers, we do not consider the term revisionism as a satisfactory explanatory tool.[116] And rather than as an analytical concept, we perceive it as a weapon used in certain historical discursive strategies.

By contrast, the term "orthodoxy" refers to the above-mentioned intellectual trend that incorporates the Second International and Soviet Marxism-Leninism (including its "mutations" in Central and Eastern Europe) and displays a much greater degree of stability. Moreover, regarding the demise of the Soviet Union, we consider its development to be closed. However, a question that we cannot answer here remains: What concept can be used in characterizing the entire development of Western and Eastern Marxism outside of orthodoxy? Therefore, in our text—for reasons of both content and concepts—we incline toward the terms "post-Stalinist Marxism" and "Stalinist Marxism" (i.e., Marxism-Leninism), which we categorize as a particular version of orthodox Marxism. Thus, in our interpretation, the term "orthodox" can overlap with the concept of Stalinism or orthodox Stalinism.

In this way, we attempt to avoid a nominalist approach. As Walter Benjamin notes, the product of nominalism can only be empty abstractions that vainly attempt to gain specific content by devouring "disorderly" particulars. Nominalism would like to respect the rights of individuals, but in creating an order that will always be only provisional and thus random, it can only find in the particulars what it has put into them. Nominalism is unable to penetrate all the way down to the intrinsic historical conditions of thought because it is extrinsic to them. At best, it can provide "a private *reservatio mentalis*, not a methodical defence."[117]

The contemporary manner of problematization therefore does not represent an "ideal" type for us, let alone a heuristic means with which we can orient ourselves in a chaotic reality. It is an epistemic field that forms real, historical, and internal conditions for the given type of thinking. It is a field upon which individual theories, concepts, or doctrines (i.e., products that we could term as the effects of differentiation into various intellectual trends and currents) have the potential to arise. Therefore, its constitutive feature cannot be either a specific theory, concept, or doctrine, but a problem that is subconsciously formulated by everyone who enters this field.

The history that we want to write, therefore, is not a history of the Czechoslovak (reform) thinking of the 1960s. We make no claim to describing all the subjects discussed within individual philosophical or scientific disciplines to a greater or lesser extent. For instance, we are not interested in mapping out the details of all the conceptions of time that arose during this period, or alternative variants for the socialist economy, from Ota Šik's economic reforms to Egon Bondy's radical project of socialist self-government. Instead, categories of thought that provided the necessary conceptual groundwork for eventual reforms or models of social organization are of paramount importance in our project.[118]

During the 1960s it began to be increasingly obvious that pressure on post-Stalinist thinking was not coming so much from the side of the party apparatus as "externally" from other philosophical traditions. The most significant of these influences were existentialism and neopositivism, which in that period, alongside Marxism, were understood as the three dominant philosophical movements.[119] There was no danger that Marxism would lose its ideologically dominant position as the state doctrine, so this was something that most of the post-Stalinist thinkers were not even concerned about. What they rather feared was best expressed by Kosík: "It's impossible to cheat in philosophy" and "the prohibition against so-called anti-Marxist tendencies, accompanied by the establishment of an absolute monopoly of thought, pronounced the death sentence of Marxist philosophy."[120] Similar to many others who were instructed by Hegel and Gramsci, Kosík was very well aware that philosophy is neither a war nor a game in which we seek adversaries' weak spots and benefit from exploiting them, but an activity that targets the adversaries' strengths. Thus, in his view, a philosophical movement worthy of the name could only emerge through a productive—though not exclusively antagonistic—engagement with other traditions and intellectual currents. This, indeed, was the path chosen by the post-Stalinist Marxists. While they undoubtedly drew inspiration from the broader philosophical landscape, they turned to Marx's works—and to Marxism more broadly—in search of their own responses to the pressing problems of their time, responses that they believed Marxism articulated more compellingly.

Josef Cibulka lamented in a typical manner, that "[M]arxist philosophers have mostly never been able to actively develop Marx's dialectical method. In the period of the cult of personality it was proscribed to them as 'Hegelian.' And as soon as this period had ended, the 'forbidden chamber' of bourgeois philosophy opened up, which still has not ceased to dazzle with its wonders and its jewels. It is no wonder that in the absence of long years of study and active development of dialectics there is also a lack of experience [so] the problem examined in dialectical movement will reveal its essence more fully than before."[121] As if, in Cibulka's view, the situation from the period before World War I was repeating itself—when it seemed to certain Marxists that Marxism alone could not resolve the philosophical questions of the time, and needed to be supplemented by other sources, primarily neo-Kantianism.

The slogan "Rehabilitate Marx!" which we have borrowed for the title of this book, thus does not mean only cleansing Marx and Marxism of dogmatic accretions, but also—primarily—raising them to the height of the period and demonstrating their philosophical superiority. Our work offers an analytical archaeology of this historically unsuccessful, though of course an intellectually very rich project.

If we have spoken above about how we are not basing our interpretation on separate discussions of individual intellectual trends, and have said that we are mainly interested in understanding how the party intelligentsia worked (within the scope of ideas about post-Stalinist modernity) with concepts such as dialectics, historical laws, practice, and so on, we must reemphasize the methodological guidelines we are applying here. In an effort to avoid subordinating our own writing to the perspectives of the thinkers we analyze, we apply an analytical framework to the period terminology, which helps our attempts to create our own structuration of the post-Stalinist epistemic field when approaching questions connected with structure, human subjectivity, collective agents, and social change.

As researchers grounded in a certain extent in the tradition of critical theory and Marxism, we admit that the categorization and the title of the first analytical chapter, "Real Structure" (chapter 2), are no accident. The concepts we discuss there (historical laws, the means of production, praxis, and dialectics) represented fundamental interpretive challenges for the post-Stalinist intellectuals, and by elucidating them we have aimed to build a firmer foundation from which to develop further interpretations. Although the individual chapters may function as independent studies on their topics, we believe that the internal diversity and common traits among their views cannot be fully understood without analysis of the real structure. At the same time, the entire book is conceived concurrently as an interconnected whole, where the individual chapters prompt or assist readers to create a holistic image of Czechoslovak post-Stalinism viewed through the lens of the party intelligentsia. Self-ironically, we can say that we have probably succeeded in creating a certain form of totality: the individual sections of this book address the issues of social development, subjectivity, the nation, and the reinterpretation of the revolution, and form an interconnected and internally consistent field. We attempt to escape from this analytical trap of cold structuring and analysis in chapter 6, where we attempt to assume a critical distance in our perspective and we sketch in the limits of post-Stalinist thought. However, readers should retain the impression that post-Stalinist thought was rich in emancipatory challenges, and we hope they will understand what we find inspiring in it. In this way, we return, via a wide arc, to the tradition that we arose from, and in this spirit, we consider our writing as an expression of engaged scholarship.

In response to our criticism in the foreword written for the Czech edition of his treatise on the social and intellectual world of post-Stalinism, Pavel Kolář mentions Boris Pasternak's metaphor, according to which making philosophy one's exclusive specialty is similar to eating nothing other than horseradish.[122] We take the author at his word and do not offer readers anything other than horseradish. We believe that its distinctive flavor will go down well.

CHAPTER 2

REAL STRUCTURE

> In fact, however, if the narrow bourgeois form is peeled off, what is wealth if not the universality of the individual's needs, capacities, enjoyments, productive forces, etc., produced in universal exchange; what is it if not the full development of human control over the forces of nature—over the forces of so-called Nature, as well as those of his own nature? What is wealth if not the absolute unfolding of man's creative abilities, without any precondition other than the preceding historical development, which makes the totality of this development—i.e. the development of all human powers as such, not measured by any previously given yardstick—an end-in-itself, through which he does not reproduce himself in any specific character, but produces his totality, and does not seek to remain something he has already become, but is in the absolute movement of becoming?
>
> **—KARL MARX**

If we speak about "real structure" within the framework of (post-)Stalinist thought, we are not primarily referring to the well-known pair of base and superstructure, which Marxism is famous or infamous for. This dichotomy, which was first established schematically in Marx's (in)famous "Preface" to *A Contribution to the Critique of Political Economy* and further elaborated in Engels's *Anti-Dühring*, has persisted since the founding of Marxism to the Second International, through orthodox Marxism-Leninism, to Louis Althusser and his students, its essence is still present in analytical Marxism (Gerald Cohen), and it is often considered an essential feature of Marxist thought as such. However, despite this, or even because of it, this conceptual distinction is neither a methodological starting point nor a guide for us. The point here is not that the primacy of the base as the determinative element in the dialectical whole had already been questioned—if not outright relativized—by certain Marxists as early as the 1920s, or that a similar move was later made by many post-Stalinist Czechoslovak Marxists.[1] The main reason lies mostly in the methodological perspective.

Henceforth, rather than following the base–superstructure imagery as the axis of Marxist thought, we are concerned with the mode of problematization and, along with it, the recurring presence of certain subjects, theses, and concepts—in short, the reference points through which post-Stalinist Marxists reflected on their own historical situation. Thus, real structure does not have to be (although it can be) the base, as defined by orthodox Marxism as the relationship of the means of production and the relations of production, or as the production and reproduction of material life. It could also be, for example, only one part (the forces of production), or a way of grasping (the entirety) of reality, or sometimes it could be the forms that govern reality (laws). At the same time, it is also true for Marxism that thinking about real structure means also thinking about the way its establishment and transformation will be accomplished. Therefore, we divide real structure (in the analytical sense of the term) into two parts: thinking about the whole, and thinking about genesis, and—by extension—activity. In Stalinism, both parts are represented by a production-determined pair of base and building, and in post-Stalinism by totality and creation.

More than we do in other chapters, we have turned our attention to the German and (especially) Soviet traditions of orthodox and Stalinist Marxism. By contrast with Bulgaria (Todor Pavlov) and Hungary (György Lukács), Czechoslovak Stalinism was missing a more significant theorist (the Czech Stalinist Zdeněk Nejedlý enters the scene as the author of the Stalinist conception of Czech history in chapter 4). The post-Stalinists thus primarily turned to polemics with the original sources of the entire orthodox tradition that had culminated in Stalinism. Here, we must issue the caveat that the conceptual apparatus and the vocabulary in the debates analyzed in this chapter are difficult to digest. However, we are convinced that it is only by understanding what had been discussed at a time that used an overly complicated vocabulary can we open the way to further topics in post-Stalinist thinking. This is not because readers would be unable to read the other chapters without this one, or that they would not be able to understand them. However, the ways post-Stalinism problematized subjectivity and social changes are inseparable from the path that the post-Stalinist intellectuals had to walk at the level of thinking about abstract issues such as dialectical laws, forces of production, and praxis.

BUILDING

It is possible to claim that Stalinism was mainly about "building," which means that it constructed plans and then built them.[2] The principle of building was the dominant metaphor in Stalinist thought for a simple reason: creating sufficient economic foundations for establishing socialism (and later, communism) was one of the young Soviet regime's primary objectives and, give or take a few details, it was imitated by the other countries of the Eastern bloc. Of course, this "building" was not just a vague metaphor, or an abstract description of activity, it was also an accurate conceptual formulation.

More than philosophy, it was Soviet debates about the economy in the 1920s that provided this form of thought with a more precise outline, and this is when two seemingly irreconcilable positions were formed. According to "geneticists" such as Vladimir Bazarov, Vladimir Groman, Nikolai Kondratiev, and Nikolai Bukharin, planning should be based in objective conditions given through historical development. The economy was understood as an organic whole, governed by specific laws and by equilibrium among individual sectors.[3] This in no way precluded the implementation of central planning, which the geneticists also considered a crucial means for overcoming the country's backwardness. However, its character should emerge from "prognoses for economic development, formulated strictly genetically; i.e., founded only upon respect for the objective rules and trends of the spontaneous economic process."[4] The "general" plan determined the approximate goal the economy should reach, and the "prospective" plan was then, taking into account the genetic perspective, to determine a degree of growth that would be as continual as possible without disruptive drops and breaks. At the same time, there was also an imperative to seek "the shortest possible path," which the authors of the plan could choose among the various predicted development curves. In any case, the geneticists were working from the assumption that besides the state-regulated area of the economy, a "spontaneous" sector would still exist uncontrolled by the state, in which the market would have a certain say.

By contrast, the "teleologists" headed by Stanislav Strumilin, Gleb Krzhizhanovsky, and Yevgeni Preobrazhensky proceeded in the opposite direction. They strongly opposed the genetic perspective, which called for respecting the economic laws, existing trends, and prognoses that resulted from them. In their own way, even these economists were based in the objective situation, but the key preconditions for drawing up the plan were not tendencies and natural laws, but the subjective will that aspires to change the given situation.⁵ Strumilin expressed the perspective of the teleologists' critique of the geneticists succinctly: "So long as we only extrapolate from the past, at best we are prolonging the past in a revised and expanded form for another five or fifteen years. However, we will not build a new social order in this way."⁶ The teleologists did not consider predictions but goals as determinative, and by prioritizing goals they wanted to drive a wedge between the past and the future. This is why they could not accept an emphasis on respecting historical laws. At the same time, they also took exception to the other core concepts of genetic theory: equal, proportional development of all sectors of the economy and its continual growth. Instead, the teleologists prioritized industry over agriculture as the leading sector of the economy, and, in so doing, they also accepted disproportions in economic development, for example, between demand and supply.

Thus, for the teleologists, thinking of economics and thinking of its planning meant constructing a building according to a goal that was set in advance: the socialist order. This is why Strumilin liked comparing the role of the economist-planner with that of an engineer, or even better, an architect, who first draws up a project and only after that seeks the means needed to carry out the construction. This process was not deemed as straightforward: it cannot even move forward in a straight line, and it requires a significant degree of flexibility as well as creative imagination from the economist, who must be able to reckon with potential shortages and unpredictable circumstances. "From now on, the difference between individual draftsmen on this field will not consist in the scope and precision of their calculations, but rather in their changing abilities to creatively combine possible elements of the planned structure as simply, cheaply, beautifully, and effectively as possible."⁷ Kondratiev, a proponent of the genetic approach, aptly captured this indifference to the underlying objective conditions of planning when he remarked on Strumilin that by disregarding the concrete forms in which these conditions are available to us, "he is tearing the thread between projection and reality. From there it is already only, however imperceptibly, a step toward creating a plan that is entirely arbitrary."⁸ Needless to say, these words were prophetic regarding the overall character of the production of Stalinist planning, which was carried on in a purely teleological spirit from the end of the 1920s.

Stalinist teleological building thus did not consist so much of a concept of "total" planning (though this could undoubtedly be its consequence) but a prioritized position of the goal (establishing socialism) compared with the current conditions, which were to be overcome. This manner of thinking allowed, or indeed absolutely required, to put it into Strumilin's terms, social engineering that was able to work creatively with the plan: to vary and "manipulate" its goals and to use any means possible as a consequence of the necessity of reacting to unforeseen circumstances, shortages (of materials, means of production, and other resources), and the ubiquitous imbalances in the development of individual economic sectors. Stalin spoke of the "state of tension" in the plans, which is the result of the rapid pace of industrial development, as "the underlying principle of, and the key to, the industrialisation of the country."[9] In this respect, Stalinist social engineering differs from the various technocratic utopias that had opposed a "chaotic" and "spontaneous" capitalist society to a society founded on strictly rational organization.[10] Here, "chaos" was considered a basic element in the construction process.[11] The decisive factor in the teleological concept was the requirement for active, voluntary behavior that could overcome the negative manifestations of chaos.

The source of the intense volatility of Stalinism as a specific mode of thought as well as a form of social organization did not consist only of the attempt to subordinate all social activity to one rational plan that would organize every single aspect of it in minute detail, thus excluding the possibility of negative tendencies as well as individual creativity and spontaneous action. The weakness of the system was embodied in the will of the planner (or "social engineer"), and this will—precisely out of reluctance to respect the initial situation—could and did degenerate into arbitrariness. It is therefore no surprise that the implementation of the Soviet planned economy in the 1930s looked more like a series of trials and errors (both successes and social and human catastrophes) than like the realization of a rational strategy that was thought out in every detail and planned. And it is no coincidence at all that in his late theoretical book *Economic Problems of Socialism in the USSR* Stalin invoked the laws of political economy "which are not created by the will of man" and thus also cannot be arbitrarily abolished as an argument against the teleological approach to planning.[12] Here, Stalin essentially ended the era of unilateral teleological planning and incorporated the genetic perspective into it.[13] He confirmed the validity of the law of proportionally planned development, which cannot be equated with the current planning itself.[14] However, this in no way exceeded the rules of Marxist orthodoxy, in which the relationship between an objectively valid law and human subjective activity—as we shall see in chapter 3—was defined in terms of control or subordination. Even in this context, the orientation remained essentially naturalistic, focused on analyzing and mastering natural laws.

REAL STRUCTURE

ORTHODOXY

Stalinist ideas about dialectics and materialism, and the conception of history derived from them, became some of the main targets of criticism in post-Stalinist Marxist thought. However, while bearing this in mind, it is also necessary to be aware of two facts. The first is that Stalinist Marxism-Leninism, as Karl Korsch pointed out in the 1930s, at the theoretical level was essentially only a peculiar continuation of the orthodox Marxism of the Second International.[15] The second fact is that this manner of interpreting Marxism proved to be remarkably long-lived, and by no stretch ended with Stalin's death or with the Twentieth Congress of the Communist Party of the USSR—and this is true to such an extent that we can observe orthodox framing of fundamental questions in Czechoslovak works on historical materialism until the beginning of the 1960s. In this part of our analysis, we are concerned with identifying the building blocks of Marxist orthodoxy so that the following sections demonstrate the ways in which the self-evidence of their assumptions is problematized. What fundamental problems of real structure was orthodox Marxism trying to solve? Two areas are crucial for our interpretation: the first concerns the way the primacy of materialism was defended against idealism, and the second is the scientificity of the Marxist method.

The first problem was often formulated in the manner of what is called the basic philosophical question, that is, a question about which of the two basic ontological instances—matter/being or consciousness—has the determinative causal force.[16] Answering it obliges one to take a position either in the idealist camp (the primacy of consciousness or thought) or in the materialist camp (primacy of matter or being). However, siding with materialism extended beyond merely affirming the primacy of matter, it also involved grappling with the very concept of matter itself. Starting with Engels, but especially since the time of Georgi Plekhanov, Marxist orthodoxy has been attempting to systematically elaborate this new form of materialism to distinguish it from the French materialism of the eighteenth century. The main issues in question were the consequential application of materialism to society, and the variability of human nature and the conceptualization of (social) development. According to the orthodox Marxists, classical materialism got itself into unresolvable contradictions in thinking about both these areas.[17] In the first case, it allegedly even yielded to idealism because it attributed a decisive role in social and "historical development" to ideas ("opinion").[18]

While attempting to solve this problem, orthodox Marxists based themselves on Hegel, who in their eyes (especially for Plekhanov) was the first to historicize the human essence, thus overcoming classical materialism. In their view, the French materialists were able to create a strictly materialistic concept of nature, but in social theory they failed to break free from a certain type of idealism, which was reflected both in the previously mentioned dominance of ideas and in their emphasis on the constancy of human nature.[19]

It was the perspective of the primacy of matter/being over thought/consciousness that allowed orthodox Marxism to further refine its conception of real structure. This idea relied on a theoretical armature of historical materialism, derived to a significant extent from Marx's "Preface" to *A Contribution to the Critique of Political Economy*. It was primarily a definition of the mode of production, which was then divided into the base (composed of the means of production and the relations of production) and the superstructure (law, politics, science, religion, art), and, last but not least, the "dialectical" relationship between the two and the related issue of historical change. Paramount for our interpretation is the fact that the "Preface" reserved a privileged position for the forces of production, whose development Marx defined as the factor that drives historical movement forward.

Naturally, the conceptual apparatus of historical materialism cannot function without one important precondition: a specific anthropology derived from the determination of the human being as a producer. Humans differ from animals mainly in that humans *manufacture* the means for producing and reproducing their own lives; or, as Marx's *The German Ideology* expresses it, to "satisfy [their own] needs."[20] This is another reason that, since its inception, Marxism has focused—as we see with Engels, and especially in Plekhanov—on the tool as the key entity for the evolution of humanity and society.[21] Therefore, according to Marxists, the starting point for human history and human thought is the activity of creating tools as forces of production. With their help, people can transform nature into *something* that it cannot accomplish through its own powers alone. This is the way that orthodoxy understands practice as the manufacture of (new) things with the help of ever more perfect tools.

The human being as a producer embodies the first mover of social existence and therefore also of historical development. In the eyes of orthodox Marxists, the producer was such a powerful driving factor that the motor of the forces of production never cooled down or deviated from the set path. Although many (late) orthodox authors have pointed out that the development of these forces cannot always be considered as moving in a straight and unbroken line, its unambiguously progressive character was not denied.

A rather different character was attributed in Marxist orthodoxy to the relations of production, which developed based on the evolution of the division of labor and determined the relationship of human individuals (society) to the means of production. These could take on a progressive, conservative, or retarding character according to how they corresponded to the degree of development of the forces of production.[22] It was only through the differentiation between the always-progressive forces and the changing character of relations that contradictions could arise—and it is this contradiction that is generally (or at least nominally) understood in Marxism as the source of all movement. However, the relations of production were at the same time considered to be the specifying factor of concrete historical modes of production (feudal, capitalist, socialist, etc.), and therefore as the basic classification units in the Marxist periodization of history. Thus, in principle, historical materialism allowed a duplication of history between the substantially progressive and continual movement of forces of production and the discontinuous movement of the relations of production. This bifurcation significantly complicated not only the unified development of history but also the assumed unity of the forces of production and the relations of production, which together were to form a specific historical mode of production.

Regardless, after all the evasive maneuvers and relativizing turns of the debates within orthodox Marxism, it was not contradiction, but the forces of production to which the role of the driving motor of historical evolution was ultimately attributed. The relations of production only had accelerating, conserving, and retarding functions. The required unity of the forces of production and the relations of production could thus only be external with a contradiction situated between them. Although they were evolving, these sets of entities and their relationships remained separate. However, the unity of both moments was considered a necessary theoretical basis for the law of conformity of the forces of production and the relations of production to function. Without this, Marxism would lack not only a criterion for evaluating the stability of individual modes of production but also a criterion for distinguishing a substantial distance between capitalism and socialism or, eventually, communism.

Another task for Marxist orthodoxy was defending the scientificity of Marxism, especially regarding practice and the conception of the natural sciences of the period. The standing of Marxism, by contrast with socialist utopianism (for example), as essentially a scientific project that rests upon positively ascertainable results of empirical research instead of upon speculative intellectual constructions was accepted without debate in all forms of Marxist orthodoxy. The question, however, remained, of how to grapple with this scientificity in such a way that Marxism did not yield entirely to positivism; in other words, how to ensure Marxism did not ultimately confine itself to the analysis of empirically verifiable facts, thereby forfeiting the capacity to transcend the social status quo.

According to orthodoxy, the scientificity of Marxism could be assured on the condition that the laws of nature and of society are of the same type. Here, Marx's proposal that society should be researched as a natural-historical process served as a theoretical foundation.[23] This was interpreted in the debate mentioned above in the terms of the homology of the laws of both domains.[24] The difference between social and natural development consisted only of the more complex character of the former. The complexity here was determined by the existence of human consciousness and differing social interests.[25]

At the same time, orthodox Marxist (i.e., also Marxist-Leninist) thought rejected a mechanical causality and distinguished its own conception of determinism from nondialectical materialist positions. Marxists understood mechanical causality in the broader sense as a relationship of causal determination between individual events, which can then be generalized and formulated as a necessary relationship or law. If something random then takes place within the framework of events that are understood to be related in conformity with the law, it can only be described as an instance of someone's ignorance or unfamiliarity with the determinative power of some causally acting series.[26] Here, chance represented a subjective category that arises based on ignorance or lack of knowledge. However, already in the phase of Marxism's formation, even as far back as Engels, and then later in the Soviet Marxism of the 1920s, we encounter an attempt to grasp chance as an objective category.[27] Plekhanov offers a particularly illustrative case, treating chance as a "relative" factor—emerging from the contingent (non)intersection of independently existing causal series—that nonetheless acquires objective significance as a real event, one irreducible to mere epistemic limitation.[28]

If man-the-producer represented one pole of orthodoxy, the other was its scientific ambition—namely, a commitment to a naturalistic understanding of reality. As we will explore in more detail in chapter 3, this orientation led orthodoxy to conceive of subjectivity primarily as a subjectivity of cognition and knowledge, considered as the reflection of objective reality in the mind. Lenin was certainly not the first to introduce this motif into Marxism.[29] It is evident, however, that he expressed this moment most concisely, not neglecting to mention its deep impact on humanity's relationship to nature: "The mastery of nature manifested in human practice is a result of an objectively correct reflection within the human head of the phenomena and processes of nature, and is proof of the fact that this reflection (within the limits of what is revealed by practice) is objective, absolute, eternal truth."[30] Lenin's *Materialism and Empiriocriticism* would later be considered an indisputable starting point, and during the period of Stalinist building of socialism it was also the horizon of Marxist-Leninist thinking about ontological and epistemological questions.

Ergo, in Marxist orthodoxy, despite explicit declarations to the contrary, the conception of practice was split into practice as a production activity (driven forward by the progressive development of the forces of production) and practice as an epistemological criterion for adequacy. The separation of the subjectivity of cognition, which is now situated outside of history, from the subjectivity of acting, whose contents are entirely emptied because there is no other way for it to proceed than to go "with" the current of history or "against" it, becomes a correlate of this double-tracking.[31] Consequently, the general result could not be anything other than the horror of every form of Marxism worthy of the name: the separation of theory and practice. The specific historical impact of this orthodoxy is embodied in the transformation of theory into voluntaristic planning that lacked any boundaries, and the reduction of practice into the designing done by engineers,[32] coupled with the emphasis on physical, mechanical manufacturing work. The concept of the leading (and thus, also unquestionable) role of the Communist Party represented a nearly requisite condition for at least a minimal degree of practical and theoretical (as well as social) cohesion. The divided world could only be reunited again by one authority—the party. Of course, this external unity had to be maintained through violence and rituals that made the party into a suprahistorical, practically sacred institution.

This difficulty is illustrated in all its nakedness in a short satirical story by Ivan Sviták about two brothers titled "Little Base and Little Superstructure." The plot revolves around Little Superstructure's disobedience and willfulness toward Little Base. The result is that on their shared journey sometimes Little Superstructure lags behind, but at other times is ahead, and then again, there are times when he is taking up the middle of the road. But the breaking point is reached when Superstructure sticks beans into his ears so that he will not have to listen to anyone else. The beans then suddenly grow so big that no one, not even Base, is able

2.1. Ivan Sviták, an iconic public intellectual in Czechoslovakia in the 1960s. Copyright National Archive, Prague.

to get them out. "So they went to see Comrade Chairman, who proceeded to solve the problem." And solve the problem he did! "He smacked Little Superstructure's left ear with his right hand so hard that the bean fell out, and then he repeated the process with the right ear. On this occasion, Comrade Chairman told the two of them that it was precisely in the handling of such matters that his leading role manifested itself." However, this is by no stretch the end of the story, and when it does reach its end the conclusion is surprising and subversive. Nevertheless, for our purposes, this part is more than telling. Little Base and Little Superstructure might be siblings, but in the end, they are two different people with different personalities, and their differences can only be reconciled by a higher power—Comrade Chairman, who serves as a metonym for the "cult of personality" or the party.[33] But Sviták also shows us here in a figurative form how Marxist orthodoxy understood the problem of mediation: the mediating moment is always *some-thing*—some concrete social institution, whether in its impersonal (the party) or personalized form (the leader), which is inserted between two instances or entities that are distinct from each other, but which have entered or must enter into some (preferably harmonious) relationship. This "nondialectical," "mechanistic" conception of mediation was problematic and unacceptable to post-Stalinist thinkers for two reasons. The first was as ontological as it was political: the moment or process of mediation was reified by this procedure—it became a manipulative and manipulable thing. The second, then, was logical and represented merely another variant of Plato's third man argument: precisely by becoming yet another thing, the mediating moment required further mediation between itself and the elements it was supposed to mediate, and so on ad infinitum.

As we have seen, post-Stalinist thinking was aware of all the above-mentioned problem areas in (Stalinist) orthodoxy. Hence, the four goals of reconstructive criticism: the post-Stalinists wanted to liberate the concept of law from the traps of causality; emancipate the concept of practice from "epistemological" subjugation; and shake the "industrial" shackles off the concept of the forces of production. The fourth goal, in which the whole critique culminated, was the notion of unity-whole, which, because of its inconsistency, orthodoxy had to reinforce, as Maurice Merleau-Ponty showed, with external, artificial instances such as the notion of an "objective social process" (in the case of the Second International) or of a party (as in the case of Stalinism). Instead of these, post-Stalinism asserted its own conceptions of the whole as a totality or as a cybernetic system, and it developed a different conception of dialectics with the de-reified idea of mediation.

DIALECTICAL LAWS

The issue of philosophical laws, with its corresponding problems of necessity and chance, is one of the central problems in orthodox Marxist and Stalinist thought. However, it would be wrong to assume that it disappeared from the party intelligentsia's conceptual apparatus with the demise of Stalinism. As we will see below, at least one of the currents that we trace in post-Stalinist thought continued to consider the category of (dialectical) laws as one of the determining elements of Marxist theory. Although post-Stalinist efforts to define a concept of law in "truly" dialectical fashion did not transcend the terminology of orthodox Marxism, these reassessments of originally Marxist concepts led to the rejection of Stalinism, or rather its philosophical forms and methods, which opened space for new models of post-Stalinist modernity. Introducing the period thinking about philosophical laws and dialectics helps us to understand the qualitative changes in the post-Stalinist thinking of the party intelligentsia, despite the complicated language of the orthodox vocabulary.

In many ways, a critique of the orthodox conception began to appear soon after Stalin's death, especially in connection with the debate on historical materialism. One of the springboards for this critique was the question of the (objective) significance, which should be attributed to individual historical events or of their causal series. Not all events could have the same significance for historical materialism when it came to identifying essential lines of development. Therefore, when evaluating historical events, authors such as Jindřich Zelený, Jaroslav Klofáč, Vojtěch Tlustý, and Miloš Svoboda introduced a categorical distinction for the evaluation of historical events, which the orthodox interpretation of materialism either confounded or failed to substantiate. In particular, it was a categorical distinction between the essence, which these authors associated with the modal category of necessity, and the phenomenon, which they associated with random occurrence.[34] By drawing this kind of distinction, they believed it would have been possible to resolve the perennial question of "mechanical" determinism that Marxist orthodoxy was struggling with but had failed to master at a conceptual level. In this respect, if we consider the case of the relationship between two events such as the "Sarajevo assassination" and the "world war," the "Sarajevo assassination" represented an event that was random in the sense of immediate causation of the military conflict. On the other hand, the "world war" was understood as a necessary event—not in the sense of this specific historical event, but rather in its *form* of conflict, which represented a necessary outcome of the contradictions of imperialism as the last stage in the development of capitalism.[35]

Thus, these Marxists did not understand events as necessarily determined in all their aspects, but as the "assertion of a tendency" or "realization of the essential."[36] However, this did not mean that there were phenomena that stood outside the effects of laws. In this respect, their conception provided nuance in the approach to determination by introducing a distinction between the necessity of a law that applies under all circumstances, and a law of necessity that only expresses a necessary relationship.[37] All phenomena are therefore determined by laws, but some of them demonstrate essential and therefore necessary connections, while others are random. For example, the authors of the compendium on historical materialism understood the law of the transition from capitalism to socialism and then to communism as general and necessary because it arises out of the irresolvable contradictions within the capitalist relations of production. Naturally, the form of transition would vary according to the specific conditions in different countries, and what needs to be done to bring about the transition to communism in one country may be unnecessary in another because its historically determined development had taken a different course.[38]

However, at stake were not only a different specific progression of a general law applied in differing conditions but also the determination of specific phenomena as necessary/unambiguous or random/ambiguous. The key to this theoretical step was to replace a strictly "mechanical" opposition of necessity and chance, where what is necessary cannot be random and vice versa, to a dialectical relationship. Necessity and chance should be interpreted as internally and mutually related. In practice this meant that seemingly identical processes or connections could be determined at one time as necessary and at another time as random, depending on the particular economic and social formation where they occurred (or perhaps even on the region within the context of this formation). It was the laws of a given formation that decided whether the (historically and socially) given phenomenon or process would take the necessary or the random form. The same model of determination was applied to the problem of the ambiguity or unambiguity of phenomena in an analogous manner. Just as there were laws that determine the necessity or randomness of specific phenomena and processes, in the same way there were also laws that determine the basis on which a given phenomenon could take on only one of several possible forms, or sometimes one or more functions or meanings. Thus, each phenomenon was considered determined, though of course not always as necessary or unambiguous.[39]

When the dialectical laws were conceived in this way, determination enabled a better understanding of differentiation in historical development (uneven development, at varying rates and speeds—the famous "law of uneven development") than was possible with mechanical causality. However, while the orthodox scheme of history itself, as we encounter it, for instance, in Stalin's theory of five stages of history in the form of monolithic development characterized by transitions from lower to higher stages, was problematized it was not abandoned.[40] Despite efforts to clear away the theoretical accretions of Stalinism, we believe this debate over determination was about deepening orthodoxy instead of transcending its epistemic boundaries. To put a finer point on it, none of the above-mentioned authors (with the exception of Zelený later in his career) has problematized the conception of determination itself, meant here as the action of one independently existing entity upon another independently existing entity, or as a generalized expression of this relationship that has the form of implication: if x and y events coincide, event z must (necessarily) also occur. The much-emphasized inequality, randomness, and fluctuations of historical development here were the result of the mere action or interaction of *many* causes, causal orders, or external factors, which nevertheless fail to capture the complex nature of the dynamics of historical formations. The attempt at a "dialectical" definition of determination was limited to a mere quantitative increase in its factors. Therefore, we do not consider the conceptualization of dialectical laws by these authors to be part of the post-Stalinist current, but as a late offshoot of Marxist orthodoxy.[41]

The concept of dialectical laws began to undergo more significant qualitative changes when it was developed by a group of authors whom we call the dialectical determinists.[42] In their efforts to overcome Stalinism, they attempted to understand dialectical laws, in their words *truly* dialectically, and thus place them on an entirely different epistemic ground. Probably the most prominent thinker in this group was Josef Cibulka, the author whose work we primarily rely upon in the following analysis.[43] Some of the other especially notable ones were Václav Černík, Zdeněk Javůrek, and Jindřich Zelený, who had already participated in earlier debates on the concept of "determination" and had been working on the logic of Marx's *Capital* since the second half of the 1950s.[44] Like Klofáč and Tlustý (and other authors as well), the determinists did not reject orthodox Marxist ideas, but focused on new ways of understanding and interpreting them. The resulting form of the newly conceptualized dialectic was to be applied, as one of the period requirements in Central and East European Marxism, to both social and natural processes. However, for our analysis of thinking on post-Stalinist modernity the social aspect is decisive and we therefore limit ourselves to its interpretation here.

According to these authors, the main problem with the new definition of determinism began where the evolution of orthodoxy ended: in the question of the relationship between determining and determined entities. As we have seen earlier, orthodoxy failed to free itself from an understanding of this relationship as a type of mechanical causal action, which, according to Václav Černík, takes the following form: "Whenever a certain factor, A, acts on the system S and there is a change in B in that system, then A is the cause of B and B is the effect of A."[45] Why did the dialectical determinists find this definition insufficient? Because they saw a fundamental problem in the external nature of the causal relationship: there is no necessary connection or relationship of mutual assumption between system S and factor A. System S and factor A can exist independently of one another and never meet. A potential encounter between them may produce effect B in the now-modified system SB, but it can also continue to exist independently of cause A. Already in his *Critique of Judgment*, Kant demonstrated that this form of causal action cannot represent the functioning and interaction of, for example, natural organisms. However, for the determinists, it was especially Hegel's *Logic* and the critical analysis of mechanical causality in it that opened new horizons for reconceptualizing (not only) the Marxist concept of historical and social formations.

Most important, the determinists had mastered one of the basic principles of Hegel's logic, according to which all external determinations are to be systematically translated into internal determinations. In practice this means that the investigated object should not only be analyzed as a set of properties and functions, but as an internally developing whole, that is, a totality. Only in this way can scientific research "reveal the process of creating the essence of objects and the process of change in the essence of things."[46] The determinists argue that causal action also contains a genetic factor, but in contrast to dialectical determination only in the second order as a moment within an already established social system, which it did not create.[47] As follows from the interpretation above, an entity created by this causal action becomes "independent."[48] It acquires independence from its own cause, and can continue to act causally in an independent manner.[49] In this sense, the causal relationship is irreversible: the cause must precede the effect in time and cannot presuppose it. However, Cibulka claims that from this position it is impossible to explain the key element of materialist dialectics: interaction. In this context, if the consequence acts retroactively to its cause, it cannot do so within the same causal relationship, but only within the framework of a new causal relationship where the former result becomes a new cause.[50] However, if it is not possible to think about interaction through causality then it also becomes impossible to think about the next key category of dialectics closely connected with interaction: the totality. Here, the individual elements-moments presuppose each other, act on one another, and thus form a developing whole. In Hegel's terminology, this kind of whole (the totality) is called a concept. The exemplification of such a concept for the determinists (and Marxists in general) was the social-historical formation. So, where then, according to the determinists, was this impetus, this genetic moment that was responsible for the inner development of a given totality to be found? And why did they believe orthodoxy had failed in its search for it?

We have already outlined several reasons for this earlier in this chapter. According to the dialectical determinists, any conception of unity within orthodoxy eventually led to an external relationship of two (however relatively) independent entities or sets of entities where one (that is privileged) acts upon the other. This was the case not only with the relationship between the base and the superstructure, but above all with the relationship between the forces of production and the relationships of production as constitutive elements of the base. These two factors were already defined in advance as two specific segments of reality, and the relationships between them were sought only subsequently.[51] However, according to the determinists, this causal scheme cannot account for how one entity emerges from another—or, in our case, how the relations of production arise from the forces of production. Here, it is precisely causality and the type of laws derived from it that had to run into essential problems in interpreting the emergence of new qualities. If, on the one hand, the causal interpretation refused to invoke a primordial (nonmaterial) mover, and on the other hand sought to avoid an infinite regress of causes, the forces of production had to be defined as a progressive historical factor and the relationships of production assigned a role that either accelerates or hinders historical movement. Their unity, which is necessary for explaining the specific historical mode of production, was then simply postulated through what is termed the dialectical relationship. In the eyes of determinists, this "dialectical" relationship was ultimately understood as a separate but simultaneously dual causal action: the base/forces of production acting upon the superstructure/relationships of production and, vice versa, superstructure/relationships of production acting upon the base/forces of production. The most essential dialectical category of contradiction was thus de facto degraded in the eyes of the determinists to a mere second-order category that only expressed the obstruction or slowing down of the forces of production by the relationships of production. The (necessary) transformation of the given relations of production took place, as we will see in chapter 5, only because the gradual quantitative growth in the forces of production broke through the tight bonds of the relationships of production. The only difference between the orthodoxy of the Second International and Stalinist orthodoxy was that the transition from one mode of production to another was, in the former case, understood as a gradual nonviolent evolutionary process, and in the latter as a sudden leap. The forces of production were thus "metaphysically hypostasized" as a set of simply already "existing" objects or actions that were understood to have the key property of being the "progressive, driving force" of development.

From our point of view, however, the significance of the post-Stalinist critique of Stalinist orthodoxy consists less in its logical relevance (to whatever extent) and more in its different manner of posing questions. Orthodoxy was more interested in the question of forms of transition between individual historical and social formations, while (implicitly) considering the very nature of the overall development as given and thus also unproblematic. Yet the dialectical determinists and post-Stalinist Marxist philosophy in genera) asked the question of the conditions of the origin (genesis) of what is new and of the self-motion of matter. From this perspective, development could not be simply taken for granted, and the issue of change could not be reduced to its possible forms. This is also where the differing roles for the conception of contradiction are derived: the role assigned to it by orthodox thinkers must have seemed both flattened and degraded to the determinists. Simplifying a little, we could then say that while orthodoxy poses the question of movement and change mainly as a problem of transition, the determinists instead pose it as a problem of genesis.[52]

All the above also factored into the different weight and character that the determinists attributed to contradiction within the framework of dialectics. Therefore, to explain an issue that—just like Marxist orthodoxy—they considered to be the key for dialectical materialism (i.e., the self-motion of matter and the genesis of new things, or qualitative change), they moved the contradiction inside the things and processes themselves.[53] Thus, in their view, contradiction was not found between things or sets of entities or actions, it was what broke their unity apart into main and opposing minor tendencies (see chapter 5). Therefore, the determinists did not pose a question about the original entity—a subject that would subsequently act as an impulse that set things into motion and could therefore (even if only potentially) be detachable from it. Movement, in the sense of its essential, basic form (i.e., the kind that leads to a qualitative change and the emergence of something new) and contradiction were therefore no different for them.[54]

With the concept of contradiction grasped in this way, the determinists then focused on revitalizing not only Marxism itself but also the concept of philosophical and historical laws—categories that, of course, already held a central place in orthodoxy as the primary explanatory framework for analyzing social movement. However, according to the determinists, orthodox Marxism was unable to overcome the limits of historization and causality. Laws (for example, the classical laws of political economy) and human nature were thus no longer understood as universal and timeless factors, but as changing over time. A (mechanically conceived) causality itself was complicated by the introduction of various external factors, as well as interaction and the like, but it was not discarded. The goal of the determinists was thus not to abandon these laws or to limit their scope as was the case with the Marxist humanists and techno-optimists, but to transform them and "truly" dialecticize them.

However, a *true* dialecticalization meant nothing other than monitoring and analyzing specific forms of movement of opposing sides within the same thing or process. The theoretical expression of this approach was then the dialectical law. According to Josef Cibulka, this type of law is different from a causal law or one that applied to relational coexistence (functional dependency). Cibulka demonstrated this specificity particularly in Marx's reinterpretation of the law of the value in classical political economy. In his view, Marx, unlike David Ricardo, proved that "it is not reduced to a quantitative determination of the amount of value by the length of the labor time," but it is determined by the socially necessary labor time.[55] Yet this law does not express either a functional or a causal relationship. Value is not a function either of the socially necessary labor time, nor is the socially necessary labor time the cause of value as a consequence. If this were the case, then the socially necessary labor time would always result in value at any historical moment. But this does not hold true in any societies other than capitalist ones. Cibulka emphatically concludes: "If there is to be a legitimately determined value relationship at all between the socially necessary labor hours and the proportions of product exchange, this relationship must take the form of a manifestation of some *third*, deeper determination."[56] And this third determination is the contradiction between social and private labor, or as the case may be, the contradiction between the degree of socialization of labor (the degree of interdependence among individual producers, division of labor) and the degree of social ownership of the means of production (i.e., private ownership of the means of production).[57]

Therefore, it is not that we are dealing with two directly given phenomena and looking for some kind of relationship (causality, functional dependence) between them, as Ricardo had done with the socially necessary labor and value. Viewed through the Marxist tradition, Ricardo was dealing in this case with an axiomatically given, universally valid relationship. Dialectical determinists, on the other hand, aimed to explain the conditions of possibility under which two given phenomena could exist in an apparently stable, consistently self-reproducing a relationship (e.g., a causal one). They located this condition in a third moment (or determination), which, however, could not be another phenomenon or thing, but a contradiction that constituted the very "essence" of the formation (or "totality") within which the given relationship could occur in the first place. As a result, a specific contradiction could not be something given that was empirically observable, but only a dialectically deducible mediating instance. Hence, each process, formation, or thing was necessarily divided into a phenomenal level (which in our case of more complex formations such as social systems will be functionally dependent relationships or causal ones) and the essential level where the determining contradiction is located.

Thus, if the distinction between the essential and phenomenal levels is one aspect of the dialectical law, a second is the previously mentioned dynamic within the contradiction itself (i.e., the dynamic between its two opposite sides—the main one and the secondary one). It is important to realize that neither of these two sides can be understood as a fixed entity (sets of things or relationships) but should instead be grasped as moments (and here the determinists again took inspiration from Hegel's *Logic*) that can merge and blend with one another.[58] For instance, one particular set of things or relationships may, in the selfsame formation, perform the function of the forces of production and at another time the function of the relationships of production.

It is precisely this dynamic that generates the internal instability—randomness, tensions, crises, and imbalance—that creates the conditions for qualitative changes in the system. Or we could also say that it drives qualitative changes of the system as such, and these are the conditions for differentiations that enable further development (or, rather, "developments"). According to the determinists, no other theory or form of thinking has yet been able to explain these internal conditions of qualitative changes as the genesis of something new without either falling into infinite regression or a vicious cycle. We have already discussed the case of mechanical causality, which could not be a satisfactory alternative for the dialectical determinists. Not only because the causal relationship is necessarily of an external nature but mainly because the chain of causes is potentially infinite and can only be broken arbitrarily—by postulating the cause of all causes, the prime mover, which has been taking various alternative forms of the divine instance and the arbitrary interventions carried out with their full ramifications by the political leader, Stalin. The second possibility was vitalism, with which dialectical determinists agreed to the extent that it located the origin of motion not outside the thing, but within it—as its immanent element. However, according to the determinists, this failed to explain motion itself, since the driving force (e.g., Bergson's *élan vital*) was once again arbitrarily introduced into the thing as a fundamentally mystical or metaphysical source of movement and change.

Similarly, the determinists were not satisfied with approaches that we could term functionalist or structuralist, including their "improved" varieties, such as the systemic or cybernetic approaches that were fashionable at that time. According to Cibulka, the main reason lay in their formalizing procedure, which deprived the given modeled sections of reality of both their qualitative and ultimately even their quantitative determination and reduced them to purely "general forms of relationships as such; the most general and formal moments common to any concrete systems of relations that are otherwise very much distinct from one another both qualitatively and quantitatively."[59] In formalized and

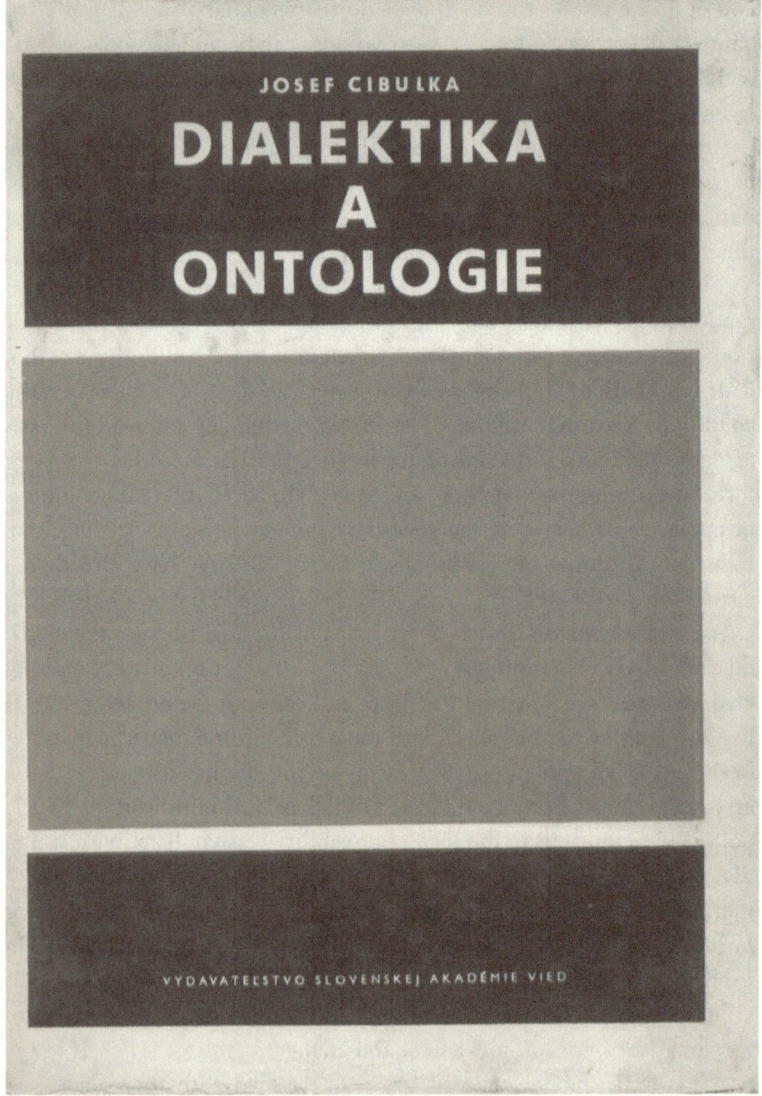

2.2. The cover of Josef Cibulka's masterpiece of dialectical determinism, *Dialektika a ontologie* [Dialectics and Ontology]. Source: *Dialektika a ontologie* (Bratislava: Vydavateľstvo Slovenskej akadémie vied, 1968).

static models, however, logical inference from pre-given axioms where the various relations among the elements are reduced to functional relationships (within the framework of which it was possible to identify only isomorphic, symmetrical, transitive, or reflexive qualities) was declared to be the only possible scientific cognitive procedure. However, any differences between models of reality constructed in this manner could be understood only based on their degrees of functional (dis)similarities and structural (non)resemblances.[60]

Of course, Cibulka did not deny the importance of either causality or the formalizing methods, including cybernetics. However, he claims that at most they play a heuristic role and do not express the deepest and most important ontological level, because functional relationships only capture the context of coexistence. Precisely because cybernetics and formalizing methods abstract from the specific historical situation, they can only represent relationships of interdependence that are able to register—at most—cyclical motion, and not the genesis of a thing.[61] In Cibulka's view, formalist reduction then "relinquishes the real knowledge of hitherto unknown relationships to intuition," which is necessarily located outside the reach of formalistic methods. These formalizing approaches must therefore limit their scope to a mere systemization of what is already known. Thus, Cibulka claims, this de facto eliminates their claims to knowledge, and true knowledge of what has not yet been known becomes "alogical in principle" for them.[62] Cibulka thus mainly reproaches formalism and cybernetics for their inadequate ontologization—"abstracting from the qualitative aspect of reality," which from an ontological perspective stems from a fundamentally misplaced problem. This is not a matter of asking how the system works, but "a question of the origin of new qualities."[63] In this respect, according to Cibulka, the cybernetic ontological conception is even "'deeply internally related' to the Stalinist liquidation of the basic Marxist principle of dialectical self-development."[64] Clearly, this did not mean blaming cybernetics or formal methods for the blunders and destructive effects of Stalinism. Cibulka only wanted to show that none of these approaches was capable of adequately grasping the nature of dialectical self-development. Consequently, they were also unable to productively cope with the challenges of the approaching period of socialist modernity. Therefore, they de facto remained closed in by the same thought horizons as Stalinism itself.

The dialectically conceived historical laws were therefore not a set of formulas that expressed fixed relationships, in which a certain series of events would necessarily be followed by another series of events or states. Nor was it a description of the behavior of a system that would attempt to maintain its own internal balance as it coped with a chaotic environment. On the contrary, dialectical totalities were internally unstable, nonequilibrium systems. However, it is precisely this "negative" character that was understood positively as an essential factor that makes the system (or "totality") a dynamic, developing entity. In this sense, analyzing dialectical laws means following the various trajectories of this dynamic within specific totalities, which do not have the nature of positivist laws that allow no exceptions—instead, they have the nature of a *prevailing tendency*. However, we should not understand this concept of the tendency empirically: as a general rule that is unable—in the face of the world's plurality—to transform all the elements in the given area into cases of its application. In other words, this is not a matter of the general being simply (in)capable of subordinating the specific. What, then, is the nature of the situation we are facing?

Cibulka generalizes Marx's reasoning from the third volume of *Capital*, where the tendency of the rate of profit to fall is analyzed as a (dialectical) law of capitalist production and then takes this line of thought to its ultimate consequences. The fact that this law is not absolute is not explained by its powerlessness to assert itself in all cases, but through its internally contradictory nature. This means that one aspect of the law acts to reduce the rate of profit, but at the same time thanks to its contradictory nature it is also producing circumstances that act against this happening.[65] Cibulka thus wants to demonstrate that the circumstances mentioned by Marx as external factors acting in the opposite direction, as in the case of the law of the tendency of the rate of profit to fall, are actually products of one and the same movement described by this law.[66] In this respect, it does not matter so much whether the law of this tendency is valid or not (which Cibulka did not doubt at all, whereas in the contemporary Marxist literature there had been a great controversy over it) as much as how the dialectical law "works." From its perspective, then, we should not understand negative manifestations, contradictory circumstances and causes as the disordering effects of the external environment but grasp them as moments of one and the same totality.

Cibulka subsequently transformed all these reflections on dialectical laws into a radical critique of the Stalinist conception of socialism, which he perceived as a misunderstanding or even a real distortion of the dialectical conception of such laws. Perhaps, the most significant flaw of Stalinist orthodoxy (and orthodoxy in general) was the grasp of dialectical development as a mere evolutionary transformation. Both structural poles of contradiction were fixed here, and the development took place as a gradual overcoming of the main side by the secondary one. The emergence of a higher qualitative formation that arose out of what was understood to be such a contradictory dynamic then de facto took place only as a quantitative increase of the already preformed core (the secondary side) and not as the origin of something truly qualitatively new. Cibulka pointed out that one of the typical cases, as we will see in chapter 5, was the orthodox conception of the transition from feudalism to capitalism. Here, he said, the main determining side (the feudal relations between the nobility and their subjects) and the secondary side (the protocapitalist relations that were arising in the commercial centers) could not represent moments of one totality (the feudal mode of production). They simply made up a composite of two separate lines of development, in which one (commercial capital) gradually prevailed over the other and became the germ of the new formation (capitalism).

In Cibulka's view, the Stalinist mode of "dialectical" thinking about development had an utterly destructive impact on the shaping of socialism and even on its very formation. Stalinist orthodoxy's fundamental deficit was that it did not understand any kind of negative manifestations in building socialism as an expression of socialism's own contradictions, but as outside interventions (hostile powers, internal diversions), that is, disturbances and anomalies caused by foreign elements. Cibulka argued that this led to the degradation of dialectical thinking to the level of evolutionism, which replaces contradictions with chaos, anarchy, and formlessness.[67] Moreover, the role of socialist relationships of production established in this way cannot consist in anything other than the "metaphysical negation" of those chaotic and anarchic elements—their removal by simple liquidation. However, it is precisely this behavior—whether purposeful or not—that results from all systems that are conceived as internally stable or directed toward stability.

Based in this perspective, Stalinist orthodoxy identified capitalism as a contradictory system, as opposed to socialism, which it believes to be a noncontradictory system or, more precisely, one that was directed toward noncontradiction.[68] However, if the mediating and therefore also the creative role of contradictions was suppressed in this way, the specific results could not be anything other than a "return to the immediate sociability of a natural economy," which in the conditions of advanced industrial production paved the way to "bureaucratic-centralist deformations of socialism." Social control over production was replaced by direct management (i.e., essentially as an allocation system) that eliminates various intermediate links, such as the market (or in Cibulka's and Marx's terminology the "sphere of circulation"). In socialist systems, these intermediate links were supposed to function as an irreplaceable corrective element that performed continuous monitoring of production. As a result, in the applications of the Stalinist system, another fundamental Marxist principle was lost that understood socialism as the dialectical negation of capitalism (i.e., overcoming it rather than abolishing it).[69] In practice, this meant that the "progressive core of the self-regulatory levers of capitalism" (such as the market, for instance) was going to be incorporated into socialist relationships of production. If this lever were to be removed, a gradual shift in the mass production of products without use value would take place, which represented an even more catastrophic type of "wasting social work than the way Marx had criticized it in pre-monopolistic capitalism."[70] Cibulka's conclusion was crushing: this mode of production "altogether loses the character of production in the economic sense and takes on the character of mere pretense at production."[71]

As a result of Stalinist orthodoxy, the dialectical mediating unity (totality) of various moments became an immediate subordination of different elements under a whole, and the incorporation of various less substantial contradictory movements into the higher ones was reduced to simple directive management. This reduction led to fixing individual aspects of the contradiction into stiff oppositions, which, Cibulka claims, had to be resolved through "tenacious overcoming," (i.e., the liquidation of one of them). The nonantagonistic contradictions of socialism were resolved in an antagonistic manner, that is, in a given situation copying the forms of political struggle waged by the Communist Party against capitalism. It followed a model in which a critic of the system (or a revolutionary) gathers forces and waits for suitable conditions to arise for a coup, which it then undertakes in a single strike by removing the criticized person or phenomenon.[72]

The fundamental error of Stalinism, then, was that socialism, which was supposed to be a higher developmental stage of social movement, was not shifted in a progressive direction but a regressive one. Stalinism seemed to return it to a developmental stage that it had already overcome (long ago) and thus even the nonantagonistic contradictions that had arisen in what was originally a progressive social system degraded into antagonistic contradictions. However, an even more serious error (and in this regard Cibulka agreed with the other post-Stalinists) was that the introduction of various centralizing and directive policies was (however justified it may have been at certain stages of Soviet development) applied in countries with quite different economic situations as their starting points.

The most flagrant case was, of course, Czechoslovakia, which after World War II had an economy based on the kind of economic relations that were typical of monopolistic capitalism. Its primary task, therefore, was to overcome the "tendency of production toward detaching itself from the development of consumption."[73] Imitation of the Soviet system, which was based in fundamentally different starting conditions (that were less developed in comparison with Czechoslovakia's), therefore necessarily had to set Czechoslovakia back several decades in the process of building socialism. For this reason, Cibulka regarded the Soviet Union as only one out of many socialist states: it could not be understood as a universally valid model, and therefore not as the one and only form of socialist modernity.

Obviously, Cibulka appreciated the fact that with the establishment of socialist regimes and the subsequent development of the entire socialist system it was possible to eliminate the fundamental antagonistic contradiction of capitalism—the contradiction between private and social labor. His principal criticism was that socialism, in its Stalinist form, was neither conceived nor practiced in a truly dialectical manner. Transformation of nonantagonistic contradictions into antagonistic ones led to a fundamental deformation of socialism, and ultimately to the gradual collapse of the entire system. One of the most significant differences in comparison with the functioning of both capitalism and Stalinism, thus, would be the way socialism "worked" with this secondary (negative) side of the conflicting movements. As products of socialism itself, these should not be eliminated but productively incorporated into the main side. However, this should apply not only to individual countries but also to the entire socialist system, which Cibulka ultimately conceived hierarchically: countries at a lower level of development were to be incorporated into the socialist order, in which the most developed countries stood at the top of the pyramid. In chapter 6, we will show how these conceptions fit in with post-Stalinism's general political thinking and what kind of (negative) impacts they had on the reflection on new socialist modernity as a whole.

It is therefore more than obvious that the decisive difference between the Marxist orthodoxy and the dialectical determinists was certainly not to be found in their use of different terms or in emphasizing different (either forgotten or suppressed) aspects of Marxist philosophy. On the contrary, the dialectical determinists did not make many changes in the Marxist conceptual vocabulary, which is reflected in the preservation of the concept of law. However, they substantially transformed and developed it as a fundamental structuring factor of reality. According to the determinists, the "truly" dialectical concept of law had to elude the orthodox Marxists because they were ultimately unable to seize the critical element of the concept (contradiction) in any way other than as an external relationship or impulse. They were therefore unable to exceed the limits of determination defined by either causality or by functionalism. By contrast, the dialectical determinists made an immanent contradiction into the central point in their philosophical reflections. It was then the activity of the contradiction that produced the other types of determining relations in a mediating (i.e., not deductive or causal) way.

However, this conviction was not shared by all post-Stalinist Marxists. For reasons that we will gradually return to, it was not only that some of them did not consider the category of law authoritative. In many regards, they perceived it as a relic of the thinking of the past. This does not mean that the category has lost all significance; however, its privileged position was replaced by other categories employed by the intellectual currents we analyze here. The humanists turned to praxis, while the techno-optimists turned to science and technology as the structuring categories for modern socialist reality.

PRAXIS

Practice is one of the key concepts in Marxist philosophy, and its understanding has undergone significant transformations over the course of history. At the beginning of this chapter, we mentioned how Marxist orthodoxy perceived practice primarily as an instance in which its initial theory should be proved, or as production activity, or—even better—as the construction (building) of things. Marxist humanists saw in the orthodox approach an impermissible degradation of practice into a simple manipulation of things and people. For this group of intellectuals, Stalinism represented a conception in which humanity's entire historical-social activity had to be subordinated to scientific laws that expressed suprapersonal and supraindividual necessity. Whereas from the dialectical determinists' perspective, the reckoning with Stalinism could be accomplished through a "true" dialectization of the category of the law, the humanists refused to accept the very concept of the law as the starting point for their philosophy. In their view, the originality and epoch-making significance of Marxism was founded on its distinctive conception of practice, which could not be subordinated to any type of historical or dialectical laws.

While reconsidering practice, some post-Stalinist thinkers oriented themselves toward Marx's transformation of this concept as a significant event in the history of philosophy. Two thinkers who grappled with these questions were Milan Sobotka and Jindřich Zelený. The latter particularly distinguished himself from other Marxist thinkers and researchers by tracing the development of the modern concept of practice backward in time: from Marx to German idealism, and even further back to Kant. It was precisely Kant's philosophy that posed with a sense of urgency the question of the relationship between theory (thought) and practice (or practical reason) in an entirely new way. For Zelený, the crux of the problem lay in Kant's conceiving of practical reason as a matter of moral obligation (i.e., in the sense of a privileged motive for action located beyond the relations of mere means and purpose, and external to sensory experience). However, this step relegated sensual, objectifying activity outside of the sphere of practical reason to the sphere ruled by natural necessity. In this conception, theory and practice therefore remained necessarily separate.

Johann Gottlieb Fichte was the first one within the German idealist tradition to renew attempts to bridge the gap by rooting the theoretical I in practical activity. However, the primacy of material and therefore nonrational practical activity was, according to Zelený, once again sacrificed to the requirement of the absolute I's freedom, which has to subordinate everything nonrational and incongruent (i.e., the sphere of material activity) under the categories of reason (and by the same token under the category of the absolute I). It thus does not matter if this reason was the individual I-ness (as in the case of Fichte and Friedrich Schelling) or the supraindividual entity (as in the case of Hegel's world spirit). Neither of the idealist thinkers managed, Zelený believed, to live up to their proclamations about the crucial importance and nonreducibility of the material world. Surprisingly, for Zelený, the result was not the manipulation of the world at the will of the reason, but affirmation of the existing "bourgeois forms of life," which were particularly reflected in laws.[74]

Against the theoretical and practical gesture of German idealism, Zelený highlighted Marx's return to empiricism, which idealists regarded as utterly unphilosophical and unscientific. Thus, the starting point for Marx, Zelený argued, was not the Cartesian "cogito" or the Fichtean I, but "the life and knowledge of practical, active, individual men in which the existence, the non-identity and the relationship of my conscious being to my extra-conscious objective (natural, social) being are posited."[75] In accordance with the *Theses on Feuerbach*, experience is not understood here as the material of sense perceptions that would be processed by consciousness. However, it is also not an irrational sphere where the consciousness or spirit realizes its freedom—instead, it represents an "onto-creative" activity that precedes consciousness. Consciousness arises only within it and primarily remains as its internal moment representing the greatest difference from German idealism.

Zelený claims that a unification of theory and practice cannot arise in the field of consciousness (theory), but only in experience, which is a "lived unity" that is impossible to substantiate theoretically.[76]

Zelený's and Sobotka's historical analyses provided a well-thought-out justification for the historical importance of Marx's concept of practice, which was not derived from the simple opposition between materialism and idealism but instead drew upon the legacy of German idealism and Kant's philosophy.[77] Viewed from this historical perspective, Marx was the first to have created a concept of practice that truly wove thought together with human existence, and at the same time enables a (revolutionary) transformation of thought and being. However, the above-mentioned analysis does not broadly encompass the form and structure of practice as such. And it is precisely this point where the Marxist humanists focused their attention.

Indeed, it is true that most of the post-Stalinist philosophers considered one and the same idea as the starting point for the revitalization of Marxist philosophy: the process by which a human being becomes objectified in the world through practical sensory activity. It was precisely the creation of concrete sensory objects as distinct and detachable from their original creator's intention that was seen as the condition for the realization of human existence and thus as a condition for the humanization process to be realized.

But in contrast to the determinists and the techno-optimists, for whom the dialectical laws or science and technology formed the basis (in our terminology, "real structure") of Marxist philosophy, for the humanists it was praxis, from which they attempted to "derive" all the other elements of human reality. When Josef Cibulka claimed that from the "perspective of Marx's dialectics and Marx's conception of social movement, objective social conditions and tendencies are nothing other than the objectification of previous human activity,"[78] it was actually the Marxist humanists who took this "objectification of previous activity" most seriously and established it as the center of their philosophy. Or, to put it another way, while the determinists privileged it in its already fixed and thus (from the standpoint of humanists) reified form (i.e., as objective tendency and condition), the humanists analyzed it as a subject–object relation in concrete, conscious action, in which man humanizes nature, shapes himself, and thus with regard to the dimension of natural necessity, also constitutes his own freedom.[79] Working within this conception, Marxist philosophy became primarily a philosophy of praxis. What was originally Antonio Gramsci's coded designation for historical materialism here acquired, especially in relation to Marxist orthodoxy, an independent status in which "the unity of dialectics, history, and man" could be expressed.[80]

It is precisely from the perspective of praxis that the humanists could look anew into one of the key antinomies of Marxist orthodoxy: the relationship of social being and social consciousness. Orthodoxy posited these entities as distinct from one another, between which it then sought to establish some essential link.[81] However, the humanists, with Karel Kosík foremost among them, entirely changed the very ground plan of the given problem when they posed the question of a relationship between being and consciousness as a product of alienation and objectification, which had its origin in being itself.[82] Kosík's main inspiration was undoubtedly the fourth of Marx's *Theses on Feuerbach*, which dealt with the specific issue of Feuerbach's criticism of religion. Here, Marx addressed the more general question of the (social) origin of seemingly unbridgeable dichotomies, which could, in his view, only be explained from the perspective of a contradictory character of (social) reality itself.[83] In the same way, the humanists did not regard the relationship between consciousness and being as a fundamental question but as a derived (pseudo)problem, the posing of which is not a product of the limits of human reason (Kant's answer) but a consequence of a fracturing in modern capitalist society that takes the form of an opposition between man and the things (objects) he has created.[84] Only this contradiction allowed an explanation of how thought could "become independent" from being, and mind from matter, and subject from object, and how the question of their relations and interactions could even be posed.

The humanists thus had to turn to an instance where the distinction still did not exist, that is, to praxis.[85] Their analyses therefore did not begin with primordial matter and its movement, from which both the orthodox Marxists and the dialectical determinists had derived consciousness and thought genetically, causally, or functionally. Instead, the starting point was where consciousness is already present in some manner—in human activity. The element of subjective intention (purpose) was thus identified as the co-structuring moment of praxis (as a causative action). In this context, Kosík was evidently opposing Kant, who would have considered it impossible that "human praxis unit[ed] causality with purposiveness."[86]

On this point, the humanists again relied on the early Marx; however, they also drew on his later work. The famous fragment included in the *Economic and Philosophic Manuscripts* titled "Estranged Labour" speaks about man as a "conscious species-being" (i.e., a being that creates objects, "produces," and is conscious of this creation as *his own* creation). What distinguishes him from animals is the ability to make productive activity itself into the object of his desire, and not just some external object. The ramifications of this idea are utterly crucial for Marx (and the humanists): unlike an animal, man is able to adopt a free and independent position vis-à-vis the products of his own activity.[87] His activity is not oriented by mere immediate physical need ("he produces even without physical need"), so this creation is therefore not one-sided (limited only to needs of its species), but instead, universal and versatile.[88] In practice, man creates a multitude of possibilities and meanings.

We meet with an analogous position in *Capital*. The "late" Marx states that man is not distinguished from animals only by creation (or production), but additionally by his conscious ability to imagine the object of his creation.[89] Human activity cannot be understood merely as production in which man creates the means for his own reproduction, but more broadly as an "onto-creative" and simultaneously meaning-generating activity. The world formed by human praxis is a world in which man realizes himself and into which he projects his intentions. Purposeless practice is no practice at all, but at most only a degraded imitation of it.

Praxis for the humanists thus represented a "mediating link," that connects intentions with the real objects that are produced as a result. Orthodox Marxists would doubtlessly think of mediation in terms of an instrument or a tool that man uses to adapt and subdue "part of matter for the struggle against all other matter" (i.e., a certain—developing—form of a means toward achieving goals).[90] All the same, for the humanists this interpretation of mediation still fails to transcend the instrumental bonds that, in their conception, human activity exceeded: while praxis is undoubtedly a mediation, at the same time within it something is happening with the human being, "something essential [. . .] that contains its own truth in itself."[91] Praxis is situated between the conscious intention and the ready-made thing, though it is not reducible to such a spatial positioning. The created thing cannot be a mere result of the projection of a conscious intention, because during its realization it encounters the resistance of an "external" matter, which is never a pliant entity that takes on any of the creator's thought forms. It is a self-reflexive moment in which "something is happening" both with the transformed matter and the transformer: both are transformed, in relative independence from their original state or order. Kosík would say this is a matter of creation, or genesis; Lubomír Nový, in turn, speaks of a "field of undecided possibilities, events without guarantees."[92] However, subjective, conscious intention here, nevertheless, by contrast with existentialism (see the corresponding section in chapter 3), is not set against the world or nature as an entity that is foreign to it. As Milan Průcha emphasized, consciousness is already objective-sensuous existence—it is the subjectivity of the objective forces that have objectified themselves and not pure (theoretical) consciousness.[93] What is dialectically sublated within the praxis is not only matter but (and maybe above all) the initial conscious intention or (with reference to Marx's *Capital*) imagined object.[94] And here also lies perhaps the biggest difference between Hegel and post-Stalinist Marxism as a whole. Whereas for Hegel, praxis is "merely" the path or detour through which the Spirit arrives at itself (to its self-consciousness), for post-Stalinist Marxists—and here they would emphatically agree with Lucien Goldmann—praxis represents the goal in itself in the sense of the transformation of the world.[95]

From all the above, it is obvious why the artist or philosopher and not the manufacturer or even the scientist represented what Gilles Deleuze would call the paradigmatic conceptual persona. Modern science and manufacturing lack or minimize this creative, genetic side of praxis, because they have a serial (in the case of production) or calculating or systematizing (in the case of science) character, which reduces the resistance of material to the absolute minimum. Quite the contrary: the modern philosopher, and (even more so) the artist make it into the main actor and even de facto the director in their works. In a parabolic shortcut, Karel Kosík best described the essence of praxis in his commentary on Jaroslav Hašek's famous antihero, Josef Švejk, and his attitude toward military service: "The master requires a servant and cannot get by without him. The master cannot eat without the servant's assistance. The master cannot enjoy himself without the servant's aid. The master cannot arrange his intimate affairs without the servant's intervention. The servant is indispensable. The master forces the servant to occupy himself with his needs and therefore the servant knows his master, knows about his strengths and weaknesses. It is enough for the master to have the power and dignity, but the servant must show ingenuity and enterprise." The master is the intention, and the servant is the execution, a material mediation that allows the desired goal (carrying out an order) to be achieved. In chapter 3 on subjectivity we will see more specifically what the process of "carrying out an order" means for Kosík. But even here it is clear that during its execution the entire relationship between the master and servant has been transformed. The servant (praxis) acquired a certain sovereign position over the master, which is found outside of the master's power. The last sentences of the passage are extremely eloquent, and it is certainly no coincidence that it ends with a question mark without a positive answer: "Who in this pair is the master and who is the servant? Who is forcing his will upon the other, and who is active in this relationship?"[96]

Now we can see even more clearly how the praxeological perspective on human activity differs from the perspectives of the other competing philosophical trends of that period, especially phenomenology and existentialism (but also the positivism of scientific activity). Above, we discussed the way that consciousness operates in the humanists' concept of praxis, and this should be compared with the phenomenological model of conscious activity. It is well-known that phenomenological consciousness is empty of contents and that it is defined solely by intentionality (consciousness is always the consciousness *of* something).[97] From the praxeological perspective, the crucial point is that phenomenological consciousness focuses on already-created, ready-made things (or, to be more precise, the essences of things). Although this consciousness can also grasp things from various perspectives, subject them to various interpretations, and give them various meanings, phenomenology leaves the objects of the world as they are and does not objectively change them in any way. Thus, we can conclude that both phenomenology and existentialism—similarly to modern science—approach things from a "distance," and their determinations cannot be defined by anything other than a correlate of phenomenological intention or (in the case of science) objective analysis. By contrast, the perspective of the philosophy of praxis is entirely different: precisely because it analyzes things from the perspective of their own genesis and reveals the process of creation as moments independent in themselves, it is therefore able to display the dynamic of this genesis as a structural moment of the things themselves. In other words, it should be able to reveal the process of things' self-creation and therefore also the process through which they become multivalent. The ambiguity or multivalency of things is thus neither the product of a subjective perspective of perception or of consciousness (intention), nor is it the product of an interpretation, but of the things themselves in their process of genesis.

As we will see in chapter 3, there is no denying that the confrontation with existentialism represented a great challenge for the humanists, especially because of its emphasis on questions of the nature of man and his relationship to the world. The Marxist humanists still significantly departed from the existentialist definition of man both as a project(ion), and as procurement and care, and in the way they understood man's meaning-giving activity. The deficiency of these determinations, as they see it, lay in the fact that the aforementioned formulations of projecting *something*, procuring *something*, or giving meaning *to something*, always implicitly worked with a world of ready-made things. From this perspective, this world could then appear to a human observer as radically different or as alien (as in the case of Sartre's distinction between the human subjective consciousness and the objective things outside of it), or instead as something that *is* known (such as in Heidegger's preunderstanding of being) but in its consequences as unproblematic and already there. According to Kosík, the existentialist way of dealing with the world did not fundamentally differ in this regard from systematic (i.e., scientific) thought.

Moreover, in the case of Sartre's existentialism, the alien character of the objective world, which Sartre introduces from the very beginning, also directly contradicted the original Marxist view because it placed the human being outside of the world and history (i.e., as a transcendent entity). The inevitable consequences of these conceptions had to lead to the reification of the world and alienation of man. In the case of Heidegger, Kosík argued, although his analysis of care succeeds in recognizing the modern human being's "lostness" in the objective world of things (manipulation), he believed that it failed in explaining how this is possible.[98]

For Kosík, this is possible precisely because human being *is* an activity that creates objects. In the process of creation, human beings separate themselves from the emerging object and thus constitute themselves at the same time.[99] If we do not reflect this moment of separation and genesis in our existential analysis, we will, Kosík believes, easily fall either into the world of the subjective (existential anxiety), or into the world of the objective (the manipulated world of ready-made objects). In both cases, the result is the alienation of man from the world and even from himself. According to Kosík, the essence of man as an onto-creative objectifying activity eludes existentialism. Therefore, it is unable to explain the process of reification as well as the state of alienation or, needless to say, to overcome it. All that is left to him is despair over the reified condition of the world, or escape into conservatively romanticizing notions of the "non-enforcing" and "non en-framing" character of pre- or nontechnological civilization with its "caring" or "pastoral" approach to reality (Heidegger's concept of "being" in a nutshell).[100] For Kosík, concepts like meaning, or by extension, the making of meaning, care, or projection do not represent the fundamental aspects of the human being, but only superficial phenomena, derived forms of human existence that have yet to be explained.[101]

However, the humanists claim that human praxis and objectivity as space for liberation from natural givennesses, as the realization of human freedom, and as the opening of horizons can easily be inverted into their opposites. This moment arrives when the newly created objectivities are fetishized and become new givennesses. Here, some humanists drew a distinction between the creation of objects and the creation of social relationships. The problem lay in the contradictory movement that the two kinds of creation could simultaneously take in the history of mankind. The creation of things (i.e., the transformation of nature through conscious human activity), amounts to nature's humanization. The same should apply to the creation of social relationships, so that the conscious transformation of social relationships should lead to its humanization. But what about the modern predicament of the humanization of nature being accompanied by the dehumanization of social relations? According to Lubomír Nový, the reason lay in the (un)conscious nature of creative activities. While we create objects with a certain conscious intention, social relations "are not the projected result of activity." Even when the resulting object, due to the resistance of unhumanized nature, may not fully correspond to the original intention, the creator may still have a certain measure of control over it (destruction, improvement). But the case is quite different in the world of social relations. Although they, too, are the product of human praxis, they are much more elusive—they escape his conscious control and thus become a source of frustration: "Behind unfulfilled desires, behind the picture of the world that no one wanted and in which they have failed to realize their aspirations, history appears to people as a boundary of activity, as *fatum* and autonomous reality, directed by its own immanent laws or by transcendent Providence."[102]

However, for the humanists, the frustration was never justified. The relationship between what is given in the present and what is created in the future, between the intended goal and the result, has never been provided in history, and by its very nature could never have provided any guarantees of full liberation or control over the course of events. Orthodox Marxism's (historical) laws were originally supposed to offer such assurances. However, the humanists no longer understood human practice as a support and a test for this law, but instead as praxis, which excluded any such type of guarantee. This was thus not just a question of (un)certain future development: man's clash with the created "givenness" also had the potential to become a source of change and liberation. Human praxis thus becomes a space in which genesis escapes the control of its creators, takes on multivalency, and transforms into a condition of openness, that is, of history.

FORCES OF PRODUCTION

The forces of production already represented an utterly essential category for orthodox Marxism and its conception of society. They were considered the driving motor of history, which guaranteed its progressive development. This is clearly why Marxists did not understand them as problematic: it would be enough to simply establish the proper conditions for the development of forces of production and then to leave the rest up to the inevitable laws of history. However, one of the most vexing problems for orthodoxy, including for the Stalinist Marxist-Leninists, was the revolutionary transformation of the relations of production. This did not mean that the question of the forces of production was no longer on the agenda. As the techno-optimists later pointed out, the Stalinist understanding of the forces of production was too tightly bound up with industrial civilization. In the conditions of the modernization project of Stalinist socialism and for the purpose of overcoming the backwardness of the Soviet Union, this orientation also had for the post-Stalinist generation "real existential justification,"[103] though in the post-Stalinist era it had already lost any kind of revolutionary appeal. Society was now facing an entirely new civilizational challenge, generally known as the scientific-technical revolution, in which the main problem was the revolutionary change in the forces of production.

However, instead of overcoming backwardness, this time the task was to set new parameters that would establish a permanent emancipatory framework out of the scientific-technical revolution. The difference between the Stalinist modernization project and post-Stalinism is quite distinct. If orthodoxy understood the development of the forces of production merely in terms of "overcoming backwardness," as exemplified by Lenin's famous plan for the electrification of the Soviet Union (GOELRO) and subsequent Stalinist industrializing projects, then the concept of the forces of production per se and their further development had not yet become a problem in the strong sense of the word. They were problematized only as a matter of implementing the level of forces of production that already simply "existed," although of course not in the geographical territory of a particular country that had proclaimed its modernization. But the techno-optimists were naturally thinking through things at a completely different level. The new concepts of the forces of production and the scientific-technical revolution existed as potentiality manifesting in tendencies that had not yet developed. It was thus a matter of devising new, revolutionary forms of the forces of production and not only of catching up to the levels that already existed somewhere else. And only the full realization of the revolutionary forms of the forces of production would enable the socialist countries to gain a decisive advantage over the capitalist countries.[104]

The steppingstone to the techno-optimistic analysis of socialist society in this period lay in the following assumption: taking over power and socializing the means of production was merely a "starting point," but this was not yet the "foundation" of a truly free socialist society, and certainly not a communist society. Thus, on the one hand, the techno-optimists explicitly drew a line against Stalinism, which, according to its own proclamations before World War II, had already laid the "foundation of socialist society."[105] On the other hand, they reproached various criticisms of modern industrial society that relied on concepts such as alienation, manipulation, and the mass society, which they considered as "humanist pathos."[106] This criticism extended not only to representatives of Western Marxism (critical theory, exemplified by Herbert Marcuse) and Western existentialism of conservative and progressive types but also implicitly to Czech Marxist humanism. They considered the common denominators of all these approaches to be an orientation toward superstructural elements and therefore also a fatal neglect of the impacts and the importance of nascent revolutionary tendencies at the level of the base. In sharp contrast to the humanists, the techno-optimists made revolutionary changes to the base, specifically in technology and science, into the starting point for their own ideas about the future development of society and social emancipation. However, the humanists' and existentialists' criticism of civilization, in their view, applied solely to industrial civilization and there was no reason to apply them to the fundamental revolutionary changes brought by the scientific-technical revolution associated with the transition to the postindustrial era.[107]

In the same spirit, the techno-optimists considered the forms of socialist revolution (i.e., the October and February Revolutions) that had gone before as insufficient. They classified these as political revolutions, which only touched on ownership of the means of production and left the very core of civilization ("real structure" in our terminology) alone. This is because industrial civilization, according to techno-optimists, is a product of capitalism, and the two are so inextricably bound that a mere change in ownership cannot transform its nature and thus its alienating character. Like the Marxist humanists, the techno-optimists had also diagnosed the alienating character of capitalism in the inversion of the positions of subject and object, where the originally active subject submits to the authority of the previously passive object. However, Radovan Richta argued that humanist criticism (even the Marxist type) did not fundamentally distinguish between various degrees of this inversion: humanist critics just took commodity fetishism as the one and only model for it and used it as their main target. In doing so, the humanists followed Marx's description of fetishism in the first volume of *Capital*, where human relations take on the form of relations between things, and relations between things assume the appearance of relations between people.[108]

For Richta, of course, this parallel represented a "lower" form of alienation, which still corresponded to the production of commodities and not actually to capitalism in the strong sense of the word. Richta argued that we could already find formulation of this kind of alienation in Ricardo, who—by contrast with John Locke and Adam Smith—did not base his theory in "human activity as such, but derived it from the governing economic relations (capital), from the production of wealth as such, and from production for production's sake, for which not only the individuality of man, but even his existence is of no concern whatsoever."[109]

Richta found the truly highest form of inversion of subject and object only in the formations expressed in Marx's *Grundrisse*, where the categories of commodities and relations were replaced with the categories of capital, value, and process.

Here we find that this form is no longer merely a matter of production for production's sake, in which the human individual is reified, but of the constitution of capital as an autonomous subject. It is a process in which value—as a specific form of wealth produced by capitalism—becomes its own object; in other words, value is concerned solely with its own self-valorization.[110] This process stands against the human individual as an external, autonomous subject in motion (a "total and mobile subject") that completely subjugates human powers. Objectified labor, of course, in the form of the machine not only subordinates the living labor of the human individual but also directly produces it as a subject. Therefore, in connection with his own interpretation of Marx's *Grundrisse*, Richta did not understand capital as reifying and alienating, but primarily as a mechanism of subjectivization. He explains that capital creates two mutually opposed subjectivities: the subjectivity of capital, a truly active power whose activity consists entirely of its own unlimited self-valuation, and the subjectivity of the human individual, whose activity is limited to mere self-reproduction.[111]

As a result, in the immediate process of production, according to Richta, the truly developing and expanding entity is only the material-

2.3. Undated portrait of Radovan Richta. Creative Commons CC0 1.0 Universal Public Domain Dedication (https://commons.wikimedia.org/wiki/File:RadovanRichta.png).

ized aspect of labor, while the aspect of living labor is gradually delegated to the sphere of its service. The crucial thing is that the developing and expanding entity is the materialized aspect of labor in contrast to living labor, which is just serving. The more the machine system is able to support an increasing number of manufacturing operations, the more the operations that must be carried out by living human individuals—workers—are simplified and reduced. The development of the forces of production here acquires a strongly contradictory character when the "continuous tumultuous upheavals on the side of the means of production" (primarily machines) is matched with "a dissipation of opportunities for the labor force's development."[112] No matter what the amount of his wages, the output of the worker's labor is essentially "inhuman" in the sense that it does not develop his strengths and abilities in any way, because they are only accessories to the machine. The problem is therefore both social and economic. Society becomes unable to use the various potentials innate to each individual. This creates a contradiction between man's social position and his position in production. Since this contradiction cannot be resolved at the level of mechanical industrial manufacturing even in socialism, the mere takeover and socialization of industrial manufacturing cannot lead to overcoming its own alienating forms. Within the framework of industrial production, this means eliminating the main obstacle to establishing a truly free communist society, the division of labor.

Hence, the second criticism of the limits of Stalinism: the Soviet leader, in the techno-optimists' view, had absolutely no understanding of the need to eliminate the division of labor in communist society because he still understood it "idealistically."[113] This was for two reasons: first, Stalin proposed to solve the problem only through childrearing and education, when the workers were supposed to be allowed to raise their "cultural-technical level" (see chapter 3), and second, he did not consider abolishing the division of labor *as such*, but only considered abolishing *essential* divisions within it.[114] In the eyes of the techno-optimists, Stalinist thinking was still fully subject to the parameters of industrial civilization, which was based on the division of mental and physical work. This led to the separation of the groups of people who manage production (in capitalism this would be representatives of capital, and in socialism the planning center) from those directly involved in the production process. The separation of physical labor from science (which was monopolized by the bourgeoisie in capitalism) was also closely connected with this problem.

According to Richta, socialism could make improvements, thanks to the socialization of the means of production and the general approach to education, but it could never fundamentally change the position of the second group (i.e., the immediate producers). The opposing positions (no matter how nonantagonistic) between scientists and managers and manual laborers were preserved even after the political revolution. In Richta's words, capital was not "abolished" in socialism, but only "socialized"—and so were the conflicts associated with it.[115] Looking at it from this perspective, we are not surprised that the techno-optimists showed a certain contempt toward the demands for active participation by workers in managing enterprises (workers' self-management and councils) within the given conditions of industrial civilization. In their view, these projects eventually had to fail because the demand for active participation in management would encounter the limitations given by the specific and specifying categorization of individuals in production. So long as workers are still chained to the machine and thus also to the immediate production process, they cannot comprehend the complexity of the entire production process, but only their own narrowly defined labor requirements.[116] Their capacity for qualified participation in the management of the whole enterprise is thus fundamentally limited.

Change within the full technological base and thus also the creation of conditions necessary for a communist society—where the division of labor will truly and completely be abolished—only arise, according to the techno-optimists, in the moment when manual labor is removed from the immediate production process. This movement is only possible with the introduction of fully automated manufacturing, which will exclude human beings from both the controlling and the preparatory phases of production.[117] Reconceptualizing the category of the forces of production had the following consequences. First, the center of gravity of development shifts from the "reproduction of objectified forces," from extensive expansion of machine manufacturing, to an intermediate phase where human labor moves out of industrial production into science, which as a result of the scientific-technical revolution was supposed to become the primary force of production. Consequently, a sufficient reservoir of free time would be created, which facilitates the personal development of individuals (for more on both these projected developments, see the chapter 5 on revolution and chapter 3 on subjectivity). Thus, not only science but leisure time itself was to become a new force of production. These would be interconnected vessels where both dimensions of human activity were closely interdependent.[118]

The techno-optimists considered it impossible to build a communist society on an industrial base, because of the persistence of the division between physical and mental labor within this industrial framework as well as the unequal positions of various groups of the population. In socialism, exploitation was no longer playing the main role in fostering this inequality—it arose from the unequal positions in the relationship between managers and managed workers. The establishment of communism is also thwarted by the very character of industrial work, which, owing to its binding and one-sided nature, prevents individuals' personal development. Within the world of industrial labor, man is bound within progressing levels of specialization and mechanization to simple abstract operations that they find no sense in performing. The orientation of human life is thus ultimately focused away from work into leisure time; however, in these conditions its significance cannot transcend its primary function—reproduction of the labor force: "Man works in order to gain leisure time; however, leisure time doesn't mean much more than freeing oneself from work—a vicious cycle."[119]

It would only be possible to fundamentally overturn this pattern with the introduction of automatization, which would bring about a convergence of the nature of the activities in both time dimensions: work and leisure time. And the latter was no longer to be primarily intended for the reproduction of the former but instead would be used for the further development of human powers. Likewise, even labor ceases to be primarily determined by acquiring the resources needed for one's own reproduction, but it becomes a goal in itself in which the individual utilizes his own abilities, develops them further, and thus finds his purpose in labor and not outside of it.

Marx himself had hinted at abolishing the contradiction between labor time and leisure time,[120] but the techno-optimists elevated the issue to a crucial step on the way toward liberating human individuals. This was the first time in history that within the base itself, not only the possibility but also the necessity for comprehensive and continual social and individual development would be created. Liberated, creative work, which is the end purpose in and of itself, was going to overcome the contradiction between the human being and society.[121]

Besides all this, the techno-optimists claimed that the general automation that would be introduced with the scientific-technical revolution would not only deeply affect the relationship between leisure time and labor time, but its influence would be just as powerful in a second area as well: in the form and development of the forces of production and in labor specialization. In the period of industrial civilization, specialization reached its maximum extent, but after exceeding the "nodal point" of development this trend was also supposed to reverse itself.[122] Automata differ significantly from industrial machines in their principles of operation, not only because they are able to serve in more of the manufacturing stages than machines can but also because they differ in the extent of their specialization. While industrial machines vary from one industry to another according to the individual branches of manufacturing, automata "have very similar features and they are often exactly the same in completely different industries."[123] This profoundly changes the demands placed on cultivating human forces. Their transfer into pre- and nonproduction phases (especially of scientific and technical preparations), along with continual revolutions in science and technology and shrinking differences in the principles of functioning of automata, all lead to "gradual reduction in the number of professions and also to diminishing the differences in the qualifications for individual professions."[124] Specialization in production (increasingly diverse products) undoubtedly goes farther; however, this does not imply specialization among the "producers." On the contrary: both processes diverge, and each one is moving in opposite directions.[125] Such a technological base thus no longer requires a fractured individual who is stuck in one line of work, but instead a "universal" individual who is "absolutely flexible."[126]

In the techno-optimists' view, it is evident that the scientific-technical revolution was going to have not only technical but also wide-ranging impacts across society, and that it would have strong democratizing tendencies.[127] But it is also obvious that the techno-optimists were modeling the future functioning of society on the basis of a generalized (and let us add, significantly idealized) functioning of a scientific enterprise in which the difference between mental and physical work has been overcome.

The techno-optimistic conception thus displays unmistakable Hegelian features. It leads or was supposed to lead to the establishment of the kind of productive and social space in which the absolute is realized and universality is achieved through a continual revolutionary upheaval in the forces of production. Here, man is eliminated from the immediate manufacturing process and acquires more leisure time for his own self-realization and for further developing his abilities. These gains are then fed back into the decisive force of production in postindustrial society: science. The division between mental and physical work is abolished, which also eliminates the fundamental basis for man's domination over his peers. It is only this revolutionary transformation in the forces of production that lays the foundations for a communist society in which the decisive role would not be played by the development of impersonal mechanical machines, but by the development of the human individual.

DIALECTICS

Marxism has professed dialectics since the very beginning. However, the debate that erupted after the famous texts by György Lukács and Karl Korsch were published in the first half of the 1920s clearly showed that there was far from any consensus on what dialectics, specifically Marxist dialectics—or as they would be called later, materialist dialectics—actually means. Even then it was evident that thinking about dialectics would be based on evaluation of the Hegelian motifs present in Marx's manner of analysis. However, the harsh verdict that the Comintern pronounced upon Lukács's and Korsch's texts relegated the issue of Hegel's philosophical legacy, and dialectics along with it, to the wayside for a long time. The subordination of these questions to others was sealed by Stalin's philosophical censure, which branded the German idealist philosopher as a conservative reactionary.[128]

The questions of dialectics and the Hegelian legacy came back more powerfully than ever in the second half of the 1950s in connection with the first critiques of the Stalinist system.[129] These criticisms gradually made it evident that more was at issue than rejecting dogmatism and the "cult of personality"—there was a struggle over the very foundations of orthodox Marxism, of which Stalinist Marxism-Leninism was one theoretical branch. At the same time, the problematization of the fundamental assumptions of Marxist orthodoxy cannot be taken for granted. The party could have suppressed further efforts to develop new ways of thinking about dialectics and resorted to simple criticism of the cult of personality. Even the leading figures in post-Stalinist Marxism could have limited their criticism to addressing the deficiencies of the basic categories Marxist orthodoxy worked with. But the fact that the whole post-Stalinist revolution pertained even to what we dare to say is the most abstract sphere of philosophy (i.e., to the categories and methods of pure thought) is testament to the profundity of the change they wanted to make.

Orthodoxy primarily based its understanding of dialectics in Engels's *Anti-Dühring* and *Dialectics of Nature*.[130] In these works we find the outlines of what would later be formulated as the three basic laws of dialectics: the law of unity and the struggle of opposites, the law of the transformation of quantity into quality, and the law of negation of negation. It is certainly true that these laws were not even close to exhausting dialectics for Marxist orthodoxy, but they formed as a kind of fundamental axis for dialectical thinking at the time.[131] The central position of these laws was derived from orthodox Marxism, which used them to think about the issues of development and (rapid, revolutionary) change.

However, Marxist orthodoxy gradually (although often implicitly) brought a certain hierarchy into Engels's triad of dialectical laws. Engels had not yet attributed primacy to any of them; and if he had, it would have been the law of contradiction, which was the first one mentioned at the beginning of the *Anti-Dühring* fragments. However, starting with Plekhanov we can already observe tendencies toward favoring the law of transition from quantity to quality. In Marxism-Leninism, this shift is even more evident. Stalin set this law ahead of the law of contradiction in his famous chapter "Dialectical and Historical Materialism" from 1938, and did not explicitly deal with the law of the negation of negation at all.[132] The same approach was also found in the Soviet manual *Foundations of Marxist Philosophy* from the end of the 1950s.[133]

We assume that this subconscious preference for the quantitative law lay in the social conception of Marxist orthodoxy (specifically in its conception of historical materialism), which was entirely dependent on Marx's "Preface" from *A Contribution to the Critique of Political Economy*. In it, Marx directly mentions that at a "a certain stage of development, the material productive forces of society come into conflict with the existing relations of production."[134] Plekhanov was probably the first who understood this formulation in quantitative and causal terms and the further development of orthodoxy, including Marxism-Leninism, only continued to expand upon this intuitive insight.[135] Here, the forces of production are the primary *cause*, which come gradually into ever greater contradictions with the relationships of production during the course of their development. Although we might expect that contradiction would occupy the premiere position as the motive force of development, it is evident that the law of quantitative growth (along with the law of the negation of negation) has been set before the law of contradiction.

At least since Lenin's *Materialism and Empirio-criticism*, the dialectical laws mentioned above were not understood only as laws of thought, but directly as a *reflection* of the true working of nature and society within the human mind. The relationship between thought and (natural or social) being had to be immediate. If mediation was found to occur within the framework, then it was a problem of tactics (in politics), of instrumentality (in the relationship between means and ends), and of the application of a general (historical) law to a specific (historical) case (in an analysis of historical situations). According to Vesa Oittinen, Lenin did not manage to exceed the boundaries of his earlier reflections on mediation, even in his late period (thus, not in the *Philosophical Notebooks*). For Lenin, dialectics primarily meant "concrete analysis of a concrete situation," but for Hegel it was a matter of a developing an organic whole—a totality.[136]

However, this relevant critical appraisal of Lenin's thought still does nothing to change the popularity he enjoyed among post-Stalinist thinkers as the initiator of the new material-dialectical thought. This fact was not only reflected in the fashion for citing Lenin's famous appeal for the need to "arrange for the systematic study of Hegelian dialectics from a materialist standpoint."[137] Some of the post-Stalinists undertook further elaborations of Lenin's excerpts and quotations from Hegel's *Science of Logic*.[138] Still, in the end it was less important whether Hegel's logic ought to be understood as the key to better understanding of Marx's *Capital*,[139] as Lenin had wanted, than the fact that a widely proclaimed return to Lenin actually also meant a return to Hegel.

In any case, similar returns to Lenin, and by extension also to Hegel, prefigured the emergence of a different conception of dialectics than the one we know from orthodox Marxism. The difference between the post-Stalinist and orthodox perceptions of dialectics is illustrated well by the insight into the thinking of the most significant orthodox intellectual, Georgi Plekhanov. Plekhanov also applied the same Hegelian critique of mutual interaction as Lenin. Is the state regime of a given nation contingent upon that nation's morals, or vice versa? This is the classic question that exemplifies this difficulty. "In order to get rid of this muddle we must discover the historical factor which produced both the manners of the given people and its constitution and thereby created the very possibility of their interaction. If we discover such a factor we shall reveal the correct point of view we are seeking, and then we shall solve without difficulty the contradiction which confuses us."[140] In this place, it is secondary that Plekhanov discovered this factor in the development of the forces of production; what is essential is the manner of formulating the problem. Plekhanov sought a *concrete factor* that causes such and such an event to transpire, and the formation of such and such a relationship. The question was then put in causal terms rather than in terms of dialectical mediation. The solution may have been materialistic in the end, but it was hardly dialectical in the sense that Hegel, later Lenin and the post-Stalinists, wanted.

Orthodoxy, including Stalinist Marxism-Leninism, thus operated in a different intellectual space. The difference lay in the emphasis placed by the post-Stalinists on the issue of dialectical mediation, which had almost no place in the orthodox conception. As Cibulka argued: "The truth of the relation consists [. . .] in mediation." In the post-Stalinist context, this proclamation inspired by one of Lenin's notes on Hegel's *Logic of Science* served as a watchword for both post-Stalinist critiques of orthodoxy's misguided emphasis on causality and the rehabilitation of materialist dialectics.[141]

For the post-Stalinists, dialectical mediation represented both an axis and a pole for Marxist thinking. In several cases, and under various names, we encounter efforts to conceptualize or define it more precisely. Along with it, the reference circle of Marx's as well as Engels's tracts also dramatically broadened. Besides the *Grundrisse* and *Economic and Philosophical Manuscripts*, which had already been abundantly drawn upon, it was especially the third volume of *Capital* and the Introduction to *A Contribution to the Critique of Political Economy* that gradually replaced the "Preface" as references for epistemological questions.

We have already seen how in this respect Josef Cibulka utilized Marx's analyses of the law of the tendency of the rate of profit to fall from the third volume of *Capital* as the foundation for an entire materialistic ontology. He was only able to do this because he placed internal contradiction as a mediating and constituting element of dialectical law in the center of his philosophical reflections. In his conception, discrepancies, exceptions, and deviations were not created by application of the law to an individual case, or by different historical conditions, but through the very action of the law of "development" or "internal contradictions."[142]

For the supporters of dialectical determinism, dialectics meant thinking and revealing the objectively functioning contradictions operating within historical-social phenomena and processes. The Marxist humanists focused more on the form of dialectics that Merleau-Ponty characterized (and also preferred) as "the discovery of an entangling relationship between the dialectician and his object," where the problem lies in "the surprise of a spirit which finds itself outdistanced by things and anticipated in them."[143] This is also the reason why the humanists, especially Karel Kosík, were inspired by Hegel's *Phenomenology of Spirit*, whose main issue is the process through which the mind/subject enters into relationship, or more precisely, intertwines with the world/object much more than by his *The Science of Logic*. Besides Cibulka, we probably cannot find any other post-Stalinist thinker who so powerfully theorized dialectics. However, unlike Cibulka, Kosík does so not by criticizing the orthodox conception of objective reality, but by examining how we approach reality itself. He elucidated the issue by contrasting dialectics with static methods (in Kosík's vocabulary, the "analytical-summative" or "structuralist" methods), which operate with already defined analytical tools, implicitly assuming that reality is a dead object that can be dissected into discrete segments. This approach, according to Kosík, does not lead to knowledge but to a deformation of reality. To avoid this, the goal of his *Dialectics of the Concrete* lay therefore not primarily in elaboration of any such (epistemological) methods, but in clarification of a certain specific human "stance" toward reality—the activity of objectifying creation, or praxis—on the basis of which any knowledge becomes possible at all. To speak in Heideggerian terms, it can be argued that while Cibulka formulated his dialectics in ontic terms, Kosík sought to assume an ontological perspective.

This is why Kosík drew outlines for a project of dialectical reason that contrasts with what he termed rational reason. Like Max Horkheimer in *Eclipse of Reason*,[144] he reproached "rational reason" (which is analogous to Horkheimer's "subjective reason") because although it created the rational reality of modern science, technology, and the rational individual, it also created the reality of the irrational, which is found outside of its reach. Entire areas of human reality that cannot be formalized and quantified (such as values, meanings, beauty, etc.) are excluded by rational reason from its sphere of their interest and thus surrendered to mysticism and religion. According to Kosík, these deficits were caused by two steps in the process of instituting rational reason. First, this type of reason focused exclusively on its own activity of positing (of objective reality), without at the same time also reflecting the fact that the reason itself is posited by something other than itself.[145] As a result, whole areas of reality slipped beyond the horizons of its perspective. The crippling consequence was the loss of the perspective of the totality, so dear to Kosík's concept of the world. This concerned not only facts such as the history of reason and the social conditions of the rational individual but also (and for Kosík above all) the very moment of man's practical activity. Second, in the conception of activity inherent in reason it only concentrated on the means and gradually excluded the sphere of purposes from the purview of its interest. By contrast, dialectical reason (Kosík's analogue to Horkheimer's "objective reason") was supposed to distinguish itself precisely by not excluding any area a priori from its investigation: "Dialectical reason is a universal and necessary process of cognition and of forming reality which leaves nothing *outside* itself, and it is therefore the reason both of science and of thought as well as of human freedom and reality."[146]

According to Kosík, by comparison with rational reason, dialectical reason should use two conceptual tools: the perspective of negativity and the perspective of totality. By acknowledging the rights of negativity, dialectical reason grasps contradictory phenomena (i.e., phenomena that oppose what is considered the "dominant tendency" in reality, and even phenomena that have been labeled as irrational) as products of its own development and as the source of its own movement. Through the concept of totality, it is able to conceive the contradictory reality as an interconnected and open "whole."[147]

While the principles of contradiction and negativity were recognized by most post-Stalinists, they had different perspectives on how to solve the question of grasping reality in its (contradictory) wholeness. Both the dialectical determinists and the Marxist humanists accepted the perspective of totality, but the ways they elaborated it differed in multiple aspects. The dialectical determinists attempted to grasp totality through the concept of dialectical laws, and their perspective was much more "objective" than the humanists'. Subjective, practical activity played for them more of a derivative, secondary role. The humanists, with Kosík foremost among them, tended to foreground the subjective moment of human objectifying activity, which in their view represented the dynamizing aspect of social reality.

Both these modes of thought placed a strong emphasis on the genetic as well as the qualitative element in the formation of concrete totalities. They also shared nearly the same concept of dialectical reason. When, for example, Cibulka pitted Ricardo's metaphysical against Marx's dialectical approach in analysis of the relationship of value and price, he wanted to demonstrate that Ricardo is essentially powerless against facts that appeared to be irrational, such as deviations from a certain norm. His solution for the existence of potential deviations of price from value is, to put it in Kosík's term, "rational" (*racionelní*):

he has to label them as an irrational antinomy—as "something that shouldn't be. By contrast, Marx attempted to capture the deviation of individual phenomena from the laws as a contradictory but also rational process."[148] The affinity with Kosík's perspective is evident on this point. They also agreed on one more important point: neither of them would admit that reality could be grasped in its essence and entirety through formalized systems (in this period, meaning intellectual trends such as cybernetics, structuralism and formal logic) that disregarded qualitative determinations.[149] This does not mean they would a priori exclude them or deny their significance, but the formalizing methods had only heuristic (for the determinists) and demystifying (for the humanists), but not ontological and epistemological value.

If, since the beginning, the post-Stalinists had originally distanced themselves from orthodoxy, soon Marxism along with the dialectical "method" were confronted with the aforementioned logical and formalizing approaches. This reality is captured very well in the debates that took place between Josef Cibulka and Zdeněk Javůrek versus Pavel Materna. At stake was the relevance and position of dialectics in relation to formal logic and the scientific method.[150] For the logician Materna, dialectics had a function that was merely "regulatory," because it was based on metaphors and ambiguous or multivalent images (he classified paradoxical and contradictory propositions among them), and these could not fulfill the scientific demands for unequivocality and reproducibility. Its role was therefore limited just to balancing out the imperfections, incompleteness, and one-sidedness of concepts,[151] so dialectics could not replace the formal logical approaches. Obviously, the dialectical determinists disagreed with such a perspective. As Josef Cibulka expressed, Materna "is not fighting only against the metaphoric expression of dialectics," but directly *"against the contents of dialectics."*[152] In the eyes of Materna's opponents, logical formalisms cannot serve as an adequate tool for analyzing reality in its dynamic genesis because its formulations directly forbid the contradiction that represents an utterly fundamental ontological and epistemological category for dialectics. If we do not want to describe the genesis of things as a mere contrast between a historical sequence of events and an already completed structure, then, according to Cibulka and Javůrek, we must adopt a conception that affirms two opposing tendencies or qualities within one and the same thing or historical formation. However, formal logic cannot accept configurations of this kind, precisely because they contain mutually exclusive ("contradictory") elements that would make such things, processes, or formations impossible.[153]

The Marxists' frequent assertions that it is necessary to grasp reality in its richness, concreteness, and fullness did not mean for dialectical determinists some kind of multiplication of empirical determinations or contextualization for the dialectical determinists. The abstracting procedure also played an important role for them in developing their own scientific method. This is why they attempted to distinguish between the formalist, logical approach and the dialectical approach to abstraction. Their initial inspiration was again Hegel's *Science of Logic* and the criticism of formalism it contained.

From this perspective, formal abstraction represented a logic of identity that can take on two basic forms. In the first type of abstraction (generally called Lockean or inductive), we proceed by separating one identical property from what is diverse, and this will serve as a basic characteristic for the given group of entities. In the second type, we summarize the diverse things under one common term.[154] In the first case, we are dealing with qualities that we can separate from within the given objects, in the second case, we are dealing with relations that we can determine among certain objects (though they are not required to have any immediate common trait). For both cases, of course, it holds true that the process of abstraction means separating out a specific form that certain objects have in common. The knowledge that we acquire through formal abstraction will analogously consist in the isolation of a certain shared form from individual, specific, and—primarily—contradictory elements.

It is necessary to emphasize again that the dialectical determinists acknowledged the relevance of formal abstraction as a scientific method. However, they were deeply convinced that the determination of an inner essence, which is the source of the self-movement of a specific entity, cannot be performed this way, because all that would be gained are solely immediate sets of opposites (abstract/concrete, form/content, general/individual) instead of mediating contradictions. This is because from the perspective of formal abstraction it is impossible to understand how one side of a contradiction can transition into another, or, alternately, how one and the same thing can contain both opposites at the same time. It was exactly this theoretical intuition that, according to post-Stalinists, formalist approaches as well as orthodox Marxism were never able to grasp.

The Slovak Marxist Oliver Tenzer discussed this problem as the difference between Ricardo's and Marx's analysis of labor as the source of value. Ricardo and Marx were both interested in certain common traits of individual forms of labor; however, while Ricardo's abstraction is based on empirical (i.e., externally observable) features (labor as a simple expenditure of energy is ultimately common to all forms of labor), Marx's abstraction is based on the trait, which is not abstractable in this manner. The social character of labor cannot be derived from social qualities, which would manifestly (i.e., immediately) apply to all of them. This character of labor must therefore be deduced via mediation. In Marx's case it was deduced from the specific arrangement of the entire society (the totality) at a particular degree of its historical development. But the social character of labor simultaneously determines the character of each individual, specific type of labor. The latter thus seemed to be divided in two: labor had its physical, natural character that creates use value, but at the same time it also contained its opposite—the social character that negates it in the process of exchange, thus creating (exchange) value. Therefore, for it to be possible to exchange two physically different things, it is necessary to cancel their concrete form and convert them into their opposite, which is the social nature (the socially necessary labor time). At the same time, however, the specific nature of labor is never abolished metaphysically (i.e., entirely), but only dialectically (i.e., only partially, in the sense that it is still operating). However, the above-described creation of value is not a universally valid procedure, but an approach that applies only in a type of society with a historically specific division of labor and historically specific property relations: bourgeois society with its capitalist mode of production. Naturally, the creation of "value" in societies with different property relations and a different degree of development of its forces of production would look substantially different. From the dialectical perspective, Marx's abstract labor thus proved not to be a suprahistorical form of value, but the product of a specific social totality—capitalism. Abstract labor can only become a measure of exchange value in a society where commodity production predominates.[155]

An even more consequential "controversy" over dialectics took place between the determinists and humanists versus proponents of the cybernetic approaches that were so popular in that period and penetrated all the scholarly disciplines including economics, sociology, law, history, linguistics, psychology, and aesthetics.[156] Even though the techno-optimists' visions of the new type of management "with the help of systematic regulation of the regulators," automatization, chemization, or atomization (massive use of atomic energy) were based in Marx's analyses of industrial society, cybernetics represented the "higher rationality of developing and mutable systems" for these thinkers.[157] For some of the Marxists, cybernetics also offered a truly scientific (i.e., formalized) expression of what dialectics itself had originally promised: grasping the nature of the self-movement within material entities with a higher degree of organization (in the cybernetic term, "systems") and the factor of interaction. Thus, there were no sharp boundaries between cybernetics and dialectics—on the contrary: cybernetics seemed to them to be a truly scientific elaboration of the principles that dialectics stood upon.[158] Cybernetics was, therefore, hailed with great hopes, as it was expected to restore to Marxism the scientific credibility that its orthodox variant had lost in the eyes of its contemporaries. However, what was at stake was not only steering socialism to a higher level of development but also explaining the origin of the higher organisms and, ultimately, of human thought.[159]

The starting premise of cybernetics as a science that deals with complex systems with target-oriented behavior lay in abstraction from the material and energetic substances of distinct organized and organizing entities. Proponents of cybernetics did not deny that in a machine, a living organism, or a society there are various types of material and energetic exchanges that are mutually nontransferable. However, they disregarded such differences to conceptualize the processes and relations that were common to all these exchanges. In the cyberneticians' perspective, it was not as important to recognize ultimate essence in the sense of one single quality as it was to grasp the factors that express behavior, interaction, and change within the framework of the given structure. Juraj Bober concisely describes this principle: "Cybernetics is the science of possible behaviors of possible structures; and not just any structures, but dynamic ones. That is, structures that are time-dependent; cybernetics does not examine specific but rather general structures of reality."[160]

Cybernetics primarily understands the dynamics of structures in connection with the relationship of the system and its environment. Therefore, the categories of input and output, through which the system communicates with the environment, play a decisive, operative role in it. The feedback then regulates the relationship between the system and the environment, as well as among its various components. We thus arrive at what is probably the most important cybernetic concept: information, which is exactly that "something" that the system and the environment are exchanging. However, cybernetics is not mainly concerned with its semantic contents ("what" is being transmitted) but primarily focuses on the degree of (dis)orderliness or (neg)entropy that the information carries.[161] Jiří Zeman evocatively characterized the value of information by its "degree of surprise" and "low probability." He says that in nature we can distinguish various organisms and systems according to the ways they cope, or rather "work" with entropy—whether they increase it (the nature of the life of an individual organism) or cause it to diminish (the nature of life as such). In the first case, the organization remains relatively stable. Schematically expressed, its function consists in evening out "disruptive" interventions from the environment to preserve equilibrium (homeostasis). In the second case, it continually increases the degree of organization "on the basis of preserving the degree of ordering already achieved" through the use of memory.[162] However, the principle of homeostasis must be maintained here as well.[163] Nevertheless, at the general level it is still true that the most vital process for the theory of cybernetic systems plays out between the system and the environment, with the environment understood here as a source of anomalies and random and disruptive elements. This is also the way that cybernetics understands one of the key categories of post-Stalinist Marxism: contradiction. "Cybernetics attempts to reveal the self-development of complex systems by analyzing the interaction of the system and the environment, which are in a dialectically contradictory relationship, while also seeking ways to resolve antagonisms between the system and the environment in favor of the system whose existence is continually threatened by disruptive effects of the environment."[164]

This conception of dynamics, contradiction, and self-development represented the fundamental theoretical achievement of cybernetics—and it also became the main target of the dialectical determinists' criticism. For Cibulka, the cyberneticians putting the surrounding environment as an element necessary for maintaining the system did not play an important role, nor did the ability to actively react and change in response to external impulses representing the nature of "openness" of the system. What was crucial was that stability or a tendency toward stability characterized the very inner nature of the system, which had to perceive external influences only as disruptions that it had to cope with.[165] However, for Cibulka this merely represented a metaphysical conception of negativity, which was incapable of conceptualizing the truly dialectical conception of internal contradiction. From this perspective, the "contradiction" between the system and the environment is not a true contradiction, but a mere *difference* between the two spheres. The political result of this perspective could only be reformism, which defines in advance what is stable and normal and attempts to eliminate any prospective negative manifestations in society either by correcting them (as in politics of the social democracy of the Second International) or eliminating them (as an alien element, as in Stalinism). Above all else, Cibulka argued that cybernetics was not able to conceptualize what represented, for materialist dialectics generally and for dialectical determinism in particular, the most essential trait of their philosophy—the *internal* self-movement of the essence of things (i.e., a kind of movement that is not dependent on something external to itself). From the perspective of dialectics, cybernetic categories thus only allow for the grasping of the "external character" of movement and change because their origin is located outside of the cybernetic system (the surrounding environment). However, the dialectical movement of the totality is not a developmental adaptation of a system to its external environment, but a qualitative change that has its source inside itself. To put it briefly (and with a high degree of abstraction), in the view of determinists, things, systems, and formations would qualitatively transform even in the case of a nonexisting external environment.[166]

From the dialectical perspective, we encounter an analogous problem in the cybernetic theory of cognition and knowledge. Jiří Zeman proceeded from the assumption that within the framework of cognitive activity we are always working with *difference* (no matter how minimal) between the subject and object; otherwise, no cognition would be possible at all.[167] From the dialectical perspective it can be stated that this difference is not the same as contradiction. However, Zeman says, "By contrast, dialectics is aware that in representation some individual aspects are torn out of context from the infinitely complex context of material reality; it [dialectics] is aware of the one-sidedness of knowledge, which leads to exclusion, negation, and the bifurcation of objective, conflicting unity."[168] Determinists would respond that despite the fact he (along with many other cyberneticians) seeks to appropriate and develop a dialectical vocabulary, in reality he advances still a formalist, (neo)Kantian conception of the cognitive process.[169] As a result, cognitive process is understood as an approach to abstraction, which separates certain aspects from an infinitely rich reality (in cybernetic terms, a "reduction of variety"), and produces a resulting concretization, or refinement of the concept.[170]

We may contrast Zeman's "formal" approach with Kosík's conception as articulated in *Dialectics of the Concrete*. Kosík does not presuppose the allegedly infinite plurality of phenomena, from a messy abundance of which the subject creates order through its concepts. From his perspective, this is exactly what a fetishizing approach to the activity of cognition would look like: an *already ready-made* subject separated from the *already ready-made* object investigates the object, organizes it, and analyzes it. Kosík's starting point is fundamentally different: it is not chaotic reality, but "pseudo-concreteness." This is a perspective in which things (objects perceptible with the senses, as well as relationships, approaches, behavior, processes, and thoughts) appear in everyday reality as unproblematic and already complete, and we only handle and manipulate them. However, pseudo-concreteness is not only a phenomenal illusion, behind which we would seek true essences, but something that is more "solid" than meets the eye.[171] Why is that?

Kosík was not a Platonist, but a Hegelian. Pseudo-concreteness always reveals the essence of things or processes to us in some way in its phenomenal nature. The phenomenon is thus always already split within itself, it reveals the essence at the same time that it conceals it. We thus see that the contradiction between the subjective conceptual tool (thought) and chaotic reality is entirely groundless for Kosík. The dialectician does not encounter chaotic plurality, but always a reality that is already ordered. However, it has been organized in a fetishized manner in which individual areas of human activity are conceived as separate sets. The approach in *Dialectics of the Concrete* consists in observing the process of the structuration of such fetishized reality. Following Lukács (and actually Marx as well), Kosík operates with a concept of "concrete totality," (i.e., a specific form of "organic" whole, in which its parts are concretized). These are revealed as both interconnected and interdependent, while also being shaped by human, subjective activity. Concrete totality comprises two faces: interconnectedness and subjective activity, structural character and genesis. Together they represent a dialectical mediation through which things reveal themselves to us in their interdependence and developments in time.

For post-Stalinist thought it was typical that individual authors did not define dialectics and questions associated with it by laying out unambiguously defined rules (e.g., as Engels had done), but instead they did this in reaction to rival approaches. Their first challenge was naturally found in Marxist orthodoxy, including Stalinism, which was not able to outrun its own shadow and develop the concept of mediation. The second was represented by formal concepts found in the breathtaking rise of cybernetics. Despite their respect toward formal approaches, in the eyes of determinists and humanists, cybernetics was ultimately incapable of capturing the most basic category of dialectics, and by extension also of Marxism—contradiction. As in other parts of this book, our intention is not to resolve the historical disputes of the period, but to highlight the fact that Marxists attributed to their method both epistemological and ontological primacy. The category of mediation can thus be understood, on the one hand, as a foundational premise of the post-Stalinist dialectical thought, and on the other, as a conceptual space through which this thought operated and which it simultaneously employed in the creation of further concepts and theories.

THE IMAGE OF THOUGHT

The Marxist conception of real structure underwent a fundamental transformation in the post-Stalinist period. All the trajectories we have examined—dialectical-determinist, Marxist-humanist, and techno-optimist—consistently challenged those elements of Marxist orthodoxy that they regarded as the fundamental determining units of (social) reality, and developed new conceptions of them. The orthodox, de facto causal conception of philosophical laws was transformed in the hands of the dialectical determinists into laws based on internal contradiction. The Marxist humanists replaced the productivist, or, more precisely, building-based and epistemological conception of practice with creative activity in the broader sense of the word, while the techno-optimistic perspective transformed the instrumental and machine orientation concept of the forces of production into science and leisure time.

However, it still seems that all these conceptual transformations could not take place without simultaneous transformation in the "image of thought," which Gilles Deleuze famously describes as follows: it is an image "thought gives itself of what it means to think [correctly], to make use of thought, to find one's bearings in thought."[172] In Marxism, the name for this correct form of thinking is (materialistically interpreted) dialectics. From the formal perspective, orthodoxy primarily perceived it through the three famous dialectical laws (the law of the negation of negation, the law of transformation from quantity to quality, and the unity or interpenetration of opposites). But, at the level of prephilosophical presuppositions of philosophy, which Gilles Deleuze terms the plane of immanence, orthodoxy understands it as a requirement for mutual interaction between the producing and produced factors. However, this aspect alone is still insufficient for its determination. As Deleuze has pointed out, the plane of immanence always has the "two facets"—that of thought and that of "nature."[173] In orthodoxy, we find that the aspect of thought consists of mutual interaction, while the other facet is made up of material activity understood as production (of tools). Plekhanov expresses this prephilosophical material assumption of Marxist orthodoxy in a remarkable passage: "Man has been called a tool-making animal. This definition is more profound than seems at first glance. [. . .] It was no longer his bodily organs that had now changed, but his tools and the things he adapted for his use with the aid of those tools; it was not his skin that had changed with the climate, but his clothes. Man's bodily transformation ceased (or became insignificant), yielding place to his technological evolution. The latter was an evolution of the productive forces, which has a decisive influence on people's grouping, and the state of their culture."[174] This passage undoubtedly brings to mind those places in Hegel's *Phenomenology of Spirit* where he discusses the process through which the man-animal humanizes itself precisely by placing an instrument between his desire and the thing he wants to devour. It is here that the concept of mediation as the moment of the birth and development of human civilization (objective Spirit in Hegel's vocabulary) is born. It seems, however, that Marxist orthodoxy could not get beyond such instrumentalized and, in the last instance, reified conception of mediation.

However, a significant transformation in this configuration takes place in post-Stalinism. Mutual interaction no longer adequately represents dialectical movement, and it is replaced by dialectically (i.e., noninstrumentally) conceived mediation, which is from now on understood no longer as a simple instrument or tool, in short, as a thing (or social instance, as we have seen in the case of Sviták's satire) placed in between two other things or entities (i.e., subject and object, or individual and society) but as a specific form of "vibrant" space filled with internal inconsistencies, differentiations, inner unpredictabilities, contingencies, and challenges.[175] Along with it, there is also a change in the "matter" of being, which is now no longer production and building, but creative activity in the broader sense—experimentation and permanent modification of the being itself. Yet perhaps the most widely shared presupposition was the idea that being constitutes a totality—conceived, therefore, as a One—and is characterized by a permanent process of transformation. This transformation was understood as the progression toward qualitatively higher and more complex formations that, despite periodic setbacks and regressions, ultimately does not move backward but advances in *multiple possible* directions. Some might argue that Marxist orthodoxy also shared this idea of progressive transformation. This is true but only to some extent. The fundamental difference was that while orthodoxy saw this development as linear and given, post-Stalinists constantly problematized this givenness and linearity and emphasized the permanent presence of uncertainty with respect to the outcome of humanity's deliberate practical activity (more on that in chapter 5).[176] The principal task of philosophy, above all, was to give conceptual expression to this idea.

This leads us to a further knot of problems. Post-Stalinism also creates its own "conceptual personae," forms of subjectivity that are the bearers of the above-described mode of thinking and acting. In the Stalinist period, certain human types were considered exemplary for the ways they represented both revolutionary ideals and the implementation of specific plans. In the post-Stalinist period these had shifted, so we see the revolutionary planner and worker being gradually replaced by the revolutionary scientist and the revolutionary artist.

CHAPTER 3

SEEKING A NEW SUBJECTIVITY

"The people" was also a constant of what was at the core of the Stalinist interpretation of history; namely, the "lawful," necessary, "unstoppable" developments in the solid riverbed of social formations and their succession from slavery through feudalism and capitalism to communism. It is thus the bearer of the "iron law of history," which was at the same time the deepest justification and rationalization of the obligation in the name of the highest historical goals and laws to clear the way for their application and before which man as an individual is a negligible quantity.

—ĽUBOMÍR LIPTÁK

The collective is not 0 + 0 + 0 . . ., but 1 + 1 + 1 . . .

—ILYA EHRENBURG

If we were to take the period texts literally, we could easily arrive at the conclusion that post-Stalinist thinking differed from the Stalinist style mainly in its emphasis on the active, dynamic role played by the individual in creating (socialist) society. Today, it should not be necessary to reiterate how erroneous this concept is. Even Stalinism, as we shall see, formed its own ideas and conceptions about the irreducible meaning of the individual and his activities, which corresponded to its internal logic of building socialist modernity.[1]

Post-Stalinism did not arrive with a radically different interpretation in this regard. In this chapter we observe how, in contrast to the previous period, post-Stalinist thought formulated its own conceptions of the function, meaning, and general form of human subjectivity—that means of active and conscious human activity, which is "irreducible to" and at the same time "necessary for" the functioning and movement of supraindividual social structures and processes. At the same time, we must keep bearing in mind that many post-Stalinist Marxist thinkers (and this goes double for the Marxist humanists) were concerned only with the difference in aspect. This means that here we do not have objective and subjective realities set up in opposition or alongside one another—we are dealing with one and the same reality. In chapter 2 we attempted to interpret how social-economic reality is viewed objectively (i.e., from the perspective of social laws and tendencies). In this chapter we look at how the post-Stalinists viewed the very same reality from the subjective point of view.

BETWEEN THE INDIVIDUAL AND THE COLLECTIVE

The formation of Stalinist subjectivity took place between two interconnected poles. One was occupied by the (Communist) Party as the dominant subject of knowledge and the leading instance in the social and political life of the state; the second is the project of the "new man," whose creation was understood as a necessary condition (and often even a goal in itself) for managing all the demands of building socialism.

The assumptions of the Stalinist conception of the party as the dominant theoretical and cognitive force in the life of socialist society can already be found, to a certain degree, in Lenin's famous formulation of the party as the avant-garde of the proletariat. While the necessity of forming a close circle of conscious and disciplined revolutionaries operating in secret serves as the practical political aspect of this model, the thesis of implanting a revolutionary, "social-democratic" consciousness of the proletariat from the outside represents its theoretical aspect.[2] Needless to say, Lenin relied not only on the specific conditions of the opposition's political struggle in the Russian autocracy and the "immaturity" of the trade union-oriented (not revolutionary) consciousness of the Russian proletariat but also on internal debates within the Bolshevist faction. This is why, regarding later Stalinist developments (both practical and theoretical) in the Communist Party, it is necessary to speak of assumptions rather than the inevitable consequences that this political institution organically grew out of.

The reason is quite clear: "Stalin's" party found itself in the 1920s and perhaps even more in the 1930s enjoying a significantly different status and conditions than it had at the beginning of the century.[3] But this is not just a matter of the obvious fact that the political situation had changed: above all, so had the party's character, which, thanks to the gradual massification, bureaucratization, and generational turnover of cadres, now contradicted Lenin's original vision. However, in contrast to Lenin, Stalin excessively increased the emphasis on party unity in both action and thought. During the turbulent decade of the 1930s this demand for unification was supposed to (and often also did) penetrate not only into internal party debates, but also into the inner convictions of individual communists.[4] As the revolutionary and Soviet diplomat Alexandra Kollontai remarked in the late 1920s, unity of will and thought not only meant submitting to party discipline, it denoted a full "fusion of one's own will with the will of the collective."[5] It is interesting, however, that in this notion of the communists as a community with one indivisible mind, instead of being more similar to Lenin, Stalin was actually closer to his rival in the Bolshevist faction, the philosopher Alexander Bogdanov.[6] Like Lenin, Stalin also did not believe in democratization or some limited form of pluralization of the party in a situation that they both described (whether or not it was justified) as being besieged by enemy (capitalist or fascist) forces. In their vision—and this goes extra for Stalin—the Soviet Union was in permanent jeopardy.[7] They perceived the return of factions, spontaneity, and internal chaos as eminent dangers and the possible first steps toward the demise of the USSR. Emphasis on unity and single-mindedness in this respect was a logical consequence of the Stalinist idea of external threat.

How the demand for unity was reflected at the level of thinking can be illustrated, for example, in the creation of the notorious *Short Course (History of the C.P.S.U (b))* in 1938. Stalin tersely explained the motivation for it as a need to create one authoritative text to replace the multiple versions of the history of the party that only caused confusion in people's heads.[8] The text also contained a famous chapter titled "On Dialectical and Historical Materialism," which was intended to provide basic guidelines for philosophy and contemporary thinking in general. The content of this text and the individual theses presented there were not as important as the way people were supposed to use them. They were not intended to arouse controversies or inspire interpretations, but to create a simple, unequivocal effect, in the way that instructions are given to workers on a building site, or orders to soldiers in a war.

The philosophy of the Stalinist era can justifiably be described as dogmatic, uninventive, repetitive, and so on. However, its form followed the logic of that time, according to which Soviet society was in permanent jeopardy (and we emphasize again that it does not matter whether this threat was subconscious, fictitious, or real) but it was also simultaneously undergoing a thorough modernization, which it was necessary to accomplish as quickly as possible, despite the shortage of means (resources and knowledge).

Unity of thought and behavior was therefore required for all these reasons. At the same time, with the overall economic, social, and ideological transformation, the above-mentioned practices were—as Peter Wagner would describe it—fixated (see chapter 1). Stalinism as a particular ideological formation thus acquired clear, permanent outlines and became a model for imitation.

In any case, it is true that the Stalinist type of Communist Party claimed for itself both the leading role in the concrete political and ideological struggle and the position of the highest epistemological authority, which considers its resolutions binding, even in the areas of science, philosophy, and art. This commitment not only applies to outward declarations but also (as we mentioned above) to party members' inner convictions. When they evinced opinions at odds with the party's, members had to undertake demanding psychological work on themselves to fully identify with the party's directives.[9] When there was an open conflict, they were forced to publicly (preferably sincerely) admit to their mistakes, or in the period vocabulary to "perform self-criticism." And there can be no doubt that this kind of "political and ethical technology of managing individuals" implied objective (from the side of the institution) and subjective (from the side of the person) psychological and ultimately also physical terror.

However, it is undeniable that one of the guiding ideals permeating these technologies was the idea of the *immediate* identity of individual and collective interests. This was supposed to be not only the goal (terminus ad quem) of the socialist pursuit of a communist society but also the current and continually confirmed starting point (terminus a quo). The party represented the only mediating element, but even this function was permanently minimized by its identification with the collective interest. Thus, in Stalinism there was a systematic shift toward prioritizing the interest of the collective, represented by the party, and therefore also toward systematically suppressing alternative interests. Certainly, one of the consequences of this practice was the stifling of intraparty, and by extension, society-wide discussion, while at the same time—and herein lies the paradox of Stalinism—this discussion was in turn provoked, requested, and supported at the society-wide and party levels; for example, in the never-ending campaigns against bureaucratism. This was among the moments that made Stalinism on the one hand a dynamic and potentially even quite explosive phenomenon, but on the other hand, it enabled a continuous and nonviolent transition to the later post-Stalinist form of internal plurality.[10]

If the party represented one pole of Stalinist subjectivity, the other was personified by the "conception" of the new socialist man. Denisa Nečasová aptly remarks that, at least in the Czech case, there was no systematically implemented unified conception, but a set of slogans, guidelines, and vaguely expressed visions. In any case, this did not detract from the strength and capability of the conception to cocreate Stalinist reality. Its ideological function was irreplaceable for the period's mobilization campaigns that were intended to arouse enthusiasm and activity among the populace for building the new socialist civilization. Ideologically, it was based both in Marx's original definition of man as a set of social relations, whose (revolutionary) change will also bring about a (revolutionary) transformation of the individual and in the conception of man as flexible material that can be shaped into the desired form.[11]

The historians Peter Fritzsche and Jochen Hellbeck correctly point out that the idea of the new man was not an invention of Stalinism (or even of Nazism), but of modernity.[12] Stalinism appropriated and significantly altered him, with regard to both prerevolutionary models and Soviet conceptions of the 1920s. The new socialist man (by contrast with his Nazi counterpart) was primarily a product of linear historical development; he was the most perfected human type to date, and his appearance should have had universal and emancipatory impact. This form of Stalinist humanism did not a priori exclude members of the "former people" (*byvshie*), or the former ruling classes. However, what Stalinism of course did require was—if possible—the complete removal of the old "bourgeois" self and the transformation of the human individual into a new, socialist individual using its will and new consciousness.

Stalinist voluntarism to some extent contrasted with the conceptions of the early revolutionary era and the period of the 1920s, when the new Soviet man was either represented as a disciplined, ascetic revolutionary (the Leninist conception), or as an individual machine, part of a unified social mechanism—or more precisely, as an integral part of the collective.[13] Stalinist theory departed from both these conceptions, and in their stead it placed a much greater emphasis on the development of the individual: "The Stalinist ideological apparatus cultivated individual biographies, emphasizing the making of exceptional personalities rather than the exceptional deeds of inanimate machines."[14] This emphasis on individuality naturally did not mean an inclination toward the liberal type of individualism, to arbitrariness and self-interest. Quite the contrary, it placed significant physical and mental demands on individuals. The new Stalinist man, according to Bernice Rosenthal was thus in many regards more similar to Nietzsche's Übermensch, a human type of hero who by the power of his will and prodigious exertions of labor manages to overcome the very limits of human (by which is meant ordinary, i.e., bourgeois) possibility.[15] Here, the first exemplary figure was the revolutionary, and then it was mainly the Stakhanovite: a shock worker who was intended to serve as a model for everyone else in society.[16]

However, as Nečasová has remarked, it is necessary to emphasize that late Stalinism was distinguished also by the (at first glance, paradoxical) "deheroization" of the original type of hero. Now, he no longer had to represent an exceptional individual with extraordinary physical and intellectual qualities (for such a one could perhaps only be properly represented by Stalin himself); instead, shock worker results were achievable even by ordinary people, but by dint of collective and not only individual efforts.[17] Of course, this fact did nothing to change the reality that pressure was exerted on individuals to mobilize their own forces for the purpose of achieving and exceeding their personal limits. Unsurprisingly, these demands could lead to various forms of critical self-questioning all the way to psychological masochism. People were required to ask themselves whether they are truly meeting the demands placed on them by socialist society, and whether they are actively taking part in creating history and the new socialist civilization.[18]

And here we arrive at the very core of the Stalinist concept of subjectivity, which was characterized by a great deal of internal tension. The individual was continually challenged and called to activity, to creative and vigilant thought, and to overcoming his own limits; however, on the other hand, he was also forced to submit to the party line, to self-discipline, and to the requirement of unifying his own interest with the social interest. And this interest was at the same time represented by and demanded by the party, which was increasingly identified with the state itself.

And as the party became increasingly identified with the state, the interest of the individual became de facto that of the state. This put Stalinist political technology in stark contrast to the liberal one, where (civil) society and individual interest is understood both as a sphere independent of the state and as a principle of its critique.[19] In contrast to liberalism, Stalinist political technology tended, with repetitious regularity to unite social, party, state, and ultimately even individual interests.[20] Without a doubt, one of the key means to create and maintain this unity was Stalin's cult and the political practices of Stalinism.[21] But at the same time, the form of Stalinist subjectivity was also determined with regard to its specific ontology and its de facto mechanistic conception of historical laws, which frequently copied the conception of the

Second International (see chapter 2). However, within this framework, human subjectivity ultimately had to find itself in a distinctly secondary, predetermined position, in which all it could manage was following the course of human history, or at most speeding it up. These consequences were contradicted by the above-mentioned emphasis on man's ability to transform and overcome his own limits by the strength of his will. From this perspective it is therefore entirely understandable why Stalinism could be accused of both determinism and voluntarism. And these supporting and at the same time problematic points became later the target of post-Stalinist critique. Given the projective nature of post-Stalinist thought, it is hardly surprising that the thinkers of the period sought to develop their own distinctive conception of subjectivity.

FROM KNOWLEDGE TO DECISION

We have mentioned that Stalinist subjectivity formed around two foci: man as a revolutionary or a shock worker, who through his self-sacrifice and extraordinary work ethic overcomes the limitations of ordinary (i.e., bourgeois) human possibilities, and the political party as the subject of knowledge, which possesses the knowledge of the historical laws. A certain group of post-Stalinist intellectuals made this latter Stalinist conception into the primary goal of their own critical revision. By contrast with the humanists, the dialectical determinists Černík and especially Cibulka did not question the fundamental determination of socialist subjectivity as the subjectivity of knowledge, as we will see below. As they had done when dealing with orthodox Marxist, or more precisely Stalinist conception of the laws (see chapters 2 and 5), they also turned their attention to the internal nature of subjectivity. However, they substantially transformed the orthodox conception while shifting it from the older teleological conception to a certain form of not only epistemological but also practical decisionism that emphasized the indispensable and irreducible element of subjective decision making. From a completely different perspective than the humanists and techno-optimists, they too arrived at an active, and to a certain extent autonomous, role of subjectivity in history.

For the determinists, the starting point for formulating human activity was the objective side of reality: dialectical laws. In this regard, they did not differ from orthodox Marxism at all. They also agreed with the nature of the attitude toward objective laws: it was necessary to possess a correct knowledge of them. However, given that they had significantly different understandings of the fundamental characteristic of dialectical laws and their functioning (see chapter 2), their conception

3.1. Václav Černík, a Slovak philosopher and one of the most important proponents of dialectical determinism in the 1960s. Copyright Department of Logic and Methodology of Sciences, Comenius University Bratislava, Faculty of Arts, Bratislava, Slovak Republic.

of active human subjectivity therefore also had to take a different form. In their view, Stalinist orthodoxy had gotten itself into an irresolvable impasse, because it proclaimed the objective functioning of "natural-historical laws," an original term Marx used, which the dialectical determinists attempted to distance themselves from.[22] This is because the "iron necessity" with which these laws asserted themselves in society and in nature *theoretically* made it impossible for man to undertake any truly independent activity, for it only allowed activity in the form of the above-mentioned acceleration (the progressive socialist subject), or deceleration (the conservative, bourgeois, or hostile subject) of the movement in the direction in which these laws were supposed to be acting. On the other hand, this necessity was weakened by the voluntarism that resulted (or should have resulted) from the characterization of the new socialist man as well as the form of planning (as we have seen in chapter 2) during the establishment of the socialist regime. The Stalinists understood social relations and human behavior in general as transparent and the laws as internally consistent, which *practically* enabled an unlimited degree of license in formulating plans and implementing individual policies.

The determinists, on the other hand, believed that a correct grasp of knowledge and dialectical laws, which contained the internal contradiction that they considered as a universally valid basic feature, was going to create the preconditions for "true human freedom."[23] Černík found the freedom in a strongly theoreticist solution and in the transformation of the spontaneous to the conscious (i.e., the manageable and controllable). In doing so, he distinguished among three forms of this transformation: the first consisted in the merely empirical, pretheoretical use of the law (the law of energy transformation has been implicitly applied by people in various cases, even if they did not know it as a theory); in the second, man acts on the direction of the law by changing the initial conditions (accelerating, slowing, blocking); and it is only in the third form that the "man's revolutionary, practical activity" takes place, because it is determined by knowing the very inner nature of the law.[24] In comparison with the second form, the difference lies in the identification of the internal contradictions in the law itself and not in the change of external conditions. Only then can the real conditions for man's practical revolutionary activity, which consists in "managing change in the essence of objects," be achieved.[25]

While for Černík active, practical activity was still a mere extension of an epistemological position that was exhausted in the categories of "management" and "governance," Cibulka also attempted to step beyond these narrow limitations. Objective development, understood as internally contradictory movement, was still his starting point, but he shifted his attention toward the nodal point in which the contradictory movement of two opposing tendencies truly *forced* the subject to active intervention: decision.[26] Thus, like Černík, he also opposed the concept of the historical subject merely following (or perhaps accelerating) a trajectory of development that was already predetermined (the orthodox Stalinist conception). However, he also defined a space for historically conceived subjectivity in which it is possible, to a certain extent, for one to "authentically" decide and implement these decisions.[27]

This conception of dialectical development that encompasses primary (conserving) and secondary (progressive) sides also implicitly includes the possibility that development left to its own devices may not, or at least may not automatically lead in a progressive direction toward a higher stage of development without active interventions by revolutionary subjectivity: "Marxist dialectical determinism understands the decision among various developmental possibilities as a necessary form of how objective nascent tendencies can assert themselves against already stabilized objective tendencies."[28] Like Černík, and in sharp contrast to Stalinism and orthodox Marxism, Cibulka here takes a position that is revolutionary-transformative and anti-voluntarist. At the theoretical level, Stalinism merely (and in the post-Stalinist vocabulary "fatally") follows or at most accelerates historical laws that are already predetermined, but at the practical level it violates reality, and thus acts against the rules of reality. In Cibulka's view, the reason for this is not ultimately the alleged Enlightenment audacity to dictate to reality, but the problem of Stalinism stems from its own conservativism and regressive nature.[29]

This was yet another reason that Cibulka considered the subjective side of social relations in its initial structure to be conservative: "The subject of decision making and the assertion of objective tendencies tends to be the most rigid link preventing nascent objective tendencies from asserting themselves more fully and effectively."[30] This is why the subject of decision making cannot be the *mere* subject of decision making, but must achieve a "maximum" transformation not only of objective reality but also simultaneously of itself. Thus, progressive, revolutionary subjectivity lies not only in the event-like nature of the moment of decision but also in the subject's transformative work done on itself.

This type of thinking about subjectivity, by contrast with Stalinism, either relegates the role of the party to the margins or is completely silent about it. Černík thus does not speak of party-directed, but of "society-wide," management of production, although he remains stuck within the originally Stalinist (and generally orthodox Marxist) strategy of transforming spontaneous development into a conscious type. Cibulka also goes beyond this one-way transformation and speaks about the dialectical relationship between "conscious" management, which would take the form of central planning, and "spontaneous" initiatives from below. Yet, neither is granted cognitive or decision-making primacy: the subject of decision is not unambiguously determined, and at most there is talk of a "progressive component of society."[31]

THE SOCIAL AND THE INDIVIDUAL

The emergence of a subjectivity that enables epistemological independence from the Communist Party was crucial for the birth of post-Stalinist thinking. From this point of view, thinking about the knowledge of historical laws is one example of a general rule. Overall, it can be said that the basic principle of the post-Stalinist definition of subjectivity consisted in reflecting on the relationship between the general and the unique; that is, about history, society, and its institutions and then examining their dynamic interactions with man as an active subject. Unlike Černík or Cibulka, for whom, in accordance with the main intentions of historical materialism, historical laws and the knowledge of them were decisive, the other post-Stalinist thinkers were focused more on the role of the individuals in their formation.

As we have pointed out, we do not want to give rise to the false impression that one is being replaced by the other. Putting emphasis

3.2. The Slovak philosopher Miroslav Kusý delivering a speech in Cuba, 1968/69. Copyright Dagmar Kusá.

on man and his subjectivity instead of on iron laws of history or society does not mean completely abandoning the search for general principles. In other words, the post-Stalinist Marxists did not eliminate either historical materialism or the holistic Marxist approach. For instance, Karel Kosík objected to the one-sided "philosophy of man," which distorts the image of the human individual because "he understands it as fragmented again, and not as a whole."[32] However, they implicitly deemed the Stalinist vision of human subjective activity as contradictory and in the last instance damaging to subjectivity itself. Hence the calls for the return of man to the playing field as a subject whose contribution to building socialism was not supposed to be a blind and pre-decreed goal, but a free and reflected choice. As the Slovak philosopher Miroslav Kusý pointed out, socialism was built in the past as an "objective system" and at the same time it was forgotten "that this objective system only makes sense if it also creates a subjective space for man." Socialism thus did not consist in fulfilling historical necessity, and man was not a mere cog in a historical machine, but the goal "for which socialism exists, and which it serves."[33]

The reorientation and reconceptualization of the human being reformulated in terms that emphasize that this human is an active and spontaneously creative individual were particularly evident in the context of relationships with the state and its institutions. This topic was part of the debates concerned with criticism of Stalinism. It was also connected with the presentation of the socialist constitution in 1960 and the transition from a "people's system of governance" to a higher stage of socialism.[34] Last but not least, this was among the main interests of Zdeněk Mlynář's interdisciplinary team in the 1960s, which was working on a theoretical elaboration of reforms that were proposed for the Czechoslovak political system.[35] The relationship between man-the-citizen and institutions is not important to us from the perspective of legal and political frameworks, as in the analyses of Kieran Williams, James Krapfl, and Michal Kopeček, nor from the perspective of the socialist concept of civil society, as in the case analyzed by Joseph Grim Feinberg, but in the sense of the requirement of the man-as-citizen's relatively autonomous subjectivity.[36] It also holds true in the case of the relationship between the institution and the individual that the difference between Stalinism and post-Stalinism consisted neither in diametrically opposed conceptions nor in a fundamental reinterpretation of the goals of society, but in a different view of the process. The Stalinists and post-Stalinists alike spoke of abolishing the difference between political power and the citizen. But while the former argued that with the establishment of socialism party politics took on an objective social character (i.e., that the interests of the individual overlap with the interests of the party and the state), the latter insisted that this state has not yet been achieved, that socialism was still in its infancy and not at the end of a trajectory of development leading to the merging of social and civic interests. By contrast with the Stalinist conception, recognition of the importance of the autonomy of the private sphere and the self-interest of the human individual were gaining in significance.[37] The subjective attitudes of man-as-citizen and his interests were supposed to be important for implementing appropriate policies in managing society and its institutions.[38] It was also essential for the expansion of socialist democracy into further areas so that it not only promoted the state's interest but also became a tool for their participation in the socialist project.[39]

The post-Stalinists assumed that there could be no arbitrary disregard for either the citizen or the state in this two-way relationship. In Mlynář's view, every attempt to ignore the interests of man-the-citizen was a "bad negation," which led to "denial of the phenomenon" and a failure to solve the problem.⁴⁰ He claimed that although socialism embodied the "real beginning of the process of overcoming the state as forces alienated from the human being," due to the real presence of the division of labor, social inequalities, the commodity nature of socialist production, and so forth, it did not permeate all of society and continued to exist as a state that was engaging in power politics instead of being an organized and nonpolitical form of administration. As soon as the latter was realized, the state would disappear, and the citizen along with it, because both of these actors—as the post-Stalinists emphasized—had to disappear simultaneously.⁴¹ Otherwise, there would be deformations of the Stalinist type, where an idealized "embodiment of the social interest" enters into the conception of the state.⁴² In this context, Kusý pointed out that the interest of the whole society cannot act as a suprahistorical objective reality separated from individual and institutional interests.⁴³ Furthermore, he explicitly formulated the existence of the socialist state as a "necessary evil" that will have to be "liquidated" when a rigorous implementation of socialism is accomplished.⁴⁴

In contrast to Stalinist legality the relationship between the citizen and the state was defined as potentially contradictory.⁴⁵ In the case of conflict, it was necessary to put both parties on equal terms, because "socialism is not only represented by the institution but also by the citizen."⁴⁶ It was therefore no coincidence that most of the authors who worked on this subject, such as Michal Lakatoš, František Šamalík, and Zdeněk Mlynář, had a legal education. Perhaps this is also why they ascribed primary importance to the legal definition of the citizen and used terms such as "socialist legality" and "legal certainty."⁴⁷ In principle, it was a legal underpinning of the relations between institutions and citizens, where the state had to commit itself to intervening in the private sphere of individuals only to the extent allowed by law.⁴⁸

The post-Stalinists derived the goals of socialist democracy from the provision of "optimal space" for the development of personality. This consisted in overcoming alienation between institutions and the citizen through the "retroactive humanization" of a socialism that had become deformed.⁴⁹ Instead of Stalin's manipulation of the state and its institutions in asserting society's interests, Lakatoš saw a shift in "self-manipulation," that is, in citizens' participation in the society's political management, including taking part in formulating legal norms.⁵⁰ But Kusý also spoke about an "institutional revolution," which was to be a gradual change in the structure and nature of institutions.⁵¹ In addition, Šamalík, in direct connection with Antonio Gramsci, emphasized the unification of humanism and politics. At that moment, man, as the object of institutional-political manipulation was to change into an entity that transcends the existing social forms while at the same time realizing himself (for more on this subject, see also chapter 5).[52]

Reflections on developing socialist democracy were focused on replacing man as a political object with an active political subject that corrects and helps shape public interests (the state and its institutional apparatus). It was Lakatoš who went the farthest in pursuit of this aim at the end of the 1960s in his thoughts on the constant corrective role for state political power played by civil society.[53] At the same time, this has always been a form of thinking in the spirit of a potentially conflicting but still interactive relationship between the state and the citizen, and it was never a matter of treating the human being as an abstract category standing outside of the institutional system. Certain authors, for example, Kusý and Mlynář, warned against a one-dimensional anthropologism, whose proponents, in their eyes, were guilty of something just as extreme as the Stalinists, but instead of the state holding the dominant position they portrayed the free development of man in an unrealistic light and perceived a manipulative element in any kind of institution or politics.[54]

If authors such as Kusý, Lakatoš, Mlynář, and Šamalík focused on the relationship between institutions (the state and the legal system) and man, who was understood as a citizen, the humanists then developed a subjectivity of a more general and anthropological character, which fit neither the category of citizen nor the concept of a socialist civil society. Karel Kosík foreshadowed the humanist elaboration of subjectivity in the 1960s in an essay he wrote in 1957. He said that Marxism here did not mean merely a philosophy of class struggle and historical evolution, he also saw it as a "philosophy of *everyday* life, a philosophy of *ordinary* relationships among people. [. . .] It not only analyzes the movements of large historical entities, such as classes and nations but also provides answers to the individual's questions—about the meaning of life, and the contents and prospects of his efforts." Although the socialization of the means of production was a necessary suprapersonal condition for stepping into the "realm of freedom," the new social relations also change interpersonal relations, including the establishment of a new freedom, sensibilities, morals, and ideals.[55] The development of these questions was one of the hallmarks of Marxist humanism in the 1960s, and even the techno-optimistic thinkers did not shy away from them.

The shift from the knowledge of historical laws and civic perspectives at the state's outer limits is a symbol of the radical demand made by Vítězslav Gardavský at the end of the 1960s. Gardavský perceived the possibilities of socialist subjectivity for overcoming the present political forms, and the Communist Party voluntarily renouncing all its power "for the benefit of all who have the meaning of the title 'man' before their eyes[.] By free choice: that is, from the awareness of the human perspective of this civilization and of this world, for the sake of which it had sought power and then seized it."[56] This statement completes the arc from the human being as the subject of knowledge of historical laws to humans as the main actors in history. And although man is formed by history, of course he simultaneously primarily shapes history and thus also socialism.

CRITICISM OF EXISTENTIALISM

Post-Stalinist thinking about subjectivity could not fail to intersect with one of Europe's most influential postwar intellectual movements—existentialism, which had massively penetrated the popular intellectual consciousness of Czechoslovak society in the 1960s. Its warm domestic reception in the second half of the 1940s as the official cultural politics of the post-Stalinist era then opened a space for similar inroads by other foreign influences.[57] Translated literary and dramatic works by Jean-Paul Sartre and Albert Camus were popular, their plays were often staged in theaters, and both enjoyed constant publicity in cultural and political periodicals such as *Literární noviny* and *Kultúrny život*. In addition, Sartre repeatedly visited Czechoslovakia and was one of the international advocates of Czechoslovak culture and "socialism with a human face." In 1963 he gave a lecture at the Philosophical Faculty of Charles University, and five years later he visited Bratislava.[58]

Reckoning with Sartre's and Heidegger's (and to some extent even Merleau-Ponty's) existentialism was typical in this period.[59] It was a time when Marxists were no longer able to simply denigrate this intellectual movement as a "manifestation of the crisis of bourgeois philosophy," as György Lukács had done at the end of the 1940s.[60] The reason that they endeavored to comprehend existentialism more thoroughly probably also lay in Sartre's self-proclamation as a Marxist at the time *Critique of Dialectical Reason* was published (1960).[61] Although criticism prevailed, the reception of existentialism was processed differently in the Stalinist era than in the period of post-Stalinism. The reasons for this change of heart were numerous, but one seems to be more crucial than the others. The economic, social, and cultural crisis of the Stalinist regimes in the Eastern bloc in the 1950s indicated to the Marxist thinkers that society in both the East and West had much in common, and that the crises felt by many on both sides had something to do with scientific and technological civilization as such. To be more concrete, what they saw as a victim of these social and technological changes was the human individual, that is, not the individual in the liberal sense as a being endowed with certain rights (this notion was seen as insufficient or as an outright ideological product of bourgeois society), but the individual in their immediate, lived contact with the world, with other individuals, and with themselves. And this was probably the main reason for the success that existentialism enjoyed on both sides of the Iron Curtain: it posed the question of the human being on a completely different basis than that proposed by previous or contemporary philosophical traditions. And not only that: the post-Stalinist Marxists (especially Marxist humanists) saw in existentialism a philosophy that espouses the personal engagement of the philosopher in matters of society and consequently an active stance toward reality as its essential feature.[62] Those were crucial and somewhat surprising observations because if any philosophical current proclaimed itself as the herald of an active and engaged attitude, it was Marxism itself. The very fact that Marxists felt the need to emphasize a feature that was supposed to be a pillar of the Marxist approach in another—by their own estimation, rival—philosophical current pointed to a crisis of Marxism per se (at least in its current state). In the context of the controversy, intellectuals of that time incorporated some existential questions into their own Marxist paradigms. Some of them even accommodated Heidegger's philosophy to such an extent that Marxist vocabulary was often replaced with existentialist terminology.[63] In this regard, the use of philosophical categories such as "authenticity," "home," "homelessness," "manipulation," and "anxiety" (*Angst*) foreshadowed the intellectual development of the Czech dissident movement in the 1970s.[64]

The critical reception of existentialism essentially became a historical necessity, mainly because no other philosophy in that period had so compellingly raised the questions of man, and human subjectivity and its forms of activity. However, these were the very topics that post-Stalinist thinking (especially in its humanist form, though also to a certain extent among the techno-optimists) wanted to broach in the face of Marxist-Leninist orthodoxy and the "bureaucratic" and "alienating" nature of the Stalinist regime as key issues in contemporary thought and society. In this confrontation, "nondogmatic" Marxism should have reappeared as the most progressive philosophy of the day in the eyes of its representatives, and one that would be able to overcome the existentialist challenges.[65]

On the more concrete level, what the Marxists appreciated most of all was the existentialist critique of the existing philosophical tradition, which, according to the existentialists, understood the human being, or human consciousness, as a mere thing among things. That is, they understood it in philosophical terms as a substance characterized by its self-sufficiency and temporal permanence. This basic assumption was not altered by the fact that specific qualities that could not be attributed to other entities, whether animate or inanimate (reason, speech, and consciousness) were attributed to human beings. According to the existentialists, the sharp distinction between the substance of thought and the substance of matter that had been introduced at the advent of modern European philosophy had essentially persisted to the present day and found its concrete expression in modern science, as its implicit assumption. The consequence was the detachment of thought/consciousness from substance/world on the one hand and the primacy of the contemplative side of human activity over active agency on the other. The cardinal problem, of course, became the question of bridging these dualities and returning the human being to the world, which, in the terms of modern philosophy, stood opposed to him as a different type of entity. Post-Stalinist Marxists, of course, immediately identified their own situation in this diagnosis and the struggle with their own orthodox Marxist heritage, which at least in one aspect identified the human being primarily as an entity that cognizes natural and social laws, with the help of which they can then direct the course of nature and society. The originally Leninist theory of reflection, which became one of the pillars of Stalinist Marxism-Leninism, was the most demonstrable proof of this. In this respect, the Marxist orthodoxy was therefore viewed as being fully consonant with modern philosophy with its reified conception of consciousness and a contemplative approach to reality. Post-Stalinist Marxists, on the other hand, argued that the character of Marxism-Leninism completely contradicted Marx's own statements about the originally practical character of human being.

This is why period Marxists appreciated existentialist efforts to de-substantialize or dereify human consciousness and thus human reality in general, and to return it to the world as an original inhabitant and active agent. One of the distinctive existentialist innovations, then, according to post-Stalinist Marxists, was the way in which existentialists sought to achieve this goal—by analyzing what the Slovak philosopher Ján Bodnár called "pre-reflective states of consciousness."[66] Thus, the human being could no longer be understood as an entity that first reflects, contemplates, or cognizes states of the world and then acts practically in accordance; rather, it was an entity that is first present in the world through immediate pre-reflective activity, from which all cognitive and reflective activities then proceed. To put it succinctly, analysis of those states and attitudes was encompassed in the conception of existence that understands the idea of the human being as an "entity" that lacks its own essence, or whose essence is entirely defined by existence (in Sartre's case existence even precedes it). The notion of existence thus underwent a fundamental change: it was no longer related to the question of whether a given thing is or is not, but was understood through activities of experiencing, projecting, taking care, and so on, and therefore, through intentionality. From this perspective, it is no longer difficult to recognize why existentialism had such appeal, and at the same time posed such a great challenge to Marxism—the analysis of pre-reflective states seemed very close to what Marx formulated in his *Theses on Feuerbach* and *Economic and Philosophic Manuscripts of 1844*; namely, that human reality consists primarily in sense-object (praxis) and not contemplative (reflection) activity.

Surprisingly, the confrontation with existentialism was even present in the dialectical determinists' works. Although it may seem that this intellectual current represented by Josef Cibulka predominantly focused on the conceptualization of dialectical law, the question of the subject, as we saw earlier, defined through its initial choices remained a crucial issue. As we will also see in Marxist humanism, Cibulka criticized the existentialist contraposition of facticity and free subjectivity (Sartre), and inauthentic everyday life and authentic "ex-sistence" (Heidegger's *Dasein*). However, in the diagnosis of existentialism he was still based in his own dialectical determinist positions, and he claimed that existentialism reproduced the Stalinist antinomy rooted in the iron necessity of valid laws (facticity) and the arbitrariness (freedom) of the revolutionary subject. And Cibulka was even less impressed by the existentialist preference for authentic subjectivity with an emphasis on the "open" and projective nature of its activity, because for him the problem of subjectivity consisted in breaking through the "limitation of its present content," and not in its projection into a "transformed objective reality."[67] Therefore, Cibulka did not place subjective choice before reality as Sartre had, nor into it as an immanent part (as we see with Heidegger and some of the Marxist humanists), but "beyond" reality in the sense of possibility determined by the inconsistent (dialectically split) character of the reality. And he did this in a(n) (onto)logical, rather than a temporal or spatial sense. This is the only way, according to him, that subjective decision could be truly realized: it had ceased to be an unconditional choice "suspended in the air" but at the same time it also didn't completely overlap with the predetermined laws of objective reality. Here, the moment of human decision was not opposed to or identical with objective reality, but instead reality itself gave shape to it, or to its possibilities, among which the human subject must choose. It is as if Cibulka wanted to say, almost in a Spinozan way, that there is no free choice without (dialectical) determination.

Conversely, terms such as "authentic being" and "irreducible freedom" were used by the Marxist humanists, for whom existentialism had powerful critical potential against the Marxist orthodoxy. They contrasted these terms with the Stalinists conception of subjectivity, which viewed it as a mere executor of predetermined historical movement. For example, Kusý used the controversy over Sartre's conception as a warning against Stalinist historical determinism, in which "the historical stage is everything and the individual is nothing."[68] In particular, as we intimated above, Sartre's conception of consciousness as a project, a free activity by which this consciousness transforms external being ("being-in-itself") into its own, humanized being ("being-for-itself"), could provide a certain interpretive model for some of Marx's statements from *Theses on Feuerbach*, especially those concerning "subjective, human sensuous activity."[69] In this respect, Robert Kalivoda found that while Sartre's approach was generally in contradiction with Marx's original understanding of freedom, his existentialist formal analysis intersected with the Marxist conception in the question of the possibilities of the human individual's projection. Kalivoda claimed that through analyzing the absolute freedom of the human individual, existentialism enriched the "real dialectics of the human subject."[70] This gives rise to the finding that the "contents of total free humanity do not fall out of the heavens nor can they be imposed upon man."[71] In socialist conditions, man thus realizes himself on the basis of his own free activity, which is tacitly contrasted with the actual role of the party in Stalinism as a mediating factor of humans emancipation.

At this point, however, the paths of post-Stalinist humanist Marxism and existentialism began to slowly but surely diverge. For the Marxists, where existentialist perspectives came up short was in the fact that they ultimately either found it impossible (Sartre) or were unable (Heidegger) to grasp the aforementioned human subjective activity as an activity that would actually transform the external world and objectify itself within it.[72] As we pointed out in the chapter 2, this objectification was not understood as a deficiency or an inauthentic expression of self-alienating "ex-sistence," but rather the highest expression of human activity. Here, the Marxist humanists went back to Hegel. From this perspective, then, the "activity" of the existentialists must have appeared to them as a reduction to mere self-projection into a dead, indifferent world (Sartre), to care for things in the external world (Heidegger), or to "giving meanings" to things in the world (Sartre and Heidegger). Thus, the post-Stalinist Marxists drew significant distinctions between the existentialist self-projection of subjectivity into reality and Hegelian-Marxist objectification (Kosík, Richta), or perhaps an avant-garde conception of freedom (Kalivoda). Whereas the first could at best acquire the form of interpretation or at worst lead to feelings of anxiety and disgust, the latter alone could lead to a real transformation of the external world. This philosophical stance was typical of nearly all the representatives of the movements we have discussed, from the humanists, to the techno-optimists, to the dialectical determinists; we encounter it with Karel Kosík just as much as with Radovan Richta and Josef Cibulka.

However, according to the post-Stalinists, both Sartre's and Heidegger's formulation of an irreconcilable opposition between being and nothingness carried further negative consequences for the understanding of human activity. Such a stark contraposition made it impossible to explain the productive interaction between the human being and the world, and it entirely closed the path (and let us add that in both cases this was done intentionally) to clarifying the dynamic of development in which the polarity of being and nothingness is—in a dialectical sense—abolished and thus resolved on a higher level.[73] It was the conceptual grasp of the possibility of this dialectical movement that was a fundamental and indispensable moment for post-Stalinist Marxism. Moreover, Sartre's absolutization of the opposition between consciousness and being had a detrimental impact even on his cherished conception of freedom. Although the Marxist humanists—particularly Kalivoda and Sviták—agreed with Sartre on the necessity of claiming the permanent possibility of free action, they took issue with the way in which he sought to substantiate it. Such absolutization, in fact, rendered analysis of objective (social and historical) material as well as the psychological conditions of using this freedom utterly impossible—and in this way it fell into a one-dimensional formalism.[74] However, from the Marxist perspective, of course man never uses his possibility of freedom existentially, which would be an empty freedom, "because he is a content-filled being, not a formal one."[75] In the end, for Marxists, the product of the openness of human subjectivity (or in Heidegger's term "ex-sistence") in resolving real social contradictions could not be anything but a blank nothingness, a meaningless position that lacked any positive content.

Nevertheless, the above-mentioned antinomy of consciousness (nothingness) and being led Sartre necessarily to the question of whether a person is first a person or something else (the world, things). This had an inadmissible implication for the Marxist humanists, because even the formulation of such an antinomy meant a de facto "splitting of the original concreteness (totality) of man," in which both aspects are only two sides of the same coin: Man "is only himself by being something else at the same time, and he is something else only because he is, or can be himself." From their point of view, this was essentially a badly stated problem that had necessarily led to erroneous solutions or dilemmas. This is another reason that Karel Kosík rejected Sartre's claim from *Critique of Dialectical Reason* (1960) that the existentialist philosophy begins where the Marxist analysis of society ends. For the Czech philosopher, it was not existentialism but Marxism that had created the "last, i.e., historically unsurpassed" ontology of man.[76]

THE HUMAN INDIVIDUAL AND FREEDOM OF CHOICE

The presence of existentialism in the Marxist discourse in the post-Stalinist era does not exemplify an isolated case of a certain shift in the thinking of the intellectuals of that time away from reckoning with orthodox Stalinist Marxism and toward the critical reception of contemporary philosophical trends. On the contrary, an inclination toward intellectual currents that transcended the bounds of Marxism was one of the typical features of thinking about subjectivity. The impact of turning away from a mechanistic conception of the individual in the realized history of socialist society was naturally considerable, though the idea of a common destiny of the Western and Eastern blocs also played a role. In the conditions of a late industrial society with a high degree of management and organization of labor together with its repressive apparatuses, as well as the awareness of the permanent threat to humanity due to a nuclear catastrophe, questions associated with human subjectivity simply had a common denominator. Additionally, the enthusiasm for absurdity, including the artistic forms and principles in cinematography of the "new waves" transcended the borders of East and West, just like the growing dialogue between Marxists and Christians.

Besides existentialism, we can also observe a whole range of referential frameworks in the Czechoslovak intellectual environment that—with a certain degree of generalization—can be collectively described as a Marxist "philosophy of man." In addition to the revival of many interwar avant-garde motifs (especially notable with Robert Kalivoda, Josef Zumr and Květoslav Chvatík), a diffusion of interest in psychoanalysis was mediated by its revival in the West, especially by the works of Herbert Marcuse and Erich Fromm. Czech translations of both of these authors' works were published in the second half of the 1960s.[77] Fromm, along with Raya Dunayevskaya, was even considered a symbol of Western, and therefore also American humanist Marxism.[78] In 1965, based on an international symposium, Fromm compiled an edited volume on socialist humanism with strong representation of philosophers from the Eastern bloc (Kosík, Sviták, and Průcha were Czech authors whose work was included). Then we can add the Slovak publication of *Marxism and the Human Individual* by the Polish Marxist Adam Schaff, and the Slovak anthology of the Yugoslav group that gathered around the magazine *Praxis*, with their summer school of philosophy on the island of Korčula, in which Czech and Slovak intellectuals regularly participated.[79] As for the Marxist-Christian dialogue, which had its strongest Czech support from Milan Machovec and Vítězslav Gardavský, one of its initiators in the West was the French Communist Party's politburo member Roger Garaudy. Garaudy's works were widely translated in Czechoslovakia, and in 1963 he visited Prague for the occasion of an international conference on Franz Kafka.[80] In the Czech milieu, Garaudy was considered one of the greatest authorities on the critique of Stalinist distortions of thought. He was additionally received as a representative of "realism without borders," which was the title of his book as well as a Marxist who was responding to contemporary trends in philosophy, including Jean-Paul Sartre's existentialism.[81]

It was the French Marxist Louis Althusser who theoretically defined himself in opposition to the subjectivizing turn within the Marxism of his time. In reaction to a personal meeting with Adam Schaff as well as to correspondence with Erich Fromm, at the end of which Althusser's text was not incorporated in Fromm's Socialist Humanism symposium,[82] Althusser began to come to terms with humanism. He considered it a dead end for Marxism, because it was unable to analyze the problems of Stalinism and even obscures the reproduction of Stalinism as such. At the same time, he saw the humanist intrusions into Marxism as revealing a limited reading of Marx's work that stemmed from the distinction between his early and late works, and which ultimately led to a shift away from Marxist class analysis to liberalism. The result was Althusser's proclamation of the project of theoretical antihumanism, which was based on a sharp distinction between Marx's early and late works with an emphasis on epistemological reading. In the second half of the 1960s, a fairly heated debate opened up on this topic, which, however—and this must be noted—was mostly limited to the French intellectual world, and often resembled the settling of scores within the French Communist Party, especially between Althusser and Garaudy. However, it is also necessary to consider the indications of an internal debate taking place on humanism within the Soviet bloc. This refers not to the anti-revisionist campaign associated with suppressing the "counterrevolution" in 1956, but instead, for instance, to the polemic over one of the most original Soviet Marxists, Evald Ilyenkov, with Schaff's conception of the total man.[83]

Althusser's critique of the humanist tendencies in Marxism is understandable not only in the context of the time but also on principle. The Czechoslovak case also illustrates a certain validity to his analyses: titles that indicated content focused on a "return" to naturalness or the exaltation of human uniqueness, which represented certain romanticizing tendencies in Marxist philosophy, were appearing on the counters of bookshops at the end of the 1960s.[84] However, at the same time, it is necessary to emphasize that despite what Althusser claimed, a great many post-Stalinist intellectuals took a critical approach to period fashions in thought; moreover, they were looking at them from Marxist positions, with an awareness of their own intellectual superiority,[85] and even when they did not apply Althusser's arguments directly, for them, a narrowly conceived philosophy of man meant a regression of Marxism and thus also of a strictly critical and holistic philosophy. For example, Kosík warned that a one-dimensional focus on the philosophy of man would come at the expense of fundamental philosophical questions, such as time, truth, being, science and nature, and would only develop the areas of personal responsibility, happiness, morality, and experience. In other words, if humanistically oriented Marxist philosophy is to achieve its goals, it cannot be perceived fragmentarily, but "totally."[86] Similarly, in a discussion about the nature of Marxist philosophy in 1967, Kusý stated: "The world, the cosmos is the highest, independent, self-sufficient, closed totality and man is only a part, a moment, or a component of this all-encompassing totality of the universe. Therefore, the world cannot be explained starting from man or with man, but on the contrary, man must be explained starting from the world and with the world, and thus define his subordinate and derived place in the entirety of world events."[87] Kalivoda likewise spoke about recognition of "human existence in its entire totality."[88]

The determinists also drew a line between their philosophy and narrowly conceived Marxist humanism, attributing to it internal problems similar to those in existentialism. In the second half of the 1960s a debate was opened about its limits even among the philosophers who were otherwise counted as its representatives. Průcha first expressed nearly the same evaluation as Althusser when he proclaimed that an inorganic supplementation of the original Stalinist ideas of the "philosophy of man" and "evolved ethics" would adapt them "to survival in contemporary conditions."[89] In his book *Kult člověka* (The Cult of Man) he directly claimed that an ontology based on the subject, even if it was also based in the subject's praxis, ultimately fails to address fundamental philosophical questions and de facto does not overcome idealistic dualism.[90]

At this point, we are interested neither in rehabilitating the Czechoslovak post-Stalinists in the eyes of Althusser's supporters, nor in enshrining the texts from that period in the most exalted chambers of Czechoslovak Marxist thought. Instead, we want to point out that the subject and his freedom of choice—Althusser notwithstanding—was the question of the day, and this cannot be overlooked from the perspective of the development of post-Stalinist thought. Unlike Cibulka and Černík, for whom choice primarily meant acting on the basis of knowledge of a general social law, or the legal philosophers' ideas about the relationship of the institution and the human individual, these authors define the human being as a unique individual who is able to realize not only himself but also his own history. While we analyze the latter authors in chapter 5, here we remain aware of the interlinkage of both topics as we focus almost exclusively on the definition of autonomous human subjectivity.

The post-Stalinist departure from Marxist orthodoxy was especially evident in the critical social analysis of the present. Especially for the humanist Marxists, the main roles here were no longer played by the figure of the "impoverished proletarian" and the "dehumanized capitalist," as they had been for the theorists of the Second International, including Lenin and his followers, nor were these thinkers concerned with builders of the Stalinist type who were creating a new world; instead they focused on the alienated nature of modern man. Modernity, as a social form shared by both East and West, thus began to gradually blur, in the eyes of post-Stalinists, the perceived differences between capitalism and socialism. It is telling that we can see similar ideas appearing at the end of the 1950s and beginning of the 1960s, which is roughly the period when socialism was officially proclaimed and thus the full completion of its legal and institutional framework had been accomplished. Czechoslovak society, as Peter Wagner would say, had achieved a degree of conventionalization, and organized modernity found itself in a relatively stable position for a while. As Vítězslav Sommer pointed out in connection with the debate over the specifics of the Czechoslovak evolution toward socialism, "The socialist state was a key result of the revolutionary process and the main tool for the administration and further development of the communist political project."⁹¹ The sense that the socialist state framework marked the completion of a historical trajectory also corresponds to the period's popularity of convergence theory based on a rapprochement between socialism and capitalism that will lead to a merger. Kalivoda aptly characterized the turn to man in the sense described above, according to which it is only with the completion of socialism, when society "begins to liberate itself from class conditions," that previously marginal questions such as the "general forms of human existence, human flourishing, and manifestations of lifestyle, ethical interests and values, or the 'natural bases' of human culture" are opened.⁹²

However, there is another important aspect, without which the articulation of a new post-Stalinist subjectivity among Marxist humanists would hardly be comprehensible (but this is also largely true for techno-optimists). We have already mentioned in chapter 2 that in praxis the human being not only humanizes nature but shapes himself and thereby creates the conditions for his own freedom. But unlike much of the hitherto existing Marxist tradition (in the East and West and in unison with new wave of praxeological approaches like the Praxis school in Yugoslavia), which identified praxis with production or more concretely with labor, the Czechoslovak humanists refused such simple conflation and introduced a crucial distinction between labor on the one hand and praxis on the other. Sviták succinctly expressed this distance and contempt toward the Stalinist conception of praxis as labor: "Finally, the most important philosophically and ideologically imperative aspect is that only through a tragic deformation of Marxist views did the idea arise that the meaning of human life is found in labor. It's as if Marxist humanism took over the Protestant view of work as a path to salvation. This view triumphed in the petit-bourgeois morality of the victorious industrial revolution, in economic utilitarianism, and in the predominance of object-oriented art."⁹³

The question now was what exactly their relationship looked like. For the humanists would be against any dualistic dichotomy in which labor and praxis were externally opposed to each other. The definition of labor then seemed quite clear. Labor here refers to the activity by which man acquires the means for his own reproduction: it is therefore a necessary activity in the sense that it is a necessary condition for the life of the human individual. Marxist humanists, in agreement with Marx and in opposition to orthodoxy and especially Stalinism, point out that in it, however, man does not yet attain liberation precisely because man is active there only under the pressure and weight of the necessity of securing the means for his own preservation. The Stalinist glorification of labor was thus de facto tantamount to a glorification of toil, drudgery, and thus nonfreedom. But man can only be free in a realm that is devoid of this necessity—that is, in the realm of freedom, where he realizes himself not through labor but through praxis as a creative activity in which he develops himself. The question remains, of course, about how to determine their mutual relationship without creating a dualistic separation of the two kinds of activity relegated into their own self-contained spheres. The humanists offered an answer that is both analytic and genetic at the same time. On the one hand, praxis was understood as a concept in which it was necessary to distinguish between the moment of labor in the sense of the transformation and humanization of nature (the realm of necessity, in which the purpose is external to this activity) and the existential moment in which the constitution of human subjectivity took place (the realm of freedom, in which the purpose is the activity itself).[94] But on the other hand, there is also a genetic relation between these moments, where the labor activity constitutes the historical condition for the possibility of the emergence of activity in its existential, subjective sense.[95] Thus, praxis as labor would be genetically primary, but in the teleological (or even moral or ethical) sense of a purpose to be achieved, the existential character of praxis as free creation would be primary. In other words, the concept of praxis comprises two moments: the moment of labor, which forms the condition of freedom as free activity, and freedom itself, which represents the ultimate purpose of the concept. Here, Marx's famous leap from the realm of necessity into the realm of freedom is not so much a leap (at least not in the spatial sense), but a twist, a revolutionizing of the realm of necessity itself, in which man simultaneously realizes himself freely in the sense that the very same activity could be both necessary and free.[96] In short, in the view of Marxist humanists, the philosophy of praxis is also (perhaps above all) a philosophy of freedom.

ALIENATION AND PRAXIS

For the post-Stalinist intellectuals, man as the main actor immediately appears in several positions that were both intertwined and distinct from one another. The human individual here, which had once been demeaned as "a consumer living in relative affluence" (Sviták), becomes the target of manipulation by the apparatuses of mass communications and entertainment, and at another time as a manipulable being, or a disposable object for modern bureaucratic regimes (Kosík).[97]

The author of the "consumerist" conception of man naturally derived his view from Western sociology, primarily from critical theory—especially Herbert Marcuse's *One-Dimensional Man*, which was very popular then. At the same time, Sviták was troubled by the same problem that we observed in the legal philosophers: the growing passivity of the individual and the consequent loss of a sense of human existence as the main form of alienation in modern society that was just as prevalent in the West as in the socialist countries.[98] As we indicated above, despite what the legal philosophers argued, the solution could not be found in equalizing the relationship between people and institutions, but in a turn to the human individual and his autonomous activity. According to Sviták, Marxism should have radically changed the perspective from which it understood man and his position in society. At the concrete level this meant breaking away from the idea of man as a "sum of social and productive relations" (Marx's definition from his Introduction in the *Critique of Political Economy*) as well as from a concept of man based in activity in the form of labor (homo faber). Sviták's understanding of the phenomenon he critiqued as a "consequence of the tragic deformation of Marxist views"—which has more in common with Protestantism, the petit-bourgeois morality of the Victorian Industrial Revolution, and economic utilitarianism than with Marxism itself—is a typical example of the humanistic conception of subjectivity.[99]

In the second case, Kosík began with analyses of the political economy of Stalinism and capitalism. He claimed that the cardinal deficit of the concept of man within the framework of the political economy lay in the wrong order in which it was questioning the nature of man. Instead of taking human "essence" in its totality as the starting point, the political economy was asking what the human being must be equipped with for the system to function. In Stalinism, this would mean achieving or exceeding the plan, in capitalism, measuring everything by costs and benefits. It is not that man was captured into these relationships before he was even able to exist: the fundamental problem was that the system became his only reality, and it enabled him to develop those qualities that it considered the only real ones. The system is thus characterized by its selection of a certain part of man that it considers essential and real, which it requires and develops. The first fatal consequence is the division of man into this essential part and one that is inessential, unreal, and suppressed by the system. The second consequence, which stems from the first, is the transformation of the living human being into a disposable, calculatable unit.[100] Kosík then poses a clear postulate: "Man *is not* reducible to a thing, he is always more than the system of factual relations in which he moves and which moves him."[101]

For Kosík, two conclusions could be derived from the aforesaid.

First, man is a totality, from which no part can be taken away without causing his fragmentation and subsequent destruction. Therefore, the determination of man cannot consist in the naming or selecting of his "essential" qualities, which distinguish him from other biological or physical entities.[102] But neither, exactly as Sviták claimed, can it consist in the classic Marxist definition of the human being as a set of social relations.[103] Second, each reduction of this kind implies an idea of man as a definable entity or, "aggregate" of relations, which can be further manipulated or perhaps developed, but only in the direction set by the system itself.[104] This perspective also formed the standpoint from which Kosík criticized techno-optimistic thinking, because it was based on science as the main driver of development (see chapter 5).

Sviták and Kosík elaborated the two interconnected motifs in similar ways. Orthodox Marxism had defined human beings through their social relations, but this conception was overshadowed in Sviták's work by the modern figure of an absurd and alienated individual, and in Kosík's by a manipulable subject. In accordance with the belief that art is one of the decisive factors in the transformation of man and society, in their considerations on modern subjectivity, both authors drew inspiration from contemporary cinema (the Czechoslovak New Wave for Sviták) and literature (Franz Kafka and Jaroslav Hašek for Kosík).

In doing so, they set the stage for the kind of antihero that replaced the Stalinist model of the hero-revolutionary and the hero-builder and became typical in post-Stalinist thinking. For Kosík, the figure of Josef Švejk represented a non-prefabricated being growing "directly from the big-city environment," who never changes and always remains himself through his series of inimitable encounters, whose result is often a grotesque inversion of some original intention or goal.[105] The system is unable to reduce him. The parallel with Sviták's understanding of the type of New Wave film that depicts "man as the object of external manipulation, chooses a down-to-earth story, and deprives the heroes of all heroic traits" is clear.[106] The characters in Miloš Forman's, Ivan Passer's, and Věra Chytilová's films also, like Hašek's Švejk or Kafka's Josef K., undergo a series of banal, embarrassing, comical, or bizarre situations that change them very little, let alone lead them to some kind of denouement or catharsis in the end. For Kosík, this tension between the characters and events caused by the system (the "Great Mechanism") was a reference to the very nature of modern society, to its crisis, and inhuman perversity.[107]

We are thus facing a certain paradox: the post-Stalinist criticism of the Stalinist conception of subjectivity focuses on the passivity that

Stalinist determinism arrives at, which is then balanced with an accent on the personal will of the individual. While Stalinism—and Stalinist art in particular—presented human subjectivity as active, and struggling against and overcoming all possible and even impossible human limitations, post-Stalinism appreciates what is nearly the opposite tendency in modern art, in which the action of individuals is replaced by "uninvolved passivity." Instead of escalating moments, the "banality of situations" emerges, and the original narrative denouement is replaced with the "open endings" of the post-Stalinist antiheroes.[108] Thus we do not see a final catharsis or liberation in any of the characters, but only the constant tension between man and circumstances, or the human subject and the outside world. Sviták describes these (anti)heroes of modern art as more like cursed heroes and romantic outlaws.[109] However, this should not confuse us. Unlike the existentialist perspective on alienation, which was effectively posed as a default and insurmountable condition, post-Stalinist understandings of human subjectivity—such as those of Kosík and Sviták—were characterized by an effort to move beyond the hopelessness and reductiveness of the modern world. Both thinkers sought to orient themselves toward determinations that allowed for the possibility of overcoming these limitations.

The Marxist humanists also adopted a similarly dual stance on modern science. In their way, they feared the fragmentation and one-sidedness in the understanding of man that could result from scientific approaches,[110] but at the same time they were not interested in a romanticizing return to the prescientific, traditionalist approach to reality. Kosík thus credited the natural sciences and technology with discovering new possibilities for "the development of humanism and researching the specifics of what is human."[111] While Kosík appreciated the shifting of the boundaries between creative and noncreative human activity,[112] Sviták creatively used the cybernetic definition of human being when he overturned one of their theses about entropy. While it generally holds true in communicative systems that during information transfers some information is lost, man, according to Sviták, is clearly the only being that escapes this law, because "only man is able in his communication with the world and with people to augment information—he is an anti-entropic agent of the cosmos."[113] Naturally, this definition had a dual nature based in its statement of the condition (description) and the projective idea (prescription). For him to be a man endowed with rights who would not fall into alienated ways of life in order not to become the hopeless antihero of modern literature and film, post-Stalinist man had to develop his own activity.

Like the representatives of the interwar avant-garde, Sviták's main concern was how man could actively constitute himself in the modern world through his "creation." In the same way, in a critical controversy with existentialism, Kosík returned to Marx, specifically to the first of his *Theses on Feuerbach*, where man is defined by objectifying and creative activity.[114] He therefore cannot be understood as a ready-made, manipulable object, but preferably through the prism of a process of subject genesis itself, which is understood as open and ambiguous. As we discussed in chapter 2, genesis is a structuring element of praxis and Kosík leaves no doubt as to the importance he ascribes to it when he writes "something essential happens in human praxis that contains its own truth in itself and does not refer to anything outside itself; something that is also of ontological importance."[115] Praxis is presented here as a process of creation that has a directional character and is held taut between intention and the ready-made result. However, what's important is that it contains the moment of reflexivity that elevates it to a determining factor that exceeds its originally transitive character. Without this objectifying praxis, man would never become *truly* man but would be reduced to a mere potency (thought) without the possibility of realization—or to a ready-made, manipulable object.

The very same problem—the relationship between the unambiguous and the ambiguous, the possible and the impossible—is also addressed by Ivan Sviták, when he says that both man and the world, or more precisely their formation, lie beyond the bounds of strict logical calculation. Therefore, neither technology nor science can become exemplary forms of creation. The only human activity able to do so represented art or more precisely poetry and modern film. It is in these two art forms that the entire condition and process of human creation stands out most distinctively. For Sviták it is the moment when human reason transcends itself and comes into contact with something that cannot be rationally grasped.[116] Following a surrealist model, for Sviták the poet becomes an "exemplary mode of human form," because the poem itself ignores the laws of formal logic and the law of contradiction. This "lack" constitutes a direct cardinal virtue—things in the poem "are and are not at the same time, they permeate one another, coexist in conflict, [and] transform into metaphor."[117] What could sound like noise or nonsense to a logical ear in the poem becomes a confirmation of what Sviták says is truly human: reaching the boundary in which what is meets what is not.

Soviet cinematography of the 1920s had achieved remarkable artistic performances, and Sviták saw similar results in contemporary international New Wave films. While for Sviták poems managed to occupy a position on the boundary between the clear and the ambiguous and the existent and nonexistent, modern film combined two seemingly opposite artistic approaches—a subjective poesis of the world and objective analysis, personal engagement, and documentary distance. This blurred the dichotomies of subjective and objective and fantasy and reality, which opened a space for man-the-creator to form an authentic statement about and through the alienation of his time. As František Šamalík fittingly remarked in his reaction to Kosík's essay, experiencing various forms of alienation from the Kafkaesque world is what finally allows a person to become fully human.[118] It was the literary scholar Květoslav Chvatík, who aptly expressed the widespread conviction of his time: "Through the artistic image of the world, life, and man, man learns to understand himself, to understand himself more deeply, and through himself to seek the answer to eternal questions: Where do we come from, what are we, and where are we going?"[119]

For Kosík, nothing seems to express the issue of human praxis as a creative activity in which an intention is realized better than the relationship between the master and the servant, as he brought it to light in the essay "Hašek a Kafka neboli groteskní svět" (Hašek and Kafka or the World of the Grotesque): "The master gives orders and the servant carries them out. The master is the intention, and the servant is its realization. However, since the order is general and takes definite shape only through its *realization*, it can be turned against the master; so many *unforeseen circumstances* arose during the execution of the order that the master no longer recognizes his intention in what the servant has done. The servant is merely a tool of the master's intention, but because he is *active*, he gives rise to situations that foil the master's original plans."[120] Here, in a parabolic summary, Kosík introduces us to the fundamental moments of his conception of praxis (see chapter 2). The intention is the master, and the realization or the implementation is personified as the servant. The servant of course is not just a gear lever of a "great mechanism," and that is not because he himself is an individual with his own intentions (Švejk is practically the opposite of such an individual), but because of the presence of another factor: the "unforeseeable circumstances" that require active agency from the servant-tool. "Activity" here, however, is activity of a very particular kind. Švejk is neither a strategist nor a boat pilot who might skillfully exploit a situation arising in a battle or react to sudden gusts of wind to arrive at a previously set goal—victory or reaching the port. The goal here is still the same one that "originated" in the master's mind, and Švejk as the servant-tool keeps this goal continuously in mind. And that is not all: Švejk attempts to carry out the intention-goal at all costs, and in his own way he succeeds. However, while he is carrying out the order he passes through a space filled with unforeseeable and uncontrollable circumstances or, as Kosík expresses it in another essay, "Švejk a Bugulma aneb zrození velkého humoru" (Švejk and Bugulma or the Birth of Great Humor) through encounters,[121] so the form of the goal also changes uncontrollably; or, if we want to keep using the language of creation, the product itself. The goal is achieved, but the result (the form) is radically and grotesquely inverted compared to the original intention.[122]

Through this arc, Kosík illustrates not only a new form of the irony of history, but above all else, what is going on with human beings when they are engaged in an objectifying activity—praxis. Just like Švejk when he carries out orders, the artist or philosopher also moves through a space that is not smooth and stable but wrinkled and fluctuating—and loaded with "circumstances," "encounters," and even challenges. In this space of becoming and creation—which holds not only an irreducible but in a certain sense also a primary position (in relation to intention and product)—what emerges is not only the object, but above all man himself. In Kosík's view, if the distinctiveness of this unique "space" of modern age is reflected and respected, no objectification and alienation of man can take place.

If Sviták declines to subject the human individual to logical calculus, Kosík speaks of the fact that human reality is not "calculable."[123] Both Sviták and Kosík situated the "essence" of human subjectivity not in the individual who recognizes and uses the general laws of human society, as orthodox Marxism (including Stalinism) would claim, but in the human being, a (self-)creator who has the ability to violate the general laws. If Sviták does not present creative consciousness as a mere reflection of reality but as a consciousness that transcends itself through the primary subconscious and creative fantasy, for Kosík the praxis itself is the primary determinant of human existence.

What is striking is that class, as an analytical category, recedes into the background in this line of thinking, giving way to an analysis of the modern world and the human response to it (see chapter 6). Here, there are no heroes who would defeat the class enemy and exceed the labor norms, but (anti)heroes. This reflects a broader post-Stalinist trend represented by seemingly disparate cultural phenomena such as Polish cinema of the late 1950s (productions of the Polish Film School) or the Soviet fashion for Hemingway in the 1960s.[124] The primary focus of questioning here is not outside of man (social relations); man himself is the biggest problem, with his unique positioning toward the world and society. "Humanism and antihumanism do not permeate classes, but man himself," Sviták characteristically comments.[125] However, it is typical for Czechoslovak post-Stalinism that the projective, future-oriented character is not lost. In art and cinematography especially, "the ideas that will take the aura of the sufferer away from the alienated hero, which will deheroize people as manipulable objects and which will do this to such an extent that they portray a new type of active, romantic, hero, with his value orientations, who is able to protest against the absurdity of alienation not only for other people and the social establishment but also for himself" is of primary importance.[126] Stalinism is not replaced by a hopeless existential skepticism but, as Gardavský would say, with a post-Stalinist "hope out of skepticism."[127] According to Kosík, modern man "never returns to the starting point of his historical movement, but aims higher. He only develops by revolutionizing relationships and by creating the objective conditions to transform himself."[128]

INSTINCTIVE MAN

The emphasis on the alienated nature of the modern world, as well as on praxis as an accompanying aspect of human existence, did not meet with unqualified acceptance by all humanists. While the author of *Dialectics of the Concrete* was warning against the reduction of the human being to a manipulable object, Kalivoda described the conception of the philosophy of praxis as a reduction of man "to his historical dimension," where he is indeed "made into his own creator," but his natural component is neglected.[129] Moreover, he reproached the philosophy of praxis as being tied to the use of "metaphysical" elements still present in the young Marx, which led to obscuring the original Marx and also Engel's intention.[130]

At the end of the 1960s, Kalivoda introduced a concept of man based on natural and instinctive determination combined with dialectical historical development. In the text "Marx a Freud" (Marx and Freud) he turned to Erich Fromm's texts spanning from the 1930s to *Marx's Concept of Man* from 1960 and to Herbert Marcuse and his *Eros and Civilization* (1955). Like Sviták, Kalivoda also vehemently professed the Frankfurt School and the interwar Czech avant-garde tradition, especially works by Bohuslav Brouk, Karel Teige, and Záviš Kalandra, and he returned to the Marxist elaboration of the human essence and nature. Just like those named above, Kalivoda also considered it a crucial point that human nature or essence is not unchanging, as it had been theorized in Marx's early works, nor is it based in a dichotomy of good (eros) and evil (Thanatos) as with Freud. On the contrary, thanks to the

5.5. Robert Kalivoda on an excursion at the Orlík reservoir in Czechoslovakia, April 1968. Copyright Eva Kalivodová.

human ability to control these instinctual forces (hunger and sex) and the possibility of their historical transformation, a "constant structure" is created that submits to historical development based on the "dialectical conflict of their basic elements."[131] On this point, Kalivoda was inspired by the theory of nonrepressive sublimation developed by Marcuse (1955) and, at an underlying level, also by Brouk's work of the 1930s. However, he considered Marcuse's solution of nonrepressive sublimation to be both too static and too idealistic (as well as too Freudian), and he called for the application of a more thoroughly dialectical conception. The reason is that every form of repressive domination arising from the transformation of instinctual drives—such as hunger and sex—entails both repression and an expansion of the space in which life's necessities can be fulfilled. Likewise, social power is not only built on the attainment and multiplication of pleasure, as Freud thought, but is also an expression of "a fundamental and decisive form of sublimation of human aggressiveness," which serves to satisfy the desire for pleasure as such. Kalivoda further elaborates on the Freudian concept of human libidinosity: since the acquisition and consolidation of social power is already libidinous, it is therefore incomparably more brutal than the original instinctive aggression of carnivorous predators. However, in Kalivoda's dialectical conception, this form of sublimation of the libido also arouses "existential counter-aggression" in the form of a humanist and humanizing "revolutionary aggression, which leads to human emancipation and which has no less libidinous charge than aggression that is the tool of social oppression."[132]

Kalivoda's concept of revolutionary change will be further discussed in chapter 5, but in his conception of man the most important element is his attempt to solve the process Freud describes as the sublimation of libidinous forces. Thus, in parallel with Marcuse, Kalivoda introduces the concept of nonrepressive sublimation, which is crucial for his vision of socialism. Based in an analysis of ideology, especially Christian doctrines of the late Middle Ages, Kalivoda arrives at the conclusion that two types of truth emerge: one that is lived, which conflicts with the original ideals because the representatives of power never behave in accordance with their proclaimed rules, and a second one that is enforced by the ruling ideology. The existence of these two truths unwittingly gives rise to the emancipatory ideal being built upon the fulfillment of the original premises of the ruling ideology. Thus, based on resistance against the character of the given social power there is a call for a real implementation of its ideology (for example, in the area of social equality). However, the aggression of the existing power can also simultaneously be challenged by its conscious negation. In this process, aggression is transformed through this negation into a "nonaggressive counteraggression," which has an intellectual rather than material character.[133] The originally aggressive erotic and instinctive forces are transformed into a utopian idea: Man "fixes himself on an ideal value and eliminates his natural egoism to the maximum possible extent."[134]

This principle allows Kalivoda to derive a philosophical historical conception of the emancipation movement (see chapter 5). More importantly, he implicitly attributes the same nature to a person living in a socialist society and thus expresses the belief that man can realize himself in the humanistic project of communism by transforming his instinctive nature into an emancipatory ideal.

The question of freedom therefore occupied the central position in Kalivoda's conception of the human individual. Here, Kalivoda again objected to Kosík's philosophy of praxis, which de facto forces man to act (and as we have seen, Kosík truly considers praxis to be a determinant) and denies him the last instance of free choice. Kalivoda had defined freedom at the philosophical-ontological and anthropological levels. In the first case, he mainly relied on the analysis of Engels's fragment on necessity and chance in *Dialectics of Nature*,[135] in which Kalivoda says the author definitively overcame Hegel's fatalist essentialism whose remnants were still present in the Marxist philosophy of praxis. The interpretation of the anthropological nature of freedom was based in analysis of texts by the "young" Marx (*Economic and Philosophic Manuscripts*) and the mature Marx (*Capital*, especially volume 3), and it demonstrates that the development of human forces and the totally developed human being "remains a goal even for the mature Marx."[136] However, in this context, he placed the critical emphasis on the understanding of freedom as variability and plurality. According to Kalivoda, Marxism concentrated its interest solely on the issue of freedom understood as the overcoming of necessity, while entirely neglecting the question of free choice—even though this aspect is already present in Marx. Freedom therefore always has a dual nature for him: as free activity, it is the overcoming of necessity and thus an affirmation of contingency; at the same time, as free choice, it is also freedom from necessity. It is precisely this second aspect that emancipates the human being from equality understood as sameness and hereby affirms the plurality of human projects. This affirmation of plurality as nonsameness is recognized, in Kalivoda's eyes, as "socialist libertinism"[137]: "Various life ideals can and must freely arise and be lived, which correspond to the specific arrangements of individuals and groups of individuals, which will probably not correspond over the long term to Marx's ideal of the total human being either as a whole or in its details. This is because the harmonization of human qualities, even if it is relative, is probably the most difficult thing a limited and conflicted human being can achieve."[138]

Marx's ideal of the "total human being" can therefore only be fulfilled based on "completely free life choice,"[139] which at the same time must also be maximally tolerant toward other contents of human existence. It is only when both dimensions of human freedom are fulfilled (i.e., if there is freedom to make one's own choices as well as tolerance for other projects) that it becomes possible to have faith in the future: "Freedom of human choice provides immense possibilities for creating unknown continents in the sea of socialist libertinism."[140] But although Kalivoda said Czechoslovakia was only at the outset of such a journey, he believed it was justified to speak of its actual realization there.[141]

Kalivoda's formulation, which is based both in the limiting natural dimension of the human being and in a radical conception of freedom, is unique in the context of period Czechoslovak thought—though not incompatible with the concept of praxis that Kalivoda himself had been criticizing. Despite the explicit way he defines it against Kosík's conception, Kalivoda's way of thinking still has several themes in common with his predecessors, most prominently an interest in various types of subjectivity in other historical times, expressed in the period's idioms as "models of human personality," "types of Man," or forms of perception.[142] Ivan Sviták agrees that history cannot be understood "as mere changes in technology, social orders, and types of art, but also—if not primarily—as changes in man's self-interpretation and as a continuum of changes in human types."[143]

In this context, as with Kalivoda, the question concerns a naturally conditioned, or if we prefer, a biological dimension of the human being. Just like Kalivoda had proposed transcending the static understanding of instinct and instead perceiving it through dialectical dynamism, here Sviták also claims that "old models of human personality [. . .] are collapsing and new ones are emerging. [. . .] A set of processes emerge, which cause a transformation of the human type, an anthropological transformation, a comprehensive, overall change in the manner of human existence."[144] Recalling Kosík, we add that not only works of art as such—symphonies, paintings, poems, and the like—belong in the category of culture, but also human hearing, the human eye, and the human imagination, which are able to perceive issues of modern reality in a particular manner: "Modern culture is a culture of the modern objective world and the modern subject; the modern-perceiving, modern-thinking, modern-seeing, modern-hearing human being. The human eye has not changed physiologically from the slaveholding era to our times. But human vision has developed, advanced, refined, and become more subtle."[145] What Kosík emphasizes here is a seemingly banal fact—one often overlooked in the over-technologized twentieth century—namely, that human activity creates "a new universe of machines, devices, apparatuses, and equipment, but also a new world of beauty."[146]

Without launching into a detailed treatise on a subject that is elaborated upon in chapter 5 in connection with the problem of social change, we can consider the assumption of creation as another common theme. Within its framework, Kosík spoke both about the disruption of the everyday world of "pseudo-concreteness" and—under the influence of German idealism—about moving toward a work of art that becomes a "Work" because it transcends the conditions of its period and breaks free of the present situation.[147] Following the interwar avant-garde, Kalivoda then conceived of creation as a permanent subversive, emancipatory, and constructive process that emerges out of the contradiction between ideal and lived reality.[148] Despite the partial differences and mutual tensions, the distinctive feature of post-Stalinism, which we identified (see chapter 2) as a shift from movement with a clearly determined and singular goal toward a common framework with creative plurality (internal plurality), reappears here. The shift from building (Stalinism) to creation (post-Stalinism) as a model for thinking about the socialist modernization project was also anticipated by the term "dialogical creationism" that was introduced by Gardavský at the end of the 1960s as part of his approach based in dialogue.[149]

THE SUBJECT IN DIALOGUE

Kalivoda's socialist libertinism allows us to approach one of the ways in which the post-Stalinist intelligentsia of the late 1960s was thinking, at a time when the formulation of a political program founded on alliances between various conceptions and interpretations of socialism was being shaped in the intellectual milieu of Marxist humanism.[150] Another version of tolerance articulated in this manner, which also called for a conscious acceptance of intellectual diversity, can be found in texts where Marxist intellectuals engaged in dialogue with Christians.[151] The definition of human subjectivity here partly overlaps with the previous interpretation and partly takes on specific features where the influence of the Christian tradition is evident. The notional turn from Stalinism to post-Stalinism is at first glance more striking among intellectuals of this type than elsewhere. To wit: participants and proponents of dialogue with Christianity had often engaged in ideological struggle against religion during the Stalinist era. To some extent, this also applies to the two authors we will be discussing in our analysis in the text that follows: Milan Machovec and Vítězslav Gardavský. However, the abruptness of the transition from ideological struggle to dialogue is naturally not as sharp as we might assume based on the contrast in meaning between the words "struggle" and "dialogue." The seemingly groundbreaking change

3.4. The Brno-based philosopher Vítězslav Gardavský, author of *God Is Not Yet Dead*, with his daughter at their family's weekend house in Prosetín. Copyright Andrea Mikitová.

in attitudes is somewhat blunted when we take into account that the "sharpened class struggle" of the Stalinist period actually led these authors to their study of Christianity.[152] Thus, as in the other cases, even here Stalinism inadvertently created the capacity (or, in Touraine's words, "historicity"; see chapter 1) for a well-informed post-Stalinism to arise from within it and overcome it.

Gardavský's and Machovec's criticism of Stalinism was mainly based on three motifs. The first, in accordance with Marxist humanism, rejected the artificial suppression of subjectivity or any type of subjectivization that required self-denial in the form of the individual "I."[153] Both authors considered the right to one's own subjectivity, including religious belief, to be an important aspect of socialist society. The second motif was related to the first, and they reproached Stalinism for its strict belief that along with the elimination of capitalism and the gradual building of socialism the class and social roots of religion would entirely disappear.[154] The basis for their argument had a core similar to that of the legal philosophers: the long process of realizing the socialist ideal replaced the short-term political decree, and "ideal, abstract goals" were inserted into the "imperfect, evolving reality."[155] Gardavský, like Mlynář, Šamalík, and Lakatoš, was also working from an acceptance of the differing interests of the citizen and the state. Just as the above-mentioned legal philosophers were expecting to maintain the category of the citizen, or sometimes of civil society until the communist ideal was achieved, Gardavský also said that until unity was achieved between the interests of the citizen and the state, "we are going to still have [religion] with us for a long time."[156]

Finally, the third motif was the most systematic and it merged into post-Stalinism's own elaboration of subjectivity. Since Stalinism set scientific evidence, rationality, and so forth. in opposition to religious thought, it automatically rejected religion and did not inquire into its actual function. By doing so, in Gardavský's view, it fell under the intellectual level not only of Marxism but also of Christianity. The result of anti-theism implemented in this way was that it participated in the "political clericalism" of the Stalinist era. In contrast, "genuine" Marxist atheism cannot be based on the idea of a priori predominance of rationality over faith, but on a profoundly self-reflexive stance.[157] In this context, Machovec introduces an important distinction between "knowledge" and "belief." Knowledge—whether in the form of ideology or science—can be disseminated, and in this respect, it is objective and collective in nature, but it cannot in itself form an engaged subjectivity. This requires a belief that is not only irreducibly individual but also subjective to the utmost degree. Persuasion, or what Althusser termed ideological interpellation, thus has (and must have) its objectively insurmountable limits, which are placed on it by subjectivity itself. As both Gardavský and Machovec contended, subjectivity is not created as a mere effect of the act of persuasion, or of ideological interpellation, because "worldview formation" has a more complex nature, is relatively independent, and certainly is not accepting of external manipulation.[158] The basis for this claim lies, as we shall see below, in a different conception of the individual's "ethical substance," to use Foucault's term, than the one that prevailed under Stalinism.

5.5. Milan Machovec at a conference of the World Christian Student Federation, 1962. Copyright Martin Machovec.

Here we arrive at the point where both authors become inspired by the Christian or broadly religious tradition. Machovec invoked certain forms of prayer or confession, whose model had to be created based on non-Stalinist materialism. This form of prayer was precisely what would play an irreplaceable role in shaping active, engaged subjectivity, because it was the only thing that could cause a "true conversion in worldview, morals, and politics" in the individual.[159] But while Machovec finds inspiration for the subject's internal dialogue in prayer or personal confession, Gardavský speaks about self-reflection as a moment of "pausing, and [of] fruitful silence."[160] By contrast with its religious counterpart, this prayer, personal confession, or self-reflection was to have the form of a nonmystified internal dialogue. Such an internal dialogue is not conducted with a "being" that was separated from subjectivity and placed outside of it as another, perfect being (God), but is consciously conducted from within the subjectivity itself). Within the dialogue, the "I" does not undergo a process of soul-searching and self-denial (or perhaps self-negation), or even of questioning its own ability to meet the demands placed on it by socialist society or by history (Stalinism). Machovec's inner dialogue represents a process where the "I," in self-reflective confrontation with itself, is developed more fully through a new belief (knowledge, ideology) than it had been through the old one. This, however, cannot be reduced to either his new or old convictions. For this reason, it cannot simply be erased in the process of conversion—as the old "bourgeois" self was within the framework of Stalinist subjectivation—and replaced by something else; rather, it must be developed and "more fully realized."

By contrast, Gardavský describes full-fledged atheism as the metaphysics of Marxism as well as its first philosophy, by which he means a mode of thinking and posing questions and answers. However, he is not interested in creating a new form of religiosity. Marxist atheism "will become a form of metaphysics by transcending, or attempting to transcend, all illusions, including religious illusions."[161] This is also the way that Gardavský's statements about self-reflection should be understood. In his view, self-reflection based on overcoming one's limitations should not be limited to contemplation in silence but must instead be rooted in everyday struggles.[162] It is, on the one hand, a matter of developing a theory of subjectivity that is not "subjectivist"—the subject cannot be abstracted from external events or absolutized—and on the other hand, a theory of transcendence that is not objectivist because it does not submit to automatism, and the subject can never be fully equated with the functioning of the external world.[163] According to Gardavský, this concept of reflexive thinking about one's own historicity and one's own self-transcendence is implicitly inscribed in all of Marx's works. However, this aspect of Marxist thinking could never come fully to the forefront during the period of establishing socialism owing to the "specific requirements of the class struggle." All the more important, according to Gardavský, is its relevance to the "present moment"—both for the development of Marxism and for enhancing its appeal, as well as for shaping a long-term social project.[164]

Nevertheless, the two authors do not end their analysis with inner dialogue or self-reflection, because they do not see them as the last instances where subjectivization is completed. For Machovec this completion is not a dialogue of "I" with "I," but of "I" with "not-I," which for him represents a world without me (death): "Dialogue with death is a dialogue with a world 'without me,' with an absolute 'non-I.' And only in this do I finally and completely find my 'I,' because it is only face to face with death that what was in my life and in my 'I' is truly existentially significant appears to me."[165] For Gardavský it is a question of a double acceptance. On the one hand, it meant awareness of continual historical transcendence (i.e., the acceptance of the legitimate character of the question "What will there be after communism?"), and on the other hand, it means looking at the future as open perspectives of all human possibilities. Subjectivity is thus completed not only in relation to one's own self or to the social past but also based on a permanent tension between the present and an open future, which does not transpire based on inevitability (historical laws), but is realized through human praxis. And because man is, in Gardavský's view, essentially a mortal being, his transcendence always has both an individual and a social dimension. Otherwise, if the dual character is not respected, every question about "purpose" either ends in mysticism or in overestimating society. In the atheist conception of subjectivity, it is only by understanding and accepting one's own mortality that it becomes possible to achieve social self-transgression. And it is only when we accept the finiteness and the material continuation of our own existence ("I myself have no hope of eternity and am at the mercy of death, but I represent hope for others who will outlive me") that we "become human beings in the true sense."[166]

Both authors are literally materializing a Christian theme here. Machovec does so (similarly to the case of the inner dialogue in the form of religious confession and prayer) by "demystifying" reflections on the transcendent, otherworldly realm, translating them back into the earthly world and assigning them a key structural role in the formation of the completing subjectivity—that is, individual existence. Gardavský accomplished the manifestation in the search for a "motif that enables this conscious, reflected acceptance of death."[167] He finds this motif to be partially present in science, but wholly present in love, as the "existential preconditions of all human relationships: as the key to its make-up, a key which is in the hands of the subjective identity wherever it wishes to let concrete relationships and its own inner life ring harmoniously together; as the code word which allows work to become creative and creativeness to become man's self-realization."[168] Here, love is the basic composite of each person conceived as a historical being.

Gardavský and Machovec, like the other Marxist humanists, invoke subjectivity, which is not reducible either to an objective set of social relations or to a space or a simple target of persuasion (interpellation), but to a dimension that has its own autonomy and is created in a process of internal dialogue or self-reflection that leads to conversion to convinced, engaged subjectivity or to true Marxist atheism as the apex of the theory of subjectivity. For both, Marxism is not, as Machovec would say, a "doctrine on the 'objectivity' of historical processes in the sense that the subject would not have to 'engage.' Quite the contrary: Marxism is a doctrine about the objective meaning of the subject in history, [and] especially about the possibility of 'personally committing' to a real path to communism."[169] However, as with the other post-Stalinist Marxists, this committed subjectivity is an integral part of objective historical processes: without it, Machovec claims, these processes would simply "cease."[170] In other words, the irreducibility of man to a set of social relations does not mean invoking an abstract subject that stands outside them: man is always an intersection between social relations and his own subjectivity.[171] And as Vít Bartoš aptly points out in a study dedicated to Gardavský, "The genesis of subjectivity with its self-confidence and idealistic-ideological background is simply not a random process" but one that plays out in history on the basis of social and natural laws that are not exclusively under their deterministic dictates.[172] František Červinka puts it this way: "A person as an individual always still has, along with all of his social, physical and spiritual determinations, a certain *possibility* of preventing himself from becoming a victim of the laws of large numbers and of the systems these laws are inextricably bound up with."[173] It is not so difficult to imagine that the post-Stalinist intellectuals intended this "possibility" to be conscious activity, praxis, or creation. In this last category Gardavský and Machovec included dialogue that not only helps build bridges from differences and mistrust but also creates a new quality. It is therefore no coincidence that Gardavský uses the phrase "dialogical creationism," and that at the end of the 1960s Karel Kosík speaks about "interactive contact, dialogue, [and] influencing," which gives rise to hopes for a post-Stalinist movement that will take the form of a "revolutionary alliance of workers and the intelligentsia."[174] We have thus arrived full circle back to the statement that the dual nature of human subjectivity spans between general laws and personal individuality, and this, as well as creation as a central motif, are two of the main themes in the post-Stalinist definition of subjectivity.

FROM LABOR TO SELF-EDUCATION

Creativity was a central category for determining the nature of subjectivity for the techno-optimists, just as it had been for the humanists. However, while the humanists attempted to shield human creation and creativity from labor activities and in many cases, they even positioned it as an opposite pole, the techno-optimists thematized the pair in close connection with production and science. The decisive role in this conceptualization was played by the transformation of civilization through the scientific-technical revolution, which was to radically change the entire character of human (re)production. The techno-optimistic perception of human subjectivity was reformulated not only at the level of the previously mentioned dichotomy of work versus creativity but also simultaneously in the dyad of working time and leisure.

According to the techno-optimists, "creativity" and the "development of all of the human individual's abilities" were only possible after a complete technological revolution had taken place in which the human forces of production were removed from the immediate labor process and shifted into a nonproduction phase. Thanks to this "liberation," a "huge fund of leisure time" was going to be created that would provide for the desired holistic development of the human individual.[175] The coming, or rather heralded technological revolution (as we will see in chapter 5) was thus going to create a key condition (leisure time), based on which human subjectivity could be fully realized. The techno-optimists claimed this process to be potentially happening for the first time in history. However, in the techno-optimists' view, a quantitative increase in free time alone would still not suffice. If there was no simultaneous change in the character of labor within industrial civilization, leisure time would remain hostage as a regenerative activity for the labor force, at best filled with passive entertainment. It would therefore be unable to contribute to the holistic development of individuals. This was exactly what was happening in capitalist countries, where increasing the amount of leisure time only led to its being filled by capital again, which provided activities organized for workers by the entertainment industry. In this case, there could be no discussion of the creative use of time. Thus, in post-Stalinism, the issue of leisure time gradually began to occupy one of the dominant places in economic, sociological, and philosophical thinking.[176]

Above all, the structural position of leisure time was going to change: it was now to be freed from the trappings of the enduring practice of industrial societies to strictly divide time spent on production and free time spent on regeneration. Here, the contents of the two time dimensions—work and leisure—were mutually exclusive. This made them into an inseparable pair in which the quantitative shifts of a mass of time from one dimension into the other could never solve the problem of introducing a qualitatively new relationship between work and leisure time. Yet the fundamental problem for the techno-optimists was not merely what quantity of time was allocated to work or regeneration but also the very nature of the activities carried out in each. In industrial civilization, these activities had their purposes on the opposite side of the dichotomy: the goal of labor was to gain the means for self-reproduction (regeneration), and the purpose of leisure time was to regenerate the labor force. Each dimension thus referred to its counterpart and found its meaning there.[177]

In contrast to this consequence of the industrial organization of labor, the techno-optimists mobilized Marx's (and, in essence, even Aristotle's) original idea that a truly free and liberating activity does not contain its purpose in something else, but only within itself.[178] However, this did not just relate to whether the purpose was located outside of or within the activity. Due to the nature of industrial labor, human subjectivity was impoverished by the inadequate position of leisure time as well as by the subordinate position of the human subject in relation to machines. For it was precisely the machine that performed the decisive function in the production process, where the human subjectivity-labor force merely assisted it, in a form reduced to simple mechanical actions.[179]

Regardless of the capitalist or socialist nature of the ownership of the means of production, the techno-optimists claimed that the mode of industrial society's (re)production was not limited to the sphere of production but had counterparts in scientific and management activities as well. Radovan Richta directly addressed the intimate connection between the machine civilization and the modern natural sciences, as well as with the former's style of labor management where the subject (the scientist or capitalist) is removed from the object (nature, the production process) and placed outside it into a seemingly independent and external position: "Everything objective is extracted, separated, and isolated from the subject. The subject itself is a pure abstraction—it no longer has any independent and objective meaning other than an external meaning assigned to it. [. . .] It loses its own quality, movement, and development, so it eludes investigation and even its objective counterpart appears to the subject as a being that is contemplated—in the form of mere categories."[180] While in modern science the abstract subject acts in relation to the abstractly understood object, in managing the labor process the capitalist (or in socialism the enterprise director or planner) is put into relation with the workers whom he controls through directives. The scientific-technical revolution was thus supposed to liberate people in industrial civilizations from the dual limitations of human subjectivity, that is, from the subordination of labor time and subordination to the object-machine, and additionally from directives issued by capitalists or planning centers. The immediately complementary and at the same time sharply contradictory character of the relationship between subjectivity and objectivity was to be abolished, and the original bipolarity of industrial society would also be bridged, or at least minimalized.

The human subjectivity of the new scientific-technical civilization was thus perceived as a function of the increasing amount of leisure time that would result from the implementation of full automation (i.e., a mode of production that could do without man's direct participation). Hand in hand with this automation, the very character of human subjectivity was also transformed and it would become able to truly utilize the liberated time for its own development. Being removed from the immediate labor process should enable the full realization of human creative potential, especially in science, culture, and social welfare, because it was only through leisure time that a full liberation of the human individual could take place—Marx's famous leap from the realm of necessity to the realm of freedom.[181]

Although the new space for the realization of human creativity was declared to be the free choice of each individual, it still placed considerable demands on subjectivity. Leisure time liberated from the immediate demands of labor became both a possibility and a task. In addition, the techno-optimists believed in the controllability of social processes and thus expected they could influence people to spend their leisure time in the way the techno-optimists intended so that it would correspond to the interests of the entire society. The contrast with Kalivoda's socialist libertinism is evident here.[182]

Owing to the nature and the speed of transformations within postindustrial civilization, the subject could no longer simply depend on the knowledge and skills it had gained in the past. To contribute to the development of society, it was necessary to react to the ever-changing challenges and continually educate oneself ("lifelong learning"). Richta formulated this principle succinctly when he said that thanks to a transformation in the production process (automation) the scientific-technical revolution was creating a "general social *need* for man to develop."[183] Man had thus become "useless as abstract labor power" and had instead become "necessary as a human being."[184] Because it was practically a force of production itself, the creativity of human subjectivity was supposed to replace the labor operations of industrial manufacturing and the directives of management functionaries. Human creativity was not only expected but required. The intellectualization of the human being was both a possibility created by humans themselves and a necessity imposed by the development of civilization and the productive forces.[185]

In this social-production configuration, the older kind of education as the transfer of a complete set of knowledge was going to be replaced by a permanent process of self-education in which people would have the possibility to freely choose their own areas of expertise for the first time in history. The one-sided development of man-the-producer that had been largely determined by the division of labor was to be replaced by a multilayered (self-)improvement of the human personality: "The school of the future will have to turn the *object* of education into the subject of his own education, the being undergoing education into the being educating himself—education into self-education."[186] At the same time, the narrow specialization demanded by the previous type of production was transformed by a new permeability of occupational fields and by the openness of the educational process, which had to adapt to the fact that man and his subjectivity were evolving historically and the scientific-technical revolution would be a source of permanent changes in the future.[187] The scientific-technical revolution became (or rather would become) a revolution in human subjectivity, which will likely "be the first in history to reveal that what man revolts against [. . .] are also [. . .] his own limits."[188] Self-transformation was to become the constant imperative of the period.[189]

Outside the category of leisure time, the notion of labor that was liberated from its dependence on machine production offered some intellectuals a sufficiently strong standpoint from which they could address the subject that the legal philosophers had been working on. Although the clash between partial (personal or group) and general rationality had led to new forms of tension and even conflicts that the individual had to cope with, the effect of contemporary capitalist society creating a "lonely mass" could not occur here. On the contrary, according to the sociologist Irena Dubská, "socialized individuality" will "multiply and increase its participation in the world," while the variety of choices will "make the personality more exclusive, unrepeatable, and unique."[190]

The human subjectivity of industrial society including its Stalinist variant was overcome here through a conception of subjectivity that was in conformity with contemporary post-Stalinist thought in rejecting man as a mere intersection or a set of social relations. The techno-optimists explicitly rejected any frameworks that would exclude the human being from the scientific-technical revolution conceived as a "total effort" to transform both the world and humanity.[191] While in industrial production man only assisted in the formation of a process based on general laws, now he both developed himself and participated in developing the nature of the continually evolving scientific and technological civilization. The Marxist ideal was thus pursued by a different path here, though the goal—human liberation—remained the same. It hardly needs to be emphasized that the techno-optimists considered post-Stalinist socialism (naturally, seen through their eyes) as the basic and necessary framework for all the above-described transformations.

VARIETIES OF POST-STALINIST FREEDOM

Post-Stalinist thought parted ways with the Stalinist and more generally, orthodox Marxist conception of the subject who recognizes objectively existing natural and historical laws and manages to control, accelerate, or decelerate them with his active will. The post-Stalinists mainly problematized what had primarily been a tacitly accepted assumption about the possibility of a direct relationship between the knower and the known in which the subject appeared primarily as a mirror in which the external world is reflected in a more or less adequate manner. In contrast to orthodox Marxism, the post-Stalinists constructed their fundamental orientation based on activity oriented toward "externalization" of the human subject into the surrounding world, or its objectification within it. In this way, they not only pointed out the shortcomings of the orthodox Marxist conception but also reacted to the existentialists, whose concept of subjectivity was in their eyes either passive or too separated from the world. The emphasis on active subjectivity corresponded to the self-confident surpassing of Stalinism in favor of the new post-Stalinist reality.

The problematization of the period understanding of subjectivity enabled the creation of a wide range of possibilities in which the solution of this problem was differentiated. However, the common denominator of all the variants remained the dialectical moment of mediation, in which subjectivity was determined not only by change as a form of "mechanical" transition from one state to another, but primarily by change as an *event*. It contained possibilities for abrupt and unexpected reversals or encounters as well as space for freedom in the sense of free choice. At the same time, the call for a dialectical definition of the relationship between subjectivity and general social laws could be heard in all the varieties of post-Stalinist definitions of subjectivity. While in the Stalinist era, man actively participated in building socialism by acknowledging the general laws of history (and sometimes focusing on how to influence or accelerate them through the party), in post-Stalinism he was not going to be a mere (co)participant in historical events, but also their creator. Post-Stalinist perception simply implied a different connection between the subject and the realization of socialism: the heroic Stalinist overcoming of oneself and of human limitations as such ("norms") within an objective historical process was replaced with a mutual influence between subjectivity and general social trends.

The dialectical determinists understood subjectivity as a moment of decision; a decision in which the subject identifies and chooses progressive tendencies within objective development. However, it was more than a question of recognizing these tendencies and decisions themselves: subjectivity had a dual nature that acted toward the realization of change (the choice of a progressive tendency) as well as toward stabilizing the given social situation. Therefore, subjectivization as a process of ethical work on oneself was also characterized by struggle to defeat the backward, conservative sides of one's own subjectivity.

The legal philosophers and political thinkers examined the space of free human activity in relation to the institutional framework of the socialist state. They came to the almost unanimous conclusion that socialism cannot develop without the possibility for human individuals to articulate their own subjectivity. The tensions between the subjective and the objective and the individual and the social represented a central theme for this type of post-Stalinist thinking.

The Marxist humanists placed "real" subjectivity into the "interspace" between intention and goal, whether this was in creative artistic activity, or the everyday actions represented by the type of the modern antihero. Here, the Stalinist Stakhanovite hero became an utterly useless if not actually even a counterproductive figure. It was no longer about overcoming human limitations that transcended the originally human activity of actively participating in production, because workers were now separated from it by technology or the organizational mechanisms of modern society. This is another reason that the main hero of the day for the humanists was an antihero, an individual who does not adapt, but protests the manipulative and fragmenting effects of modern civilization. Such types were exemplified by Švejk or the "accursed" avant-garde modern creative artists. And despite his critical reproaches of the Hegelian determinism of the philosophy praxis (the necessity of activity), Kalivoda's project of Marxist libertinism pursued similar intentions. His conception of a subjectivity based on creative reflection of the instinctual character of human subjectivity represented the most radical Marxist vision of its time, the "harmonized" project of humanistic socialism ultimately remained the intersection point for the different projects of human subjectivity.

By contrast, the techno-optimists, who had started from the same situation using the same initial assumptions, arrived at nearly the exact opposite conclusion. The humanists were undoubtedly aware of the significant differences between industrial and fully automated technology, but automation did not mean the same thing for them as it did for the techno-optimists—the ticket to a new epoch of civilization. The latter believed that only the fully automated production process in socialist society allowed for the creation of sufficient conditions (leisure time) for the fullest self-realization of the individual. It can be said that ultimately both camps were aiming for the same goal, which was the most complete and comprehensive development of human abilities. While for the humanists the projective nature of subjectivity grew out of resistance toward the negative effects of modern civilization, techno-optimistic self-modulation tended to accept the demands brought by modern civilization's challenges.

The common denominator in all these definitions of subjectivity remains a certain form of necessity that the development of the post-Stalinist project of socialism could not have done without. The philosophers of praxis "had to" perform unmasking and thus also projective activity, and Kalivoda's human individual man ultimately "had to" make a free choice and—despite the proclaimed freedom gained through free time—the subjectivity of the techno-optimists necessitated permanent (self-)education as both a personal and social activity.

The post-Stalinists did not create some new concept of human nature that would correspond to their ideas about shaping socialism. On the contrary, in their eyes, man was subject to historical development, and his subjectivity also changed depending on his own activity and shifts in the forces of production and social structures. Awareness of human historicity allowed all these seemingly opposing intellectual currents, despite their discrepancies, to speak about various human models and types (Sviták, Průcha), changes in human emotionality (Ota Klein), and in human perception (Kosík, Klein); in short, about continual human (self-)formation.

A further common denominator, but certainly not the final one, among the post-Stalinist definitions of subjectivity is a phenomenon that we could describe—with reference to Michel Foucault—as an attempt to develop a specific "technology of the self" (i.e., practices or techniques that enable individuals to create from themselves the subject of their own conduct). By this, we mean that post-Stalinism was not only limited to the theoretical determination of the nature of subjectivity, the conditions of its constitution, and the goals it was to achieve, but also examined its practical and ethical side. The development of this kind of technology is indicated by practically all the above-mentioned projects of post-Stalinist subjectivity. For the dialectical determinists, this meant struggling against the conservative dimension of subjectivity; for the legal philosophers, it meant establishing an equal and mutual relationship between human individual and socialist institutions; for the humanists, it was primarily artistic activity understood in the broader sense as creative activity; and for the techno-optimists, it was ultimately about a process of self-education as a permanent response to the new civilizational challenges.

The most-elaborated form of the ethical side of post-Stalinist subjectivity represents Vítězslav Gardavský's and Milan Machovec's dialogical thinking, where they formulate a kind of "materialist spirituality" through their critical dialogue with Christianity. Both refer to a certain type of "dialogue with oneself" (variously termed "confession," "prayer," or "a moment to pause and be silent"), in which the individual reflects upon himself, and by overcoming his own limits actively participates in historical and social events. However, unlike in Christianity and Stalinism, here the process of overcoming one's own limitations did not mean repudiating one's old (pagan, bourgeois) self and accepting a totally new subjectivity, but developing one's own, original uniqueness, which cannot be reduced to any form of religious "belief." In their eyes, this dialogue enabled self-reflection, without which any truly active subjectivity would be unthinkable.

Returning to the beginning of this summary, the post-Stalinist conceptions diverged from the originally orthodox Marxist idea of the subject as an individual or collective acting in the direction (or sometimes perhaps against the direction) of historical laws, or of an individual who overcomes his own limits. As the starting point for their inquiries, they chose the originally Hegelian conception of subjectivity in the sense of active (self-)objectification in the external world. If post-Stalinist subjectivity generally understood its own individual act of creation as participation in objective social and historical events, it is then necessary to illuminate not only subjectivity as such but also the conceptualization of subjects as specific bearers of this activity who are aiming toward bringing post-Stalinist socialist visions to life. We will do so in chapters 4 and 5.

CHAPTER 4

BETWEEN FOLKNESS AND THE NATION

> Thus, since the beginning of this new existence, the Czechs as a people have been connected with culture more fatefully than practically any other European nation, so in this half of Europe they are a people who are by far the most educated and contemplative, who cannot be easily taken in by some cheap propaganda.
>
> —MILAN KUNDERA

Despite the rejection of the Stalinist idea of man as a set of social relations, the post-Stalinists' thinking about subjectivity did not lead to an absolutization of the human individual that would have resulted in rejecting efforts at capturing general laws. On the contrary, the constant connection of thinking with the social and historical connotations, along with an emancipatory perception of this dimension of man, revealed an affiliation with the Marxist world of thought. And let us not forget that Marxism was originally characterized by an attribution of subjectivity to collective entities and social classes more than by concerning itself with individual subjectivity.

Based on their analysis of society, Marx and his followers explained the behavior of individual social classes in relation to the means of production, or sometimes based on their awareness of their own positioning and historical role (e.g., Lenin in *The State and Revolution*, György Lukács in *History and Class Consciousness*). In the period when Soviet Marxism-Leninism was forming, the original class analysis was mixed with the Russian revolutionary democrats' ideas about people and folkness as a driving moment in history. We can already see this aspect in Lenin's positive evaluation of Alexander Herzen and Nikolai Gavrilovich Chernyshevsky.[1] The people and folkness were also topics brought up by Stalinism, though in the 1930s they were joined by the category of the nation, which was given preferential treatment. In this context, historiography speaks of the Stalinist turn from the class to the nation,[2] with the second category ascending to dominance in the following periods. For many reasons, we doubt the absolute validity of this thesis, as well as the claim that the national aspect completely overshadowed the class or folk elements in the Stalinist project of modernity.[3] Instead, we incline toward a softer picture of Stalinism, in which these three collective subjectivities were not mutually exclusive, and despite the strong emphasis on the nation (for example, during the Great Patriotic War campaign), they complemented one another.

THE COLLECTIVITY IMAGINED IN CZECHOSLOVAK STALINISM

From the perspective of collective subjectivity, Czechoslovak Stalinism was mainly defined by the phrase "the Czechoslovak people," which could be found, for instance, in the Ninth-of-May Constitution of 1948. The concept of "the people," which here pertained to the romanticized Czech and Slovak language community, actually brought together class and national dimensions.[4] Members of the "reactionary classes," whether Czechs or Slovaks, were excluded from the revolutionary process that led through people's democracy to socialism. Of course, an exclusivist conception of the people was nothing new. Its tradition reaches back to the ethnocentric conception of a "people" as defined in the pages of the journal *Český lid* by the ethnologists Čeněk Zíbrt and Lubor Niederle at the end of the nineteenth century. The postwar democratic period of the Third Republic (1945–1948), which focused on building a people's democracy, was also ethnocentric and excluded those who had sold themselves out to the previous Nazi occupation regime, which includes all the right-wing parties.[5]

As part of the framework of the class definition of Stalinism, the concept of the people was primarily applied within the Czechoslovak state with the aim of creating social changes and removing class antagonisms; however, at the national level it tended to be defined outwardly, with the goal of achieving a pan-Slavic unity. "We brought a Slavic, East-facing orientation to our politics," the doyen of the Czechoslovak Stalinist national-historical story, Zdeněk Nejedlý (1878–1962), stated in 1948.[6] In the years after World War II, he connected the revived, albeit semantically relabeled set of pan-Slavic stereotypes both with building the new order and defending this endeavor against external German (or imperialist) threats. Besides Nejedlý's concept, the gradual acceptance of the officialized Stalinist interpretation into Czech linguistics and ethnography also played a role.⁷

It was Nejedlý who created the canon in the era of Czechoslovak Stalinism for how to work with the concepts of "people" and "nation." In his interpretation of the nation he referred to František Palacký, who was a Czech historian and one of the cofounders of modern Czech politics and national identity, and to his concept of two opposing tendencies within one nation, the protestant (Hussite) and Catholic, considering this divisions to be timeless: "It is so ingrained in our nation that we still have to overcome it today, and this is very important in our struggle against reactionism."⁸ A dualistic definition of this type was entirely complementary with Stalin's or Lenin's conception of two national cultures: bourgeois and democratic (or reactionary and progressive), which are in continual conflict.⁹ Nejedlý was already very well aware of the Stalinist combination of national and class elements ("proletarian content, socialist form"), and it is also reflected in the analysis by the Polish historian Maciej Górny, who finds a fundamental tension between class-oriented inspirations driven by Marx and Palacký's nationalistic legacy in the Czechoslovak historiography of the 1950s.¹⁰

The "people" or the "popular classes" always had only a positive connotation with Nejedlý, as an integral part of the progressive component of the nation throughout history (i.e., from the Middle Ages through the Hussite movement to "Victorious February" in 1948: "They also led in this way, and even today they are still leading the nation forward."¹¹ These categories made it possible to demonstrate continuity between the historical efforts of so-called progressive traditions and building socialism. The people and the popular classes were characterized by democratic and revolutionary tendencies, national self-sacrifice, patriotism, and natural wisdom, thanks to which they were able to replace academic philosophy and make relevant judgments about art.¹² However, their main trait was supposed to be a class-defined unity ideologically based in progressivism. Nejedlý's concept of the people represented a connecting link between the categories of class and the nation that allowed the temporary attribution of progressiveness—in the name of historical evolution within the nation—to other classes (such as the Czech aristocracy or bourgeoisie) before the proletariat came into existence.¹³ This folkness was considered a positive quality of the progressive classes, with a focus on smallholders and the proletariat, which represented a contrast with the way the concept was used in the nineteenth century and the interwar First Republic (1918–1938), when the emphasis was instead on the "rural element." The concept was then adopted as an analytical category in

4.1. The doyen of Czechoslovak national Stalinism, Zdeněk Nejedlý, delivering a speech in Havlíčkův Brod in memory of the one-hundred-year anniversary of Karel Havlíček Borovský's birth, 1956. Copyright Masaryk Institute and Archives of the Czech Academy of Sciences.

Stalinist scholarship. Less than a year after Stalin's death, on February 26–27, 1954, a conference about folkness in Czech literature was held, at which the Czech structuralist Jan Mukařovský discussed folkness as a category superior to realism, idealism, and artistry.[14]

At the same time, Nejedlý's intellectual background cannot be associated only with Stalinism because it also includes the interwar intellectual milieu and the Czech University in Prague before World War I (where he had worked since 1909).[15] This is why, in his extensive interpretation of Nejedlý's concept, Michal Kopeček, who is a historian of Central and Eastern European political thought, highlights the existence of least two intellectual traditions that intertwined and fed into the Czech national version of Stalinism. In addition to Lenin and Stalin, the native understanding of collective subjectivity also drew upon debates about national destiny and the philosophy of history that had accompanied the shaping of modern Czech national identity since the last third of the nineteenth century.[16] Nejedlý was an original supporter of formal Herbartist aesthetics as well as the neo-Romantic conception of culture. As a figure rooted deeply in Czech modern cultural and intellectual life, Nejedlý embraced and represented the ambiguity of the Stalinist relationship to a cultural heritage that was partially rejected and partially appropriated. As Nejedlý's biographer František Červinka aptly pointed out at the end of the 1960s, when discussing Nejedlý's personality it would be inappropriate to speak of "a 'break' . . . a sudden change from an independent critic and thinker into an official and uncritical representative of the regime,"[17] because Stalinism and progressivism were not mutually exclusive. Although Nejedlý gradually rejected most of his early inspirations embodied by the philosopher and founder of the formalist school Johann Friedrich Herbart, Richard Wagner, and Friedrich Nietzsche, he remained true to the culture of the national revival exemplified by the composer Bedřich Smetana.[18] Michal Kopeček has convincingly demonstrated in the above-mentioned study referring to Polish historiography that Nejedlý is more exceptional in the Central European context for his broad spectrum of interests than for his nationally colored conception of Stalinism.[19] Let us add that the seeming incongruence among his multiple modes of thinking was not dissimilar to Soviet Stalinism, which drew upon its own theoretical sources in combination with the intellectual legacy of the Russian revolutionary democrats (Alexander Herzen, Dmitry Pisarev, and Vissarion Belinsky).

The relevant questions are whether and to what extent post-Stalinism was even related to collective subjectivity. The Czech Germanist Alexej Kusák established an influential and attractive interpretation, in which young communist radicals began to define themselves against Nejedlý at the end of the 1940s and beginning of the 1950s. In Kusák's view, the rejection of Nejedlý's concept represented the first step on the way toward reevaluating Stalinism and breaking free of its black-and-white manner of viewing the world. Kusák distinguishes mainstream Stalinism, as represented by the interwar party functionaries and cultural commissars such as Nejedlý and the literary scholar Ladislav Štoll, as well as an avant-garde poet, Vítězslav Nezval, from a radical left ring that recruited young authors who gathered under the patronage of the communist functionary Gustav Bareš and the magazine *Tvorba*. It was claimed that the radicals mainly disagreed with the conservatively flavored conception of Czech history from the period of the national revival. And instead of wanting to emphasize the category of the nation, Kusák believed that they preferred internationalism and cosmopolitanism, naturally viewed through the period's Soviet lens.[20] The literary historian Petr Šámal subsequently applied Kusák's interpretive key in evaluating Karel Kosík's early works when he used these texts as a counterpoint to Nejedlý's traditionalism, and Kopeček did the same thing in comparing Nejedlý with Karel Kosík over a period spanning two decades.[21]

We are not interested here in questioning the existence of a radically oriented young intelligentsia under the auspices and authority of older communist cadres such as Arnošt Kolman, Pavel Reiman, and Gustav Bareš. Nor do we intend to whitewash the period controversies over the basic dimensions of cultural politics as manifested in the mockery of Vítězslav Nezval as a representative of the conservative status quo (1949), and in the ostracization of Bareš and Reiman after the culmination of the Stalinist show trial with general secretary of the Communist Party of Czechoslovakia, Rudolf Slánský (1952).[22] And we do not want to deny that Nejedlý was criticized in the Stalinist and post-Stalinist eras and that Marxist intellectuals have been reckoning with him and his legacy since then. However, we consider the relationship of the above-mentioned radical intelligentsia to the Stalinist national narrative and therefore also to the figure of Nejedlý as more complicated than certain authors have frequently presented in an exaggerated manner ("radicals often commented on the work of 'Grandpa Nejedlý' with irony and sarcasm").[23] In our opinion, the leftist-Stalinists but also, and even more so, the post-Stalinists distancing of themselves from Nejedlý is far from being such an important turning point in the conception of Czech history and culture as has been generally accepted.[24] Like Maciej Górny, who finds no evidence of a boundary line having been drawn between Nejedlý and the young radicals in the historiographical production of the 1950s,[25] we too fail to find it in the post-Stalinist texts. Instead, we agree with the most recent biographer of Nejedlý, Jiří Křesťan, when he says: "The connection between Nejedlý and the revisionists of the 'sixties exists even where it is not directly reflected,"[26] even if he is speaking from a point of view different from his younger contemporaries.

Although a strong break with Nejedlý would be convenient for our previous interpretation of post-Stalinist subjectivity based on a preference for the human individual, by highlighting the rift between post-Stalinist thinking and the romantic idea of the people (from J. G. Herder to Nejedlý), we want to demonstrate that post-Stalinism did not relinquish its connection to collective subjectivity. Indeed, its thinking along these lines was complemented by reflection on human subjectivity, similar to the way Stalinist thinking on class had been complemented by thinking on the nation. Although the category of class lost its relevance at the end of the 1950s and beginning of the 1960s with the proclamation that the socialist stage of development had been achieved,[27] the categories of the people and the nation did not disappear from Marxist intellectuals' sights. As in the case of the notions of law, humanism, and the individual, the semantic poles changed, and concepts took on specific post-Stalinist meanings, even though the category of nation and folkness still remained in conformity with a progressive interpretation of Czech history and therefore to a certain extent also with Stalinism.[28]

POST-STALINIST FOLKNESS

The anthropologist Joseph Grim Feinberg notes in one of his essays on socialist realism that the doctrine proclaimed it was "combining mass activity with the activities of intellectuals."[29] It is more than obvious that in contrast to Stalinism, post-Stalinist thinking had given up on achieving this kind of unity. The Marxists of the time rejected the romanticizing concept of the people implied by Nejedlý as much as they refused the uncritical overuse of precepts excerpted from his writing about the people as the determinative force of history or the people as the fairest judges of art. From diverse positions and in various forms, by rejecting the unity of socialist realism they spoke in favor of the autonomy of artistic and intellectual creation, which cannot be subjected to authorial self-censorship in relation to the people as the privileged consumer of the culture or to "popular" objections to art that is too distant from the masses.[30] This does not mean, however, that the post-Stalinists relegated the categories of the people and folkness to some imaginary graveyard of ideas. On the contrary, it seems that thanks to the reconceptualization of the relationship to human subjectivity, they were aware of the pitfalls of exaggerated and uncritical extrapolations of individuality. As we will see in chapter 5 on revolution, although classes or the people were no longer considered to be the agents of transformation of post-Stalinism, the Marxists of that time still returned to these concepts in one way or another and attempted to reembrace them. It was as though they were constantly attempting (albeit not always consistently, as we will see in chapter 6, to reflect the tension between their own exaltation of the autonomy of intellectuals, who remained essentially the spokespeople for historical progress (in our case, especially in the form of Marxist humanism), and the danger of being too distant from those on whose behalf they were speaking. Viewed through this lens, post-Stalinism thus became one of the moments in the history of socialism when certain intellectuals intuitively feared that they "would [find themselves] above the masses, and thus [violate] the principle of the self-movement of the masses upon which the entire movement is founded."[31]

This is why Kosík spoke at the end of the 1950s about the two poles of Czech culture of the nineteenth century: the aesthetically pleasing art of the patriarchal society that did not problematize anything, and the intellectual elitism of the so-called high culture. In his view, it was possible to create a bridge to connect both poles in only one way—by creating a modern socialist culture that could not be old-world or provincial, but had to be truly popular. Kosík resolutely drew a line against Nejedlý's concept of folkness as the sum of the wisdom of simple country people, which manifested itself immaterially as a collection of handed-down ideas and proverbs. Externally it also took the form of folk costumes whose industrial production in what were called the cooperatives of the folk industry, torn out of a functional social context (re-)presentation, was among the iconic elements of socialist realism.[32] In contrast to the unity and organic understanding of the development of folk culture, Kosík argued for a permanent and dialectical overcoming of the old by the new, where folkness was an "elixir of life that continually rejuvenates and revives culture."[33]

At the same time, Kosík remained an advocate for Nejedlý to the extent that he ascribed paramount importance to the idea of folkness. He considered it an expression of democratism because it made it possible to build a bridge between unproblematically pleasant decoration and elitism, and thus it was also the basis of every true humanist culture. In his view, modern socialist culture should repudiate the people's earlier artifacts of superstitions, mythology, and religious obscurantism as part of the process of its historical progression. However, in the same breath he added, "This shift only means that the creativity of the people is inexhaustible, that the folk creations of previous eras are not the only or even the supreme expression of the folk's initiative. . . . [Socialist] culture will not confine folk activity to rigid historical forms, but will instead create organizational and material conditions for the birth of a folkness of a new character, which corresponds to the position of the popular masses in socialism."[34]

Kosík did not further specify the nature of this folkness. However, he certainly did not prefer either the concept of the rural people promoted by the editors of *Český lid*, which Nejedlý had sympathized with, or the concept of the people as the urban proletariat (Karel Teige).[35] In any case, the people did not appear to him as something like Nejedlý's timeless collective where the social groups changed (the bourgeoisie replaced the petty aristocracy), but the progressive quality born in the Hussite movement remained the same. Kosík consistently integrated the people into the dialectical movement of historical formations: "In historical development, the concept of folkness also changes along with the change in the objective composition of the people."[36] In connection with transformations in the nature of the forces of production and the ownership of the means of production, the socialist people had to take on new qualities because socialism as a modern social form brought with it a new perception of reality.

In the context of post-Stalinism as a modernization project, a progressive folkness stripped of static forms was thus considered to be the basic building block of the historical process. As in the case of individual subjectivity, history was not supposed to be realized through teleological necessity (the self-motion of historical laws) or by accelerating these effects, but through the conscious activity of the collective subject—redefined as the people—by their actualization of their folkness (i.e., their praxis). As Červinka put it in the mid-1960s: "Of course the creator of history is the people. . . . Only through historical creative work can the people change the world and themselves."[37]

At the end of the 1960s, when most of the protagonists of our treatise had begun to think about collective subjectivity within the category of the nation, Kosík appealed for a new alliance between the classes. The crucial connecting link was to be a new activation of people according to citizenship and the principle of what he called "integral democracy," based on an equal alliance of communists, socialists, democrats, and other citizens as well as on the self-management of socialist producers.[38] In Kosík's view, this was the only way it would be possible to revitalize the profaned politics that had emerged from the dichotomy of party versus nonparty actors. In his essay "Naše nynější krize" (Our Current Crisis), he drew attention to the "crisis of classes and society," noting the success of the ruling bureaucracy that had led to the social isolation of members of the common people: laborers, peasants, and the intelligentsia ("workers to the factories, peasantry to the villages, and intelligentsia to the libraries"), even in their transformation into a "uniformed, featureless mass."[39] He envisioned the new constitution of the collective consciousness through working class, which would reflect on the very contradiction "between ideologies and illusions on the one hand, and its real *political* position on the other." Such a process required the complete freedom of information.[40] In this way, he was making an explicit return to the class perspective and considering the working class as the representative component of the redefined people to be the avant-garde of the new social alliance formed with the peasantry, intelligentsia, employees, and youth.

Immediately after the military invasion by the "friendly" armies in August 1968, Kosík mainly called for an alliance to be formed between workers and the intelligentsia.[41] Healing the above-mentioned tension between them would, in his view, create a truly revolutionary unity, because both groups would once and for all put aside their mutual antipathy and class prejudices and guarantee wisely conceived activity that the Communist Party could rely on.[42] In coining the expressions "wise revolutionism" and "revolutionary wisdom," Kosík continued his reflections on the parallel nature of pre-Marxist development, when both popular and educational efforts to reform society were working side by side.[43] But he said it was only the idea of communism that created the space for removing this division, which neither the European Renaissance nor the Reformation had accomplished: "Communism tackles, on the modern foundations of the twentieth century . . . the unification of reason and the people, the establishment of a republic in which reason would have the effective force of popular power, and the people will have the acumen of contemplative reason."[44]

Kosík designated his direct inspirations in "Our Current Crisis." While Nejedlý is not among them, he mentions Tomáš Gariggue Masaryk, Rosa Luxemburg, Lenin, and Antonio Gramsci. Referring to the last name from this list, Ivan Landa even speaks of Kosík's effort to constitute a Gramscian "historical bloc" that would establish a revolutionary hegemony.[45] At the same time, the undeniable influence of the Italian Marxist's works represented a connection (and it does not matter if it was unarticulated or unconscious) with the concept of the people, which, moreover, Gramsci was familiar with. The title of the speech Kosík gave at the November session of the Central Committee of the Communist Party—The Only Chance—An Alliance with the People also suggests this.[46] Within the framework of what he called "wise revolutionism," Kosík attributed qualities to the alliance between the intelligentsia and the workers (the people) who bore some resemblance to Nejedlý's conception, even though they were set into the entirely different context of the post-invasion situation.

Kosík redefined the people as a unified, sober, progressive body in their collective judgments. On this basis, a folk wisdom would emerge that would inhibit opportunism and sly cunning, as well as excessive radicality and superficiality, and it would become a counterweight against the hysteria, demagogy, ambitions, and vanity of individuals, "cowardice, prudentialism, and the proverbial Czech earthiness and joviality." Here, the people no longer acted not only as the subject of creation in the sense of the modern culture of socialism but also as a decisive creative political force guaranteeing the maintenance of democratic socialism (i.e., as the very principle of progress). If, at the end of the 1950s, Kosík declared folkness historically variable; exactly ten years later he added that constituting a new collective (whether we call it a historical bloc or the people) must take place based on "dialogue, contention, tension, and the interplay" of individual strata of society. In the late 1950s, folkness had been "an elixir of life that constantly rejuvenates and revivifies culture," but for Kosík this forged alliance became an "inexhaustible source of inspiration, initiative, and political energy, a source which inspires and enriches the progressive development of society in all its spheres."[47] Shortly afterward, he added that the meaning of 1968 was specifically that "gestures and words either awakened or expressed the *popular movement* and only took on historical significance in connection with this movement."[48]

The revived interest in collectivity combined with a belief in the unity of the people are not exclusive only to Kosík. In his article "Český úděl" (The Czech Destiny), Milan Kundera referred to the society-wide unity after the military invasion.[49] He also updated the category of the people in downright Nejedlýan fashion: "Yes, the Czech nation has already lost its direct connection with the heroic tradition of Žižka's mace, but Hussitism also means a popular tradition in which 'each of his grandmothers was a better expert on scriptures than an Italian priest,' and this tradition of popular education and contemplation is still at home in our country."[50] In the same way, we can also observe it among the party intelligentsia in the declarations and resolutions issued by artistic and creative associations. For instance, the "Solidary Agreement" of October 1968 spoke of an alliance between cultural workers and laborers; similarly, the declaration of cultural and scientific workers in November of the same year explicitly identified the people as a political subject and called for the unification of intellectuals with laborers and students.⁵¹ The legitimacy of the further progression of democratization policies was seen in society-wide (popular) unity, which at that time was often combined with national unity in the Czech context.

THE PROGRESSIVE TRADITION IN CZECH HISTORY

It is precisely this "progressiveness," which the post-Stalinist intellectuals attributed to democratic socialism, that leads us to examine the broader commitments of post-Stalinist thought to reflections on the sense of Czech national history, or to what is called the philosophy of Czech history. However, first, it is necessary to return once more to the compelling image of the radical Marxist intelligentsia rejecting Nejedlý's conception at the end of the 1940s and beginning of the 1950s and never crossing paths with it again. Although the original categories of "the people" and "folkness" were no longer used, the focus on the historical-philosophical principle of "progress(ivism)" did not fundamentally change in post-Stalinism.

At the beginning of this chapter, we outlined the thesis that the relationship of the post-Stalinist Marxists to the doyen of the Czech national-Stalinist conception was more layered than what has been described in the scholarly literature to date. If we consider, for example, texts by Karel Kosík, who has been framed by Petr Šámal and Michal Kopeček as a certain counterbalance to Nejedlý, more complicated connections begin to emerge. Apart from Kosík's admiring and celebratory text about Nejedlý from 1953,⁵² we primarily turn to his *Česká radikální demokracie* (Czech Radical Democracy) from 1958. We again agree with Kopeček that Kosík primarily differs from Nejedlý in his dialectical analysis based on class criteria, in the concept of concrete totality, and in the context of the European history of revolutions.⁵³ Upon closer inspection, however, it becomes clear that *Česká radikální demokracie* grows out of the motifs that Nejedlý himself had recommended expanding upon.⁵⁴ The book analyzes the thinking of figures who—among other projects—focused on the categories of people and folkness,⁵⁵ and here Kosík expresses a high opinion of Nejedlý as a thinker who was not interested in schemes, but primarily in concrete truth. We believe that references to him are justified in Kosík's interpretive line, and that he is not doing it to adhere to official lines for his own benefit.⁵⁶ At the same time, the author views Czech radical democracy through the lens of a "revolutionary act" that is entirely in accordance with Nejedlý's views, and he also finds these acts in culture (as Nejedlý had before him), more precisely in the works of a writer Jan Neruda and of a composer Bedřich Smetana. Unlike Nejedlý, he presents both manifestations as the "unity of the social consciousness of the bourgeois democratic revolution," however he considers Nejedlý's analysis of Smetana's music to be "penetrating."[57]

Naturally, certain authors were uncompromising in distancing themselves from Nejedlý. One example is Ivan Sviták, who called the "traditions" Nejedlý developed, as well as the "cult of personality" and the "schematism" of the period a "mass illusion."[58] However, the ambivalent positions of Kosík, Kalivoda, and Červinka toward Nejedlý overlapped with the fundamental principles of the post-Stalinist dissociation from Stalinism. Rather than a rejecting, negative attitude, there is a critical relationship here, where they reject some motifs, but develop others. In this case, the analogy of the relationship of post-Stalinism to Stalinism does not hold true: Nejedlý is respected as a distinctive intellectual and remains a point of reference even during the search for new perspectives.[59] At the beginning of the 1960s, in a debate with Machovec on methodological problems in intellectual history, Kalivoda stated: "Today—after Nejedlý's death—one of the great, immediate tasks of our philosophy is to truthfully evaluate the great intellectual phenomenon of Nejedlý, to elucidate the uniqueness and unrepeatability of his philosophical development, and to explain the great value of his works in more depth."[60] At the same time, he described Machovec as an author who nominally endorses Nejedlý, but does not follow in the footsteps of his truly creative method.[61] In the same spirit, Červinka wrote in 1967 that "Nejedlý's work as a living whole and complete organism defends itself against any vulgar and one-sided criticism."[62]

The return of the discussion of the conception (and meaning) of Czech history is closely connected with the expression of collective subjectivity, and by extension with questions relating to Nejedlý. In interpreting the Czech communist intellectuals' rejection of Nejedlý, Kopeček notes that in an anti-Masaryk article of 1954, Kosík refuses the principle of humanity, and thus indirectly rejects Nejedlý's "inversion of Masaryk's original idea of humanism into his peculiar vision of folksiness," in order to replace it with the revolutionary struggle for liberation.[63] Kopeček also draws attention to the reckoning with Nejedlý in the concept of the historiography of the nineteenth century and to the controversy over the ideological legacy of the Hussites, and in the latter issue he names Robert Kalivoda as the chief critic.[64] Regardless of Kosík's fairly complicated relationship with the category of humanity and Kalivoda's multidimensional relationship to Nejedlý's interpretation of Hussitism, we still believe that this was primarily a discussion focused on determining the sources of the progressive movement in Czech history that joins both poles into one whole. Even though Kalivoda reproached Nejedlý for lending Jan Hus and revolutionary Tábor an artificially constructed radicality under Palacký's influence, he agreed with him in the basic assessment of the historical and philosophical significance of Hussitism: "However, it is at the same time a perspective that exalts the Hussites' *truly most precious* values and achievements; it is the perspective of a revolutionary thinker—of a socialist who seeks in Hussitism precisely the sources that lead in a direct line from them to modern socialism."[65] The fact that Masaryk's understanding of humanity and Nejedlý's conception of folkness were rejected as historical principles does not mean that the authors cited here refused the idea of historical movement founded on progressivism. Quite the contrary: like Nejedlý's view, the interrelationship of the past, present, and future are also viewed by Kosík and Kalivoda (and even by Josef Zumr) in such a way that the past is charged with the burden of progressiveness, which plays an extraordinarily important role for the present and future. This is also the reason that Kosík wrote about radical democrats (Josef Václav Frič, Emanuel Arnold, and Karel Sabina) and why he continually returned to the works of Czech writers and journalists such as Jan Neruda, Božena Němcová, and Karel Havlíček, in whom he sought the principle of democratism.[66] Červinka also justified his interest in Nejedlý by pointing to his emphasis on progressivism. According to Červinka, he thus deviated from the norms in period thinking, because he was returning to sources "in the spirit of the positivist method as well as in the spirit of revolutionary romanticism."[67]

At the same time, the above-mentioned debate between Machovec and Kalivoda certainly did not revolve around overcoming Nejedlýan dogmatism and distancing from this conception of the history of Czech thought. Despite the shifts back to Nejedlý, there was certainly not a resignation to "revelation" of the sense of Czech history, measured in terms of its progressiveness. Kalivoda and Zumr traced the line of Czech history from the radical peasant-plebian Tábor of the Hussite movement to the evangelic community Unity of Brethren of Jan Chelčický, a humanist philosopher John Amos Comenius, a romantic poet Karel Hynek Mácha, the revolutionary democrats of the nineteenth century, and the interwar avant-garde all the way into socialism and Marxist humanism: "If there exists a direct continuity between the revolutionary legacy of the far left of 1420 and the far left of 1848, the same continuity exists between the Czech radical democracy of the mid-nineteenth century and the Czech working class in the mid-twentieth century."[68] Both were essentially adhering to the progressive line of interpretation of Czech

4.2. The philosopher Ivan Sviták and the historian František Červinka (on the left) were regular participants in the intellectual salon that convened in the apartment of the grandparents (on the right, Zdena Votrubová and Antonín Votruba) of this book's coauthor, Jiří Růžička, 1960s. Copyright Vanda Růžičková.

history that was founded by Masaryk and more fully developed by Nejedlý. However, there were also certain differences: they openly incorporated Czech Herbartianism into this line, which was one of Nejedlý's original points of departure, but that he later kept silent about.[69] They also drew upon the interwar avant-garde (both Zumr and Kalivoda) and eccentric figures like the Czech Nietzschean writer Ladislav Klíma, and they perceived human emancipation as the main historical logos (see also the following chapter).[70] Of course in unison, both rejected Nejedlý's reserved attitude toward the avant-garde after 1945.[71] Furthermore, they took particular exception to his idea about art, in which folk styles merged in the 1950s with intelligible realistic styles.[72]

Both Zumr and Kalivoda focused mainly on nonconformist authors. Regarding Ladislav Klíma and the avant-garde theorist Karel Teige, they highlighted a creative focus that maximizes the autonomous position of the artist and either liberalizes or directly and radically denies a relationship with external reality. However, neither the differences in approaches to art, nor amended lines of development (e.g., Klíma instead of Alois Jirásek, whose novels celebrated Czech history), nor the substitution of folkness for emancipation can overshadow the fact that the principles of Czech history may be different, but the "place remaining after Nejedlýan-Jiráskian 'meaningfulness,'" was not left vacant, despite Karel Bartošek's convictions, the basic logos remained.[73]

Just as for Masaryk humanity and for Nejedlý folkness were the principles in Czech history that drove it toward interwar democracy or postwar communism, a revolutionary urge and democratism (Kosík) or emancipation (Kalivoda and Zumr) became the fundamental drivers of progress on the way to achieving the communist ideal.[74] "The belief that national culture is inherently progressive . . . , meant that both Frič and Palacký, and the Adamites as well as [Jan] Žižka, could be evaluated positively in their texts. . . . The ideas Nejedlý had given shape to had fallen on too-fertile ground,"[75] Maciej Górny writes at the conclusion of his study of Czechoslovak historiography. In our opinion, this finding has a broader validity that is not limited only to professional historians or to the 1950s. Progressivism, including its grounding in folkness, undoubtedly remained a central category used to evaluate historical material until the end of the 1960s in post-Stalinist notions of socialist modernity.

Červinka aptly captured the timeless relevance of the philosophical-historical moment in an article of 1968 on T. G. Masaryk: "When sometime in the future certain historians engrossed in the archives wrinkle their noses at the philosophy of our history, and at what they'll call mere ideologists and essayists—don't take them too seriously!"[76] We present this quote here to emphasize at the conclusion that it was the philosophy of Czech history that, along with thinking about the people and folkness, co-shaped post-Stalinist ideas about collective subjectivity. If we accept, at the same time, that the post-Stalinist conception of Czech history is following in the footsteps of the progressivist interpretation,[77] it is not surprising that as in Masaryk's and Nejedlý's times (including the Stalinist period), the constant tension between universal and national dimensions of historical progress can be considered one of its hallmarks. In the Czechoslovak case, however, the two lines often intertwined, because—as we shall see—the fulfillment of universal emancipation was often supposed to take place through the nation.

THE NATION AS A SOCIALIST COLLECTIVITY

The tension between an emancipatory process tied to the category of the nation and ideas of universal progress has accompanied the history of European modernity since its beginning, especially in the culturally and ethnically diverse Central and Eastern European region.[78] Similarly, since its inception, both the socialist movement (Marx's reflections on this topic from 1848 are well known) and Soviet socialism have also had to reckon with this. Lenin commented on national emancipation in relation to the revolution; Stalin followed in his footsteps after 1913, and the "national question" was tackled by party theorists in the post-Stalinist and real socialist eras.[79] In the 1960s the Austromarxist ideas promoted by Bohumír Šmeral (especially cultural autonomy) also returned on the scene.[80]

Although the general historiography of Stalinism suggests that the Stalinist version of the national story seemed exclusively national in many respects, the links to universal progress were still present. Before the elections in 1946, Nejedlý wrote, "Czech democratism has an indisputable tendency to develop ever further in accord with world development."[81] Naturally, the measure of worldliness and thus of progressive universality was determined by the Soviet version of modernity. At the same time, it would seem that as a result of overcoming Stalinism, the national dimension would gradually be displaced in favor of the universal message of socialism, yet the opposite was the case. In the 1960s, the Slovak and Czech party intelligentsia even amplified the national aspect of socialist development.[82] In many variations there was talk about the uniqueness of Czechoslovak development, its democratic traditions, the national path to socialism, and so on. Debates about the Slovak nation and its right to political self-expression then represent a chapter of their own. At this point, we are not concerned with a comprehensive analysis of the national dimension of Czechoslovak reformism, but with capturing these aspects in our protagonists' expressions.[83]

One of the participants in a debate between Milan Kundera and Václav Havel on the significance of the Czechoslovak Spring of 1968, Jaroslav Střítecký, was undoubtedly right when he observed that "until 1967, in the ideology of Czech liberal [reform] communism, the word 'nation' appeared at best only by chance."[84] However, this should not obscure the fact that for a long time the Marxist humanists had an indirect relationship to national collectivity through reflections on the continuity of "traditions" of Czech culture and Czech thought, on their nature, and on their relationship to foreign countries. If we read, for example, Kosík's *Česká radikální demokracie* (Czech Radical Democracy), revolutionary events and ideas of progress are set into a broader European intellectual context.[85] Kosík considered the fundamental questions of Czech political thought to be "seeking a solution for the relationship[s] between nationality and Europeanness, nationality and progress, and the people and democratism," which in his view the radical democrats were trying to find a political solution for, and at the artistic level it was being attempted by Jan Neruda and Bedřich Smetana.[86]

A tension between a passive reflection of European development in Czech intellectual and artistic production and its own contribution to European movement accompanied Czechoslovak post-Stalinism from the 1950s until the end of the 1960s. For example, in 1954 Kosík wrote: "It has been rightly emphasized countless times in our literature that only art that is deeply national can take on a world character. However, at the same time, the opposite side of this truth, which is mentioned by Neruda, is often forgotten: that art can only be truly national if it does not isolate itself from progressive world trends, and independently approaches the most important problems of European development in its own country."[87] He certainly would have known that in his time, Nejedlý had defended Neruda and Smetana against accusations that they were introducing foreign elements (the Young Germany movement in Neruda's case, and Wagnerianism in Smetana's).[88] However, at the time, Kosík was still articulating precisely the dimension that Nejedlý had reduced to the Czech(oslovak)-Soviet relationship in the 1950s.[89] Also illustrative in this respect is the essay "Modernost, lidovost a socialismus" (Modernness, Folkness and Socialism) that we have quoted several times here, in which Kosík summarizes the ratio of backwardness and modernity—or Czech philistinism and cosmopolitanism—that he develops in *Česká radikální demokracie.*

The end of the 1960s brought a significant revival of this theme of the relationship between the local and the international. First, we see it in the effort to legitimize the autonomy of contemporary artistic work at the end of Antonín Novotný's era, and it reappears during 1968 and after the military invasion. At the Fourth Congress of Czech Writers in June 1967, Kundera, with reference to the Czech German journalist Hubert Gordon Schauer (1862–1892), raised the classic question of the legitimacy of an independent national existence. His conclusions were similar to Schauer's at the end of the nineteenth century: the legitimacy of a collective in the form of a nation can only be derived from its ongoing and original contribution to European development, and localness cannot remain confined within its own borders.[90] Kundera consequently evaluated the Czechoslovak year 1968, or more precisely, the efforts to create a democratic socialism, as a significant Czechoslovak contribution of a universal nature. In his essay "The Czech Destiny," he remarked that when he had formulated his question a year ago at the writers' congress he had no inkling that the entirety of Czechoslovakia would provide an answer for it in 1968, when "for the first time since the end of the Middle Ages, Czechs and Slovaks stood at the center of world history and addressed their challenge to the world."[91]

This concept of the year 1968 representing the possibility of fulfilling the potential of Czech history, or that perhaps being its culmination, was generally shared among Marxist humanists. For a nation that does not want to resign its existence "and permanently reconcile itself to servitude," the "renewal and scientific justification of the ideal of the free man in a free society . . . is a basic necessity of life," Josef Zumr wrote in a review of Kalivoda's book *Moderní duchovní skutečnost a marxismus* (Modern Spiritual Reality and Marxism). And the author of the book himself considered the democratization of development as aiming toward the highest social model, "socialist self-government of a socialist society."[92]

Many drew connections between the positive tradition of building postwar socialism in the years 1945–1948, the period of the People's Front in the 1930s, and even the traditions of parliamentary democracy and the legacy of T. G. Masaryk and the national distinctiveness of Czechoslovak post-Stalinist socialism.[93] According to the Marxist humanists, no other nation in Central Europe had such a deep experience with bourgeois parliamentarism and with Stalinism.[94] Moreover, the native democratic traditions distinguished the quality of Czechoslovak socialism from the other socialist countries.[95] Using the same rationalization, the Brno philosopher Lubomír Nový wrote: "I consider uniqueness to be a stark fact" in 1969.[96] In this context, there was a growing conviction that Czechoslovak development was externally defensible while remaining exclusive at the same time, and that in its own way the country was the avant-garde of socialism within the East bloc, as it was enriching and qualitatively surpassing the Soviet model. According to this interpretation, the democratization project meant an "appreciable contribution by this small socialist country to the treasury of those hitherto innumerable experiences of the world, which confirm that our socialism is its truly desirable next model."[97]

At the writers' congress in June 1967, Kundera was seconded by Kosík when he used the example of Jan Hus, who was burned at the stake for heresy in 1415, to explain the unity of reason and conscience.[98] Preserving life while sacrificing truth, reason would be a mere technical instrument without conscience,[99] and conscience without reason would be nothing more than purely subjective insight. In a way, in this speech he anticipated the principal meaning of the country's national existence. A year later, in an essay "Our Current Crisis," he further explained that the "Czech question" is "inquiring into the totality of national life, which ought to be built upon a firm foundation of truth and sincerity."[100] Similarly, national life without truth and sincerity as a common bond of "politics and individual action, public affairs and science, culture and morality, education and the everyday atmosphere" would turn into "a helpless fluctuation between megalomania and grandiloquence on the one hand and narrow-mindedness and mediocrity on the other."[101]

This need to define the meaning of collective subjectivity arose out of the conviction that a self-evident and unreflected national existence detached from considerations of its meaning and the role of culture carries the threat of degrading the people into "a Czech-speaking population that produces steel and grain."[102] Therefore, Kosík arrived at the conclusion that even if the original standpoints in the debate on the meaning of Czech history, "in one point Palacký did not disagree with Frič, [or] Nejedlý with Masaryk, [or] Konrad with Pekař. All of them respected the *basic fact* that can be expressed in modern terminology as a nation that does not even think that it could produce and own atom bombs or compete for world leadership in oil production must justify its existence and purpose in a manner that corresponds to this reality."[103] Although this was a typical manner of writing about nation at that time, his contribution indicated a small change in the accent. Kosík inadvertently replaced Kundera's "condition" for national existence with a "necessity." While Kundera still considered the possibility of free choice to create or not create a full-fledged national existence, Kosík claimed that a small nation simply "must" prove the reason for its existence. And this "necessity" here is not only some form of moral or existential imperative but is explicitly supported by a reference to the issue of fact itself, expressed in his formulation "respect[ing] the basic fact."

Just as Kosík's individual subjectivity was realized through one's own praxis, the national form is also determined through a process rather than being suprahistorically given by a collection of traits: "The nation is continually fighting for its character and as a nation it constitutes itself daily only through this endeavor."[104] And just like an individual, a nation too—if it does not want to be an object, a mere plaything of history—must transform itself into a subject that is able to bridge the tension between localness and cosmopolitanism. Hence, "what we can do today and in the near future in this country remains crucial."[105] At this point, Kosík was consciously following in Masaryk's (and therefore also Nejedlý's) footsteps, and postulating the "Czech question" as an international question.[106]

At the same time, Kosík was one of few Czech party intellectuals who (like Robert Kalivoda and Karel Bartošek in another context) had noticed the Slovak part of the republic.[107] Moreover, he declared that the "Slovak question," or more precisely its substantive and political solution, was a practical test and a precondition for further national existence as well as a matter of the character of the state.[108] After the August invasion, he linked cosmopolitanism with a conception of politics that would represent a "liberating and revolutionary alternative to the system of general manipulability in all of its forms, varieties, and manifestations."[109] The Czech question formulated as the question of the historical subject then necessarily consisted in whether, within the given geographical field of Central Europe, the creation of such a conception of politics and of the political nation is possible. And if the political nation is not realized, the nation as an active historical subject sinks "into a mere object of pressures and powers" with a common language, and Central Europe disappears as a "historical reality" as it transforms into a geopolitical space of superpower interests.[110] If it should fail to realize itself as a political nation, the population of the state per se is doomed to take an interest only in its economic productivity and in mere survival.[111]

By recalling the Slovak side, here we arrive at an aspect of post-Stalinism that differs from those previously and subsequently discussed. In the analysis of structure, the individual, and even revolutionary change, it is possible to take members of the Czech and Slovak party intelligentsia into consideration without distinguishing between them, but this is far from the case when approaching the question of national collective subjectivity. We do not intend to delve into the mutual disproportions and misunderstandings between the Czech and Slovak parts of the intellectual scene;[112] however, we need to draw attention to the national question within the Slovak party intelligentsia. This is because at least two approaches can be identified within the Slovak intellectual milieu, which overlapped but still had a mutually centrifugal effect on each other. Although both referred to earlier debates and regarded Stalinism as a constraint on national activity,[113] they definitively separated into two streams at the end of the 1960s. Both agreed on the need for political enforcement of the Slovak national question (federalization), but their views differed on the nature of national collectivity.

For the first group, which we can term "national communist" in accordance with previous research, the decisive factor was the determination of collectivity through the nation.[114] Intellectuals such as Vladimír Mináč, Ladislav Novomeský, and later, the first secretary of the Communist Party of Czechoslovakia, Gustáv Husák, simply perceived post-Stalinist socialism as a path toward the goal of political confirmation of an independent national identity. In their eyes, this imagined collective subjectivity was not defined in any way other than nationally. They considered any other qualities except participation in the socialist project to be low priority; or, to put a finer point on it, in their view the qualitative development of the nation (democratization) could only take place hand in hand with federalization. "There will be no democracy in Czechoslovakia without equality of the nations and nationalities: there will not be equality of the nations and nationalities without socialist democracy," Vladimír Mináč declared somewhat tautologically, although his ideas were in a clear sequence in 1968.[115]

The second trend, which could be termed "democratic-socialist," also called for the political confirmation of the Slovak nation, but hand in hand with this it sought a more nuanced definition of collective subjectivity. Like the Czech case, this mainly concerned the democratic nature of the national body: the national and democratic dimension of the Slovak nation was represented by two connected vessels, two inseparable aspects of its qualitative definition.[116] One of the most prominent exponents of this trend was the Slovak writer Dominik Tatarka, who (along with other writers including Zora Jesenská, Ľubomir Lipták, Július Strinka, and Pavol Števček) in this spirit elaborated an image of the nation as an active subject that takes matters of national and democratic liberation into its own hands and does not leave its own emancipation to outside (Czech) interventions.[117] Tatarka understood the national collective as a community of God, as a continually evolving and changing body that relates to its own ideals. Since man creates deities according to his own ideas, and in the previous era the state and the hierarchical functioning of power and public life had been deified, Tatarka proposed culture and creative work as the program for the contemporary "community of God." As a writer, he did not limit himself only to the arts as such—on the contrary, he mainly emphasized their broader importance and spoke about freedom of association and about civic activities: "the stem of national culture is the culture of society, social culture."[118] In this sense, national and cultural activities included the verb "communing" (*obcovanie*). National subjectivity here consisted in the awareness of participation in the creation of a shared community, which was to become an expression of historical consciousness, conscience, and humanist, national, and universal ambitions.[119] The linking of the national and the universal led, as in the Czech case, to an attempt to instill a certain form of cosmopolitanism. In an interview for the daily of the Communist Party of Czechoslovakia *Rudé právo*, Pavol Števček expressed this feature saying that it was—among other things—an "orientation of the spirit toward European civilization—toward . . . modeling socialist democracy for an open society of free people who are open to everything that created the world for man,

4.3. The Slovak writer Dominik Tatarka delivering a speech at a conference of the Slovak Writers' Union in Bratislava, April 30, 1968. Copyright Literary Archive of the Slovak National Library.

and people for a world of new humanity." He also issued the appeal: "Let us be modern Slovaks, citizens of a society like this, and not only a Slovak one."[120] Like Kundera and Kosík, Tatarka also believed the national existence of either Czechs or Slovaks did not make sense if it were going to be subordinated to a "standard of living [and] imaginary security."[121] "Our national defense, which is called nationalism, has a lasting meaning only if we defend the national culture, which means creation, the expression of each of us."[122] On the other hand, the awareness of belonging to cocreation creates the feeling of a shared national existence that might be defended "at all costs."[123]

All these efforts to create a new definition of national collectivity naturally stemmed from the feeling of a Soviet threat to the democratic socialist project. Binding democratic socialism together with the nation (as did Kosík and Kalivoda as well as Tatarka) was supposed to definitively legitimize it and protect it in the sense of mobilization against attempts to regulate it. At the same time, we cannot ignore the fact that in the Czech case the above-discussed trend was also associated with debates around the formation and transformations of the modern Czech national identity, which we can trace from the last third of the nineteenth century through the interwar and even postwar eras. "To return to the source of this nationality, to grasp the moment when the nation enters political and cultural reality, such is the program of this 'historization,'" reads the evaluation of Zdeněk Nejedlý penned by the French Bohemist Xavier Galmiche.[124] How typical for Czech post-Stalinism, which drew inspiration from the progressive tradition of interpreting Czech history and, by emphasizing a harmonization of the local and the global, sought to create a modern national character corresponding to the image of democratic socialism. At the same time, it was true for both Slovak national-democratic and Czech authors that modernity was—as it had been for Nejedlý—given by progressivism and the non-Stalinist democratic and creative nature of the (national) socialist project.

Hand in hand with this went the idea of exceptionality—one of the main attributes of thinking about Czechoslovak post-Stalinism—which was rooted in the idea of Czech democratism and, accordingly, progressivism. "And it is truly a typically *Czech* democratism, as we shall best see, if we compare it ourselves in this way with other nations."[125] This quotation could have been written at the end of the 1960s by any of the above-cited authors instead of Zdeněk Nejedlý (see Kundera's quote introducing this chapter). At the end of the 1960s, the historian Karel Bartošek asked himself the question: "What will be the nascent

4.4. The historian Karel Bartošek, the author of one of the most radical political programs of the end of the 1960s. Copyright National Archives, Prague.

'meaning of Czech history'"? And he answered himself, that it will clearly be "'old-new.'" However, Bartošek was one of the few party intellectuals who warned against a romanticizing "escape to history," against the horizon of the "national sky" and also against "black-and-white patriotizing."[126]

Returning to one of the introductory statements that although the post-Stalinists preferred the individual and their autonomy—while at the same time not forgetting collective subjectivity—it seems that besides the historical continuities outlined here, there was one more reason for their manner of thinking. If during the period of officially proclaimed socialism, the party intellectuals had given up on the category of class, the only categories left to them for capturing collective subjectivity were the people and the nation. While the "people" has always remained a vaguely defined concept that post-Stalinism, despite some brief attempts, did not manage to provide a more satisfactory definition for, the nation was available without any necessity for further adjustments or reinterpretations. So, stealthily—and then quite determinedly after the military invasion—the nation asserted itself into thinking about collectivity as a hegemonic concept.

From the perspective of the intellectual history of post-Stalinism, the following is also worth mentioning. The subject of the nation or the people is almost entirely absent in texts written by the techno-optimists and determinists. At most, collectivity was mentioned in connection with the form of a society's structure or as a relationship between the general (social) and particular (individual) interest, as addressed by period sociology, legal philosophy, and reform economics. Unlike law, science, education, leisure time, the structure of society, and so forth, questions of peoples or nations were not part of their register. It was as though in the context of the establishment of a classless society in its definitive version with a thorough implementation of the scientific-technical revolution, they no longer needed to ask such questions, or the concepts of people and nation simply lacked functionality in modern socialism. This is suggested by the laconic comment of Ota Klein that the civilizational movement of the scientific-technical revolution was clearly leading to the creation of some kind of "new collectivity" where the individualism of capitalist modernity and Stalinist collectivism would meet in the middle.[127]

Thus far, we have gathered a number of materials that testify to Marxist humanists' surprising affinity for collective subjectivity, but we still need to more systematically investigate the relationship that connects questions of the human individual and its total realization and reflections on collectivity with ideas about the "people," the nation, and the tradition of Czech history. However, first we will touch upon the ideas about change, or rather, revolution that we have already mentioned (see chapter 5).

CHAPTER 5

THINKING REVOLUTION

> The socialist revolution and revolutionaries will therefore protect themselves only if they are able to create a model of social power capable of permanently producing situations in which people can and must become revolutionaries every day without submachine guns in their hands: revolutionaries of thought and revolutionaries of action.
>
> **—ZDISLAV ŠULC**

Analysis of thinking about change as a problem in and of itself has an indispensable place in our interpretation, mainly because the concept and content of this thought are transformed in post-Stalinism. Therefore, we will devote attention to the conceptions of historicity and development as well as focusing on the concept of revolution, which does not disappear from the thought horizon of party intellectuals but even takes on new aspects. In this chapter we offer an analysis of shifts in thinking about the areas of human activity (technology, science, and culture) that were expected to become the primary loci of revolutionary change, thus shifting socialist society to a qualitatively higher level. These reconceptualizations also implied a need to rethink the relationship between the basic moments of chronological sequence: the past, the present, and the future. As in chapters 1–4, here we also open our interpretation by discussing Stalinist orthodoxy for the purpose of comparison. In the final part of this chapter, in accordance with our conception of post-Stalinism as a modernizing project, we balance the divergent—and primarily shared—motifs in techno-optimistic and humanist thinking on revolution. We thus respond to the dichotomous reading of humanism and techno-optimism, as well as to the uncertainty and instability that Pavel Kolář attributed to the post-Stalinist era in his analysis.¹ This chapter concludes our elaboration on the conceptual formation of post-Stalinist modernity. Chapter 6 is devoted to the limits of post-Stalinist thought.

REVOLUTION AND CHANGE

Although the post-Stalinist period is mainly associated with "reforms" of the state-socialist regime, or perhaps with "reform" discourses or the "reform" movement, from our point of view this is a distortion or even a heavy-handed sanding off the edges of post-Stalinist thinking, precisely in the intentions we defined as having a negative or privative nature in the thought of the time (i.e., mere de-Stalinization or criticism of the cult of personality). Nor is it the case that reforms were not discussed, and their social necessity had not been formulated—even the upper echelons of the party's leadership had to agree with this need to a certain extent, especially after the crisis of 1961–1963—but there was another aspect that was decisive. The party intelligentsia had not stopped thinking about revolution,² but the term took on a significantly different meaning from the one it had in Marxist-Leninist orthodoxy.

It is precisely when it is set in comparison with Stalinist orthodoxy that post-Stalinist thinking emerges as a movement that went beyond merely eliminating mistakes and correcting injustices. And moreover, it also took decisive steps in a fresh direction that was supposed to give socialism a new character and launch its next phase of development: real socialist modernity. At the same time, the relationship to the old Stalinist socialism was not understood either as simple rejection or simple continuation, but in the sense of a dialectical overcoming. And it was the adjective "dialectical" that was to express this tension among the party intellectuals themselves when they approached the Stalinist legacy. Undoubtedly, even Stalinism itself planned for its own development and a shift to another level (toward communism), while at the same time being unable to resolve its own internal contradictions or the externality of its development,³ which significantly complicated the "straight" trajectory of the state socialist regimes and led to its reassessment. Thanks to the "restart" of socialist modernity that we have diagnosed, and despite frequent positive references to the past (the interwar democracy and the short period of the popular-national front in 1945–1948), post-Stalinism was not without a certain revolutionary flavor and an atmosphere of something "new."

Part of the post-Stalinist transformation was also a critique of the Stalinist conception of revolution and temporality. In this respect, the Marxist historical perspective, or its understanding of the revolutionary transitions between individual modes of production (primarily capitalism and socialism), entered the equation. Post-Stalinism held the conviction in common with Stalinism that the abolition of capitalism and the establishment of socialism (or more specifically, the dictatorship of the proletariat) can only be achieved through a coup d'état—which implies a turning point, a discontinuous moment at the level of ownership of the means of production. The party intelligentsia espoused the assumption of the antagonistic character of capitalist society, which was inherently incapable of resolving its own contradictions in a nonviolent manner. However, for the post-Stalinists, it was crucial that the model of revolution as a discontinuous break was only valid at the moment of violent takeover of power—and not necessarily in all historical cases—and its scope was limited to the political aspect (i.e., the installation of the dictatorship of the proletariat and not the building of socialism itself).[4] So while culture was to play a significant revolutionary role, unlike in the Western New Left, the concept of Maoist cultural revolution was not present in Czechoslovak post-Stalinist thought.[5]

Thus, on the question of the construction of the socialist system, the paths of Stalinism and post-Stalinism began to diverge diametrically. The post-Stalinists agreed with the thesis that to promote Stalinist modernization and overcome the backwardness inherited from tsarist Russia, it had been necessary to accede to mobilizing economic policies—and the same applied to laying the foundation for the Soviet Union's international position at the end of the 1920s and beginning of the 1930s. This perception of Stalinism can be considered a certain form of developmentalism whereby an economically less developed country attempts to catch up to the developed countries in the shortest time possible. In cases corresponding to this model concept, mobilization policies and strong state-centralizing measures are typical—and in many respects, these were better ways to reach the desired goal than they would have been in the market economies. In the Soviet Union, these policies were implemented not only in an effort to overcome backwardness but primarily to establishing a just and egalitarian society, which, according to period interpretations of Marxism, could take place only after a certain degree of development had been reached.

Lenin often used vocabulary that described abrupt leaps and sudden changes within his understanding of Hegel's dialectics,[6] as well as, naturally, in the process of building socialism in a backward country, as Soviet Russia was at the beginning of the 1920s. However, Lenin's—and later Stalin's—leaps were not supposed to have the nature of headlong plunges, but only a speeding up (however radical that might be) of the entire developmental process. Using another metaphor, they were not supposed to be making a leap over a chasm, but only lengthening their stride to a run.[7] In this way, Leninist-Stalinist developmentalism could defend itself against charges of voluntarism, which we have already seen—especially on real structure and subjectivity (see chapters 2 and 3)—were often brought against them by post-Stalinist intellectuals. The conscious management and steering of social (and soon thereafter natural) processes were legitimized based on Lenin's and Stalin's belief in the possibility of recognizing social and natural laws. From their perspective, this was not a matter of arbitrary governance, but of behaving in accordance with the regular course of society and nature. Both Leninism and Stalinism were founded on a scientistic belief in the significance or even the decisive role of science and a scientific approach to governing society. In the post-Stalinist era, this mindset was partially shared by both the techno-optimists and the dialectical determinists.

The second characteristic feature of Stalinism that became a target of post-Stalinist criticism was the infamous thesis about intensification of the class struggle under socialism. Its essence lay in Stalin's interpretation of what was originally Lenin's statement on the bourgeois class, which—although it would objectively decline with the establishment of the dictatorship of the proletariat—would be motivated to a furious final opposition against the emerging social order as it became aware of its weakening position.[8] This was the reason for the periodically recurring Stalinist operations against "internal enemies" (saboteurs, agents of foreign powers) launched against threats that were relatively real, or sometimes even entirely imaginary.

This fact also had a major impact on the functioning and international self-reflection of the Stalinist system. The situation escalated at the moment when the whole project of modernization (and therefore also of Stalinist modernity in its entirety) began to encounter failures caused by excessive speed, faulty planning, a lack of technology, or (what mainly interests us here) the orthodox conception of dialectical laws. The occurrence of any of these "disruptions," "shortages," "errors," or—in dialectical language—"negativities" was then interpreted entirely consistently with the thesis of sharpening the class struggle as a result of the activity of (internal or external) enemy classes and powers. Both the incredible resilience and the (self-)destructive and (self-)regenerative power of Stalinism were to be found in this train of thought.

If the premise was that successfully building socialism would arouse an increasingly determined resistance by the historically "extinct" classes, then any actual error in the functioning of the socialist system could be (and often was) labeled as enemy sabotage. Their increasing frequency, and the growing resistance of the enemy classes thus confirmed the legitimacy of the choices made. In this way, Stalinism created an iterating sequence in which the crisis of the system essentially equaled the system's success through the intermediate element of sabotage. This meant entering not only a vicious cycle, but even accelerating into a spiral, culminating in violence that could ultimately only be ended by Stalin himself. It is a system is generated by the conception of change, which in the form of Stalin's decisions can only take on sudden, abrupt, and therefore irrational forms. Hence, the post-Stalinist critical distance toward the abrupt, discontinuous model of change, which they saw as inevitably reliant on the arbitrary interventions of an external authority, sustained by a cult of personality. To be clear, however, the criticism does not concern social and economic change in the form of expropriating the means of production, but precisely the space for such interventions by an individual who stands at the top or even beyond the society's pyramid (i.e., Stalin, or in the Czechoslovak case, Gottwald).

The differences between Stalinism and post-Stalinism inhere in the overall conception of change and later also in the conception of the functioning of the individual modes of production (particularly socialism). As David Priestland points out, Stalinism was noted for several waves of mobilization policies (here, Priestland is referring mainly to the 1930s), which oscillated between emphasis on a popular democratizing strategy and the political element, and a technological-managerial strategy and scientism.[9] These policies were alternated in the absence of a dialectical linkage of the scientific and political aspects within the framework of a unified conception of building socialism. This is precisely why the Stalinist manner of building socialism seemed so voluntaristic, haphazard, and uncoordinated to the post-Stalinists. According to them, it emphasized one aspect or another depending on the success or failure of specific mobilization policies. In other words, it reflected a way of thinking that understood revolution and revolutionary action only as sudden, disruptive events. For the post-Stalinists, violent coups, mobilizations, and shock worker movements were, at best, valid means during the transitional stage between capitalism and socialism, or in exceptional cases necessitated by historical and cultural circumstances for the first stage of socialist modernization (e.g., overcoming the USSR's backwardness).[10]

The post-Stalinists considered the paradox of the mutual implication of irrational discontinuity and the Stalinist naturalist (strictly evolutionary) conception of history—where socialism was supposed to be the necessary outcome—as specious. In their eyes, it was a product of the tension between the rational construction of successively evolving historical formations and the naturalistic thesis of the sharpening of the class struggle for socialism. As we have seen above, if this combination gives rise to the perception of any negative phenomenon as the work of forces that are hostile to socialism (nondialectically, according to post-Stalinist criticism),[11] the result cannot be anything other than a simultaneous self-reinforcing spiral of violence and reinforcement of belief in the legitimacy and inevitability of the development that had been initiated and implemented—the Stalinist version of modernity. The discontinuity, which at first appears to be an external, nonintegral part of historical development (when it is thus conceived) functions in two ways: as a mobilization element and as a brake that slows down the self-destructive operation of processes that had already been initiated. The question was thus not whether the Stalinist conception of revolution based on a combination of Lamarckian evolutionism and discontinuous interventions could be maintained for the operation of an already-established socialist system,[12] but how to preserve the principle of revolutionary change as an integral aspect of post-Stalinist socialism.

HISTORICITY AND DIALECTICAL DEVELOPMENT

The post-Stalinists criticized the Stalinist conception of change particularly focused on the above-mentioned moment of discontinuity, which they considered to be one of the defining traits of Stalinism. This critique not only rejected the application of discontinuity to existing socialism but also interpreted it as a paradoxical product of the dialectic of the naturalistic-evolutionary concept based in a model of history as a timeline of social and economic formations (feudalism—capitalism—socialism) that must follow in a predetermined order. At first glance, the mutually exclusive moments of continuity (the evolutionary order of history) and discontinuity (Stalin's interventions) are perceived in post-Stalinist criticism as complementary elements of the same Stalinist development, which was built from the beginning on a faulty understanding of dialectics.

Thus, in this spirit, the post-Stalinist intellectuals sought to challenge teleological necessity ("naturalistic evolutionism") and to disrupt the determinism that stemmed from a mechanical conception of causality (see chapter 2). Here, the debates within historical materialism and period historiography on the crises of feudalism, the rise of capitalism, and the nature of dialectical development in historical materialism and period historiography became the starting point. And as in other cases, the intelligentsia did not stop only with criticism of the past (i.e., Stalinism), but attempted to develop their own, as they said, "truly" dialectical conception of historicity.

Probably the first more painstakingly elaborated approach to overcoming the negatives of the Stalinist conception was the philosopher Robert Kalivoda's historical analysis. To demonstrate the novel post-Stalinist character of his attempt we must turn our attention to his considerations regarding the origin of capitalism out of contradictory development within the "feudal mode of production." Kalivoda rejected the claim that the origin of capitalism was to be found in the urban environment, or respectively in the seminal forms of capital—commerce and usury—which for him merely represented "special forms of feudal rents."[13] Neither the Italian city states nor the Netherlands in the seventeenth century (and—as Josef Cibulka was later to emphasize—not even Great Britain in the eighteenth century) could yet be considered fully developed capitalist states because their wealth was the product of an economic boom and military dominance rather than industrial manufacturing for a stabilized domestic market.[14] To put it more formally, Kalivoda opposed those ("dialectical") conceptions of the genesis and extinction of social and economic formations that seek the origin of developmentally higher formations in particular elements of developmentally lower formations. Such elements are believed by others to bear a matrix of the inevitable code of the formation that is going to emerge already within them. According to this line of analysis, all that is necessary is to sufficiently enable the development of these embryonic elements, and the definitive transformation from one social and economic formation to another will take place. In the eyes of both Kalivoda and Cibulka, these are the basic traits of the evolutionist and naturalistic scheme espoused by Stalinist orthodoxy.

However, trade, money rent, commodity capital, banks, and credit are not the embodiment of capitalism, nor are they embryonic elements of it; instead they represent an integral part of feudalism (as products of its contradictory development).[15] Kalivoda argues that capitalism "does not arise because medieval commercial capital is all of a sudden 'internally impelled' to transform itself capitalistically, but rather because on its long path to finding profitable application it finally arrives at the possibility of being profitable in industrial production."[16] Therefore, the change here is given neither by teleological movement nor by a "spirit" (such as a capitalist one) that would already be present within individual, specific elements; rather, it is enabled by the contradictory movement of the formation itself. In any case, it is explicable but not understood as inevitable within the framework of a developmental order. Kalivoda formulates this change more specifically as the crossing of a certain threshold ("it finally matures into the possibility of effectuation"), which is achieved "spontaneously."[17] Here, the dismantling of Stalinist determinism led to the possibility of socialism being grasped as a contradictorily developing whole, as well as enabling thinking about change beyond the framework of historical necessity. This critique of the inevitability of historical development afforded the authors of that time a theoretical tool for thinking through the account of history's movement in a different way, which at the same time also opened space for new interpretations of socialism.

Kalivoda's concept of change was based on the idea of human liberation. In his view, it was most precisely formulated by Marx, but during the course of history it had been expressed in various forms with the same degree of urgency and originality. In history, there has been a tension between the historical development of the ideal of freedom and emancipation (for example, in early Christianity and peasant-plebian Tábor) and the social and economic reality where the emancipatory ideal has not yet been realized,[18] or is even suppressed. Historical turning points and revolutions are therefore the results of emancipatory efforts aimed at what should (*soll*) be. Ideas of liberation often precede the emergence of the social and economic formations that, according to the Stalinist canon, are supposed to enable them. Thus, social consciousness does not necessarily have its origin in social being, as Marxist orthodoxy would like to have it (see chapter 2); instead, emancipatory ideals attributed to the social superstructure can precede the development of the economic base and thus, via real revolutionary movements, act to transform them. To put it even more precisely, according to Kalivoda, the idea of freedom generally considered to be inherent to the French Revolution had already appeared in the Hussite revolution in the fifteenth century, when for the first time in human history an attempt was made to fulfill human beings' natural needs in a social context.[19] The roots of Jacobin radicalism can thus essentially be found running deep before the social and economic formation that bourgeois revolutions are associated with—capitalism—came into being.

Kalivoda claims that this moment of tension between a specific emancipatory ideal and its failure to be implemented—which is given by historical reality—can also be found in socialist development. It is not sufficient only to create a social and economic formation (socialism) founded on the socialization of the means of production. Real socialist development, if it is to meet the obligations of liberating man, must make changes that bring it closer to fulfilling the ideal: the main emphasis here is on *aiming* toward the utopian goal instead of on achieving the goal itself (the turn to the present through which the future is perceived is explained in the section "The Turn to the Present"). This is the understanding of change that will enable Kalivoda to support the spontaneous creation of workers' councils through which the emancipatory idea of democratic socialism, consisting of radical political and economic democratization, would be established in 1968.[20]

Kalivoda's analyses and interpretations of the crises of feudalism allowed him to transcend the framework for conceptualizing historical change that had been widely accepted until then. Josef Cibulka further elaborated upon Kalivoda's observations by (among other projects) developing his own conception of dialectical totality that was based mainly in a perception of reality as contradictory development (see chapter 2). As with Kalivoda, Cibulka's reconceptualizations not only took aim at the Stalinist conception of history and historicity but also worked to formulate the nature of the change that even (post-Stalinist) socialism should be guided by.

In chapter 2, we have seen how and why Cibulka criticized the Stalinist conception of social and economic formations as well as various other structural and systemic approaches. Although both perspectives argued for the contradictory nature of the formation, structure, or system to varying degrees, Cibulka claimed that neither was ultimately able to grasp its own *internally* contradictory movement. Based on the confrontation with systemic and structural approaches, Cibulka introduced the pair of concepts *prehistory* and *history*, through which he explained the concept of the dialectical totality (see chapter 2). The dynamics of prehistory and history as two phases in the development of a totality is caused by their contradictory character. The difference between them lies in the relationship between the internal and the external, which, however, is not understood as an opposition between the transitional state when the system arises and disappears (*not yet* governed and *no longer* governed by its laws) and the stabilized state of a structure or system that is characterized by cyclical motion. In Cibulka's dialectical conception, the emerging dialectical totality depends on external conditions in the prehistoric phase, whereas in the phase of history—that is, of the fully formed dialectical totality (e.g., capitalism, socialism)—it is already fully determined by the movement of *its own* contradictions. However, this can in no way be considered cyclical, with the implications of a certain regularity and thus also stability. Here, the moment of stability is not at all an original state and is merely derived, whereas the dialectical totality is distinguished by its permanent internal contradictions.[21]

This theoretical step was important not only within the critique of capitalism and as a contribution to debates on its origins but also within the framework of critiques of Stalinism. In both applications it was a critique of mixing the prehistoric phase of creating "preconditions" with the phase when a capitalist, or, later, a socialist dialectical totality actually functioned. In Cibulka's critique, the Marxist-Leninist orthodoxy interpreted the preconditions as already being an internal moment in the first phase of the functioning of the historically subsequent totality instead of perceiving them as merely external conditions. In this context, Cibulka, following Evald Ilyenkov, referred to one important rule that was typically applied in the dialectical conception of historicity: the external condition or precondition for the functioning of the totality cannot be considered the cause of its origin.[22] This can be illustrated by the following example. At odds with the interpretations of Stalinist as well as classical economics, which understood any form of savings and accumulation of money capital as the main cause for the origin of capitalism, Cibulka considered this to be an external condition that became an internal condition (an integral aspect) only with the establishment of capitalism, that is, retrospectively (the concept of mediating determination), as a result of the already historical functioning of totality. The situation is exactly the opposite of a simple causal relationship—accumulation becomes a "cause" only within the functioning of the totality, and therefore cannot be the cause of the totality's emergence. As we have seen above, neither developed trade, sophisticated financial instruments, nor even manufacturing for export necessarily had to engender capitalism when dialectical development is conceived in this way. Instead, it arises only with the separation of most of the immediate producers from the means of production, with the mass commodification of their productive forces and with the integration of its own domestic market in commodity manufacturing.

Thus, for Cibulka, none of the previous Marxist interpretations were able to meet the original requirement of Marx's (and Hegel's) dialectics, because their conception of the negative side of the dialectical contradiction did not present it as an internal aspect of the totality (structure, system), but merely as a disruptive external element that threatens the otherwise internally stable character of its organization (see chapter 2). Thus, change could not be grasped as a product of the organization within a system, and in Cibulka's view, therefore, it also could not explain qualitative transformations of the totality (i.e., of the given economic and social formation). Thus, if the previous Marxist trends recognized the existence of contradictions, they were then unable to understand them as a source of internal systemic revolutionary change, i.e., as a self-negation of the system, but implicitly only as disruptive elements. While in the evolutionism of the Second International the question of revolutionary transformation remains unanswered, or is reduced to a simple gradual development, Stalinism delegates the origin of change to the political takeover of power (for example, by the proletariat in the case of a socialist revolution). For Cibulka, in the Stalinist-evolutionist perspective, this means that such an act is classified as an act of a systemically external nature: "Against evolutionism, which falsely interprets qualitative change as merely quantitative rearrangement of an old, given quality, the Stalinist conception only *supplements* the evolutionary conception with the moment of a turning point."[23] Similarly, in his view, the contemporary cybernetic approach understood the system as internally stabilizing, or as having a tendency toward equilibrium or stability, and the origin of change was a product of interaction with the external environment.[24]

It was the appreciation of the internal contradictory nature of dialectical totalities that should have a deep impact on the functioning of the (post-Stalinist) socialist system. As we stated above, in Cibulka's view, Stalinism's fundamental conceptual mistake was de facto considering the socialist system as a system inherently free of contradictions and therefore perceiving any kind of dysfunctions or negative phenomena as manifestations of an external (hostile) environment. Thus, from the orthodox perspective, the laws of dialectical development in socialism ceased, or, rather, should have ceased to apply in socialism because the achievement or the process of achieving socialism meant a process of eliminating the negative crisis elements (for instance, there was the expectation that the liquidation of enemy classes would abolish antagonistic social relations). Consequently, he went on to claim, idealistic and even utopian inclinations were practically inevitable within Stalinism. Yet he also claimed that the laws of dialectical development have a universal character and are valid for capitalism and socialism alike. The difference lay in the way that the social system provided opportunities to resolve its given internal contradictions. Here, Cibulka fully agreed with the thesis about the diametrically opposite nature of the contradictions within capitalism and socialism.

In the end, the antagonistic contradictions in capitalism did not allow for another form of transformation to a qualitatively higher level than discontinuous leaps. This contrasts with the nonantagonistic contradictions in socialism, which were supposed to allow for continuous transformation without violent or irrational leaps: "Discontinuous changes are moments of uninterrupted dialectical transition from a given qualitative differentiation of reality into a developmentally higher one. A constant dialectical transition of this qualitative differentiation into a developmentally higher qualitative differentiation necessarily arises."[25] Thus, the contradictions in socialism do not stand against one another as irreconcilable elements; rather, they represent the motor of socialist development that propels it toward permanent qualitative transformation. In this respect, socialism is not moving toward a utopian goal but is continually overcoming its own contradictions.

For the dialectical determinists, including Cibulka, the transition from capitalism to socialism, and from socialism to communism, is embedded into an overall development of human society, progressing from lower levels to higher, more complex ones. In this respect, post-Stalinist Marxism is no different from orthodox Marxism, which works under the same assumption. Nevertheless, they do differ in the way they understand the individual levels. The difference between them is clearly shown in Zdeněk Javůrek's criticism, which took aim against the overall framing of the debate on historical materialism in the second half of the 1950s and beginning of the 1960s (see chapter 2). Javůrek mainly took exception to the formal separation of historical and dialectical materialism, in which the former was to investigate social laws and the second investigated the most general laws governing all levels of reality. In Javůrek's view, this perspective had an especially devastating impact on the concept of development, because it seemed like a progression from general to particular laws. In contrast, Javůrek proposed a thesis inspired by Ilyenkov, concerning the general and the particular, which are present at all levels of reality. General laws are undoubtedly present in all forms of movement (physical, social), but not in the manner of an essence, with specific laws being merely an added contingency. Rather, they appear in the form of a concrete totality of general and particular laws.

The fact that the more general laws governing physical nature are overcome (dialectically negated) in dialectical development by laws of a higher type—those that control the more complex levels of reality of a biological and social type—was therefore pivotal for Javůrek's conception of historical development. Through Javůrek's work, we thus obtain an image of unified dialectical development of all nature, whose highest stage is the human being and human society. Both "agents" can dialectically negate, incorporate into their functioning, and thus also (dialectically) determine the developmentally lower biological and natural laws. Social and historical laws thus ultimately subordinate lower-level laws and therefore provide unity to the entire natural-historical movement.[26]

Thanks in particular to Robert Kalivoda, Josef Cibulka, and Zdeněk Javůrek, the post-Stalinists attempted to create a conception of historical change that would avoid the deficits of Marxist orthodoxy—remnants of evolutionism and a strict division of the general and the particular. Despite criticisms of one-dimensionality, linearity, and the assertion of their differentiation, they still shared one essential trait: they understood historical movement as a unified or unifying process that proceeds from lower developmental stages to higher ones. However, the post-Stalinist reflection on the issue of change not only was restricted to historical development but also broached questions associated with time and temporality itself.

THE TURN TO THE PRESENT

Post-Stalinist reflections on change culminated in a reconceptualization of temporality: thinking about the relationship between the past, present, and future. While the debates on historicity were still primarily based either in implicit or explicit criticism of Stalinism, later reflections on temporality went beyond this framework. This was a reaction not only to the original orthodoxy but also to social and technological changes and the Marxist understanding of non-Marxist stimuli such as existentialism (see chapter 3).

For Karel Kosík, the critical overcoming of existentialism manifested especially in the concept of temporality stemming from his critique of Heidegger's understanding of practice and labor.[27] First, from Kosík's—and more broadly, from a Marxist—perspective, Heidegger idealistically inverts the relationship between time and human activity. For Heidegger, a human being is primarily defined as a temporal being based on their awareness of their own death. In contrast, Kosík sees temporality as derived from human practical activity itself—it is only on the basis of such activity that one can distinguish between past, present, and future. Second, Heidegger's definition of the human being (though Heidegger, of course, speaks of Dasein) through projection, and his view of activity as procurement and care, implicitly distorts the human understanding of time, because he structures these modes of activity in fundamental relation to the future, where the present is assigned a subordinate status—understood merely as something to be overcome or negated. "The temporal dimension and the being of man as a being in time opens up in care [*Sorge*] as a fetishized future and a fetishized grasp of temporality: for care, the present is not the authenticity of existence, 'being present,' but an escape, because care has already outdistanced the present."[28] Thus, according to Kosík, the authentic nature of human time cannot manifest itself in this Heideggerian "care" because in it the human being does not live in the present but exclusively in the future (i.e., as a being that is *always* oriented toward the future). And because the future by its very nature *is not yet* and can never be present in a strong sense of the term, it is always in a negative relation to the present. In the end, according to Kosík, Heidegger forcibly inverts their relation: what is not yet (the future) determines (and thus negates also) what currently exists (the present). Yet, as we will show and specify later, it should be the other way around: what is not yet (the future) should be determined from the standpoint of what currently exists (whereby actual existence is not to be confused here with mere facticity). Only in this way, according to Kosík, can we avoid human individuals being consumed by nothingness (i.e., by what does not yet exist).

For our purposes, it is not of crucial importance whether Kosík's analysis and interpretation of Heidegger are correct and whether they take all the aspects of his philosophy into account. What matters is its significance in post-Stalinist thought. The critique of practice as procurement focuses not only on existentialist thought but also on Stalinism, which is oriented toward a future from which both the present and the past are understood. This is illustrated in certain contours in Kosík's critique of the idea of the economy as an independent factor that determines other factors, which is the classic Marxist doctrine about the relationship of the base and the superstructure. The concept of the factor is problematic because the economy is understood as a complete (closed) and separate product; it is a clearly defined area of human activity that exists independently of other elements or factors. In Kosík's view, this is essentially an already fetishized idea of the reality, where individual forms of human activity act against one another as though they were independent and complete things. A Marxism that accepts this concept of reality would not differ by nature from the thinking of bourgeois political economics.

According to Kosík, for a truly Marxist conception of human time to be freed from orientation toward a ready-made thing, it must prefer the present time, which needs to be ripped out of the templates of immediate experience. He uses the term "pseudo-concreteness," by which he means that which appears to us in our unreflected daily lives where we take things for granted. However, this "uprooting" or upending of the present cannot come about with reference to the future, or from the perspective of the future, because in that case it would be a product that was always already ready-made (only ideally, of course, not materially). Kosík had already programmatically formulated this perspective in 1958 in an article with the somewhat ambiguous title of "Tomorrow Is in Our Hands" (*Zítřek je v našich rukou*): "The goal of life is life itself, not the idea of a future, never-experienced life, even the most beautiful one. The idea of tomorrow may be a part of real life today, but it cannot replace it."[29] The perspective of the philosophy of praxis is and must be the viewpoint of a philosophy of the present, because only from here can things be captured in their dynamic genesis. But, as we have indicated above, it is necessary to stress that in his conception (and the same applies to other post-Stalinists), it is not the present in the sense of a mere positively given facticity (see also chapter 2). It was a Hegelian conception that contains both facticity (now seen as a mere "ruling" tendency or ready-made things) and tendencies aiming against or outside of it (in the sense of nonactualized possibilities or negativities structuring the process of creation). In any case, the facticity along with these tendencies makes up one and the same present time.

These reflections on the relationship between the present and the past are also evident in Kosík's conception of history. According to him, history is determined neither by the future (utopian ideal) nor by the operation of historical-natural laws, but by totalization, in "which human praxis incorporates and thus revives moments of the past."[30] In this sense, human reality is not only the production of the new but also the critical and dialectical reproduction of the past. The continuity of history is guaranteed, but now it is contingent upon the existence of objectifying activity and from the perspective of the present. It is no longer the "iron laws of history" that shape social reality, but human everyday practice (see chapter 2). The present is thus understood not as a "sacrifice" for a still nonexistent glorious future (Stalinism), but as the everyday realization of the human being, which, as praxis, has an ontologically formative character.

Kosík was not alone in thinking about new, revolutionary forms of temporality: another champion of Czech Marxist humanism, Robert Kalivoda, also attributed a decisive role to the present, but approached the issue from the perspective of the historical forms of emancipatory ideologies. He contrasted the evolutionary line of emancipatory thought that aimed at true freedom (Marxist libertinism) with the abstract idea of liberalism. We have already seen that his conception of historical change is based on a conflict of present reality with the ideal of "human happiness that man does not find in his reality."[31] Libertinism in its historically original form (peasant-plebian Tábor) was still working with the idea of restoring a lost essence, which, despite its orientation toward the future, it had substantially reified. Or, in Kosík's words, the

5.1. Robert Kalivoda on a vacation that, by chance, fell during the days of the military invasion in Czechoslovakia in August 1968. Here he is shown with his son Jan. Copyright Eva Kalivodová.

followers of libertinism "fetishized" an originally existing state. However, this is where its deficiency became apparent: the inability to create a new reality, and the mere reproduction of the lost emancipatory ideal, led to stagnation. In Kalivoda's view, Marx's historical merit was in relieving libertinism of its metaphysical utopianism, and he formulated the struggle for a better reality as the consequence of objective historical necessity.

However, in Marx's conception, even capitalism's internal self-negation as a social system did not mean eliminating the remnants of romantic utopianism. It was only when Kalivoda found a surrealistic reformulation of Marxism in Karel Teige's conception that space was created for the realization of human freedom in the development of a "harmonious totality of human irrationality and rationality, as the fullness of human pleasure."[32] Similarly to Kosík's conception, Kalivoda's Teige first deflected attention from the future (where it is unconsciously projected as a finished state) to the present as the desirable goal of revolutionary action. At the same time, the future dimension was not abandoned; on the contrary, it is, in Kalivoda's words, deepened by *dialectical concretization*. Only from this perspective can it be understood as a matter of permanent struggle: "Future freedom is born in the present as its moment, a romantic utopia ceases to be a utopia if it can identify itself as this moment, which even a movement that is realistically striving for man's future freedom cannot do without if it wants to definitively step out of the realm of utopian metaphysics."[33] Just as with Kosík, we see here in what sense a turn to the present opens up the future. It is no longer a "ready-made" and concrete state that is to be achieved and to which everything must be sacrificed on the basis of a metaphysically posed utopian ideal; it is the result of orientation toward moments of "future freedom" in the forms that unfold in the "unfree present."[34] By diverting attention from the future to the present (even in the socialism of the time), the struggle for a harmonious content for freedom was to take on the character of a "perpetually dynamic moment," which is available both for the not yet entirely free present as well as for the future communist society.

In the same spirit, Vítězslav Gardavský, the author of the international bestseller *God Is Not Yet Dead*, contemplated a present that would project Marxist atheism as a Marxist metaphysics that transcends the finitude of human beings through conscious creation. The future is open instead of inevitable, because it unfolds based on its fulfillment in the present, which ceases to be a place of expectation of what is coming in the future. Instead of a necessity, the future here appears as a "construction principle of conscious creation,"[35] which, within the awareness of

5.2. The philosopher Vítězslav Gardavský was employed at the Antonín Zápotocký Military Academy in Brno. (Today, this is part of the University of Defence.) Copyright Andrea Mikitová.

individual finitude, is accomplished now. It is a "high point of my life as if I were to die tomorrow."[36] In a similar way, Milan Machovec, another participant in the Marxist-Christian dialogue, criticized the Stalinist idea of communism and its separation of the present and the past. He claimed that the isolation of the longed-for future state allowed and justified the use of any extreme measures whatsoever in the present.[37] And not only that, but with the postponement of communist society Stalinism also pushed aside "man," whom Machovec said had always been inherent in the foundations of Marxism.[38]

If the starting point of the humanist conception of temporality was a criticism of the future as a privileged site from which the position and entire content of the present and past are retroactively determined, the starting point of Radovan Richta's techno-optimistic approach was the exact opposite end of the time series.[39] In his view, what has shaped our thinking about time so far and characterized our conception of historical development and the nature of its processes was not the future but the past. Nevertheless, Richta did not blame the previous understanding of temporality on some kind of a priori misconception, as Kosík had in the case of Heidegger's philosophy of "care" and "procurement." Instead, he directed his critical attention to the foundations of the Stalinist conception of history.

The Stalinist conception of temporality, by its nature, stemmed from the character of certain real historical processes—"industrial civilization," in Richta's terms—which, according to him, was shaped by the accumulation of past labor. Only on this basis was it possible for the subsequent cycle of production in which "the process of expanded reproduction is known to have been the starting point for all surmises about the future and for speculations."[40] Richta claimed that the paradigmatic theorist for this type of theory was the French thinker Henri de Saint-Simon. He would most likely also include many of Marx's reflections on capital as well as all the Marxist conceptions of history based on the assumption of the position of human beings, who are always born into relations that they cannot choose and are a product of previous generations in the same line. History understood in this way still retains the character of a necessary process in which "free human endeavour can cross the frontier set by the mere use of chance within the necessity of historical development."[41] In a conception of this kind, creativity and the creation of something new are only exceptions, and not the rule.

The epoch of the scientific-technical revolution was going to bring about the turning point, when the justification for the above-described conception of time and history would weaken because it was incapable of breaking through the historical fatalism of industrial civilization and liberating human creative powers.[42] The deterministic power of the industrial era is undoubtedly given by the nature of the labor involved, in which all the labor processes that human beings immediately engage in are reduced to simple expenditures of energy. However, in Richta's view, the scientific-technical revolution will bring radical changes to the nature of labor: there will be a significant reduction in the number of human laborers who must participate in immediate production, hand in hand with a significant increase in the number of those originally in nonmanufacturing or premanufacturing sectors—mainly in science, but also in education and the arts. In Richta's conception of the new civilizational epoch, time ceases to be governed by abstract quantities (energy output), and the past loses its determining function in a time series in which the future is conceived as the last, derived point. The present time becomes essential, because it gives meaning to the past and opens the future as an unlimited field of possibilities. Analogously to Kosík, Richta also sought the origin of certain historically specific temporalities in labor. However, while the former extracted human temporality from labor, Richta observed how a historically specific form of labor—simple, abstract labor characteristic of industrial production—shaped the prevailing conception of historical time. This conception, however, must be overcome, as it no longer corresponds to the new demands of the emerging era of the scientific and technological revolution.

By shifting the accent from the outlying moments in the time sequence to the present (Kosík and Kalivoda from the future, Richta from the past), post-Stalinist authors took a significant step to breaking up the inevitable linearity of (historical) time. Time could no longer progress unproblematically from a starting point—the past (accumulated labor)—through the present—into the future as the end point of the series. Nor could it move from the final point in the series, the future (the eventual result as a complete thing; communism as the future state of society)—through the present—back to the past. The foundation for any transformative activity lay in the here and now: the post-Stalinist present. As the Slovak philosopher Miroslav Kusý affirmed in the 1960s, socialism is not the fulfillment of an abstract historical principle, but efforts made by specific people who are acting in this way for themselves.[43] Even if at first glance the orientation to the present along with denial of the abstract historical principle seems to exclude any revolutionary alternatives, we should not forget that it is exactly the revolutionary nature of socialist efforts that the post-Stalinist intellectuals had in mind.

THE ROLE OF TECHNOLOGY

We have already mentioned the basic features of the concept of the scientific-technical revolution. The analysis of Vítězslav Sommer particularly address this issue from the perspectives of temporal and thematic overlaps and transnational history.[44] For us at this point the manner of conceptualizing the nature of revolutionary change and its subject are the crucial aspects. For adherents of the techno-optimistic way of thinking, and especially for Radovan Richta, the starting point was analysis of transformation in the type of production process. The focus here would be on technology, and especially in changes in the practice and position of science.

Richta's argument about the fundamental changes brought about by the scientific-technical revolution was particularly emblematic of the post-Stalinist era. As we already hinted earlier in this chapter, his explanation of this shift was grounded in both the historical and conceptual transformation of labor. In doing so, he drew a distinction between craft and industrial forms of work: in the former, the specific nature of the activity—centered on skill—predominated; here, the subject (human) maintained control over the object (tool). By contrast, in industrial era, labor acquired an abstract nature and became simple and serial; here, the relationship between subject and object was reversed and human beings became mere appendages to machines. According to Richta's theory, societies in which craft and later industrial production prevailed were— due to the nature of these forms of labor—internally limited, because neither craft workshops nor industrial factories were able to continually develop human powers. Moreover, these powers tended to be destroyed in industrial production. Due to the depletion of human forces, societies with preindustrial and industrial production succumbed to recurring

5.3 AND 5.4. The lead author of the book *Civilization at the Crossroads*, Radovan Richta, explains the principles of the scientific-technical revolution in connection with social and political changes on Czechoslovak TV, 1968. Copyright Archive of Czech TV.

crises and they were only able to begin new productive cycles after their regeneration. And when a development of human powers somehow did take place, it was only a by-product of these forms of production (period bourgeois science and culture).[45]

For Richta the process of industrialization was characterized by stability and invariance in integral productivity.[46] Growth was based on a quantitative expansion of industrial production with a stable structure of the productive forces.[47] Thus, creating new economic value required more factories, more machines, more labor force, and more capital.[48] The advent of science as a critical productive force was predicted to lead to both a radical restructuring of production and a transformation of (not only) socialist civilization. Science enabled the replacement of industrial extensive growth with intensive growth where quantitative factors yielded to qualitative ones. The gradual phaseout of human productive forces from immediate production would allow a massive transfer of human resources into the preproduction phase, where science would dominate. As the economist Zdislav Šulc pointed out in 1968, the goal of socialism was not the proletarianization of society: "The purpose of uniting the proletarians of all countries is instead that they cancel

themselves as proletarians, as assembly-line workers subordinated to the rhythm of machine production, in order to transform themselves from assembly-line workers back into a whole personality."⁴⁹ The Stalinist apotheosis of labor was supposed to be replaced by its abolition in manufacturing, and this process was going to radically transform the entire basis of the current society.

The emphasis on the word "revolution" was not accidental here. While human civilization had not been able from the time of its inception until the scientific-technical revolution to transcend the extensive form of growth and it thus succumbed to cyclically recurring phases of rise, crisis, and regeneration, for the first time in human history the scientific-technical revolution—as the first true *revolution*—was supposed to open the way to a state of *permanent* qualitative transformation of the forces of production. Clearly, one of the basic motifs associated with the conceptualization of post-Stalinist modernity is repeating here: a continual revolution replaces the irrational, uncontrolled, and abrupt changes of industrial modernity, and therefore also of Stalinism.

For Richta and the techno-optimists more broadly, the success of revolution lay primarily in the qualitative transformation of contemporary industrial production, in which cybernetization ("automation") was going to be massively utilized. Within the framework of production this meant implementing the principle of autoregulation: machines are equipped with their own "nervous and sensory system" that enables them to direct the entire process of production with minimal interventions by human beings, or with none at all (Richta's "highest form of automation").

Cybernetization was also supposed to affect the development of the forces of production, which in Richta's conception mainly meant science. In post-Stalinist thinking, the conception of science transcended a mere technological principle of management that would be implemented in manufacturing. As a theory of the system, cybernetics was going to help Marxist theory grasp the higher developmental levels of reality more precisely, and as a science of management and information it was expected to enrich Marxist dialectics with the aspect of the surrounding environment. It was cybernetics that indicated the need for inputs and outputs (feedback) to allow for better regulation.[50] The dual form of change in the cybernetic system was enormously important for post-Stalinist ideas about socialism. If a system is closed (i.e., without a relationship to its surroundings and lacking feedback, according to the second law of thermodynamics the degree of entropy—disorder—increases and the given system spontaneously disappears). Conversely, if the system is open, changes take place within it based on interactions with the outside environment as a result of receiving information and feedback from it. However, for cybernetics, no truly functioning system exists without a relationship to a surrounding environment that causes changes in the system. These changes do not necessarily have to be degenerative in nature, as is the case within closed systems, but they depend on the system's ability to react to external impulses or to feedback. Thus, there is a certain internal tendency of the system toward stability and to self-preservation; however, this tendency is of necessity relative because of the necessary relationship with what is outside it.[51]

In the broader sense, findings from cybernetics should encourage the ongoing acceptance of critical impulses leading to changes in the socialist system, and in the narrower conception, cybernetized machines were—by contrast with their counterparts in traditional factories—able to regulate themselves to the changing external environment and adjust their own functioning. They exist, therefore, in a continuous state of transformation, permanently reconfiguring their original principles of functioning. Mutatis mutandis, the same holds true for the human labor force, which is now "liberated" from its bonds to the immediate production process by this automatically controlled production.

Richta never ceased to emphasize that the scientific-technical revolution serves (or should serve) primarily for the development of human beings as the accomplished revolution's own subject and object (see chapter 3). On this point, he consistently adhered to Marx's perspective, and he considered the development of human beings in the new scientific-technical epoch as a self-evident purpose. This, naturally, could only be achieved upon the bedrock of a communist society where the forces of production "which were previously externally united and set into motion against one another by capital, receive (on the basis of the economy of social labor) the foundations for their own internal self-propelled movement."[52] Given that for Richta the complete and unlimited application of the scientific-technical revolution essentially fell into line with communism itself, this self-evident purpose eventually took on the form of a continual and automatic movement of the development of human creativity. Human beings no longer have to work to provide for basic life necessities, the purely economic character of work disappears, and labor transforms itself into a "field of man's active self-realization."[53]

Along these lines, Richta spoke of a wondrous dividing line of growth, "beyond which the fundamental associations and proportions in the march of civilization are inverted."[54] Crossing this "line" changes the modal organization of contemporary society: what had seemed impossible becomes possible, and what had seemed well-established becomes antiquated and preposterous. In the case of the transformation of industrial society into a scientific-technical society, this nodal line represented a threshold beneath which growth is achieved through the concentration and transfer of the available productive forces (including capital) into immediate production, whereas above this threshold growth is determined by the "resources released from production proper to the pre-production phase and to the cultural and social services."[55]

Thus, even at the socialist level of the development of the productive forces we still encounter the concept of continuous qualitative changes (revolution) in the form of permanent scientific progress. The development of human creativity was simultaneously understood as an integral part of this movement of transformation of the forces of production (science), in a very similar sense to the way an automatic production system reacts to changes and stimuli in the surrounding environment and modifies itself in accordance with them.

The techno-optimistic notion of modern progress was thus conditioned by the interconnectedness ("dialectical relationship") of the development of technology and creative human potential. However, the initial impulse of the revolutionary movement was of course not primarily the human being, but technology based on the cybernetic principle that, after its implementation, would free up an unprecedented amount of space for the full realization of human creative powers.

THE ROLE OF CULTURE

While for the techno-optimists in post-Stalinist Czechoslovakia, science symbolized social progress and a qualitative transformation of socialism, for the humanists, it was culture that embodied these ideals. Unlike cybernetic technology, culture was not defined in theoretically sophisticated ways; nevertheless, there was still a fairly strong consensus that it was mainly represented by art in the forms of literature, film, theater, the fine arts, and music.[56] František Šamalík termed this understanding of art as a definition that refers to "authentic culture," which in his view analyzes real conditions and "provides countless models of human experience, motives, and emotions, mediates knowledge of what is outside a person's own experience, [and] provides a deeper meaning for this experience."[57] However, the peculiarity of the post-Stalinist definition of culture lay in the fact that in addition to art in the narrower sense, it also included thought (or philosophy), which was supposed to provide modern art with a sufficient theoretical framework for self-definition and creation, and which—just like traditional art forms—had society-wide impacts.

The conception of art as a significant agent for shaping society was not new, nor was it unique within the framework of state socialism,[58] and in Czechoslovakia it represented a further development of several traditions. Thus, in a way, party intellectuals were returning to the times of the shaping of the modern national identity, when art—especially literature, because it was bound up with language—represented a significant factor in the life of the nation. They also turned their attention to the interwar avant-garde and the idea of art as a means of liberation from the snares of bourgeois society. The crucial role was the interpretation of modern art as a specific activity, in which—by contrast with premodern art (especially realism)—the process of creation itself is captured. By means of experiments, modern art reflected on itself, as well as on the position of artists in relation to their products and to society,[59] thus creating a matrix applicable to modern society as a whole.

Finally, it was important to challenge the mediating function between party elites and the popular masses that orthodox Marxism—and in its hypertrophied form, above all Stalinism—assigned to art. The problem with this idea was not so much that the post-Stalinist intellectuals had given up on a social role for art, or even that they would have preferred art for art's sake over various forms of artistic engagement. Rather, they expressed disagreement with the conception of artistic forms that was determined by the socialist realism of the second half

ANTONIN LIEHM

5.5, 5.6, AND 5.7. The journalist and film critic Antonín Jaroslav Liehm, one of the leading figures of the cultural political weekly *Literární noviny*, conducted interviews with Czech and Slovak writers in the years 1966–1968. These were to be published as a book in Czechoslovakia; however, due to the military invasion and subsequent purges of the Czech and Slovak intellectual scene, it was first published in French and English with a foreword by Jean-Paul Sartre (the English translation is titled *The Politics of Culture* [New York: Grove Press, 1970]). In this book we cite passages from the post-1989 Czech editions of works by the writer Milan Kundera, the philosopher Karel Kosík, and A. J. Liehm. Source: *Generace* (Prague: Československý spisovatel, 1990), 48, 322, 7, respectively.

of the 1940s and refused to take the measure of reality through party resolutions. Ivan Sviták concisely summed up this principle: Art "serves but does not obey."[60] A statement made by Antonín Sychra, a musicologist and former advocate of Andrei Zhdanov's concept of socialist realism, in the mid-1960s is also significant in this respect: "I attempted to prove that the aspects of content and ideology in music cannot be considered only as cultural-political postulates. They are scientific categories. Giving them up—that would mean disparaging the social and generally human reach of the art of music. . . . Such nonconformism does not rule out principles and partisanship [*stranickost*] even an iota."[61]

Hand in hand with the redefinition of the original Stalinist function of art, which was now interpreted as a noncritical "servitude," a sidelining of the distinction between bourgeois and socialist culture in favor of an understanding of art as a universal language was also taking place. A certain tension between bourgeois and socialist art never completely disappeared, but within the framework of the post-Stalinist departure from the Stalinist sharpening of antagonistic class relations, it was themed rather marginally.

In the following section we will attempt to gradually clarify how the Marxist humanists understood art in the context of socialism, how they conceived of it in relation to modern civilization in general, and to what extent they considered it an agent of fundamental social change—of revolution.

AUTONOMY

Ideas about autonomy, or more precisely, about the peculiarity of art in socialist society stemmed to a certain extent from a feeling of exclusivity of the art sphere, which despite the Stalinist ethos of folkness (*lidovost*) had survived in cultural circles. The conviction that the artistic product, literature, film, or theater changes reality was shared by party and nonparty intellectuals, admirers of the avant-garde, and even Catholic writers.[62] However, it was also related to the transformation of post-Stalinist subjectivity and the thematization of the free and active subject (see chapter 3) as well as the question of the relationship between ideology and theory that was opened up in 1956 on the pages of the weekly *Literární noviny*. Authors such as Karel Kosík and Ivan Sviták postulated there that ideology cannot fully and completely determine the nature of theory and the needs of politics cannot shape the nature of science. These theses were easily transferable to the area of culture and art. When Sviták declared that the "relationship of the man" to cognition of the objective laws of social development "is a direct relationship of the theorist to the object of knowledge," it meant abolishing the mediating role of the party with its exclusive access to knowledge of reality.[63] According to this interpretation, artistic trends should not be influenced by politics, or, more specifically, by party resolutions and regulations, but by the artists themselves. By contrast with the Stalinist model of culture, there was now a retreat from the obligatory commitment to one aesthetic and an openness to internal diversity ("the 'unity' of socialist art cannot be based on the uniformity or dominance of one conception, but on diverse personal, group, and generational concepts"),[64] as well as an undistorted (true) reckoning with the Stalinist past and the socialist present. Along with this, the post-Stalinist intellectuals also sought the greatest degree of financial and political independence from influential party and state authorities.[65]

Although the intensity of this kind of characterization of art declined or grew in connection with official ideological campaigns (such as those against revisionism in the second half of the 1950s, against cultural and political magazines after 1964, etc.) and pressure from the party apparatus on the cultural sphere, the idea of a specific nature and thus also a special position for art in socialist society was still one of the crucial traits of the post-Stalinist conception of it. For example, the literary scholar Jan Cigánek proclaimed in 1957 that politics and art are two separate forms of social consciousness.[66] Whereas, ten years later, the cultural journalist A. J. Liehm called for the abolition of existing dictates of power and dictates of the market, which would have meant that culture could be realized as an entirely free sphere for the first time in history, transcending both the socialist and capitalist models.[67]

The activities of individual artistic and creative associations naturally developed out of this conception, and while proclaiming their independence from politics in the post-Stalinist era, they actively and relatively confidently entered into it. However, for our purposes it is more important that this concept made it possible to view art not only institutionally, at the level of artistic associations, but also as a creative act with the potential to change the present social reality. If, as Ivan Sviták had it, the axiom of artistic creation is *"creative freedom, unlimited by either internal or external censorship,"* art was also going to become a basic condition for the emergence of a society that would be richer and more diverse in all ways than the previous one.[68] As Kalivoda wrote, "socialist art not only can endure, but downright requires a number of 'aesthetic standpoints' in its programs."[69] At the same time, art's direct and unlimited contact with the surrounding reality arose from an explicitly formulated awareness "of the recognizability and changeability of the world."[70]

A MIRROR OF MODERN CIVILIZATION

To what extent contemporary art speaks to the nature of the modern era and of modern human beings, and to what extent it can shape and change them were among the questions advanced by Karel Kosík. He discerned a seemingly incongruous pair of authors—Jaroslav Hašek and Franz Kafka—as distinctive native contributors to this discussion. Kosík considered Hašek's humor and satire and Kafka's anatomy of the alienated world of offices as high-quality testimonies about the modern era and human destiny in general. Both authors reveal and disrupt the absurd machinery of contemporary civilization, but at the same time they also bring its human dimension to light. In the face of the alienated mechanisms of bureaucracy, power, and state violence—whether military or administrative—both Hašek and Kafka depict an individual who refuses to submit to them. If man has created this world, only he can change it, even if his experiments meet with varying degrees of success. While Kafka's protagonists do not break through the shell of the objectified world, Hašek's character Švejk manages to maintain his humanity amid general havoc and ruination. In this way, Hašek wants to illustrate that man is not reducible "to a thing, to objectified products and relationships."[71]

In this spirit, the Marxist humanists turned their attention more toward questions of alienation and an alternative to total self-destruction instead of analyzing ideological differences between socialism and capitalism. By contrast with their critical relationship to existentialism (see chapter 3), the universality of art was one of the basic criteria for their understanding of culture in discussions of that period.[72] Both Western art and art from the Soviet bloc were evaluated without distinction in most of the period cultural and political magazines.[73] This means that it was approached without a priori judgments that assigned "quality" to socialist productions and "limitations" to bourgeois ones.[74] In this spirit, the art historian Luděk Novák declared, "There is not a double perspective for humanity, for [humanity] is one."[75] Hence, the effort to introduce modern art from capitalist states in Czechoslovakia and to showcase Western "progressive," though not necessarily exclusively communist, intellectuals and artists such as Jean-Paul Sartre and Ernst Fischer.[76] For example, the former stated at the World Congress on General Disarmament and Peace in Moscow in July 1962 that in the face of the threat of humanity's self-destruction in an atomic conflict, the obsolete era of confrontation must be replaced by peaceful coexistence and constructive overcoming of differences. If the recent militarization of culture was characterized by the defense and isolation of one's own viewpoints, then peaceful coexistence must be accompanied by a new form of competition—"struggles within unity"—expressed through open discussion.[77]

In 1964 the monthly periodical *Plamen* organized a debate aptly titled "Peaceful Coexistence and the Battle of Ideas," in which Ernst Fischer followed up on Sartre's speech by labeling the Stalinist era a period when Marxists "failed to receive, assimilate, process, and enrich our Marxist view with all the new things that happened in the world, in the economy, in science." Sartre spoke about dialectically overcoming the intellectual products of the West (sociology, psychoanalysis, and the Nouveau Roman), which "scientistic Marxism" (Stalinism) had defended itself against in the era of confrontation and now had to be honestly reckoned with.[78]

The thesis of peaceful coexistence in culture did not just mean importing bourgeois ideologies, as later "normalization" (post-1968) analyses claimed. It arose out of a sincere belief in the universality of art that can identify problems of the time and contribute to their resolutions. Naturally, the sense of threat that grew stronger after the Cuban crisis in 1962 was also found outside the circle of Marxist humanists. It was concisely expressed by the director Jaromil Jireš in his explication of the film *Křik* (The Cry): "We live in a time when man's most intimate experiences are connected with the mainstream of world events. This has always been the case, but the intensity of this connection is more immediate than at any time previously. . . . Humanity has never been faced with such divergent possibilities for development: before a war so destructive. And so disgraceful for its futility. At the same time, before the prospect of a society that would eliminate the causes and justifications of wars. These two outlying facts powerfully affect our conscious and unconscious mindset."[79]

The literary scholar Květoslav Chvatík spoke in a similar way about how a great deal of effort would still be required to master humanity's destructive tendencies.[80] And in his turn, Ivan Sviták interpreted small-stage performances of satirical improvisation (*divadlo malých forem*) as pitting humor against "absurdity, against the possibility of humanity exterminating itself."[81] The real possibility of self-destruction was also among the main motivations for the Marxist-Christian dialogue that developed in western Europe as well as in Czechoslovakia, after starting in the second half of the 1950s. As far back as April 1967, the topic of "collective amnesia" was one of the main questions at the international dialogical conference in Mariánské Lázně.[82]

The alienation of human beings in modern society, which was the second universalist point of convergence, was also discussed at the above-mentioned symposium. The scope of the topic of alienation not only encompassed the economic dimension of *alienated surplus value*, but also the overcoming of the absurdity of human existence and modernity's alienating mechanisms. While Marx demonstrated that alienation has a dual character—on the one hand, a portion of the value produced by the immediate producer is appropriated by the owner of the means of production (surplus value); on the other hand, due to the repetitive nature of labor in industrial production, the worker cannot and does not relate to the product as an expression of their own creative powers—both the humanists and the techno-optimists primarily drew on the latter aspect of Marx's conception. The Marxist humanists were thus less interested in the alienating effect that arose out of the division of society into the owners of the means of production and the owners of (mere) labor power. Instead, they were more concerned about the alienation that was the product of the mass, consumerist, and instrumental nature of modern industrial society, as we have already touched upon in chapter 3. However, this question transcended the division into the Eastern-socialist and Western-capitalist blocs, and thus formed a kind of keystone for common critical reflections on the destructive impacts of the modern era.

In the shared beliefs of the humanists, progressive artistic trends of their periods expressed "alienation and objectification, in order to warn man and rouse him to fight for true humanity."[83] It is no coincidence that the author of the above statement, Květoslav Chvatík, considered Franz Kafka's works an example of this kind of art; nor is it surprising that at the international conference on Kafka that took place in Liblice in May 1963, the theme of alienation was much discussed. In accordance with the contemporary interpretation and with the personal participation of Ernst Fischer Kafka was characterized as a "poet of our absurdities," and proclaimed to be a supremely relevant creator, whose work was a "tragic document of the situation of man in our times" that disrupted the world of alienation by breaking the walls of ideological rigidity.[84] Even though a statement like "because alienation exists, Kafka is relevant in our country as well" seemed bold at the time and led to a cultural and political rift with the German Democratic Republic,[85] it was entirely in keeping with the above-discussed concept of art and culture as a universal sphere that identified the negative aspects of modern civilization at a general level. At the same time, we cannot overlook a certain shift from the general (modern civilization) to a specific historical form (the socialism that existed at that time) and to a critique of it. In the same spirit, Chvatík pointed out the fact that the destructive nature of modernity is not foreign to socialist countries and, in connection with Herbert Marcuse's Freudian Marxism, Robert Kalivoda spoke of a necessity to neutralize the destructive tendencies found within socialism: "It is obvious that social aggression, a tendency towards power and to social oppression will also manifest itself in a society founded on socialist ownership."[86]

THE SUBJECT OF REVOLUTIONARY CHANGE

Modern culture not only identified alienation, the post-Stalinist intellectuals were also convinced that it actively accepted the challenge of modern civilization, humanized it, and created space for the consummation of Marx's ideas of the free self-realization of the human individual. As one of the key elements of Marxist humanism, culture was thus perceived in a processual spirit as a continuous liberation of human beings aiming toward a "new historical type of man," which was distinct from an animal or a machine.[87] The idea that this radically humanizing process is accomplished through art was shared across the post-Stalinist humanist intelligentsia: it appears in Sviták, in Kalivoda, and in the documents of the Union of Czechoslovak Writers (Svaz československých spisovatelů), and in 1968 we even find it in official materials produced by the Ministry of Culture.[88] As Chvatík put it in 1965, socialist culture is about overcoming alienation, fetishism, and the negative impacts of the technicist world, and about abolishing the opposition between high and low culture and all in support of "strengthening the new social bonds of emancipated, fully developed personalities."[89]

However, if art were to fulfill a humanizing function, the relationship to a nondeformed portrayal of the past and the present had to be clarified. In the effort to overcome the Stalinist conception, the post-Stalinists did not offer a new and more truthful description based on an undistorted reflection of reality. Despite that—or perhaps because—socialist realism only nominally embraced the theory of reflection and instead of the reality of the Stalinist period it merely captured a fictitious reality, the criterion of truthfulness could no longer be judged on the basis of a direct correlation of the work of art to reality. Although those who aimed to capture truth did not give up the ambition of a holistic view, at the level of art this tended to mean a right to identify deformations and the fragmentary character of the modern world. In this regard, some of the Marxist humanists departed from the demand for a holistic capture of the work of art from approaches promoted by György Lukács,[90] who was among the prominent, sought-after authorities at that time.

In connection with the relationship between modern art and reality, Ivan Sviták aptly applied the metaphor of a "shattered mirror," which can fulfill cognitive and social functions only if it arises as an inherent need from within art itself.⁹¹ In other words, the humanizing aspect of art would be lost at the moment when humanism became a program determined from the outside. For Sviták, modern art was primarily about the capturing of beauty—the concreteness of truth—of the modern world, which "must . . . be contradictory, brutal, tender, superficial and deep, must be a reflection of the conflicts of modern people, have the cacophonic jazz rhythm of our life, the horror of concentration camps and the mushrooms of atomic explosions, must be everything, just not a harmonious idyll of toothless happiness."⁹² In this regard, Kalivoda went even further. Building on a Marxist development of Mukařovský's structuralist approach to the aesthetic function—which he presented as a "pure anthropological value"—he asserted that art can exist only as an autonomous shaping of reality, as its aesthetic-deformative appropriation, which, even when based on factually mistaken premises, can still be seen as a "real humanity that arouses and deserves human attention."⁹³

The Marxist humanists did not understand culture only as a means for liberating themselves *from* Stalinism. Despite a strong social need to reckon with Stalinist injustice, they did not consider the past as binding. This was one of the reasons that Sviták admired contemporary art. In his view, it was mainly cinematography that was able to dialectically connect objective-analytical and poetic visions, which is why it replaced the artistic-critical function of the novel in the modern society of the twentieth century. The Czech New Wave, oriented to the present with its tragicomic or existential absurdity, represented exactly this type of art for him.⁹⁴

The humanists perceived emancipation *into* a fully developed human being as part of social-human praxis,⁹⁵ which meant not as a passive recorder of an already-created and stable world at the level of conventionalization (in Peter Wagner's term), but above all as an active project. To a significant extent, this claim overlapped with the ethos of Stalinism (i.e., with the artist's active engagement in creating the new world). This was similar to the process of cognition; however, here the relationship of the artist and the intellectual to reality itself had changed. If Stalinism was founded on the mediating role of the party, or perhaps on the authority of Stalin himself, now there was an active grasp of reality by actors who give shape and form to social reality through their cultural activities.

If we go beyond Michal Kopeček's monograph *Hledání ztraceného smyslu revoluce* (Quest for the Revolution's Lost Meaning),⁹⁶ we could say that in Czechoslovak post-Stalinism a process of seeking the revolutionary subject instead of seeking the sense of revolution was taking place. This is similar to what was also happening in the West, where—at least in the eyes of the Marxist humanists—culture (in the sense of art and critical thinking) had replaced the working class. However, except for considerations of workers' self-government in 1968, the revolutionary transformation did not consist in bringing about fundamental social and economic changes, but in realizing the Marxist ideal of the attainment of the "harmonious and fully developed human being." Not only was the cancellation of the proletariat after the elimination of division of labor absent among subjects addressed by Marxist humanism, but the nature of the nationalization of the means of production under socialism went practically unchallenged (see chapter 6). Additionally, it was implied in post-Stalinist texts that with the completion of the social revolution, the proletariat had "fulfilled" its historic task and in socialism the formative revolutionary process would arrive at a new level, where it was going to be realized by different agents: science, in the case of technooptimists, and active artistic, or by extension also philosophical work for the humanists.

If we return to Kalivoda's reference to the presence of destructive mechanisms in socialism, it was accompanied by a program proposal to transform the various forms of inevitable social aggression into a principle of permanent "emancipatory counteraggression" (see chapter 3).[97] This actually meant the creation of an emancipatory "revolutionary aggression" with an "optimal humanistic and humanizing" value,[98] which Kalivoda considered the most difficult task along the way to a human individual's full self-realization. Emancipation is understood here principally as a creative activity that emerges out of the liberation of the aesthetic principle from conformity to social demand ("the servile feudal relationship to truth").[99]

Specifically, it was a matter of bringing about a state in which artistic creation would not be conditioned by any external influences and where, as Květoslav Chvatík summarized, its "practical functionality" is denied.[100] Only when this condition is fulfilled can art act as an epistemological and shaping subject, as an "extreme humanization of reality."[101] The concept of an aesthetic function as an "empty principle" (Mukařovský) was thus exalted in reaction to Stalinism, not as purposelessness and radical relativization, but as an opening up of the true formative productivity in the relationship between human beings and their creative work. For Kalivoda, this was not the closed subjectivity of the artistic perspective, of art for art's sake, but an interference into social reality in which art revealed itself as a "great potential social force" that continually expanded "human freedom" as a "reservoir of forces to defend the fullness and freedom of human existence."[102] Only art was able to achieve this kind of emancipatory character because (by contrast with technology) it was able to rid itself of the attachment to external functionality that was so typical for modern society. Consequently, art was supposed to be simultaneously autonomous and socially engaged.

Therefore, the revival of interest in the function of "accursed" (*maudit*) and avant-garde poetry. Kalivoda saw it as the fulfillment of Marx's originally abstract idea of the "liberation of man with concrete human content."[103] Even though avant-garde art itself speaks out against culture, Kalivoda sees it as having high cultural value as a contemporary form of self-realization. In connection with socialism (economically speaking) these are works that fulfill the permanent need to fight for the freedom of human individuals, a struggle that is never completed and always heading into the future.[104] Karel Kosík spoke similarly about modern art at the end of the 1950s and beginning of the 1960s when he considered it a principle that, in socialist union with the human element, would create a "new renaissance; a new historical synthesis."[105]

Chapter 4 has dealt with attempts to connect modernity, which is always contaminated with a certain kind of elitism at the political and aesthetic levels, with the concept of folkness (*lidovost*). In chapter 6, we will elaborate on the tension between calls for a broader socialist collectivity and elitism of post-Stalinist intellectuals. However, at this point we want to emphasize the direct connection between culture and social change. This was not alien even to Stalinist party intellectuals and artists who shared the idea that they were taking part in the revolutionary transformation of human beings and society. If post-Stalinism again took after Stalinism in this respect, it still differed in the role it attributed to criticism. The difference between them is aptly characterized by Marx's eleventh thesis on Feuerbach: "Philosophers have hitherto only interpreted the world in various ways, but the point is to change it."[106] Whereas the Stalinist era was founded on change that was determined by official party lines, now there was spontaneous grassroots criticism of contemporary socialism. Thus, unlike during Stalinism, engaging in philosophical thinking was an activity that stemmed from one's own cognitive ability and not from an impulse passed down from higher party echelons. Ivan Sviták aptly characterized the principle of post-Stalinist engagement in the mid-1950s: "If today's philosopher is not a critical thinker about the need for transforming the world and about the real problems of our time, if he is not a person who lives an idea and examines it with his own life, then the only thing that makes him deserving of our respect is his gray hair, nothing more."[107]

Karel Kosík developed a similar idea in *Dialectics of the Concrete*. His exposition begins by introducing the category of "pseudo-concreteness" (*pseudokonkrétnost*), which we already presented earlier as the petrified world created by man with seemingly fixed and unchanging rules. In Kosík's view, such a world—a product of human praxis—must be known ("demystified"), broken apart ("destroyed"), and overcome by revolutionary praxis. Destruction of pseudo-concreteness must follow these three steps: the "humanization of man" in the sense of a social revolution, a process of dialectical thinking that pulls back the veil of deformed reality, and the realization of truth as a process in which every human individual participates without representation.[108] Its application can serve to illustrate what a post-Stalinist dismantling of the Stalinist world might look like.

The first step, in the form a social revolution, was considered to have been fulfilled to all intents and purposes through the existence of the socialist state itself. The second step, consisting of revealing pseudo-concrete reality, could be perceived as a disruption and "demystification" of the official party discourse and the obligatory nature of party politics. The third step, which relies on the human individual for realization of the truth in completing the revolutionary process, could potentially disrupt the Leninist concept of the Communist Party as the avant-garde of the working class with its epistemological superiority and internal authoritarian hierarchy.

Here, the human being stood as a self-assured existence, aware of their historicity in the sense of the ability to transform surrounding reality despite inherited historical conditions. Post-Stalinist socialism thus did not consist in a mechanical overcoming (a simple rejection) of Stalinism, but in a specific dialectical revolutionary process that transforms the entire society.[109] Kosík claimed that there are two ways of getting to the heart of reality and revealing it in its entirety (*concrete totality*). He put the main emphases on philosophy, specifically dialectical-critical thinking, and on art, whose purpose was to break apart pseudo-concreteness. The demystifying role of modern art here functioned as a main theme accompanying thought during the revolutionary transformation of the world. It was in *Dialectics of the Concrete* that Kosík, with reference to Franz Kafka and Bertolt Brecht, claimed that "one of the main principles of modern art, poetry, and theatre, fine art, and film is 'violence' against the stereotypes of everyday life, that is, the destruction of pseudoconcreteness."[110]

For Kosík as well as the other Marxist humanists, culture does not stand alone as an area independent from society, where it only produces artistic artifacts or timeless masterpieces. Rather, the Marxist conception is as a sphere of human activity that can have a revolutionary character, and thus also an eminently political one.[111] Although Kosík would have preferred to oppose the second characterization because he himself decried the replacement of politics with culture, his concept of the relationship between culture and social change affords the best-elaborated example of this type of period thinking.

Despite his distrust of the artistic avant-garde, which was in contrast with the positions of Chvatík, Kalivoda, Sviták, Josef Zumr, and Růžena Grebeníčková,[112] he remained a thinker who defended revolutionary change in which modern art participates. This not only made it possible for art (along with philosophy) to expose the absurdity and manipulative nature of modern civilization, but at the same time to transform it in the spirit of emancipatory progress, and thus cocreate a new type of socialist modern society. Kosík's statements from the late 1960s aptly illustrate the overall concept of Marxist humanism's relationship to culture: "In the fundamental question of Who is man? lay a key critical and political moment in Czech culture. That is its politicalness, criticalness, and revolutionary nature. . . . The man of Czech culture of the previous decade is a potential revolutionary because he simply cannot live in this disposable and manipulable system."[113]

TECHNOLOGY OR THE HUMAN BEING?

The trite attribution of science as the techno-optimists' premiere value, and culture as that of the humanists whom we presented in the preceding section forces a perception of post-Stalinism as a clash of two opposing conceptions, as if in Czechoslovak post-Stalinism there had been a choice of a socialism that would be founded either on technology or on the free human being.

Despite the internal plurality of Marxist humanism, a relationship to modern civilization—or more precisely to a techno-optimistic interpretation of it—was very critical. Květoslav Chvatík, Robert Kalivoda, Karel Kosík, Ivan Sviták, and Josef Zumr all drew attention to the pitfalls of a modern civilization with technology and science as the prime drivers of social progress. On the one hand, they granted science an important place in the development of socialism, but on the other hand, they also pointed out the treacherous moments when it had been overestimated. Miroslav Kusý tersely summarized this attitude in a manuscript of the late 1960s: "The scientific-technical revolution extraordinarily multiplies man's forces, possibilities, and abilities, but man is still often unable to solve the problem of how to use these new forces, possibilities, and abilities to his benefit."[114] Thus, neither technology nor science could have the necessary liberating power to break through uncritical immediate connections with things and thereby create the necessary distance for critique or free creation, because for Marxist humanists both technology and science were still moving within the element of manipulating ready-made things.

Naturally, this does not mean that the humanists would have rejected technological and scientific progress as such in a romantic spirit, or that they would followed Heidegger's footsteps into hopeless tenets of *Zivilisations* or *Technologiekritik*, as we can observe happening in the West at that time. Neither science nor technology was denied the right to transform, or more precisely, engage in a certain form of active intervention in the world around. As Sviták wrote, "Contemporary technology has ontological significance as a formative force in the process of transforming the human type," and, "The modern fact is not a god, history, or politics, but technology." However, for the humanists, the result of technological activities could not be anything but a product with an instrumental character, whose only essence can be utilitarian function, that controls human individuals through "alienated forms of manipulation."[115]

Karel Kosík spoke directly about the danger that the original bureaucratic form of dictatorship would be replaced by a new mystification, a type of expert dictation that would generate new forms of manipulation and alienation. In his view, optimism for the concept of the scientific-technical revolution was entirely out of place, because the heralded change could not represent a qualitative historical breakthrough but could only copy long-established forms of modern European thinking based on the dominance of technical reason. Narrow scientific specialization leads to fragmentation of knowledge, which makes a comprehension of reality in its complexity and totality impossible. For this reason, modern science cannot become a revolutionary subject either: scientists are mere specialists who work in their narrow fields with specific types of exact knowledge but no awareness of the meaning of the whole. The absence of this awareness in the project of the scientific-technical revolution created the threat of negative developmental alternatives or degeneration that run counter to the liberating purpose of socialism.[116]

The humanists pitted art and philosophy—as spheres where human beings have the possibility to relate truly creatively (art) and critically (philosophy) to their present time—against the techno-optimist vision in which the primary agent of revolutionary change was technology and science. Culture, then, in the sense of art and critical thinking, was to become a regulator for the alienating character of technology.[117] This was a kind of cultivating counterweight,[118] which not only affords human individuals space for their own development but also protects this space from the manipulative nature of technology. Kosík's essay "What Is Central Europe?" ends with the question of whether "Europe, including its center, will someday become one great *caricature* or Europeanism, because it succumbed to the *Gleichschaltizing* power of a new, modern symbiosis."[119]

The techno-optimists, in turn, clearly took exception to various forms of humanist criticism of technology and science. This was not because they considered them to be substantially in error or because they viewed themselves as enlightened advocates of a scientistic faith in technological progress. For them, the critique of technology was justified in a certain sense, but this sense had historical limits that ended with industrial society, which they saw as having truly pitted human beings against machines, or perhaps into an unnaturally inverted servile relationship to technology. And the techno-optimists particularly emphasized that the criticism was aimed against a *specific* (i.e., historical) form of technology, which with the advent of the scientific-technical revolution would lose its justification (Richta). The old form of technology ruined human power, but the new one was going to develop it and afford it sufficient space for self-development. The necessary rational reorganization of human society—including the integration of science—was therefore not a "utopia" in the eyes of the techno-optimists, nor was it "machinism," but the "possibility" and even "necessity" of simultaneously transforming industrial civilization.[120]

In relation to the above, the following motto of Radoslav Selucký was typical: not less, but "more automation," and more technology was needed. In this view, the problem is not "overtechnologization, but rather undertechnologization of our society."[121] According to the techno-optimists, criticism aimed at the alienating and manipulative nature of technology was also unjustified because it was based on an overly abstract understanding of technology that failed to consider its qualitative determination and the social relations in which its individual forms arise. On the contrary, the true origin of the alienating effects of technology must be sought where technology is lacking, or where it is at a low level that cannot bring about full automation and thereby create sufficient leisure time for human development for its own sake.

It was precisely science and technology that embodied the areas of human activity within which and through which the techno-optimists claimed that fundamental transformations were to take place both in social organization and individuals. As Selucký put it, "Technology is an essential means to transform socialism into communism. Therefore, the mission of technology in socialist society is human to the utmost: it should be an aid to the development of the human personality." Kosík also agreed that "with the complexity of civilization, man must submit further and further spheres of his activity to automation in order to free up space and time for real human problems." However, in contrast to the scientific-technical revolution's claims, he also emphasized that there is also a sphere, "which cannot be automatized in the interest of mankind."[122]

5.8 AND 5.9. The economist and journalist Radovan Selucký (left) in a debate with Jiří Hermach on Czechoslovak TV in 1968. Copyright Archive of Czech TV.

Although each of these standpoints was based in entirely different perspectives, it cannot escape notice that a basic Marxist position advancing the ultimate aim of the full liberation of human creative potential is maintained in both. The essential difference lies in their starting points. Whereas the humanists thought of human development unconditionally, or perhaps located the "condition" as well as place and source of liberation within human beings, the techno-optimists were relying on an external condition that was finally going to liberate them. Nevertheless, this "outer" element was not found entirely outside of human nature. Science as a tool for change was one of the high points of human activity for the techno-optimists, but it was never supposed to be an end in itself.

This difference in conditionality and nonconditionality most strongly manifested itself in the position of art and culture that the two movements attributed to them. The techno-optimists based their view in the scientific revolution as an essential external condition for a cultural revolution. However, the humanists—as we have seen with Chvatík and Kalivoda—were themselves relying on an externally unconditioned development of art as a reservoir of "social forces" that led toward freedom. The relationship between technology and culture or, to put a finer point on it, the aesthetic artistic sphere was usually formulated in terms of utility and enjoyment during leisure time; that is, in a radically different capacity than it had with the humanists, for whom the sphere of art (and philosophy as well) had become a privileged approach to questioning and problematizing human (social) existence as such. From the perspective of the scientific-technical revolution, art and culture more generally were always to be found in a position that is dependent on or at least socially constructed on the basis of technology, which practically excluded it from any critical significance. In a contrasting approach to the connection between art and its aesthetic function, the humanists attempted to break through the close association of the category of enjoyment with its counterpart, the category of utility, and to prove that art can (and should) also contain critical and creative potential, which fully enables the holistic development of human beings. They believed that science and technology fragmented individuals, because they necessarily subjected them to the division of labor and thus to potentially alienating effects.

Yet, despite the differences described above, it is impossible to miss the way that both these intellectual currents still shared the same intellectual space, where the idea of the fully liberated human being stood at the very center. Whereas one group (the techno-optimists) arrived there on the basis of a full development of external conditions (science), the second group situated the movement of liberation within the internal condition, within the human being itself—or more precisely, within that sphere of human activity that alone can posit its purpose within itself, and thus directly develop creative human capacities.

Both approaches worked simultaneously with time and the historicity of the realized ideal. For the humanists and techno-optimists alike, the Stalinist past delimited a space that was not merely a negation (rejection), but a truly dialectical overcoming of a previous stage of development. Their reflections on the development of socialism were equally focused on the future and envisaged a progressive, though not teleological realization of the ideal of human liberation. Of course, the emancipatory goal was not supposed to be realized from a future perspective to which the present should be subordinated, but through the present. Moreover, as in the analysis of conditions for liberation, here too, the same goal was reached from opposite ends of the time series analyzed. For the techno-optimists (Richta), the initial target of criticism was the past, from which the progressive ideal of industrial civilization was constructed, but for the humanists (Kosík and Kalivoda), it was the future that was criticized as a starting point and determining moment.

Thus, in our opinion, post-Stalinism is not characterized by processuality, which, according to Pavel Kolář reluctantly and ambiguously leads to utopia; it is a mode of thinking that displays anything but the wavering uncertainty caught between the "sins of the past and the promises of the future." If post-Stalinism could be described as replacing the programmatic processual utopia, as Kolář has suggestively indicated, then it is not in the sense of deprioritizing the goal in favor of "openness of history, contingency, and ambivalence,"[123] but in the sense of a process that is a continual—or dare we say truly "permanent"—revolutionizing of the present, which must again and again create and reformulate its goal (as we saw in all the studied intellectual currents—in Kosík and Kalivoda, as well as in Richta and Cibulka). Hence, uncertainty and randomness as two aspects of post-Stalinism are not only external, empirical determinations, which insert themselves between the present and the overshadowed goal, as Kolář's interpretation suggests, but entirely internal and reflected moments of the process itself. For post-Stalinism, Kolář de facto assumes this kind of conception of the process, which is determined by a goal that lies outside of it. It is therefore teleological, even though this goal is constantly postponed. Its present achievement is exposed to uncertainty or skepticism and the resulting turns to a "purer" or "more authentic" past, or by extension away from a great sweep of history and the masses to everyday life and individuals.[124] Here, and in chapter 2, we have attempted to demonstrate that the post-Stalinist conception of the process intended by the party intelligentsia was significantly different.

The internal reflexivity of its own processes is one of the key traits of organized modernity or historicity in the sense used by Peter Wagner and Alain Touraine. If these sociologists speak of modernity, or perhaps historicity, as stances that continually reevaluate their perspectives along the way to modern progress, then post-Stalinism—without regard for the partial differences between techno-optimism and humanism—is an example of precisely this. Taking inspiration from Wagner, we dare say that Czechoslovak post-Stalinism reacted to the challenges of modernization with its own conceptualization of modernity. In our estimation, this was an autonomous and distinctive emancipation project.

CHAPTER 6

BEYOND THE HORIZONS OF POST-STALINISM

Our present period is the result of a match lost by an entire generation, who had staked their lives on it—the generation raised on Stalinism failed to cross over and bring their country into non-Stalinist and post-Stalinist socialism. This goal, which was the only real objective in this country, was unclear to them; moreover, they didn't manage to develop a strategy for Czech society's further transition. Modern Czechs have been failing in polemics since even before March [of 1848] and in this sense, the most recent modern Czech Thermidor is more normal than abnormal. However, nothing is fated in human history, and we suffer from being excluded only because we have allowed ourselves to be excluded, because we failed to imprint a different shape on the course of things.

—ROBERT KALIVODA

The previous chapters of this book, divided into four basic topics, dealt with the post-Stalinist problematization of real structure (chapter 2), the definition of subjectivity (chapter 3), the paired categories of folkness and the nation (chapter 4), and revolutionary changes (chapter 5). In this chapter, we are no longer addressing Marxist orthodoxy with an emphasis on Stalinism. We also set aside neutrality in our analysis of post-Stalinist thought.

THE UNITY OF HISTORY

In the analyses offered earlier in the book, we demonstrated the importance of the party intellectuals' efforts to separate themselves from Marxist orthodoxy in shaping post-Stalinist thought. However, a certain paradox inheres in their idea of the unity and direction of history, which remained truly (orthodox) Marxist. Understandably, post-Stalinist thinkers criticized the Stalinist conception of history; however, they mainly reproached it the way its unity and historical development were conceived rather than for its essence. Neither the humanists nor the dialectical determinists or even the techno-optimists went beyond this horizon, though in their own ways they all gave it a more solid theoretical foundation and social significance.[1] And yet, as we shall see below, this had the negative consequence in a conviction of civilizational and national superiority.

A comparison with intellectual movements in the West at that time is relevant here. During the 1960s the West's left began to distance itself from the intellectual horizon of Marxist orthodoxy. However, the unity of history was not the only target of their critique: they also took aim at the concept of unity per se within philosophy. This change in the outlines of thinking took on its clearest contours in France, but it was also evident in Germany and outside Europe. Its most tangible consequence was the effort at a philosophical reflection on that which always escapes any systematization or totalization, but which remains its "basis."

In France this trend was personified in Michel Foucault, with his historical-philosophical analyses of the borderline experiences of madness, crime, and sexuality, which in Western (modern) civilization had been subjected to exclusion, normalization, and control. Besides his works on these topics, his powerfully discontinuous model of the history of Western thought was also very influential. In his late work, Roland Barthes came up with a concept of fragmented desires that defy their originally unifying function. Jacques Lacan introduced the "Real" as that which is displaced by foreclosure (rejection) from the symbolic order but, paradoxically, returns to the same place. Jacques Derrida created the concept of *différance*, which denotes not only the concept of differentiation but also the eternal postponement of the wholeness or fullness of meaning. Theodor W. Adorno had followed a similar inspiration in the conception of negative dialectics, which he applied in an effort to "save" the nonidentical, which Hegelian dialectics necessarily had to exclude in the totalizing process of concept formation. Here, it is noteworthy that, in contrast to Czechoslovak (and we dare say even all East European) Marxism, where Hegel's materialized dialectics enjoyed a renewed popularity, Hegel's legacy occupied a somewhat ambiguous position in the West and the Third World.

Foucault and Gilles Deleuze held the view that it is necessary to throw totalizing dialectics overboard as a historical burden; for Foucault, this is accomplished with the help of a very nontraditional version of positivism, whereas Deleuze attempted to replace Hegel's dialectics with a broadly conceived "vitalist" philosophical current. For Derrida, Lacan, and Adorno, totalizing dialectics had a dual nature: it was simultaneously the culprit and the liberator. Their perspective on dialectics is that it culminates the totalizing, unifying tendencies of philosophical thinking, while at the same time completely new horizons open within it.[2] However, we decline to create hierarchies here and proclaim the intellectual development of the West's left as superior or even more adequate to the era's social development. We consider assessments of this kind to be misleading; moreover, they fail to respect the differing political and historical contexts of Central and Eastern Europe.

In this context, we should not forget that regardless of the differences in approaches to the future direction of socialism, what the party intelligentsia all had in common was the idea of the superiority of the current trajectory of the socialist countries (especially Czechoslovakia), which they saw as confirmation of the progressive character of historical development. This idea, moreover, manifested in the smooth adoption of the official proclamation of socialism, which appeared to the post-Stalinist intellectuals as the materialization of an obviously more advanced reality than the previous stage of so-called people's democracy. It was also reflected in thinking about the humanist and techno-optimist varieties of socialism. In both cases, there was no doubt that Czechoslovak post-Stalinist development was part of the progressive arc of history. It was also the basis for "overcoming" (not rejecting) Stalinism, which ultimately led to accepting the Stalinist revolution as an essential and indeed necessary socioeconomic transformation. The same conception of the unity of history then prevented (not only) the Czechoslovak post-Stalinists from subjecting their present socialism to a more radical critique, which would focus on the ownership of the means of production or on alternative possibilities for historical development. Indications of such considerations only appeared briefly in the helter-skelter publication activity in Czechoslovakia in 1968. The scant reflections on socialism as state capitalism were therefore located outside the post-Stalinist party intelligentsia.[3]

In this book, we have tried to show how Czechoslovak post-Stalinists, in contrast to Marxist orthodoxy, have promoted a different conception of mediation that would contain a space for internal inconsistency, differentiation, internal unpredictability, and contingency. It is these moments of thought that should have shaken the understanding of history as a unified, total movement. Rather, it seems that post-Stalinists have here again encountered one of the antinomies they have failed to resolve, let alone articulate. It is as if, in the end, the aforementioned moments always had to give way to thinking in totalities in which contradictions, differentiations, and deviations ultimately existed only to drive the unified machine of history or at least keep it running. When such problematization did eventually occur, especially in the eventful years 1968–1969 (and it was far from a general phenomenon), it tended to take the form of skepticism, which sometimes took on a conservative tone expressed in various critiques of modern civilization (Kosík). That in the end this kind of thinking must have had devastating consequences, especially for political practice itself, seems obvious.

POLITICS

Although we have not dedicated even one chapter of this book primarily to political thought, we consider it necessary to comment at least briefly on the issue here at the end. In state socialism, the products of science and the arts became a political question. Some of those who could testify to this include Ivan Sviták, who was dismissed from the Institute of Philosophy and expelled from the Communist Party in 1964, the editors of the magazine *Tvář*, whose publication was stopped for political reasons at the beginning of 1966, or the New Wave cinema directors, who were occasionally pilloried for being ideologically unprincipled. Additionally, in the post-Stalinist era, many of the figures we have discussed took on the roles of public intellectuals and operated in the highest echelons of politics in 1968. Here are a few examples: in 1968 Miroslav Kusý accepted the position as head of the ideological department of the Central Committee of the Communist Party of Slovakia; Karel Kosík was a candidate for the Vysočany Congress of the Communist Party of Czechoslovakia, and in September 1968 he was co-opted into the Central Committee; in 1968 Ivan Sviták was one of the leading personalities in the civic-oriented group KAN-Klub which brought together engaged nonparty members; Radovan Richta took part in drafting the Communist Party's Action Program; and Zdeněk Mlynář, the only one among those named here who had been involved in elite politics for a longer period of time, was a member of the Presidium of the Central Committee in 1968. Several of our protagonists, such as Ján Bodnár, Irena Dubská, Zdeněk Javůrek, Robert Kalivoda, Ota Klein, Milan Průcha, Radoslav Selucký, Július Strinka, and Josef Zumr, also prepared the theses of the long-term program of the Communist Party of Czechoslovakia in 1968. This program, which was elaborated for an extraordinary congress of the KSČ, was prepared in a commission headed by Radovan Richta.[4]

However, we do not intend to devote ourselves to the communist reformists' political thought.[5] Instead, we will attempt to represent certain deficits that we perceive to have accompanied it. We consider the relationship of political thought or let us rather phrase it as "political imagination," to Leninism to be of crucial importance in this context. By "Leninism," we do not mean the entire theoretical complex derived from Lenin's writings on the functioning of the state and its mechanisms, on national issues, on the theory of revolution, on international relations, and so on; instead, we are referring to the way that the relationship of the Communist Party as the vanguard of the working class (and, after 1960, of socialist society) has been captured. The question is therefore to what extent the "leading role" of the party was criticized in the post-Stalinist intelligentsia's thinking, and if the critique did not play a role, what the consequences were.

In chapter 1, we discussed the importance of overcoming the original Leninist epistemology that was based on a privileged approach to cognition of reality for the sake of defining post-Stalinist reflexivity and internal plurality. This resulted in a multiplication of epistemological subjects, in which the party leadership lost its sovereign position, and the political dimension of Leninism was somewhat more ambivalent. On the one hand, as in the case of cognition, there was a disruption of Leninism as an avant-garde movement in the strict sense and demands appeared for participation in the establishment of political strategies. On the other hand, this post-Stalinist disruption did not lead to a rejection of Lenin's understanding of politics as a whole. Based on an analysis elaborated by Pavel Machonin's sociological team, Michael Voříšek demonstrated how—contrary to Lenin's idea about the Communist Party—the so-called progressive core, which was supposed to look beyond the intelligentsia and also recruit the most qualified, soulful, and politically engaged workers, was coming to the fore in sociologists' conceptions of the 1960s.[6] However, we should not be confused by Voříšek's legitimate claim that in this concept the party's leading role was taken over by this progressive core and the party was left with more of an organizational role. Despite the revision of Leninism formulated in this way, even for Machonin it was impossible to think about politics without the party. For example, we use Lubomír Nový's reflection on philosophy and politics, in which he rhapsodized about highly qualified management, about the concept of party spirit as a pure and practical expertise, and about the communist solution for the scientific-technical revolution, naturally with the proviso that the party is the "leading political force of the entire socialist community."[7]

One element of the activation of party members after the Twentieth Congress was the proclamation of a return to Leninism, which at least rhetorically supported the activities of the lower echelons of the party hierarchy. As we have already stated several times, in contrast to Stalinism by that time, an overarching normative interpretation of what Leninism really means was lacking. Nikita Khrushchev did not simply begin writing new "questions of Leninism" after which the vacant space was filled with interpretations by party intellectuals acting in the spirit of party activism. Thus, the expression of "true Leninism" could not continue being limited only to the official lines given by the KSČ, but became part of a broader party debate, which the ideological authorities tried to correct from the top down, but their attempts at regulating it always failed. Post-Stalinist Leninism took on various forms, although at least in the years 1956–1960 the irreplaceable leading role of the KSČ remained their basic touchstone. There are "three cornerstones of Marxism," Karel Kosík wrote in 1957: "The dictatorship of the proletariat, the leading role of the party, and proletarian internationalism."[8] A year later, Ivan Sviták reassured his critics that "the leading role of the party" is unquestionable for him.[9]

Party intellectuals welcomed the officially proclaimed return to Leninism through the decentralization of the party's management, especially the state agencies, and the renewal of the principles of internal party debate at the level of "democratic centralism." However, while the leaders of the KSČ were very careful not to be swept away by a rigorously applied "Leninist critique," the post-Stalinist Marxists took the concepts seriously all the way to their final ramifications, including an open debate within the party before the adoption of a resolution (democratic centralism). In contrast to the vaguely worded strategy put forth by the party leadership, the intellectuals called for the application of Leninist principles here and now. Kosík declared that "a return to Leninism cannot be a step backwards. [. . .] The entire problem consists in tackling issues in the *present time* using the Leninist method and in a Leninist spirit."[10]

However, as in other areas of thought, the post-Stalinist intelligentsia's approach to political Leninism also underwent some changes. While in the second half of the 1950s party intellectuals referred to documents from Chinese congresses when defining "true Leninism,"[11] backed by the claim that this doctrine represented the alpha and omega of political thought for the overwhelming majority of the post-Stalinist intelligentsia, a clear retreat from this position can already be observed in the early 1960s. Until 1968, this retreat was not manifested in a direct polemic with the Leninist conception of politics, but took the form of a change in vocabulary and topics. The journalism in cultural and political magazines provides many examples of this, such as debates over Hegel's intellectual legacy or about bureaucratism—these were in keeping with the period renaissance of Leninism and were accompanied by several references to Lenin as an unquestionable authority. Yet, after 1960, treatises on specifically Leninist aspects of politics become rarer, which can clearly be seen in debates on enterprise management or the scientific-technical revolution, and in journalism by the Marxist humanists, where we can trace a tendency toward public engagement through the arts and culture from the beginning of the 1960s (see chapter 5).[12]

Besides the different intellectual development within the post-Stalinist intelligentsia, there was a range of other factors that influenced this development. The proclamation of the socialist constitution, which we have mentioned before, played a certain role in bringing the sense of a new socialist quality. So did the permanent conflicts and disputes of the party intelligentsia with the ideological apparatus of the KSČ Central Committee, which attempted to establish its right to hegemonic interpretation of Leninist political principles through repeated campaigns within the Czechoslovak de-Stalinization development (for example, the campaign against revisionism in 1957–1959). Last, but not least—and the critique of "actually existing" socialism was probably right in pinpointing this motif—there was the influence of non-Marxist intellectual traditions. It is also necessary to reckon with a transfer of ideas from the new Western left, which had jettisoned the Leninist vocabulary of communist parties.

Of course, all the above does not mean that post-Stalinism had done away with Leninism altogether after 1960; this is where the normalization criticism of the early 1970s was wrong. For instance, when we focus on the works of the legal philosophers it cannot escape our notice that the definition of politics remains Leninist in a certain sense. The space dedicated to the human individual and his participation in the institutional improvement of socialist society—beginning with law (Michal Lakatoš) and state organizations and ending with the National Front—should not tempt us into hasty evaluations. In chapter 3, we already pointed out that the human being is always meant here in relation to institutions, and never as an entirely autonomous subject. Despite the calls for multiplicity and internal diversity, the last resort of political unity, which was an essential condition for the existence of the socialist establishment, was not forgotten. In this spirit, a primary topic for Mlynář, František Šamalík, and Kusý was the question of governance—not in the narrow sense of management, but in the sense of setting basic social priorities and policies. In accordance with period sociological understanding of modern societies, the authors address subjects of participation, activity, efficiency, bureaucracy, and so forth, but in the end they still placed the main emphasis on the social dimension of governance because it was one of the fundamental features of state socialism. As Mlynář aptly pointed out, "The requirement to abolish the social conducting of the social forces of production (conducting that is done by the state) in the name of the 'liberation' of man as a citizen and holder of an independent 'inalienable right' to private ownership of anything (and thus also of the social forces of production) would be a ridiculous requirement [that is] utopian in a reactionary way, [as well as] politically counterrevolutionary."[13]

The fact that the social dimension of governance, despite the ways its content might be discussed and negotiated, was always guaranteed and expressed for them by the party, testifies to Leninist affiliation of these authors more persuasively than anything else. This was the reason that Šamalík, on the one hand, spoke of the unique role for the free activities of intellectuals, but on the other hand, he related intellectual value to "conformism to the organic goals of the institution, to the historical process, and to the powers that the institution 'expresses.'" Inspired by Antonio Gramsci, he interpreted this "organic conformism" as "responsible freedom." The control of intellectual activity should take care not to disturb the unity, but at the same time it must not hobble the activity of thinking. This duality in the functioning of an institution founded on controlled reflexivity—activity and its critical evaluation, discipline, and initiative—should have been inherent in post-Stalinist socialism.[14]

Lenin's direct or mediated presence cannot be circumscribed only to the circle of legal philosophers. It also appears in Lubomír Sochor, who is mainly associated with Marxist humanism, thanks to his translations of the works of KarlMarxism with those of Korsche, György Lukács, and Antonio Gramsci, and in Jaroslav Šabata, a party intellectual and functionary from Brno who later become a politician in 1968. Despite differing evaluations of Lenin's philosophical legacy, Šabata and Sochor agreed that Lenin was the type of thinker who was capable of "perfectly penetrating into the inner structure of revolutionary praxis" and that he "reached the greatest maturity as a theorist of imperialism, revolution, and the dictatorship of the proletariat."[15] The fact that Šabata's and Sochor's texts are equally dedicated to Lenin and Gramsci is not just coincidence. As we have already indicated with Šamalík, interpretation of the Italian Marxist played an important role in relation to Lenin. Referring to Palmiro Togliatti, Šabata called for a "correct reading" of Gramsci as a Leninist thinker, noting that the process of overcoming Stalinism ought to consist of nothing other than a semantically updated "revolutionary praxis."[16] In Mlynář and Šamalík's reception of Gramsci, they did not take inspiration from his theory of cultural hegemony or of the historical bloc, as the new left in the West and the Czechoslovak Marxist humanists had; instead, they drew upon the interpretation of the Communist Party in the spirit of a modern Machiavellian prince, which meant the primary strategist and guarantee of unity. It was compared with an orchestra conductor who "has the entire score in front of him and creates the conception of social activity," because "consent and activity assume an organic connection between the leaders and the led."[17]

Some of the post-Stalinists relied on Gramsci's realistic observation that no politics can manage without manipulative techniques.[18] From

6.1. Zdeněk Mlynář, the head of an interdisciplinary research team that was working on a theoretical elaboration of reforms proposed for the Czechoslovak political system. He is pictured here with his daughter Milena at the Prague Zoo. Copyright Milena Bartlová.

this perspective, in June 1965 Mlynář criticized the main thesis, or rather the conception of politics contained in Karel Kosík's *Dialectics of the Concrete*. He considered its fundamental shortcoming to be the assignment of politics to the sphere of "pseudo-concreteness," which is distinguished by a fetishized praxis of everyday living. In Mlynář's view, this conception only affords politics manipulative functions in the form of "dirty haggling [Marx]," which deprived it of any share in human emancipation or in the realization of the individual within socialism. Even though in socialist politics, forms of manipulation that benefit the whole at the expense of the interest of individuals do and must appear (and they are immanent in all forms of politics), it does not not necessarily mean that politics as such should be confined to the sphere of pseudo-concreteness, in which the human being is necessarily and solely an object of manipulation."[19]

BEYOND THE HORIZONS OF POST-STALINISM

In chapter 5, we pointed out that Kosík's revolutionary idea (the destruction of pseudo-concreteness) was not a program in the Leninist sense of the word. This vision of change depended on authentic human activity that overcomes the "conception of politics as a calculable and rational technique, as scientifically predictable manipulation with human material."[20] Thus, the party politics that put human emancipation into practice in the name of the proletariat was not considered to be a revolutionary activity, but critical thinking in the form of a real dialectical philosophy (authentic Marxism) or free artistic work, primarily modern art was.

However, Kosík was aware that if art and philosophy did not want to risk losing their critical value they should not simply stand in for politics, as had been the case of Czech culture in the nineteenth century.[21] Therefore, even in the late 1960s, he sought a new definition of politics that could come to life in the redefinition of the original revolutionary people: an alliance of workers, students, and the intelligentsia (see chapter 4). Even though our dear colleague Ivan Landa justifiably speaks of a Gramscian search for a "historical bloc," in this place we assume that Mlynář's criticism of Kosík's (non)conception of politics also had its rationale.[22] If Kosík indirectly defines politics as a sphere of manipulation in *Dialectics of the Concrete*, in "Our Current Crisis," its concept is unclear, or at most there is an evident search for new forms. On the one hand, it seeks to establish a historical bloc of "revolutionary wisdom and wise revolutionary" spirit; but on the other hand, definitions that are too abstract prevail: politics means nonmanipulation, unlimited activities by members and nonmembers of the party, and both nations share the implicit goal of creating a unified political nation that realizes a socialist Czechoslovakia. Similar ambiguity is typical not only in Kosík's work but also in that of the other Marxist humanists. A positive definition of politics is ultimately only to be found in a few vaguely phrased journalistic pieces about workers' self-management.[23] Under the influence of Machiavelli and Gramsci, the post-Stalinist definition of politics was limited to the idea that it would be necessary to consciously shape the kind of politicians who would not be afraid to work toward the abolition of politics in its original Machiavellian and therefore manipulative form.[24]

We agree with Ivan Landa that unlike the legal philosophers and the Leninist reading of Gramsci, Kosík was looking for a new type of politics that went beyond the original Leninism.[25] However, it seems to us that although such efforts can be described as radically democratic, this concept of creating a model of "truly" democratic socialism has ultimately not been fully developed.[26] The abandonment of Leninism as a framework for political thought led the humanists to seek new ways for politics to operate. Kosík called for a political nation as a historical subject, and this clearly could have replaced both the party and the proletariat; however, this concept was never thought through completely. It worked out similarly with the turn to the Gramscian theory of hegemony, which the Marxist intellectuals (especially humanists like Sochor and Kosík) had already been advocating in the 1960s. Even though we repeatedly admit that Landa was correct about Kosík's having been inspired by Gramsci and that he had called for the interpretation of the people as a historical subject, we do not see the development of a new conception of politics at this moment. The vision was not only theoretically incomplete, it simply did not find fulfillment and sufficient capacity for action in the months after the August military invasion in 1968. It was then to completely collapse during the first waves of purges in the party and the society, when individual parts of society began to represent themselves and attempted to preserve their own privileges. Thus, the historical bloc cannot be discussed either on paper (in theory) or in reality (in practice). Moreover, the idea of cultural hegemony was still applicable even in the era of post-Stalinism, when the party intelligentsia enjoyed a good deal of autonomy and had inexhaustible production possibilities (e.g., magazines, cultural and artistic associations, universities, and the Czechoslovak Academy of Sciences). However, the Czechoslovak restorers of order in the early 1970s well recognized this circumstance, and therefore the regulation of productive possibilities and the elimination of any sign of alliance ("false solidarity") were among their goals.[27]

The ambivalence of this approach to politics is also clear from the real political actions undertaken by the thinkers we are following in 1968 and 1969: with almost no exceptions, they participated in the Communist Party of Czechoslovakia extraordinary congress. At the moment when Kosík entered high politics in September 1968 and accepted his co-optation into the regular central committee of the KSČ (he had been elected during the invasion days at the Vysočany Congress, which was of course later proclaimed as invalid), he was probably aware that he was opening the gate to "pseudo-concreteness" with its own mechanisms, unwritten rules, manipulative practices, and process of decision making. His speeches from the November plenary (1968) and especially the April plenary (1969), at which the new leader of KSČ Gustáv Husák was elected, are undoubtedly extraordinary in comparison with the other speakers, and in the second instance, also courageous. At the same time, however, it cannot be overlooked that Kosík's emphasis on seeking a new

6.2. Karel Kosík delivering his paper at a youth meeting in the Congress Palace in Prague, March 20, 1968. Copyright profimedia, photograph ČTK, Josef Nosek.

historical alliance across Czechoslovak society was not supported by his own political activity. From his position in the Central Committee, he did not formulate any concrete political tactics or alliances that could actually support the visions of the Marxist humanists. It is as if he had a dual relationship to real politics: on the one hand, he did not hesitate to really get involved and he entered the Central Committee saying that "whoever takes part in politics must be aware of what he's getting into and where he'll be operating,"[28] but on the other hand, his influence remained limited to presentations of his own essays. His own reflection, that "it's possible to go into politics with ethical principles that dictate to me that I mustn't be a criminal, an enemy occupier, or a traitor, but I'll only be operating at a peak level politically if and to the extent that I can anticipate these phenomena and know how to fight against them," thus remained more or less unfulfilled.[29]

After all, clinging to "political innocence" was typical of party intellectuals who were oriented toward intellectual and cultural production, and in most cases, it was inextricably linked with their activities until they faced utter political defeat that culminated in their expulsion from the party and bans from engaging in public activity. It was not just a reluctance to engage in tactical political maneuvering and seek compromises: owing to their resistance to the manipulative side of politics it was practically impossible to establish any real political opposition. We do not deny that the effort to build coalitions with workers and students was justified: it was probably the only possibility for taking on the encroaching normalization process after the military invasion; however, all activities of this type remained at the level of the written word. Although the approach to politics described above emerged from noble motives, the reluctance of this segment of the party intelligentsia to embrace politics fully, including its "dirt" (manipulative parts), was also its greatest weakness, or even a conceptual deficiency. In the end, it meant that the humanists, despite their various efforts, never created a truly new political project.

If, in this context, Kristina Andělová poses the provocative question of what happened to reformist political thought after its proponents lost their previous positions because of deinstitutionalization,[30] it is fair to ask the same about the fate of Marxist humanist political thinking. In our view, it is no coincidence that the representatives of this current found themselves on the outer margins of political opposition during the period of "actually existing" socialism, or they were entirely disconnected from it. In fact, their tools of political thought did not afford them the means of an effective response to the changed situation, either in terms of analyzing it or in bringing about any desired changes. In other words, no equivalent idea replaced the Leninist concept of politics that would enable the post-Stalinists to cope with a possible political defeat and thus to accept full political responsibility for it. While keeping the faith with Gramsci meant one thing in Western Europe in the 1970s for the Eurocommunists, it was an entirely different matter in Czechoslovakia in the era of "actually existing" socialism, when the original post-Stalinist party intelligentsia no longer belonged to the party after its purges—let alone having the possibility of engaging in institutional intellectual production or public activities. When Karel Bartošek declared on July 4, 1969, at a lecture where the program was going to be set for the new Czechoslovak left, that it is necessary to take the Gramscian strategy of trench warfare "that demands intellectual hegemony, and conquering one enemy trench after the other," he had no idea that in a few months this type of strategy would already be obsolete, because the situation had changed entirely and trench warfare was not possible in an atmosphere of widespread cleansings.[31]

The humanists simply did not understand politics as a power struggle. In early 1969, the monthly literary periodical *Plamen* organized a roundtable event on Machiavelli and Machiavellianism. All the participants in the post-invasion situation agreed on the necessity of taking the power dynamics in politics seriously, but instead of discussing this they spent the time primarily discussing their thoughts on morality, philosophers' and politicians' responsibilities to the people, and analyses of the present crisis. Karel Kosík even raised the question of the relationship between philosophy and politics to the original principle of "destruction of pseudo-concreteness," mediated by dialectical thinking in clarifying basic philosophical categories such as "the question of truth, time, the essence of nature; in short questions upon which everything depends," and which politics cannot do without.[32]

In an article on T. G. Masaryk, the Brno philosopher Lubomír Nový wrote: "The struggle for this socialism with a human face has become the meaning of our present history. It is not an ephemeral matter for a few bamboozled heads or a refined import. We do not even consider this to be our national idiosyncrasy, and on the contrary, we are convinced that through our efforts we pose general problems of the contemporary world as well as the contemporary communist movement. We do not force anything on anyone, and here we stand and we cannot do otherwise."[33] Here, however, a politics based on "general problems" already extended toward the center of national existence, whose humanistic nature—confirmed by "democratic socialism"—took on the contours of inevitability. "It was not primarily a political, but rather an existential revolution, which was for the first time going to create the conditions for appropriate political action," was Michal Kopeček's apt evaluation of the moment discussed above.[34] The exception at the end of the 1960s was Bartošek, who proclaimed in the spring of 1969 that the problem is not culture, but autonomous politics.[35] He sought to develop a conception for it in the lecture "Naše nynější krize a revoluce" (Our Current Crisis and Revolution). Bartošek's analysis represents a fairly unique attempt to go beyond the post-Stalinist horizons. The above-mentioned Gramscian-Šmeralean tradition rooted in cultural and national aspects of socialism was fused with theses from the anti-colonial movement (Régis Debray), the emphasis on anti-bureaucratism, and inspiration from Yugoslavia's concept of a self-managing society.[36] Those who ended up in exile (such as A. J. Liehm, Ivan Sviták, Lubomír Sochor, and Karel Bartošek) and adopted the totalitarian paradigm as an analytical framework for socialist Czechoslovakia in the era of "actually existing" socialism in the 1970s also stepped outside the box of then thinking of socialism in Czechoslovakia.

In contrast to the humanists, people like Zdeněk Mlynář and Jaroslav Šabata entered high-level politics without qualms, and they did not hesitate to promote their own model despite public opinion, which in the spring of 1968 had already transcended the Gramscian-Leninist idea of unity in diversity guaranteed by the party (the KSČ's Action Program). Of course, in contrast to the humanists, these intellectuals had clear tools for political action at the beginning of the 1970s. Even when they found themselves excluded from office or from the party itself, the international communist movement and the party itself still represented their basic framework of political thought and practice. As Kristina Andělová convincingly demonstrates in her analysis of the exile group around the journal *Listy*, ultimately this certainty led to a dead end.[37] We argue with her that the cause was to be found in an absence of significant philosophical personalities (Kosík and Kalivoda)—instead, it inhered in a lack of political imagination and an unwillingness to explore any other approaches than the tried-and-true "Leninist" ones. And here again, we arrive at the fundamental problem of the understanding of political Leninism. The humanists decided to abandon it, and after the military invasion they found themselves in a certain intellectual and political vacuum. As Kalivoda later self-critically stated, "They let themselves be excluded because [. . .] they failed to imprint a different face on things as they unfolded."[38] Those intellectuals who relied on the party as a guarantee of unity continued onward along these same lines but ended up with the same result. What both groups then had in common was that in the 1970s and 1980s they entirely resigned the search for new theoretical tools that would allow them to elaborate a concept for significant socioeconomic change. In the end, this change came about without them, and—unlike in 1968—these former actors became rather unwelcome observers after 1989.

The ideas of the techno-optimists, who theoretically stood apart from politics, or perhaps only accepted it as a necessary framework for the implementation of the scientific-technical revolution, came to an even more straightforward end. It is not that they avoided the contemporary movement for reforming and democratizing politics: on the contrary, they welcomed and supported it, but they still placed their main emphasis on structural and civilizational change, which was inherently superior to politics.[39] However, the belief that this social change is ultimately achievable regardless of the level of real politics naturally led them to a dead end similar to that of the thinkers discussed above. As Vítězslav Sommer demonstrated, political acquiescence to "actually existing" socialism by Radovan Richta, who was one of the leading representatives of the Czechoslovak techno-optimist movement, meant transferring this concept into the era of the 1970s and 1980s, but because of the political consolidation the vision also lost what was most valuable in it. While post-Stalinism created a great deal of space for spontaneous party activities and even for the intelligentsia within the state socialist form of civil society, and it seemed that the techno-optimistic idea of developing science as a productive force based on the human creative process gained traction, the "actually existing" socialism was only counting on the development of science itself, and not on spontaneous creative activity. This radically changed the position of techno-optimistic thinking. Only the elements in it that the humanists had been issuing warnings about remained: namely, sociotechnical mechanisms that served efficiency for its own sake and oversight instead of creativity.[40]

Let us add that the political debacle of post-Stalinist political thinking was not only to be found in its absence of a sufficiently powerful conception of politics, it also had broader theoretical causes. In chapter 2, we focused on the moments when the post-Stalinist Marxists attempted to critically reinterpret Hegelian dialectics in materialist terms. They criticized Hegel's dialectical movement as a movement of thought (Spirit) and not of matter—the practical, active side of human existence. However, they did not damn the movement itself, but focused on its form and on the movement of the whole. It must be emphasized that post-Stalinist Marxism never managed to step out of the notion of unity of history. The concept of the totality, which was used by the dialectical determinists and Marxist humanists alike, is the best example of this. As Karel Kosík tellingly expressed, dialectical rationality leaves nothing "outside of itself." Similarly, Josef Cibulka did not understand other nonsocialist systems as standing outside of the socialist system, but only as relics of other historical stages that had already been overcome. And that is why this kind of thinking was completely defenseless against any kind of political catastrophe that came from outside. The invasion in 1968 was exactly this kind of catastrophe, even though it came from the Soviet system—which the post-Stalinists believed that Czechoslovak Marxism had already overcome! This only deepened the resulting paralysis in political thought and action.

THE NATION

The story of Marxist humanism, at least as it has been portrayed in the literature thus far published on the year 1968 in Czechoslovakia, ended under the tracks of Soviet tanks and the ensuing normalization purges. This external intervention allows its protagonists to be seen as romantic heroes promoting a noble vision of human freedom. However, at the same time, it is an opportunity for us to look at the humanist content with different eyes.

The Brno-based intellectual Jaroslav Střítecký, who as a member of a younger generation (born in 1941) had been influenced by the German New Left, wrote the following words on the account of the Marxist humanists at the end of the 1960s: "The moment of restoration has matured. The romantic conception of the 'nation,' a dark bond uniting all the parts of the community in a single ur-essence of blood, has again become a flexible tool for the fictitious unification of the post-revolutionary 'we.'"[41] In the polemic between Milan Kundera and Václav Havel he came to the defense not only of the latter but also of the entire nonparty intelligentsia, a different generation that was defining itself against the cultural hegemony of the post-Stalinist intelligentsia of the 1960s. Although his negative judgment is influenced by the period context of the clash between generations and their values (and the "ur-essence of blood" was not really something being discussed in connection with the nation at that time), the author's observation about a discourse of a new collectivity does correspond to our findings. And while in chapter 4, we have attempted to reconstruct post-Stalinist thinking about collective subjectivity, now we are concerned with the questions of where this turn came from and, above all, what its consequences were.

In several examples, we could see the double tension present in post-Stalinist thinking. Despite the abundant and obvious affinity for the human subject as the actor of history, the party intellectuals encountered the problem of the relationship between the subjective and the objective, and the humanists likewise faced a tension between particular, national, and universal emancipation within the framework of their progressive ideas about socialist development. Yet both elements were projected in the way the category of the nation was present in the period's vocabulary.

In a text on Kosík's conception of man and concept of radical democracy, Joseph Grim Feinberg points out that in the essays "The Nation and Humanism" and "Our Current Crisis" the author arrives at the characterization through a definition of humanity which thus places his reflections within the tradition of Masaryk's political thought. Feinberg convincingly demonstrates that humanity precedes and determines the nation in the sense of a historical subject.[42] In our view, the fulfillment of humanity as a national principle (or the logos of Czech history) versus the emancipation of the individual is a vexed pair. In chapter 5, we stated that in the Marxist humanists' conception, the vision of a radical socioeconomic transformation was substantially replaced with the realization of the human individual. From another point of view, we can add that the goals of eliminating exploitation, abolishing the division of labor, and rendering the proletariat obsolete were deprioritized before the development, fulfillment, or emancipation of the nation. And then at the end of the 1960s, some of the humanists were considering shifting the real control of the means of production to workers' councils, this moment was implicitly incorporated into a realization of the so-called Czechoslovak model of socialism (i.e., a national history). Going beyond Feinberg's findings, we believe that the shift to the category of nation also has other causes within the context of Marxist humanism. Elsewhere in this book, we have repeatedly noted that class had been abandoned as an analytical tool in favor of analysis of the human individual living in the modern world, and his alienation and subjectivity, at least since the 1960s. As Bini Adamczak remarked, the theme of exploitation was generally replaced in the 1960s with the theme of a struggle against alienation, or—to put a finer point on it—against alienation's existential dimension, at the expense of the class dimension.[43]

We cannot find any split in the period thinking from the overall socialist project with its progressive dimension or from a defense of democratic socialism. However, we believe that clinging to Marxist social progressivism without the class perspective had led the Marxist humanists to a dead end. In their eyes, only real democratic socialism could satisfy the conditions for the full development of the human individual, but it could not be left up to automatic historical processes: it could only take place through active, collective intervention by creative people (historical practice). Not only does the goal here (socialism) somewhat overlap with the means toward it (the human individual), but Marxism simply cannot do without collective subjectivity. Although the Marxist humanists did not reflect on this problem, they at least had to be aware that no kind of creative activity, whether artistic or intellectual, can play the role of a decisive actor in history by itself. As Zhivka Valiavicharska notes, "To be fully realized, the holistically developed person had to be part of and an expression of the social whole."[44] Obviously, this unity could not be the proletariat, which the post-Stalinists saw as having already fulfilled its historical mission. And in reply to the question of the overriding interest of individual social groups (keeping in mind the efforts to overcome Stalinist historical determinism), the answer could not simply be "socialism"—so the collective unity of the nation appeared to be an unproblematic certainty that has not been sufficiently reflected by period thinkers.

In chapter 4, we pointed out that debates on the local and the universal in Czech culture were not an effort to move beyond the national dimension so much as part of the definition of the qualitative content of the nation. Similarly, it might seem at first glance that the search for a Central Europe defined by a common cultural and historical experience, as Karel Kosík had already undertaken using the examples of Hašek and Kafka at the beginning of the 1960s, or the revival of the idea of a Central European federal body (Bartošek), transcended the narrow national framework.[45] Ultimately, however, this geographical spread has consequences similar to relating the nation to European culture, because it is still a qualitative definition of content: we exist as a nation only insofar as Central Europe, which we help to create, also exists.[46]

Thus, despite Central Europeanism (the "center" between Germany and Russia), the basic reference framework for the determination of the nation and national existence remained the horizon of the Czech-German encounter. This applied not only in the context of the historical figures the humanists referred to (Karel Havlíček, František Palacký, Tomáš Garrigue Masaryk, etc.), but also thematically in the form of questions about national existence, nonexistence, meaning, fate, and so forth. This trend naturally culminated after the military invasion in August 1968, when along with Central Europe, the theme of Czech society in the era of the Nazi Protectorate of Bohemia and Moravia becomes relevant.[47]

The automatic locking of the category of the nation in the intellectual forms of the emerging modern Czech national identity movement in the nineteenth century led to an interesting misidentification. Unlike the Western New Left, and except for the eccentric Zbyněk Fišer, alias Egon Bondy, who at the time was independently supporting Chinese Maoism, the Marxist humanists were treating the category of the people as the equivalent of the Czech nation. They thus overlapped not only with Nejedlý but also with the entire tradition of national historiography and ethnography (see chapter 4). And their focus on the "Czech question" within the framework of the original Czech–German, or, comparably, the Czech–Russian encounter made it impossible to interpret the people in the spirit of the anti-colonial struggle in the Third World. It was not even so much the humanists' reluctance as it was a "blindness" (in the sense of the feminist expression "gender blindness") that prevented recognition of the motives that moved Europe at the time, which, for example, were starting to interest some members of the Czechoslovak student movement and the younger nonparty intelligentsia.[48] And this impermeability to the new ideas probably had something to do with the generally shared notion of superiority that Czechs and Central Europe enjoyed as part of the West.

The fact that the Czech Marxist humanists moved almost exclusively in a Czech-German framework, prevented most of them from thinking about a national collectivity in a Czech-Slovak dimension. Michal Kopeček notes in his analysis of "Our Current Crisis" that "despite his sensitivity for Slovak requests, Kosík remained, similarly to most Czech intellectuals of the time, deeply bounded to his own national context. He expressed the Czech part of the wished-for transformation from ethnic to political nationhood," and he did not seek to understand the Slovak side of the issue.[49] We entirely agree with the author on this point, adding that even though Kosík's performance was perceived positively in the period context by the Slovak national communists, this accommodating understanding ended with a somewhat patronizing statement about the Slovaks as an "awakening historical subject."[50]

When we defined post-Stalinism in chapter 1, we identified one of its traits as the principle of reflexivity. However, we must state that it was the category of collective subjectivity represented by the nation that the humanists used in an unreflected and conventionalized manner, without significant indication of real assessment taking place. We even find that the renewed journalistic production of many authors in the 1990s reveals a marked continuity with the post-Stalinist era. These authors sparred with the terms "the nation" and its "existence" with no less intensity because they perceived the developments after November 1989 and the breakup of Czechoslovakia as a threat to the Czech nation. The basic Czech-German axis also remained the same—and it was more consequential than before, because the united Germany was seen as a power that the Czech elite were already selling out their nation's interests to. The only difference was probably that in the meantime many of the authors had "liberated themselves" from Marxism: although they usually criticized the socioeconomic conditions after 1989, they did not formulate an explicit demand for progressive social change, and thus the nation came to the fore.[51]

Note, for example, that both Karel Kosík and Ivan Sviták compared the partitioning of Czechoslovakia in 1993 to that of 1938 and called it a "third Munich."[52] Sviták blamed the step on the political elites of both states, adding that the Czech elite "ostentatiously and even proudly entered foreign services [...] for the benefit of foreign managers."[53] He also simultaneously evaluated it as a consequence of external strategies, such as an "insult and betrayal by the West comparable to Munich."[54] Kosík summarized the experiences from 1938 and 1968 and spoke of

"Munichism" as an aspect that, unlike Nazism and Bolshevism, had survived the twentieth century.[55] Such a feeling of the national existence being under constant threat ("To the sound of amateur marching bands the shadows of the Protectorate come alive again. Long live Havel, our people cry out. And the Bavarians join them") illustrates that the confinement between the Czech and German horizons of the modern Czech identity was a permanent condition for the post-Stalinists, even after 1989.[56] Let Jan Tesař's sympathy for Vladimír Mečiar's post-1989 Slovak nationalist populism serve as an overwrought example of a nationally oriented position shared by those who did not agree with the division of Czechoslovakia, but still saw Slovak nationalism as a barrier against the restoration of capitalism and European dictates.[57]

Joseph Grim Feinberg demonstrates that Kosík's reading of Johann Gottfried Herder was inconsistent and that while the German philosopher spoke of a multiplicity of humanities in connection with individual nations, Kosík emphasized a universal humanity that individual nations ought to be responsible to.[58] It seems that the emphasis on creating a universal category of the human individual in the midst of a modern world, and the idea that this individual is relegated to overcoming alienation and achieving his own full personal development, were the greatest weaknesses of humanist thought. The universality of the given category conceived of this way within the framework of the Marxist solution of collectivity, in addition to other problems that we will draw attention to below, allowed for a reorientation from universality to particularity. After all, it is ultimately within the nation that the realization of the individual and therefore of individuality takes place.

In a way, it is possible to perceive this turn back to the nation as a return. It seems that the Czechoslovak or Czech case was no different from the Russian intelligentsia's attachment to the nation, as identified by Alexandr Genis and Petr Vail. The difference is that in the Czech case there had not been a turn to the nation at the expense of Khrushchev's cosmic utopia, but instead a continual presence of this category in post-Stalinism humanist discourse.[59] In their texts, Zhivka Valiavicharska and Nikolay R. Karkov treat the question of a systematic connection between Bulgarian and Yugoslav Marxist humanism and the adherents' tendency toward nationalism, and in both cases even toward ethnonationalism. As one of the main arguments, they pose the problematic definition of the human individual, which is abstract and universal.[60] We can agree with them that category definitions of this type, whether they refer to a universal human being with well-rounded development, a universal idea of humanity, or a search for a progressive line in Czech history, opened up space for the further development of Marxist humanism.

In Marxist humanism we do not find an inevitable cause leading to some form of nationalism, and we agree with Martin Profant that this development does not necessarily "have to" happen under any circumstances.[61] But in our opinion, this is not the question that lingers in the end. The decisive factor is that the space is already opened as one of the real eventualities, as we already witnessed in the Yugoslav case, and we need to remain aware of this fact when evaluating this strain of post-Stalinist thinking. If we look at the fate of Mihail Marković, who ended as Slobodan Milošević's main ideologist,[62] it does not surprise us. The space that Marxist humanism opened for similar vicissitudes and never closed was truly enormous.

CIVILIZATIONAL SUPERIORITY

The internal contradiction of the emancipation of the human individual did not just manifest in the questions of collective subjectivity, the nation, and the people. The problems with the definition of the human subject (the one that was supposed to undergo well-rounded development) were also linked to other issues, such as the question of how to look at human beings based on their membership in certain civilizations, genders, or social classes. Although these are interconnected attributes that in some respects have much to do with the above-mentioned collective framework for the realization of the liberated human being, by contrast with the nation as a category, gender, and class concerned not just the Marxist humanists. The difference is not only in the large set of party intellectuals who were addressing such questions but also in how they approached them. While the nation became a ubiquitous element in period essays and debates, the thematization of civilization, class, and gender took place only unintentionally. That is to say, defining these categories was not on the post-Stalinists' agenda, they did not figure as questions for them, and their contents are only contained implicitly in period texts. Just as the Marxist humanists did not subject the concept of the nation to a greater degree of reflection, they also neglected to reflect these concepts.

The question of civilization is connected with the very approach based on which we consider both Stalinist and post-Stalinist socialism to be part of European modernity. Just as the story of modernity and modern thinking is accompanied by a feeling of the teller's civilizational superiority, this conviction also shaped ideas of post-Stalinist socialism. Whether determinists, techno-optimists, humanists, or legal philosophers, everyone in unison considered socialism to be a superior socioeconomic form.

In the Czechoslovak case, the feeling of civilizational superiority was connected to at least two wellsprings. In comparison with the possibilities of bourgeois science, it was derived from the generally shared conception of Marxism as a qualitatively more valuable platform of knowledge (see, for example, the section titled "Criticism of Existentialism" in chapter 3). Hand in hand with this, it drew from a conviction of the maturity of Czechoslovak socialism as a model that represented a contribution to the "treasure chest of countless experiences of the world." They considered their version—along with the Yugoslav one—to be one of socialism's most prominent avant-gardes, and superior to the Soviet type.[63]

The same pattern also applies to the relationship with the Third World, which is always established in the terms of a clear relationship of the more advanced to the more backward. At this point, however, we must mention that this assumption was shared among all socialist countries, with the Soviet Union as the premier example. In practical policies it manifested in various forms of military, economic, or expert assistance to "developing" countries.[64] Josef Cibulka spoke about the fact that the world socialist system enables a qualitative shift for Third World countries from a backward phase into an advanced phase. It thus helps the development "so that their feudal or other [type of] economy transitions into a socialist one without a capitalist intermediate stage,"[65] and the socialist system can back this up economically and on the world political stage. In the end, revolutionary movements in the Third World were relegated to a role as mere "facilitators of the transition to socialist relations of production" without the possibility of imposing their own conditions for development or autonomous decision making about their future.[66]

A similar paternalism toward the Third World or certain national entities was among the deeply rooted values of the world of "actually existing" socialism, and we also find it in the pedagogical relationship of Czechs toward Slovaks, and Russians toward non-Russian ethnic groups. The fact that Josef Cibulka did not ask himself what kind of socialism is actually achieved in the Third World thanks to this "socialist system" confirms a deep conviction of his nation's civilizing mission, which had been present in the Marxist vocabulary of socialist countries since the time of Lenin.[67]

The concept of the scientific-technical revolution also involved the achievement of a qualitatively higher level of modernity that is best

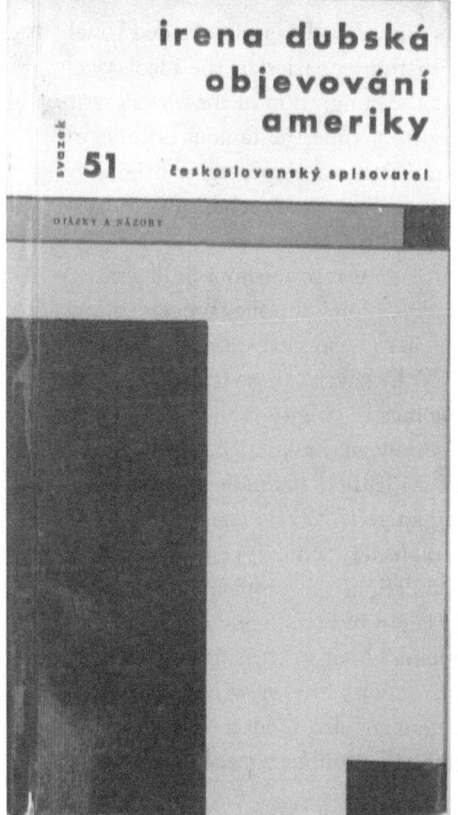

6.3. Based on research she conducted in the US, the Czech sociologist Irena Dubská published one of the first accounts of Western sociology in 1964. The cover of *Objevování Ameriky* [Discovering America] (Prague: Československý spisovatel, 1964).

managed by socialism. In this spirit, Irena Dubská spoke of the "socialist system" as the bearer of "dialectical reason," which at the "international level is the background and the basis of all other forms and degrees of the rationalization process."[68] It may seem that thanks to their emphasis on the human individual this mindset will not be found among the Marxist humanists. However, as in the case of the nation, the first glance provides a misleading image. In the end, among other reasons, it was the awareness of the uniqueness of their national experience or of the Czechoslovak path to socialism that led the Czechoslovak humanists to their feeling of being exceptional. To this must be added the fact that in Marxist humanist thinking the human individual and his alienation are integral to modernity and the modern world, which itself is inextricably linked with socialism. Nikolay R. Karkov claims that apparently the perception of socialism as a product of European modernity led to the definition of the individual as the human type of Western civilization. He went on to say that their own projections of themselves created a dehumanizing effect on others, who were described as "tribal cannibals" or "Albanian Muslims" (Mihailo Marković).[69]

Although the Czech humanists did not take the same contemptuous approach toward the Slovaks as Marković did to the Albanians, the Czech party intelligentsia's uncritical attitude toward Israel in the Arab–Israeli conflict in 1967 can be considered a variation of the same theme. Many party intellectuals, especially writers and journalists, spoke out at the time against Czechoslovakia's official policy and defended Israel. This brought them into conflict with functionaries in the ideological apparatus, which had fallout such as the emigration of the Slovak writer Ladislav Mňačko, the author of at that time the famous critique of Stalinism titled *Oneskorené reportáže* (Delayed Reportages, originally published in 1963), to Israel in protest against the Czechoslovak foreign policy toward it.[70]

However, this was not just a unilateral reaction to a unilateral official party policy. Compared with official foreign policy proclamations, the Czechoslovak party intellectuals often expressed strong a priori cultural and civilizational evaluations: "Why haven't these refugees [Arabs who had fled to Egypt] built their homes in twenty years?" Statements such as "Israel is economically, culturally, and mentally at the level of the European countries" contrasted with their evaluation of Arabs as a nation "much more primitively organized." While Israel was an "extremely dynamic country," the "pharaohs left [Nubia] yesterday." There were even arguments about overpopulation: the problems of the root cause of the "backward Arab world begin in bed."[71] Such comparisons overlapped with Marković's statements about Albanians in the early 1990s.[72] Humanists formed a contrast with the view of the techno-optimists, whose vision for their system enabled them to transcend the East–West dichotomy and to recognize the conflict between the affluent North and the poor South.[73]

At the same time, in comparison with the West, an interesting inversion arrived at the same result. While in its stance toward Israel, the Western New Left is often accused of uncritically accepting propaganda spread by representatives of the Arab states,[74] the same can be said about the Czech and Slovak post-Stalinist intellectuals, but with the positions reversed. Thus, the Czechoslovak intellectuals referred to proclamations about the liquidation of Israel with comments on the "hateful Arabs" and "tolerant" Israelis, and they spoke about Arab support for political genocide. Applying an analogy based on the experience with the Munich Agreement of 1938 and all of Central Europe, the Arab states were considered a potential occupying power.[75]

From this perspective, it is quite understandable that only those who have already "achieved" the given, "higher" degree of civilization could reach true humanism, defined as the abolition of the alienating forms of modern society ("manipulation"). The others had to be denied this "privilege" because they could not emancipate themselves from something that had not "yet" subjugated them. It is therefore clear which of the two civilizational stages had to be afforded priority in their eventual conflict, in the interest of human progress. To wit, the humanists' humanism was not for everyone.

Besides the connection with the abstract idea of Western modernity, there was also the question of cultural membership in the West that had accompanied the formation of modern Czech national identity since its beginning. It is possible to say that with the end of Stalinism, or during a certain phase of post-Stalinism, the Czechs witnessed a reversal of ascribed values in the East–West polarity. During the Stalinist era, the party intelligentsia considered the Soviet version of modernity to be the most advanced model, and therefore worthy of following. Even in the first years after Stalin's death, intellectuals still paid attention to Soviet and sometimes also to Chinese debates.[76] Later, however, references to Soviet authors began to taper off in popular and professional publications. Simply, the post-Stalinist intellectuals seemed to have less contact with the Soviet intellectual world than in the previous era. Soviet debates were no longer a framework of reference for the Czech or Slovak post-Stalinists (one of the few who clearly paid close attention was Josef Cibulka), let alone was there space for a significant intellectual exchange between the Czechoslovak and Soviet intelligentsias. Moreover, members of this intelligentsia began to criticize Stalinism as a model of modernization corresponding to the conditions of the Soviet state that was imported into the more industrially developed Czechoslovakia. The East thus ceased to be "our model," and the West began to replace it as a reference, which is not surprising in the context of the Czech debates that had been organized on this subject since the second half of the nineteenth century.

In chapter 4, we have seen that in the 1960s, the discussion about the role of the link between Czech and European culture, which was always implicitly associated with the West, played a significant role. This is why Ivan Sviták, despite the way he fought against the Western economic system as an obligatory model for transformation, used pejorative expressions connected with the Third World ("toboggan to Bolivia," "Nicaragua of vulgarity") in his writing in the early 1990s.[77] As Nikolay R. Karkov points out, the enduring notion of belonging to the West has always led Eastern Europeans to define the East as being on the other side of their borders.[78]

Thus, if it seemed that the humanist invention of Central Europe attempted to build a unique identity, Kosík's and Kundera's emphasis on cultural unity and a shared experience with the absurdity of the modern world (Hašek and Kafka) served to strengthen the Western identity. Kalivoda, for example, also clung to the concept of Central

Europe. He shifted the definition of "center" as a shared experience to the position of a non-Eastern, non-Soviet reality. In a discussion at a conference on Creativity and Freedom in a Humane Society that took place in Mariánské Lázně in 1967 as part of the Marxist-Christian dialogue, he lodged a protest in a symptomatic manner: "Don't keep calling us 'Eastern,' we are in Central Europe."[79] It is also no coincidence that one version of Kundera's later essay "The Tragedy of Central Europe" (1984) bore the title "The Kidnap of the West."[80] In his efforts to prove its membership in the West, the already world-famous author defined Central Europe as a cultural bulwark against Russian barbarism.[81] It is typical within a certain type of humanist orientalization of Eastern Europe that Kundera also used the confessional differences between the Christian democratism of Western Europe and the Byzantinism of the Orthodox countries.[82] We can only agree with the author of the analytical study on the shift in meaning of Kundera's Central Europe when he claims that these efforts "can sketch new boundaries after the abolition of the old ones."[83] It seems to us that the humanist understanding of this region had contained exactly this possibility since its very beginning.

Post-Stalinism was by no means alone in its feelings of uniqueness. The historical development sequence and hierarchy were undoubtedly just as present in the minds of Lenin's contemporaries, including his opponents in the Second International, as they were in the post-Stalinists'. The broad consensus that even "the worst socialism is better than the best capitalism," expressed by György Lukács, the doyen of authentic Marxism, in the summer of 1968,[84] was not invalidated among the Czechoslovak post-Stalinists even by the military invasion. The relationship with "actually existing" socialism only began to change in the 1970s. A shift is especially evident in the Czech exile community in France, where under the influence of the local intellectual milieu, a critique of state socialist regimes as totalitarian began to appear.[85]

We should also not lose sight of the fact that from the beginning, the sense of civilizational superiority outside and inside the Soviet bloc was connected with a feeling of national uniqueness based on the historical experiences of the Czechoslovak path to socialism. These experiences could include vicissitudes ranging from the Austro-Hungarian monarchy to the interwar democracy, the German occupation, and Stalinism to Czechoslovak post-Stalinism. Up to this point, the Czechoslovak path to socialism represented a theme that we can track in Czech society and its (non)reflection. The benchmark of maturity becomes whatever its own idea of itself was at the time: the interwar republic as the most advanced economy and democracy in the region; post-Stalinism as the most effective and freest socialism; the post-November development as an example of postcommunist transformation; and so on. Regardless of the wanderings of these ideas in the historical collective memory the same unwillingness to engage in more critical self-reflection also appears here.

CLASS CONSCIOUSNESS

Civilizational superiority is clearly visible in post-Stalinist thinking, however, the pervasive silence on questions of social and gender equality is impossible to overlook. We believe that the consensus on the civilizational superiority of socialism as a social model related to this absence of questions concerning any form of social inequality. In the eyes of the post-Stalinists, socialism simply eliminated class differences and opened a space for society-wide development. Testimony about these ideas is essentially interwoven throughout this book. As we have seen in the other examples, the determinists believed in sufficient cognition of historical laws and in human intervention in their operation; the techno-optimists and legal philosophers believed in the correct establishment of essential social processes and in making the administration of economic and political affairs more effective;[86] and the humanists believed in the possibility of transforming the world through human activity, or sometimes human collectives including the nation. Without exception, all of them were deeply convinced that their form of socialism would eliminate inequalities, or at least that it was attempting to eliminate them, but none of them were thinking along the lines that this system was reproducing old inequalities or producing them anew.

In chapter 1, we argued that the change of the epistemological subject from the party to the intelligentsia was the condition for the possibility of internal plurality to arise. While in Stalinist intellectual production the party had the final word as the focal center for a privileged access to truth, which created a framework in which Stalin himself could engage in interventions, in post-Stalinism the access paths to truth multiplied. At this point, however, we must note that the approach to the epistemic subject, whether it is the party or its intellectuals, shows structural similarities. We believe that the social prominence of the intelligentsia in socialist society is also part of the answer to why social and gender inequality are absent in the post-Stalinist vocabulary.

The sociologist Michael Voříšek connects this sense of social exclusivity with the generational hegemony that arose with the establishment of Stalinism; that is, the liquidation of inconvenient students and the interwar intelligentsia. The hegemony then emerged to the forefront in the 1960s, when this generation was at the height of its creative powers.[87] The same author also notes the class origin of the party intelligentsia, the vast majority of whom, despite Stalinization-era attempts at creating a new man, came from bourgeois families.[88] As was the case of the thinkers Voříšek investigated in the field of historical materialism and sociology, those we were nearly all recruited from the middle classes.[89] They included Irena Dubská, Vítězslav Gardavský, Ivan Sviták, Karel Kosík, A. J. Liehm, Radovan Richta, Radoslav Selucký, Milan Kundera, Josef Zumr, and others who were mostly from families of officials, teachers, lawyers, and so on, and they all attended academically oriented high schools (*gymnasia*), often before 1945. Their social, moral, and aesthetic values had roots in the milieu of a Czech intelligentsia perceived as the traditional bearer of Czech identity, and this later grew into their communist engagement. It is certainly no coincidence that the culture of intellectual salons, such as the group that met in the home of reform communist KSČ lecturer Klement Lukeš, was cultivated in party intelligentsia circles.[90]

We can track the uniqueness of intellectuals and the feeling of elitism in the legal philosophers' reflections on the role of the intelligentsia in modern society, in the Marxist humanists, and in period sociological concepts.[91] Naturally, this aspect is also present in the concept of the scientific-technical revolution, which by elevating science to a productive force practically required that man improves himself to the level of epistemic subject and demiurge all in one.

The motor of history was no longer man-the-producer, but instead the creative and continually educated human individual, and the heroes of the new era would not be shock workers but scientists, inventors, artists, or philosophers. Not only should the intelligentsia play a much larger role in these optimistic conceptions than it had before, but its ranks should continuously grow. Typical in this respect is František Šamalík's statement that the value of intellectuals "lies in their individuality and singularity: scientists, artists, journalists, organizers, administrators, etc. should see, feel, and know more deeply, and transcend the boundaries of what is known."[92]

In post-Stalinism, however, the intelligentsia not only had an extraordinary calling in building socialism, but also an attitude that can be described as contempt for the materiality of everyday life. Although Robert Kalivoda was one of the few who referred to the need to procure what was necessary to satisfy basic instincts—*Bedürfnisse*, according to the *Economic and Philosophical Manuscripts*—in the form of satisfying hunger and sexual urges, his starting point was mainly in the sphere of art. Although he emphasized his own image of rural-plebian Tábor as a libertine folk movement, his approaches were rather elitist in what art is and should be. If Karel Kosík defined himself in *Dialectics of the Concrete* against the dictates of economic and material procurement, which prevent man from transcending the sphere of pseudo-concreteness and leave him at the level of a manipulable object, by the end of the decade he was already utterly contemptuous of the concrete forms of the materiality of life.[93] When considering the political nation he concluded that in the event of failure to establish themselves as a historical subject, the inhabitants of the state are condemned to captivity in "concern over acquiring things, gathering them into barns, worrying about watering and feeding troughs" so they "have neither the time nor the need to discuss metaphysical questions—which naturally includes inquiring into the meaning of human and national existence."[94] Intellectual arrogance is similarly evidenced in a diary entry by Jaroslav Putík, the editor in chief of a cultural-political magazine called *Orientace* (Orientation) that was about to be terminated. "Riding in a train with two old classmates: both fat. They talk about cars, about digging a ditch and [getting] a pipeline to their houses, about rabbits and chickens. Not a word about politics." One day later: "Still a bad taste in my mouth after yesterday's class reunion, when classmates reminded me of things I've known for a long time but don't want to acknowledge: our working class grumbles a bit, but it eats from the [party's] hand."[95]

The party intellectuals considered themselves a social group that looked after its own interests as well as its own ideas about socialist society and hegemony in the production of post-Stalinist thought. In a period reflection, Benjamin Page described this post-Stalinist moment as a shift from the dominance of "a centralized bureaucracy with a no class basis, toward domination by intellectuals within the Party, tied by training, outlook, and interests to the class of owners of the factor of professional managerial and technological [and let us add, cultural and intellectual] knowledge."[96]

In addition to the fact that we can deduce the class position of the party intelligentsia from their own interests stemming from a privileged position in society, it is also necessary to take their economic situation into account. It was not even the salaries paid at scientific institutes and universities as such, but the generous fees paid by the state socialist media and publishing houses that afforded the party intelligentsia a decent standard of living. The radical Marxist Egon Bondy, who stood outside the party ranks as well as the cultural and social mainstream at that time, described this unspoken aspect faithfully in a poem dedicated to the most influential cultural and political magazine of the reform communist intelligentsia *Literární noviny*:

> If you've made well sure that nothing will happen to you—
> to you, such dear bourgeois flowers of love for man
> i.e., to you yourselves
> to your refrigerators, weekend cottages, televisions
> (when you have just started saving for a car
> which—God willing—you will have saved up for after a few more articles
> for *Literární noviny* on the subject of pan-human humanism) . . .
> now you proclaim generous justice freedom brotherhood etc.
> till you're out of breath
> or until the moment when you begin to be afraid
> and cower
> and only underhandedly engage in skullduggery
> the way you've been used to doing it
> until you suddenly begin to suspect
> that time is turning
> But I'm probably unnecessarily afraid
> Most of you
> —I firmly hope—
> will be traditionally stupid
> and will fiddle the music of your class interest
> all the way to the interesting end.[97]

Bondy's poetic criticism is naturally both fitting and one-sided at the same time, but we are citing it practically in full length because it also captures a more general feature of the post-Stalinist intelligentsia: just as a fish swimming in water cannot see the water from outside,[98] the post-Stalinist party intellectuals were not able to reflect upon their immediate milieu. And even when they attempted it, they ultimately did not pass over the threshold of their own interests. Karel Bartošek was one of the few to attempt a greater degree of introspection. However, despite trying to get out of the rut of post-Stalinist intellectual production and look at the ranks he belonged within through the lens of the "elitist illusions" that were cured by the military invasion, he, too, returned to his origins, and in the same text he declared that the KSČ was "getting rid of honest, engaged intellectuals," thus depriving itself of the "possibility of an internal regeneration."[99]

As we have seen in the case of the nation, the longevity of a strong class consciousness within the party intelligentsia also reveals itself when a broader time perspective is applied. Karel Kosík, for example, argued in an interview for the magazine *Concordia* at the beginning of the 1990s when he expressed certain distrust toward the original Marxist subject of revolutionary change: "However, the working class proved unable to discharge the tasks Marx expected of them."[100] According to other statements, he was not intending to seek either a new eschatology or a new revolutionary subject, but wanted to try to critically analyze the present to determine whether the connections between the economy, science, and technology could also contain liberating elements. Although he still pleaded the case for the Marxist tradition, according to which citizens establish the free world, here Kosík also ultimately arrives at himself as a destination, because he considers analysis of the conditions of things from which freedom could emerge as fundamental and determining. As in the 1960s, the central historical actor remains the intellectual who ruthlessly analyzes reality and thus opens space for liberation. Despite his interviewers' urging, he did not intend to consider the subject of change in categories other than intellectual praxis (*Dialectics of the Concrete*), and he ended with the laconic pronouncement that it is necessary above all else for philosophy to think.

Michael Voříšek also discovered that intellectuals and artists considered themselves to be the only seekers of truth and were convinced of their justification in "bringing the rest of society to reform" in his analysis of period sociology.[101] This fact was already reflected by period observers, as some of the reactions to the Fourth Congress of the Union of Czechoslovak Writers in the summer of 1967 were critical of the party intelligentsia. One stated, "The working class can understand the honest wandering of an honest artist but does not understand the vulgarization of Marxism by those who pursue the idea of perfection and raise themselves up to the role of monopoly custodians of truth."[102] As with Bondy's poem, a statement of this type naturally only offers a glimpse into one part of social reality. However, it seems as if the post-Stalinists repeated the same mistake that happens in most modern political movements when they take the lead in the democratization process, the movement of national history, and ultimately in the nation itself, which was supposed to fulfill the historical process on their behalf. Jaroslav Stříteckýpointed out that more than with the nation, they were concerned with filling a social role connected with the modern national identity, which was about keeping with the "frame of the image, in which all being and non-being depends on the self-sacrifice of Czech intellectuals taking the sins of the world on themselves!"[103]

The rhetorical question then remains of whether one of the successes of "actually existing" socialism, whose restoration of order was explicitly based on the liquidation of the part of the intelligentsia that "eluded" control, was not precisely the recognition of this moment. The wariness of the average citizen toward the intelligentsia was already manifesting strongly in 1968 in statements such as "intellectuals are crap!"[104] The sociologist Ivo Možný speaks of this rift between the ordinary people and the intelligentsia (dissidents) as a factor in the eventual real demise of state socialism at the end of the 1980s.[105]

GENDER INEQUALITY

It would be naïve and unproductive if we approached the subject of gender inequality based on the keywords "woman" and "man." Nevertheless, readers of most of the texts we discuss will be surprised by the astonishing absence of these categories. As in the case of the social inequalities discussed above, we believe this was caused by a blindness associated with the sociocultural background of the post-Stalinist party intelligentsia.

By now it is clear that post-Stalinism cannot be perceived as a homogeneous field—and it was even quite rich in thematization of gender questions. Recently, this topic has attracted the interest of many Czech scholars; however, the issues relating to gender were mostly reflected outside the works of the authors we analyze here. Libora Oates-Indruchová links the post-Stalinist articulation of gender themes with the unfulfilled promise of women's emancipation in Stalinism.[106] Period journalism, including *Literární noviny*, addressed, for instance, the shortage of apartments, the role of women in the household, and parenting.[107] A cultural historian, Květa Jechová, draws attention to the debate "The Controversy over the Woman of Our Time," organized in 1967 and 1968 by the magazine *Vlasta*.[108] The film scholar Petra Hanáková speaks about Věra Chytilová's films, which she worked on with the director and with the artist Ester Krumbachová (*Sedmikrásky* [Daisies], 1966; *Ovoce stromů rajských jíme* [Fruit of Paradise], 1969), as "gender critical" cinematography that is possible to read as a "feminist testimony."[109] The art historian Marianna Placáková understands the expressions of female artists (including Naděžda Plíšková, Eva Švankmajerová, Běla Kolářová, Zorka Ságlová, and Soňa Švecová) in the 1960s and 1980s as "critical expressions of 'female voices.'"[110] Hana Havelková, based on data provided by the State Population Commission, demonstrates how that the empirically and essentially technocratically inclined expert community was only standing in for a missing women's emancipation movement.[111]

The absence of gender-structured topics is even more striking in the texts written by members of the post-Stalinist party intelligentsia that we have analyzed in this book: for instance, the legal philosophers and the determinists were entirely silent on the topic, perhaps because they did not consider it a problem. Surprisingly, though, a certain gender sensitivity appears among the techno-optimists. Although in most cases they were tackling questions of science and automation, when they carried out an analysis of leisure time it was not a broadly defined human individual that emerged from the results, but women and men separately, and the gaping disproportion between women's and men's participation in household chores did not go unnoticed.[112]

The research conducted by the secretary of Richta's team, Ota Klein, whose studies on the crisis of emotionality were published posthumously in early 1969 represented a fairly singular approach.[113] Against the background of the relationship between mother and child as the fundamental determining factor of human emotionality, he attempted to sketch some points of departure that would correspond to the rapidly changing civilization. He forthrightly labeled "women's emancipation [in] itself" as one of the reasons for tackling this problem because "the handicap of the woman-mother in demanding professional careers [. . .] is all too clear."[114] Klein's text was based on the fundamental assumption that if human emotionality undergoes historical development, as he proved through the analysis of transitions from traditional to capitalist societies, it is necessary to also consider the changes that will take place within the framework of the scientific-technical revolution.

In the future there was to be a regulation of emotionality, a kind of rationalization of emotions that corresponded to the changes in the "structure of society-wide human reality," and thus also to a change in the relationship between mothers or other caregivers and children. Despite the previously cited motivation, a techno-optimistic effort to optimize social relationships shines right through Klein's text. In the transformation of the relationship between mother and child, he was clearly not as interested in women's emancipation as in freeing up social capacity to launch the intellectually demanding transition into a scientific-technical society. On the other hand, it is clear from Klein's text that his techno-optimistic visions relied upon women no less than men. Similarly, the sociologist Dragoslav Slejška spoke of the difficult conditions for women participating in the management of enterprises, because besides their own work and taking care of their households, they no longer wanted to be burdened with the extra mental stress and the ongoing education required in managerial positions. And like Klein,

Slejška called upon society to remove these barriers; he was also relying on larger numbers of women "participating in management" when more people overall would be involved in it in the future.[115]

By contrast, the occasional ruminations by Marxist humanists who foregrounded the project of the "fully developed man" had an entirely different nature. For consideration of the mutual interlinkage of humanity and gender, the late remark by Predgar Vranicky (1976) is striking. As Una Blagojević presents it, this representative of the philosophical school centered around the magazine *Praxis* said in a lecture titled "Marxism and the Social Position of Women" that Marxism did not divide mankind into two parts, but was always concerned with the human individual as a "social and historical being" and with "emancipation of the working class and liberating mankind, always meant in the sense of holistic freedom."[116] In the subtext of Vranicki's dictums there is a clearly legible general humanist assumption about a universally defined humanity. However, we believe that it is the abstractness of the definition of man that is, as J. G. Feinberg rightly points out, always self-explanatory (man is determined by his own humanity),[117] and ultimately leads to an unconscious implication of a human model based on its own image. The case is similar, moreover, with the definition of the fully developed man, whose totality is conceived of universally, but is still always defined negatively, as the opposite of the "fragmented" man of the modern era (see chapter 3). We therefore cannot shake off the impression that this human universality in the conceptions of Czechoslovak humanists then more or less culminated in an image of the human individual that essentially copied the social position, gender and ethnic identity, and Eurocentric orientation of the given authors. Their image of the human being thus corresponds to the context of how the male members of the state-socialist middle class perceive the world. Thanks to continuities with the presocialist period, the socialist middle class remained firmly rooted in bourgeois culture; however, their defining trait was not their economic background and material assets, but their possession of substantial symbolic capital. In connection with the ethnic position of the writer, this implicitly meant their position as a Czech or Slovak and self-identification with European culture—and thus with the West. As Jaroslav Střítecký would add, it was essentially about middle-aged, middle-class Czech men and "dissatisfied breadwinners."[118] The fact that this universal humanity corresponds to a purely masculine image was unwittingly revealed even by Ivan Sviták. In one entry in the intellectual diary he kept from 1959 to 1961 titled "Man" (Člověk), he speaks of mistaken escapes from the "emptiness of being" to a "comely woman," a "fast car," or a "flock of young ladies."[119]

The occasional appearance of gender categories in period Marxist humanist texts certainly gives form to this kind of image. In the early 1960s, in an entry on Božena Němcová for an annotated calendar, although Karel Kosík wrote that she was not only a great Czech writer but also the "first modern and emancipated woman,"[120] he did not elaborate any further. At the end of the same decade, however, when he conceived a reflection on Havlíček's democratism, he reconstructed the author's use of the terms "masculinity" and "femininity." We certainly cannot anachronistically reproach Kosík for failing to apply the tools of gender critical analysis that are offered today to the political thinking of the nineteenth century. However, his nonchalant appropriation of these terms is rather striking. At the same time, his conception of the essentiality of "masculinity" and "femininity" was distinct from the post-Stalinist elevation of femininity as an antithesis to Stalinist universality.[121] Kosík stated that thanks to a strict separation of both categories in Havlíček's world, "the monsters that have inundated the 20th century, the effeminate, weak man and the mannish woman, devoid of charm" cannot appear. If Kosík, based on Havlíček's work, accepts masculinity as the "measure" of man, and if he defines democracy as the "unity of masculinity, clairvoyance, and humor," in his reflections, femininity only appears as one side of the above-mentioned "monster" of the twentieth century, or as "charm."[122]

However, the unconscious reproduction of prejudices against women was not the only consequence of an abstractly defined humanity. They also appeared in magazine interviews with women intellectuals in that period,[123] and these could even go as far as the ventilation of open and patronizing arrogance of someone's own sense of (not only gender) superiority. When a Czech translation of the French philosopher Simone de Beauvoir's book *The Second Sex* was published in 1966, a heated discussion broke out in the pages of *Literární noviny* in which Ivan Sviták, Jan Patočka, Irena Dubská, and Helena Klímová all joined. Its contents were reconstructed by Dana Musilová and again more recently by Marianna Placáková, who also analyzes the letters of readers who responded to the debate. In addition, she draws attention to the circumstances surrounding the Czech edition, which was prepared by Jan Patočka.[124]

In the above-mentioned debate, Sviták, in conformity with the period Marxist critiques of existentialism (see the section "Criticism of Existentialism" in chapter 3) draws lines against excessive subjectivization of human individuality and against its exclusion from social and economic relations. However, he combined this stance, which is legitimate from the Marxist position, with phrases not dissimilar to those we saw from intellectuals who had a sense of their civilizational superiority over the Arab population of the Middle East. Instead of engaging in debate, Sviták heaps a pile of invectives upon the author of *The Second Sex* with the goal of diminishing her philosophical credibility to an absolute minimum. Accusations that she is uninformed as a scholar, or overly ideological or speculative are among the more substantial "arguments" presented, but by contrast with the blindness of his peers, Sviták's texts are distinguished by an unprecedented aggression that reaches even obsessive proportions. For example, he sees de Beauvoir as showing off a "plush salon in her head" instead of thoughts, and accuses her of understanding Hegel in the same naïve manner that she might serve "female immanence" to a "woman preparing a steak," and that the most that emerges from her work is that she "knows how to count to two," and so on.[125] He crowns his patronizing remarks toward the author and the issue itself with a concluding statement that philosophers and poets are "perceptive of the essence of life. [. . .] Without symbolism or transcendence, they understand precious femininity, from which Mrs. de Beauvoir and Mrs. Dubská have, for a change, unshackled us, even though we are having a beautiful spring."[126]

6.4. The Czech philosophers (left to right) Jan Patočka, Irena Michňáková, and Karel Kosík in 1976. Copyright Jan Patočka Archive.

Furthermore, Sviták's method of fighting against female perspectives is inconsistent in a particular way. Like the other post-Stalinists, he paid no attention to his own social, racial, or gender conditionality in his texts, but of course he damned de Beauvoir (to a certain extent justifiably) for reproducing the prejudices of her social class.[127] While in other essays he speaks of the power of poetry, which is the only thing able to overcome the limitations of the scientific perspective,[128] here he is suddenly helping himself out with contemporary expert discourse ("Anthropological research has proven that for a child's first three years, childrearing is an irreplaceable human good") and he spoke of the dubiousness of infant day care. In his texts on culture, Sviták called for the absolute autonomy of art, artists, and the human individual as such, but here he considered the female question to be mainly a problem of "socioeconomic structures."[129] His economic position was certainly not distant from the one advocated by the de Beauvoir herself, for she did not avoid the problem and she considered the elimination of economic inequality to be the essential condition for women's emancipation; however, Sviták was not considering her perspectives. For him, de Beauvoir was not a counterpart worthy of engaging in a serious discussion with.[130]

Sviták also refused to acknowledge motherhood as an issue, instead arguing that this subject was inflated every year in speeches commemorating International Women's Day. But he still would not hesitate to suggest some original instructions in line with the abstract humanism of his time: "The solution to the female question will finally arrive with a structural transformation of the human species, which contemporary history is working on with a hectic intensity, in order to [. . .] create such a human scenario for modern man that would be commensurate to the reality that people are capable of flying to the cosmos and mastering nature outside themselves."[131]

We also find it quite interesting that women who were active in the public sphere in the post-Stalinist era did not always view themselves through a gendered lens. In her analysis of the debate mentioned above, Marianna Placáková illustrates the dual nature of their perception of gender inequality. The first overlaps with our findings and is based on the idea of the civilizational maturity of Czechoslovak socialism, which in many regards was not afflicted with the gender inequalities described in the Western world (Dubská and Klímová). Placáková even proves that for this reason, letters from readers of *Literární noviny* often sided with Sviták's "Marxist critique."[132] The second feature would require a deeper analysis, but it still shows that although Dubská and Klímová criticized Sviták and espoused feminist or at least feminine viewpoints, at the same time, together they established a professional human-oriented sociological and psychological discourse in the 1960s. This scholarship reacted to the one-size-fits-all solutions under Stalinism with a post-Stalinist expertise.[133] As work by other female scholars has indicated, the emancipatory dimension of expert discourses was at least controversial and the 1960s are often considered to mark the beginning of a conservative turn in this regard.[134] Incidentally, though for different reasons, Ota Klein took a similar view on the contemporary expert discourse that advocated a greater role for mothers in childrearing. He considered it a conservative-romantic escape from the necessary social changes that would take place with the shift of a larger number of people into "super-qualified labor."[135]

In her study, Petra Hanáková presents Ester Krumbachová's typical statement, which calls for conceptualization. At the end of her answer to the question of a specific female perspective, the leading artist of the Czech New Wave in film unwittingly identifies with one of the basic assumptions of Marxist humanism when she says "not only thinking inspires respect, whether it's from a woman or a man: true, real thinking that is not pressed into pre-made forms. But it goes, it pushes itself wherever it can."[136] We can also see similar examples in the activities of the female philosophers gathered around the magazine *Praxis*, who—according to Una Blagojević's findings—reported on Lucien Goldmann and Herbert Marcuse, but with the exception of Simone de Beauvoir did not deal with feminist topics and literature.[137] From this point of view, the interventions of, for example, Irena Dubská and Helena Klímová were fairly rare within the framework of the post-Stalinist party intelligentsia, and they can be read as contributions to a Marxist debate on gender questions.[138] Blaženka Despot's efforts to connect authentic Marxism with feminism in Yugoslavia represented an even rarer phenomenon within state socialism.[139]

Searching for and analyzing period gender motifs and the modes of their conceptualization exceed the intentions for this work, so let us arc back to our post-Stalinist protagonists. It would be utterly impossible to overestimate the significance of the debate on *The Second Sex*, on account of its uniqueness as well as Sviták's eccentricity, but at the same time we do not believe that the author's outbursts could be described as coincidental. Moreover, they were far from exceptional. In his analysis of period novels, Jan Matonoha demonstrates the extent to which authors such as Josef Škvorecký, Ludvík Vaculík, Arnošt Lustig, and Kundera conceived of women as objects, as beings who lack their own voices and are incapable of independent action (Kundera).[140]

Until the end of his life, Sviták perceived women as inferior beings who are incapable of rational analysis or of transcending themselves through creative work. Instead, they are the objects of male activity: "Man aspires for women only in passing, on the path toward his calling. Women are not his program; his work is actualizing something outside himself. It is precisely this disregard that women love: the more he is fundamentally a stranger, the more he attracts them."[141] A woman is unable to decide for herself, and she only encounters the value of freedom through love, when she is "forever infected by the right man."[142] In an essay on the Czechoslovak New Wave, Ivan Sviták compares Chytilová's *Daisies* with Jiří Menzel's *Closely Watched Trains*. Even though he positively assesses the originality and contribution of both films, he reproaches the first for excessive subjectivity and escapes into the self, and says it is characterized by "esoteric symbolism" and that its universe is entirely subsumed within the author, while Menzel, by contrast, "acts" and "changes his surroundings," and his film is "full of interest in objectivity, depicts the hero against the most civil background, alternates comedy with lyricism and the loving and smiling humanism of Bohumil Hrabal's model."[143] Thus, a woman, when she gets around to creating something, focuses on her private life, encloses the cosmos into herself, while a man with his openness to the world and his activity fulfills a humanist calling. Despite the professed humanism of Sviták and other like-minded authors, we think that humanism and the abstract (non)definition of the human individual open space for feelings of civilizational superiority, of belonging to a nation, and ultimately for writing such as Sviták's in which he discussed female "subjectivism" as leading to a particular humanity. In other words, in many cases, the "humanism" of the post-Stalinist era inadvertently changed into its opposite: what was supposed to be emancipatory and progressive became—at the very least—traditionalist.[144] Unlike Libora Oates-Indruchová, we do not believe that the main enemy of the development of critical thinking on gender was "actually existing" socialism preventing an epistemological breakthrough.[145] Instead, we believe, it is an internal (in)disposition of post-Stalinist thinking within the party intelligentsia, especially within Marxist humanism.[146]

In the context of the above, it is surprising that besides the techno-optimists, some of the few party intellectuals who reflected on these selected moments were the Slovak national communists. While Ladislav Novomeský criticized the uncritically accommodating stance taken by Czech and Slovak intellectuals toward Israel and when asked for support for the Arab side said that "humanity is all one,"[147] Vladimír Mináč showed much greater social and gender sensitivity than any of the Czech or Slovak humanists.

> It's a job for the whole epoch. The inequality is still too great: individual nations and ethnicities are unequal in political, legal, and social terms: some districts are at the level of Hungarian feudalism—in all respects: hundreds of thousands of women are bound to abominable mechanical activity for literally a beggar's wage. It matters in which family, in which region, in which nation, and which gender a person is born in our country! Inequality still prevails in the most basic things: from the possibility of subsistence to the possibility of education. Until everyone has the same opportunity, until the time when there will be a real democracy, let the present-day democratizers think what they want.[148]

It is a pity that the humanists, in the heat of the struggle for a real socialist democracy, did not take some of the Slovak national communists' and the techno-optimists' ideas more seriously at the end of the 1960s. If they had, their ideological current would have taken on more specific and truly liberating contours.

THE OPENNESS OF EMANCIPATION

While evaluating the Socialist and Communist Parties in relation to Marxism until roughly the 1960s an important fact must be kept in mind. These parties, or the regimes established by them, relied for the most part on orthodox Marxist conceptions as they had emerged within the Second International and in Stalinism, and their appearance and their limits corresponded to these. The Czechoslovak Marxism of the 1960s attempted to understand the circumstances of this tradition's origin, and then to critique and overcome it. That they did not bring their efforts to a successful conclusion and instead fell apart (in the case of Marxist humanism), or were co-opted and shorn of their radicalism (techno-optimism), or only survived at the margins of academic circles (dialectical determinism), was the fault not only of occupation by the "friendly" powers and the regime of "actually existing" socialism but also of the unreflected theoretical and practical limits of this type of Marxist thought. However, this does not mean that nothing at all remained from them. Although Czechoslovak Marxism as a coherent field of thought within post-Stalinist modernity has disappeared, the form of problematization and attempts to solve it remain.

The period conditionality of post-Stalinist thought is utterly evident. Its very definition as an effort to overcome the previous period locked post-Stalinism in a modernist-progressivist mode of thinking. Even though the Stalinist-type modernization project failed, it was not rejected by the party intelligentsia as a whole. All the problems associated with civilizational, social, or gender supremacy arise out of accepting the idea of a socialist project in which an abstractly defined universal human individual played the main role, especially for the humanists. However, the internal contradiction of post-Stalinist thought, to which we have tried to draw attention in this chapter, naturally should not lead us to reject the emancipatory nature of post-Stalinist thinking as a whole. If we do not want to consider the epistemic field of post-Stalinism a dead object of intellectual history, we must also illuminate it from the other side and point out the positive aspects of its internal contradiction.

In critiquing Stalinist Marxism, the post-Stalinists not only indicated the more general problems of the Marxist orthodoxy that had reigned until that time but also were able to come up with their own inspiring solutions. If we accept the claim that Stalinism hindered the creative development of philosophy and the humanities disciplines, the Czechoslovak party intelligentsia managed to overcome the obstacles quickly. Since at least the 1960s, Czechoslovak post-Stalinism did not lag behind the development of either Eastern or Western European Marxism at all.

Based on the analyses presented here, we dare to claim that Czechoslovak Marxism can be presented as an autonomous form of thought. In the effort to overcome Stalinism, it processed ideas on its own theoretical ground and often also came up with similar formulations of questions or solutions like those that were discovered abroad, while at other times it created relatively original answers in reaction to non-Marxist intellectual traditions. The resulting picture of Czechoslovak post-Stalinist thought certainly does not represent a kind of eclectic collage composed of countless foreign impulses.

In an effort to problematize the central position of causality and functional relationships within the framework of the problem of determination of historical development and the functioning of social formations, the dialectical determinists created their conception of dialectical laws based on the immanent conception of contradiction. In many respects they were tackling almost the same problems that Evald Ilyenkov was working on in the Soviet Union, and that Louis Althusser dealt with in France a few years later.[149]

The Marxist humanists succeeded in developing the Marxist conception of praxis as an onto-creative activity, the originality and seriousness of which they managed to defend in confrontation with the existentialist conceptions of projection and cares, as well as the (implicitly) behaviorist concepts in Anglo-Saxon pragmatism. At the same time, the emphasis on the fully developed human being did not always have to be problematic. Although its abstract definition may have been constructed in such a way that it caused the interests of specific social, gender, and other groups to be overlooked, at the same time, it also contained positive potential. It is this aspect that played an unmistakable role in the successful emancipatory efforts of the Czech and Slovak cultural and intellectual scene of the 1960s. It is also significant that Kosík received positive contemporary praise from Edmund Husserl's disciple Jan Patočka, who declared *Dialectics of the Concrete* as a "breakthrough" symbolizing a new "epoch" in Czech philosophy of the time.[150]

If we read the texts from the end of the 1960s consistently, we cannot ignore signs of a critique of state socialism as a system. Although they are incomparable with, for instance, Bondy's vision of a self-governing society or Jacek Kuroń and Karol Modzelewski's critique of "state capitalism," they demonstrate that humanism was also open in this regard. It is also already possible to recognize the rudiments of efforts to name the structural deficits of state socialism as well as developed capitalism in the period's thinking, which are evident in post-1989 texts. In the 1990s, in a critique of capitalism's restoration and the absolutized idea of the market, Karel Kosík introduced the concepts of the "lumpenbourgeoisie" and "supercapital" and rejected the economic thinking of "actually existing" socialism and capitalism.[151] After returning from exile in the autumn of 1991, Ivan Sviták delivered several lectures at Charles University in Prague and Comenius University in Bratislava in which he took a stance against the Soviet bloc's Leninist path, but even more powerfully against the reintroduction of capitalism. He described the rejection of Marxism and socialism in the name of a campaign against communism as an "epochal illusion" that arose out of the region's early postcommunist hopes. By contrast with this, he attempted to rehabilitate Marx's thought, relieved of accretions, and to advocate for a democratic socialism based on "growth of human freedom, humanism, and liberation of labor" as an alternative model for Czechoslovak transformation.[152]

In many cases, the post-Stalinists had even anticipated the themes of their period in advance. The techno-optimists, exemplified by Radovan Richta, certainly were not the first to point out the importance of the scientific-technical revolution and its social impacts, but they probably were the first to think it through in Marxist concepts and to present it as an ambitious philosophical concept. While it could sound too optimistic and utopian in some respects, at the same time, thanks to its radicalism, techno-optimists foresaw many of the problems we are dealing with today. Lukáš Likavčan, for example, shows the extent to which topics analyzed by Richta's team still resonate in the contemporary philosophy of technology.[153]

In connection with Kosík's texts from the end of the 1960s, we pointed out several problematic moments that were also projected into his late work. On the other hand, we ought to acknowledge the inspiring moments of a timeless nature that he has provided. We have already commented on the humanists' concerns about the manipulativeness of technology and the fragmentary scientific view of the world. It is in this context that Kosík, in an interview with A. J. Liehm in 1968, called for a new human relationship with nature: "It is said in recent years that man 'humanizes' nature. Yet this claim ignores the fact that modern man also

6.5. Milan Machovec (left) at the conference of the Church of the World Christian Student Federation, 1962. Copyright Martin Machovec.

devastates it, and that his relationship to nature therefore consists in antithetical processes of humanization and destruction. It suffices to point to the pollution of the air, the poisoning of the waters or to the ruthless exploitation of the soil—the destruction of those elemental things which make it possible for man to inhabit the earth."[154] He already indicated negative aspects of modern civilization in "Our Current Crisis." In the 1990s, he openly discussed European rationality and the symbiosis of the economy, science, and technology as a threat to humanity because it "is already on its way toward destroying both itself and nature."[155]

Kosík's starting points thus come close to a reevaluation of what Moishe Postone termed classical Marxism.[156]

> I would like to particularly emphasize here the fundamental aspect of responsibility for nature, because here is a reference to a correction of the Marxist perspective. Marx still speaks about controlling nature. For Marx, industry was a means for controlling nature. Here, Marx was still thinking in an entirely Cartesian sense. However, today, based on his own experiences, man is learning

to develop another relationship with nature. He is learning to encounter nature not only as an object (i.e., he is learning that the relationship with nature should no longer be organized according to the "subject–object" pattern, but as an interplay). We even find some inclinations toward the development of this new relationship in Marx himself. For instance, in the *Grundrisse*, he speaks about nature as man's extended non-organic body. For Marx, nature is also the human body.[157]

Milan Machovec also chose the same perspective in his monograph *Filosofie tváří v tvář zániku* (Philosophy Faces Extinction), where he demanded a radical reevaluation of the human relationship to nature in the 1980s.[158] Although techno-optimist critiques, as Lukáš Likavčan points out, were only formulated in economic and aesthetic categories, we can find earlier hints of reflection on the ecological crisis in their works.[159] Jaromír Klaučo and Emil Duda noted the ecological impacts of socialist industrialization and explicitly stated that in addition to developed technology, society also needed "a clean environment, the original condition of nature, clean waterways, sufficient water, safe air, and an environment without excessive noise."[160] In this orientation we can perhaps catch a glimpse of the positive openness of post-Stalinist thought, which, as Erazim Kohák claims, would ultimately have pushed back against technology's self-directed development; at the very least in the humanist interpretation.

In conclusion, let us turn our attention once more to the interrelationships among individual intellectual currents, and to their tensions and similarities. The dialectical determinists reproached the humanists for neglecting the determination of subjective agency by objectively existing material conditions of practice, which brings them dangerously close to idealism. In turn, the humanists criticized the deterministic reduction of subjectivity to the level of a mere sociological factor that is solely reactive to already-existing conditions. The techno-optimists considered the underestimation of the civilizational role of science and technology by the humanists and determinists to be a fatal misunderstanding of the social processes of postindustrial modernity. In contrast, the humanists regarded the techno-optimistic uncritical admiration for science as a blindness to its potentially manipulative and therefore even enslaving effects. The determinists, for their part, were vexed by what looked like naïveté in the techno-optimistic approach, which suppresses the internally contradictory nature of socioeconomic relations—from which this new role for science and technology should arise. On the other hand, all these schools of thought had in common the Hegelian-Marxist starting point, which considered the humans' active transformation of reality as the essence of human reality. Unconsciously, as we pointed out in chapter 2, they also thus formulated a contradiction that we could consider to be the antinomy of post-Stalinism.

Mediation, a concept intended to resolve the basic ontological question of primacy in post-Stalinist Marxist philosophy, was placed by post-Stalinists into not-yet-entirely-objectified and not-yet-stabilized activity itself (praxis as creation for the humanists). At other times, however, it was placed into the objective conditions of this activity, which were instead defined as already-objectified and stabilized activity itself (objective tendencies for the dialectical determinists).[161] Thus, post-Stalinist thought found itself in an onto-logical circle, from which it could not find (and did not seek) a way out—either it moved from actual praxis to conditions or vice versa. This circle, which is otherwise perfectly permissible in Heidegger-inspired hermeneutics, should of course, as Hegel and after him Lukács already knew well, be taboo in dialectical thought, which any treading on the spot or spinning in a circle should precisely transgress. This unarticulated and unseen crisis or impasse in the post-Stalinist field of thought may seem fatal from today's perspective, but at the same time, we believe that it represents a so-called great mistake from which contemporary materialist and emancipatory thought can learn a great deal. The question also remains, however: To what extent have post-Stalinists not only encountered their own limits here but, consequently, also the limits of Marxist philosophy per se.

We recall, therefore, the claim that for us post-Stalinism represents a unified epistemic field that is shaped by the same form of problematization whose common denominator is the identification of the moment of mediation, which—from the perspective of post-Stalinism—was either suppressed or deformed by the previous epistemic field of Marxist orthodoxy. The intellectual currents that we have followed here—dialectical determinism, Marxist humanism, and techno-optimism—formed diverse but equally autonomous modes of approaching mediation. As we have seen, the emphases, the questions posed, and the varieties of solving given problems have differed, but together they form a unified constellation.

At the beginning of this book, we claimed that post-Stalinist Marxist thought can be considered a reflection on, but at the same time one of the outcomes or symptoms of what Peter Wagner terms the crisis of organized modernity. It questioned the previous way of solving social conflicts and the form of social organization that had been established during the first half of the twentieth century in the First and Second Worlds. Stalinism was one version of this modernity.

The post-Stalinists were aware of the limits of organized modernity, whether in the crisis of existing forms of production (abandoning Fordism and the advent of automation), social organization (the party and class institutions or corporative associations in general), management (central planning), or consumption (the mass society). At the same time, they formulated their own critical stance in progressivist terms as a unified historical movement that—with whatever limitations—ultimately confirmed their ideas, or ought to confirm them in the future. While voices appeared, especially at the end of the post-Stalinist era, that questioned this form of legitimization through history, their tone at most reflected various forms of pessimistic critique of civilization. However, as we see it, this did not represent the overcoming of historical progressivism, but only its opposite side.

We have thus come full circle back to the thesis that we outlined in chapter 1, which is that the post-Stalinists did not want to dismantle organized modernity of the socialist type, but to reconstitute it on new foundations. At the same time, post-Stalinism was also characterized by a particular ambiguity. Even though post-Stalinist Marxist reflections transcended Stalinist thought, and in doing so created a distinctive field of thought, their relationship to modernity was similar. While criticizing Stalinism, modernity and modern civilization remained both progressivist and modern in the post-Stalinists' diagnosis. Thus, post-Stalinism, rather than overcoming organized modernity, represented its culmination.

NOTES

CHAPTER 1. CZECHOSLOVAK POST-STALINISM

Epigraph: Nový, "Metakritika krize," 16.

1. In this respect, we take an approach similar to the one used by Michael David-Fox in the context of Russian/Soviet history. See David-Fox, *Crossing Borders*.

2. As a philosophical concept, "praxis" differs from the more commonly used term "practice." While the latter refers to ordinary reproductive activity or activities, the former is understood as a mutually intertwined relationship between a conscious human being and their activity, with an emphasis on the productive side in the sense of creating something new and also on its emancipatory aspect. However, both terms should be understood in their intertwined aspect rather than as opposites.

3. A shortened version of this chapter was published as Mervart and Růžička, "Czechoslovak Post-Stalinism."

4. Stephen Kotkin is a historian who began to understand Stalinism as a grandiose modernization project that enjoyed broad public acceptance in Soviet society. Stalinism, he said, was not a conservative reaction, as certain "post-Trotskyite" interpretations claim, but a "revival of revolutionary utopianism" that had the goal of creating "a new civilization." See Kotkin, *Magnetic Mountain*, 14, 16.

5. On the concept of "developmentalism" or—more precisely—"developmentalist dictatorship," see Losurdo, *Staline*, 241–49. On various theories of ("developmentalistic") development, see Prebisch, *Economic Development of Latin America*; Bairoch, *Révolution industrielle*; and Chew and Lauderdale, *Theory and Methodology of World Development*. See also Růžička, "Poststalinismus jako (ne)stalinský projekt modernity?"

6. Pinsky, "Origins of Post-Stalin Individuality." The origin of the "thawing" process has also been traced to late Stalinism by Denis Kozlov and Ele-

onory Gilburd, who date it to after 1953; see Kozlov and Gilburd, "Thaw as an Event," 26–27.

7. For the context of "thawing," see Kozlov and Gilburd, *Thaw*; for the continuity with Stalinism, see Olšáková and Janáč, *Cult of Unity*.

8. To learn more about the debates on how socialist ownership was shaped, see Horvath and Sommer, "From Nationalization to Privatization." The authors state that the most important legal enactments from the perspective of ownership were the promulgation of the socialist constitution in 1960 and the civil and economic code passed in 1964 (102).

9. With this statement we do not want to marginalize what has been called the national path to socialism, which was thematized in the 1940s by Polish, Czech, and Slovak communists. Placing an emphasis on local cultural and historical conditions was supposed to lead to a slight diversification, but the positive approach to the Soviet version of modernity did not change as a general principle.

10. "Backwardness" here refers to historical underdevelopment. Because it was so pronounced in the Soviet case, a considerable degree of state involvement was needed in the process of modernization. However, this underdevelopment is partially a hypothetical question, because the Soviet Union was not integrated into the world economy in a standard manner at that time, and certainly not in the sense assumed by the theorists of this concept (i.e., as a country that becomes "backward" only because of its integration in the world economy). On the other hand, as Robert C. Allen explains, due to its economic and population structure, the USSR had much more in common with countries of the Third World than with the West, so it is appropriate to ask to what extent it is possible to speak about it as a country that was not only historically but also systemically backward. See Allen, *Farm to Factory*. Lenin viewed Russia as a second-rate country with a high proportion of foreign capital that was seeking to create colonies out of it. Lenin, "Imperialism," 259–62.

11. This moment is well illustrated in the Czech magazine *Lidová kultura* (subtitled "list pro kulturu pracujícího lidu" [a paper for the culture of the working people]), published in 1945–1950. This magazine reported on the specifics of Czechoslovak development as well as on the progressiveness of Soviet culture, economics, and theory.

12. In many ways, Stalinization had strong domestic roots. Often, approaches were applied that had been abandoned a long time ago in the USSR. See Heumos, "*Vyhrňme si rukávy*," 44; and Connelly, *Captive University*. On the continuities of post-February social policies, see Rákosník, *Sovětizace sociálního státu*.

13. For example, James H. Satterwhite defined Marxist humanism as the antithesis of the orthodox Marxism of the Stalinist era. See Satterwhite, *Varieties of Marxist Humanism*, 8.

14. The historian František Červinka's introduction to his monograph on

the Czech Stalinist scholar Zdeněk Nejedlý, which he wrote in June 1967, is typical in this regard. The author states that he will neither celebrate nor comprehensively criticize the Nejedlean 1950s: "I will disappoint readers who expect [. . .] that the period of socialist reconstruction of our society, in which Nejedlý was an active participant, was replaced by a period of free criticism, which only concerns mistakes and tragic deformations of socialism in this immediate 'past,' whose revolutionary significance in our history will be increasingly felt in its own historical, revolutionary sense." Červinka, *Zdeněk Nejedlý*, 8. At the same time, it should be noted that in this regard a shift took place in post-Stalinist thinking during the 1960s, toward criticism of Stalinism as such (or, at the very least, toward its application in Czechoslovakia). With increasing frequency, voices were pointing out the unsuitability or outright error of applying the Soviet model of socialist modernity to the Czechoslovak case—and not only this, but at the end of the 1960s, Karel Kosík and Robert Kalivoda, for instance, issued a challenge to rethink socialism completely from its foundations. See Liehm and Kosík, "A. J. Liehm's Interview with Karel Kosík"; and Kalivoda, "Demokratizace a kritické myšlení."

15. Minutes of the discussion on the results of the Twentieth Congress of the Communist Party of the USSR at the membership meeting of the KSČ Cabinet for Philosophy, dated March 19, 1956. (Personal archive of J. Zumr.)

16. Berman, *All That Is Solid*, 98.

17. Wagner, *Modernity as Experience*.

18. Wagner, *Sociology of Modernity*, esp. 101–3.

19. Kolář, *Der Poststalinismus*.

20. A typical example of this is Sviták's retrospective interpretation of the 1960s as "squaring a circle." See Sviták, *Czechoslovak Experiment*. The authors of this penetratingly analytical book on the 1960s also attribute internal contradictions to post-Stalinism: Genis and Vail, *60. léta*, esp. 140–55.

21. Árnason, "Communism and Modernity," 65.

22. See Sommer et al., *Řídit socialismus jako firmu*.

23. Árnason, "Communism and Modernity," 68.

24. Árnason, "Communism and Modernity," 78, 89n10.

25. Wagner, *Sociology of Modernity*, 76.

26. In this case, our understanding of the term "reflexivity" significantly differs from that of Stefan Guth, who relies on theoreticians of modernity such as Ulrich Beck. In Guth's view, "reflexivity" and "reflexive modernity" denote a period in which where a single vision of one future is abandoned in favor of many possible futures. The theorists of scientific and technical revolution, as well as party leadership in the Eastern bloc (Guth focused particularly on the case of the Soviet Union), were unable or unwilling to frame the future in more pluralistic terms. See Guth, "One Future Only."

27. It is necessary to note here that in the 1960s this process went much farther than just the circles of the party intelligentsia—it also affected non-Marxist intellectual circles (for example, those who were involved with the magazine *Tvář*) as well as noncommunist political groups. For both examples, see Špirit, *Tvář*; and Hoppe, *Opozice '68*.

28. Intellectual activities of this type are the subject of further analysis. However, let us at least share a typical statement made by Radovan Richta, who claimed that the Stalinists were intoxicated by revolutionary intervention into the structure of the relations of ownership, which led to a loss of their capability for self-reflection. See Richta, "Ekonomika jako civilizační dimenze," 12. From the artistic clique of the party intelligentsia, we suggest Ladislav Helge's film *Stud* [Shame] (1967), Milan Kundera's novel *Žert* [*The Joke*] (1967), and *Démon súhlasu* and *Oneskorené reportáže* by the Slovak authors Dominik Tatarka and Ladislav Mňačko (both published in 1963) as examples.

29. Touraine, *Self-Production*, 19.

30. Touraine, *Self-Production*, 15.

31. Touraine, *Self-Production*, 27.

32. Touraine, *Self-Production*, 27, 49, 63.

33. Touraine, *Self-Production*, 58–69.

34. On the Czechoslovak Academy of Sciences, see Hoppe, Škodová, Suk, and Caccamo, "*O nový československý model socialismu.*" On artistic associations, see Mervart, *Naděje a iluze*; and Mervart, *Kultura v karanténě*.

35. See a statement made by a Slovak historian Ľubomír Lipták at the congress of the Slovak Historical Society in July 1968: "It is thus a certain paradox—for Stalinism a typical 'narrowing' of the field of view of the society in *our* specific conditions generally meant its expansion, even temporally, and not only in the area of the most recent history, but especially for the entire period of feudalism, where the previous historiography that was understood in a narrow national context—apart from a few topics—could not find the *subject* of Slovak history. A knowledge of older periods of Slovak history, even though it's in a relatively narrow thematic section, has greatly expanded in the past twenty years. True, it is difficult to call this a 'contribution' of the ruling historical conception; rather, this conception only *made it possible*. However, this only created the preconditions for creatively overcoming the original narrow ideological boundaries, albeit in rather complicated ways." Lipták, "Úloha a postavenie historiografie," 102. We are grateful to Adam Hudek for the reference to this text. On the question of reflexivity before 1956, see the following texts: Debates in the Cabinet for Philosophy ČSAV; Notes on the situation on the philosophical front, January 23, 1955; On the Current State and the Tasks of the Work of the Department of Dialectical Materialism, 1955; The State of and the Tasks of Historical Materialism in the Cabinet for Philosophy, 1955. (Personal archive of J. Zumr.)

36. Rowley, "Bogdanov and Lenin," 2–3.
37. Steila, "Lenin's Philosophy in Intellectual Context," 102.
38. Fitzpatrick, *On Stalin's Team*.
39. Rockmore, "Marx, Marxism, and Philosophical Modernity," 184.
40. Rowley, "Bogdanov and Lenin," 13–15. Rowley, like Rockmore, thus argues that Lenin's insistence on his own epistemological views expressed in *Materialism and Empirio-criticism* had a dimension that went beyond his own philosophy. He convincingly shows that Bogdanov's and Berdyaev's different epistemologies led these two proponents of Russian social democratic theory to entirely different political implications. It should be added that a more accommodating reading of Lenin's philosophy is offered in David Bakhurst's work, "On Lenin's Materialism and Empirio-criticism"; and, most recently, also by Marina F. Bykova. Like Bakhurst, she does not consider political-ideological motivation to be a sufficient explanation; she evaluates Lenin's philosophical concept from the perspective of period Russian Marxism and finds it to be both original and at the same time successful. See Bykova, "Lenin and the Crisis of Russian Marxism." Although we consider the debate over the philosophical significance of Lenin's oeuvre inspiring, for our historical perspective the question of his motivations is not crucial. More important are the consequences of Lenin's legacy in Stalinism, where the link between knowledge (philosophy) and politics is unquestionable.
41. Ree, "Stalin as a Marxist Philosopher," 280.
42. Pinsky, "Origins of Post-Stalin Individuality," 458–59. In this sense, a statement of a party political theorist, Miroslav Kusý, is typical for the Czechoslovak case: "Neither party discipline nor party resolutions bind me to find the truth somewhere that it isn't." Kusý, *Filozofia politiky*, 173.
43. See Kolář, *Poststalinismus*; and Kristina Andělová, "Intelektuální dějiny reformního komunismu jako jedna z možných perspektiv výzkumu post-stalinismu," a chapter in "Intelektuální dějiny českého reformního komunismu 1968–1990."
44. Pinsky, "Origins of Post-Stalin Individuality," 482.
45. See, for example, Mlynář, *Stát a člověk*; and Kosík, *Dialektika, kultura a politika*, particularly the section in the first part of the book under the title "Marxism a přehodnocování stalinismu" [Marxism and the Reevaluation of Stalinism].
46. See, for example, Ladislav Mňačko's statement of September 1964: "I am an old and responsible communist. I am not willing to have my things censored by an exceptionally idiotic censor." Cited in Mervart, *Naděje a iluze*, 8. Or the statement by the sociologist Vladimír Maňák: "If we have objective facts in our hands that prove that a resolution is unrealistic (and at the same time, the authorities that adopted it are unfamiliar with these facts), what kind

of person, our person, would not address them and would leave the resolution unsolved?" Maňák, *Kultúrny život* 18, 4, cited in Andělová in "Intelektuální dějiny reformního komunismu," 41.

47. Pinsky, "Origins of Post-Stalin Individuality," 460–61. For example, in one of the period documents there was discussion of "unification of all the creative forces of our philosophy around the party," while the "philosophical front" was also supposed to serve as the party's cognitive faculty, whose conclusions would be used "more than previously" in the party's practice. See Proposal for a Party Committee, in reference to Comrade Zelený's report, 1958. (Personal archive of J. Zumr.)

48. Ivan Sviták's remark in one of the party debates. See Protocol from the session of the party group division of historical materialism in the Philosophical Institute of the Czechoslovak Academy of Sciences, held on May 18, 1959. (Personal archive of J. Zumr.)

49. See, for example, Miroslav Kusý's interpretation of the party line: "The party tells me: here is a problem that is socially important; without solving it, it's impossible to go further toward realizing our ideals. If you are acquainted with it, you're an expert, an ideologist, or a writer, seek the truth that will help us solve the problem." Kusý, *Filozofia politiky*, 173. At this point, it should be noted that for some time, thanks to the space that was consciously created by the highest echelons of the party, the party intellectuals indeed became, in their own way, cocreators or co-participants in official politics. This was the case with the expert academic teams in the 1960s, the artistic associations that consulted on press law, and the ad hoc groups brought together in 1968 to help create materials for the planned extraordinary Fourteenth Congress of the KSČ.

50. Certain members of the party intelligentsia were of course already aware of this in the post-Stalinist period. For example, in a study she produced at the beginning of the 1960s, a Czech literary scholar, Růžena Grebeníčková, analyzed the Soviet debates on the Russian formalism of the 1930s. She concluded that the foundations of truly scientific ("objectively valid and scientifically verifiable") Marxist literary studies had already been laid at that time, "which brought social-historical and class aspects over to the other side, from the field of causally deterministic interpretation to the inner background of the literary work." Grebeníčková, "Cesty marxistické literární teorie," 101. We are grateful to Roman Kanda for drawing our attention to this text.

51. See, for example, Knapík, *V zajetí moci*.

52. For a similar development in the Soviet Union, see Guth, "One Future Only," 359, 362. In the Soviet case, Guth particularly emphasizes the new role that scientists and science claimed as "an independent and impartial judge of political initiatives."

53. On this subject, see Landa and Mervart, *Proměny marxisticko-křesťan-*

ského dialogu. At the same time, it is possible to provide solid demonstrations that Marxism not only absorbed but also influenced it. The diaries of the young Catholic intellectual Jiří Němec provide eloquent testimony of this. See Němec, *Zápisníky I (1960–1964)* and Němec, *Zápisníky II (1965–1969).*

54. If we remain with the example of the Marxist-Christian dialogue, it is no coincidence that the participants from the Marxist side were recruited from party intellectuals, who in the Stalinist era had worked from a paradigm of "scientific atheism." Institutionally speaking, we can see that the Department of Scientific Atheism at the Institute of Philosophy within the ČSAV, which was founded in 1960 under the leadership of Erika Kadlecová, gave rise in 1965 to the section on the sociology of religion in the ČSAV's new Institute of Sociology. Kadlecová, who during the Stalinist period had been engaging in intellectual struggle with the remnants of religion, became the leading sociologist of religion in the post-Stalinist period, and she conducted relevant research into religiosity. See Kadlecová, *Úloha Křesťanství,* and Kadlecová, *Sociologický výzkum religiozity.* For more on this subject, also see Nešpor, "Význam Eriky Kadlecové." The same also holds true for other leading figures in the field, such as Milan Machovec and Vítězslav Gardavský. See Nešpor, *Ne/náboženské naděje intelektuálů.*

55. See Kopeček, *Hledání ztraceného smyslu revoluce.*

56. Let us share a personal testimony here: it was probably in 1957 when Růžena Grebeníčková began working on her study of the Soviet debates concerning Russian formalism. In this context, she wrote a letter to György Lukács in which she asked whether it is possible to include his early writing in the Marxist tradition, and what to do with Lucien Goldmann and Merleau-Ponty so the result would not be hybrid pseudo-Marxist. See the Lukács Archive in Budapest, Letter by Růžena Grebeníčková to György Lukács dated June 21, 1957. We are grateful to Ivan Landa for helping us access this document.

57. Skilling, "Background," 78.

58. Schmarc, *Země lyr a ocele.*

59. An analogous movement can also be observed within the framework of the great Stalinist architectural projects that were usually only built in the post-Stalinist period. See Olšáková and Janáč, *Cult of Unity.*

60. For an analysis of Erika Kadlecová's book as a source on Stalinism, see Mervart, "Czechoslovakism and the Party Theory"; and Cvekl, *Lid a osobnost.* This trend is also indicated in records from some party discussions where criticisms of "revisionism" came up. See esp. statements by Karel Mácha, Erika Kadlecová, and Irena Dubská, in Minutes of the meeting of the party group of the Department of Historical Materialism in the ČSAV Institute of Philosophy held on May 18, 1959. (Personal archive of J. Zumr.)

61. Sommer, *Angažované dějepisectví,* esp. 200–229; and Kanda, "Strukturalisté dělají marxismus"; and Kanda, *Český literárněvědný marxismus.*

62. In this respect, Sommer mentions the collectively authored *Přehled dějin Komunistické strany Československa: These* (Prague: Státní nakladatelství politické literatury, 1957), and Stalinist signs of propagandism can still be found in the final synthesis of party historiography in *Dějiny Komunistické strany Československa* (Prague: Státní nakladatelství politické literatury, 1961), which was prepared under the leadership of Pavel Reiman. As an example of the complicated relationship to the structuralist background, Kanda mentions Felix Vodička's monograph *Cesty a cíle obrozenské literatury* (Prague: Československý spisovatel, 1958).

63. However, in his study, in connection with Felix Vodička and Jan Mukařovský, Roman Kanda suggests that speaking about "pure" Stalinism is problematic in the Czech case. Both the domestic traditions of non-Stalinist Marxism and the structuralist influences operating here brought a certain multivocality in certain Marxist concepts and colored the methodology of the entire Stalinist doctrine. Besides the "Stalinist structuralists," Zdeněk Nejedlý also probably represents a good example of this.

64. Sommer et al., *Řídit socialismus jako firmu*; and Kopeček, *Architekti dlouhé změny*. Kopeček states in the introduction that "a striking continuity is shown [. . .]in all cases between the 1960s and 1970s" (32).

65. Kopeček, "Vládnout právem."

66. See Sommer, "Zkoumání budoucnosti socialismu," 74–82.

67. Andělová, "Reformní komunismus po roce 1968: Nástup normalizace," a chapter in "Intelektuální dějiny českého reformního komunismu," esp. 61–77.

68. Kolář, *Der Poststalinismus*, esp. 91–142.

69. Access to the Twentieth Congress and the experience of ordinary party members were of course different matters. For example, Matěj Bílý draws attention to the "strong, and often repressive suppression of criticism from within the party." Bílý, "Debata o XX. sjezdu KSSS," 250. Of course, the party debates were also regulated at the level of scientific and academic workplaces, and in no way were the higher echelons of the party launching an open and welcome debate—for more on the atmosphere at institutes of higher education, see Hájek, *Paměť české levice*, 161–70.

70. See the Report from the Plenary Meeting of the KSČ Cabinet for Philosophy from March 5 and 19, 1956; and the entry on the discussion of the results of the Twentieth Congress of the Communist Party of the USSR at the membership meeting for the KSČ Cabinet for Philosophy, dated March 19, 1956. (Personal archive of J. Zumr.)

71. Notes on the situation on the philosophical front, January 23, 1955. (Personal archive of J. Zumr.)

72. Resolution from the Plenary Meeting of the KSČ Cabinet for Philosophy ČSAV company organization, held on April 16, 1956. (Personal archive of J. Zumr.)

73. National Archives, Prague, fond Ivan Sviták, box 60, "O projevech a překonávání takzvaného kultu osobnosti ve filozofii."
74. Kolář, *Poststalinismus*, 91–142.
75. Sviták, "O projevech a překonávání takzvaného kultu."
76. Nový, "Filosofie a politika," 188n3.
77. Dubská, *K problematice stranickosti*; Dubská, *Auguste Comte*; and Dubská, *Objevování Ameriky*. In this context, Michael Voříšek states that three prominent sociologists in their countries (Vladimir A. Yadov in the Soviet Union, Julian Hochfeld in Poland, and Pavel Machonin in Czechoslovakia) originally criticized the idea of a Marxist sociology, until they made it their own. See Voříšek, *Reform Generation*, 183.
78. Krylova, "Soviet Modernity."
79. Harding, *Leninism*, 239.
80. Yurchak, *Everything Was Forever*.
81. On this point, we agree with the approach used in later Hungarian analysis. See Konrád and Szelényi, *Intellectuals*.
82. Regardless of the different levels of modernization between the Czech lands and Russia, the Czech intelligentsia played an "enlightening" role in their country like that of the Russian intelligentsia in theirs. See David-Fox, "Intelligentsia."
83. On the parallel division within the "physicists versus lyricists debate" in the Soviet Union, see Guth, "One Future Only," esp. 366–67. It should be noted that while the Soviet "physicists" roughly overlap with the Czechoslovak techno-optimists, it seems that the Soviet "lyricists" differ in some respects from the Czechoslovak Marxist humanists. The latter were definitely much less anti-scientistic and more progress-oriented than the former.
84. On February 25, 1948, the Communist Party of Czechoslovakia completed the political coup. In their official interpretations, the communists' seizure of political power was styled as "Victorious February."
85. Paradigmatically, see Kosík, "Přeludy a socialismus" (originally published in 1957).
86. For alienation, see *Franz Kafka*, especially the contributions by Ivan Sviták and Eduard Goldstücker; Sviták, "Hrdinové odcizení"; and Průcha, "Marxism." For modern art, see Kalivoda, "Tikal a český surrealismus"; Kosík, "Hašek and Kafka" (originally published in 1963). For the critique of ideology, see party meeting of the Cabinet for Philosophy ČSAV March 19, 1956. The entry on the discussion of the results of the Twentieth Congress of the Communist Party of the USSR at the membership meeting of the KSČ Cabinet for Philosophy dated March 19, 1956. (Personal archive of J. Zumr.) Later, in 1956–1958, the discussion spread to the pages of *Literární noviny*, the weekly publication of the Union of Czechoslovak Writers; for a summary of the de-

bate, see Kopeček, *Hledání ztraceného smyslu revoluce*, 239–55. For the Marxist approach to Christianity, see Gardavský, *God Is Not Yet Dead*, and Machovec, *Marxismus und dialektische Theologie*; for self-governing socialism, see Bartošek, "Naše nynější krize"; Kalivoda, "Demokratizace a kritické myšlení," 10:13, 11:6; Kalivoda, "O perspektivách"; and Kosík, "O dělnických řadách—kriticky." An English version was published as "A Word of Caution on Workers' Councils," in Satterwhite, *Crisis of Modernity*, 209–10.

87. Since there is no accurate translation of the Czech term *lidovost* into English, we coined the term "folkness," which is close to the meaning of the original concept. In Stalinist theories, folkness was understood as a positive feature of the popular masses and of their thinking, artistic expressions, and political activities. Since the popular masses were interpreted as the core of the national body, folkness was therefore perceived as a quality of the nation, and, in Nejedlý's interpretation, specifically of the Czech nation.

88. One could object that the above-mentioned emphasis on culture stemmed from the disciplines themselves (philosophy, history, or aesthetics) from which the great majority of Marxist humanists were recruited, while the techno-optimists generally had backgrounds in more technologically oriented fields (economics or cybernetics). However, a closer look shows that this objection does not hold up. Richta's team—known for its focus on technology, civilizational change, and its strong support for techno-optimism—was highly multidisciplinary. It included not just economists and cyberneticists but also philosophers and historians.

89. Kalivoda, *Moderní duchovní skutečnost*; and Kosík, *Dialektika konkrétního*. For English translations, see Sviták *Dialectics of the Concrete*; and Sviták, *Windmills of Humanity*.

90. Auerhan, *Technika, kvalifikace, vzdělání*; and Richta et al., *Civilizace na rozcestí*. For the English translation, see *Civilization at the Crossroads*. See also Selucký, *Ekonomika*.

91. Richta et al., *Civilization at the Crossroads*, 46–47.

92. Richta et al., *Civilization at the Crossroads*, 34–40; and Selucký, *Ekonomika*, 32–33.

93. See, for example, Sommer, "Scientists of the World, Unite!"; and Guth, "One Future Only."

94. Richta et al., *Civilization at the Crossroads*, 219.

95. Kosík, *Dialectics of the Concrete*.

96. In this respect, *Dialectics of the Concrete* bore the revealing subtitle "A Study on Problems of Man and World."

97. At first glance, it sometimes seems that the main driving force of post-Stalinist Marxism, especially in its humanist strains, was Marx's *Economic and Philosophic Manuscripts*. Johann P. Árnason, however, speaks of the unrecognized critical potential of Marx's *Grundrisse*. See Árnason, "Perspectives

and Problems," 73, but he draws attention to its influence only in the context of Ágnes Heller and Robert Kalivoda's historical analysis of the transition from feudalism to capitalism (Árnason, "Perspectives and Problems," 78). By contrast, Nick Nesbitt's work agrees with our findings in his recapitulation of the reception of the *Grundrisse*, mentioning Karel Kosík right next to Louis Althusser. See Nesbitt, "Grundrisse," 45.

98. Selucký, *Ekonomika*, 94.

99. See Sommer, "'Are We Still Behaving as Revolutionaries?'"

100. See Kopeček, *Architekti dlouhé změny*; Sommer et al., *Řídit socialismus jako firmu*; and Rindzevičiūtė, *Power of Systems*.

101. Trencsényi et al., *History of Modern Political Thought*, vol. 2, part I, 416, 419.

102. This was one of the Marxist humanists' shared convictions that was propounded across the state socialist countries. For the Yugoslav case, see the study on a member of the Yugoslav Praxis school, Danko Grlić (Hočevar, "Art as Praxis") We can recognize another shared belief among Marxist humanists in the Gramscian approach of culture as something that replaces the former Leninist conception of politics. Thus, for example, the Polish sociologist Zygmunt Bauman was convinced of the irreplaceable role culture plays in the critique of a given social order. See Brzeziński, "Human Praxis," 67–73. In his way, Ivan Landa, who labels techno-optimism as technological determinism, also adheres to this interpretation, and thus he evaluates the humanistic vision of radical democracy as a more open concept of emancipatory politics. See Landa, "Technology and Politics."

103. Erazim Kohák, "Filosofický smysl Československého jara 1968," manuscript 1981 (National Archives, Prague, fond Zdeněk Mlynář, box 24). For more on this subject, see Trnka, *Filosof Erazim Kohák*. In historiography, the Czechoslovak democratization movement in 1968 is usually called the "Prague Spring." To avoid its Prague-centric or Czech-centric implication, we prefer the term "Czechoslovak Spring," which includes Slovak historical events and processes along with the Czech ones.

104. On the concept of thinking as an in-no-way natural feat of a certain disposition or power, but as an activity forced by things (events) that lie outside thought, see Deleuze, *Proust and Signs*, 94–102.

105. For discussion of the Czechoslovak case, see the stimulating book by the Social Democrat Karel Hrubý, who was a contemporary of the Czech post-Stalinist figures: Hrubý, *Cesty komunistickou diktaturou*, esp. 221–51. Regarding the following, it is typical that the author spoke in the context of the Stalinism of a generation of young communists, and then in the post-Stalinist period he discusses individual authors: Karel Kosík, Robert Kalivoda, František Graus, and others, as though a member of the party intelligentsia only became a full-fledged thinker when he discarded the Stalinist baggage.

106. The concept of a generation as the determining moment of post-Stalinist thought is brought forward by Antonín J. Liehm in *Generace*. The work was translated into English by Peter Kussi as *Politics of Culture*. Liehm's influence can be clearly seen on Michal Kopeček (*Hledání ztraceného smyslu revoluce*) and Miloš Havelka ("Česká kultura a politika." Probably the strongest and conceptually most elaborated version is found in Voříšek, *Reform Generation*.

107. Wagnerová, "Ještě o Karlu Kosíkovi." In the second half of 1944, Předvoj [Vanguard] was the largest anti-Nazi resistance group in the Czech lands. Two of the major icons of Czechoslovak post-Stalinism, Kosík and Richta, were members.

108. Voříšek, *Reform Generation*, 297.

109. There is a rapidly growing body of literature on this subject but see especially the collectively authored works by Kopeček, *Architekti dlouhé změny*; and Sommer et al., *Řídit socialismus jako firmu*. Several papers also address the issue of experts: see Havelková and Oates-Indruchová's edited volume *Politics of Gender Culture*.

110. Our approach is based on the results of the historical analysis of several of the social sciences and humanities fields. See Hermann, "Biologický ústav ČSAV," 543–45; Mervart, "Filosofický ústav ČSAV"; Franc and Dvořáčková, *Dějiny Československé akademie*, 602–13; and Sommer, *Angažované dějepisectví*.

111. Špirit, *Tvář*.

112. Voříšek, *Reform Generation*; Sommer, *Angažované dějepisectví*; Hoppe et al., *"O nový československý model socialismu"*; and Olšáková and Janáč, *Cult of Unity*.

113. Árnason, "Perspectives and Problems," 216–17; Kohák, "Filosofický smysl"; Kovanda, *Experience with Democratic Self-Management*; and Landa, "Technology and Politics." See also Landa, "Historical Bloc and Revolution."

114. See, e.g., Golan, *Czechoslovak Reform Movement*; Golan, *Reform Rule in Czechoslovakia*; Kaplan, *Kořeny československé reformy 1968*, vols. 1–4 ; Kusin, *Intellectual Origins*; Kusin, *Political Grouping*; and Skilling, *Czechoslovakia's Interrupted Revolution*.

115. In our use of the terms "epistemic field" (*épistémé*) and "field of problematization," we have been very loosely inspired by Michel Foucault and Louis Althusser. Naturally, it is necessary to mention that our use of these terms does not always exactly match their conceptualizations. For more on these terms, see Foucault, *Order of Things*, and Althusser, *Reading Capital*. The passage that perhaps most accurately reflects our methodological perspective is to be found in Foucault, "Polemics, Politics and Problematizations," esp. 118.

116. Kopeček, *Hledání ztraceného smyslu revoluce*; and Satterwhite, *Varieties of Marxist Humanism*; Suk, *Veřejné záchodky ze zlata*.

117. Benjamin, *Origin of German Tragic Drama*, 41. On the criticism of

nominalism in historiography, see Benjamin, *Origin of German Tragic Drama*, 39–44.

118. In a review essay on the original Czech edition of this book, Juraj Halas convincingly showed that our concept can also be successfully applied to post-Stalinist economic thinking, specifically to works of Ota Šik and Čestmír Kožušník. See Halas, "Intelektuálne dejiny československého poststalinismu," esp. 152–57.

119. Kusý, "Systém a štruktúra zofie," 425. In our treatise, we present a critical relationship to the "outside" through existentialism. The period manner of relating to neopositivism is an independent topic that would exceed the framework of our research. However, it is still clear that for Karel Kosík, for instance, this trend presented a lesser challenge than existentialism, and that his rejection of neopositivism was very indiscriminate. For more on the subject, see Hříbek, "Kosík's Notion of 'Positivism.'"

120. Liehm and Kosík, "A. J. Liehm's Interview with Karel Kosík," 406.
121. Cibulka, "Rehabilitovat Marxe!" 375.
122. Kolář, *Soudruzi a jejich svět*, 8.

CHAPTER 2. REAL STRUCTURE

Epigraph: Marx, *Grundrisse*, 411–12.

1. Even though some have good reasons not to consider him a "full-fledged" Marxist, let us offer the example of the early György Lukács in *History and Class Consciousness: Studies in Marxist Dialectics* (1923) to stand for all the rest, and Walter Benjamin in *On the Concept of History* from 1940. See Lukács, *History and Class Consciousness*; and Benjamin, "On the Concept of History," 389–400.

2. Stephen J. Collier uses the Soviet conception of urbanization as an example of this manner of thinking in *Post-Soviet Social*, 65–67.

3. Bazarov, "Methodology of Perspective Plans," 366–67.
4. Bazarov, "Methodology of Perspective Plans," 365.
5. Sharov, "Goal of Plan," 380.
6. Strumilin, "Perspective Guidelines," 431.
7. Strumilin, "Perspective Guidelines," 433.
8. Kondratiev, "Critical Remarks," 442; cited in Collier, *Post-Soviet Social*, 59.
9. Stalin, "Industrialisation," 256. Of course, it is necessary to add that Stalin would have vigorously defended himself against any accusations of "arbitrariness" or "autocratism." His introduction of such a rapid pace of industrialization was not some kind of random, discretionary decision, but was based on his evaluation (however twisted it might seem) of the domestic and external situation of the USSR. For more on this, see Stalin, "Industrialisation," esp. 257–67.

10. Sommer et al., *Řídit socialismus jako firmu*, 19.

11. This is undoubtedly also evidenced by the strict rejection of Bukharin's original conception of equilibrium, which was one of the cornerstones of the genetic principle. In addition, see Stalin, "Concerning Questions of Agrarian Policy," esp. 149–52. On Bukharin's theory of equilibrium, see Bukharin, *Historical Materialism*, 242–43.

12. Stalin, *Economic Problems*, 4.

13. Czech philosopher Lubomír Sochor very keenly observed this moment at the beginning of the 1960s. See Sochor, "Filozofie a ekonomie," 96.

14. Stalin, *Economic Problems*, 7.

15. Korsch, "Present State of the Problem," 100–101.

16. On the distinction between idealism and materialism from the point of view of the Marxist orthodoxy, see Lenin, "Materialism and Empiriocriticism," esp. 23–33.

17. As Plekhanov notes, although the French materialists admitted in theory that transformation (of species, or societies) is possible, this never became a fundamental perspective for their thinking. In Plekhanov's view, they were simply unable to formulate a satisfactory theory of development (that is, if they were even interested in doing so). See Plekhanov, "Development of the Monist View," esp. 537.

18. Plekhanov, "Materialist Understanding of History," esp. 603–4; and "Development of the Monist View," esp. 537–38.

19. See Plekhanov, "Essays on the History of Materialism," esp. 51–52. Among the post-Stalinists, this perspective was most painstakingly developed by Jindřich Zelený. See Zelený, *O historickém materialismu*, 16–24.

20. Marx, "German Ideology," 42. The fact that satisfying these needs leads to creating new needs, and thus to further development of the forces of production is only possible under the assumption that the "first" act of manufacturing has already taken place.

21. Plekhanov, "Essays on the History of Materialism," 145–46; Plekhanov, "Materialist Understanding of History," 619; and Engels, *Dialectics of Nature*, 330, 457.

22. Klofáč, *Materialistické pojetí dějin*, 189–90.

23. Marx, *Capital, Vol. I*, 18, 751.

24. Klofáč, Tlustý, and Svoboda, *Problémy determinismu a pokroku*, 20–21, 40–41, 99–100; and Klofáč, *Materialistické pojetí dějin*, 58–61.

25. Klofáč, Tlustý, and Svoboda, *Problémy determinismu a pokroku*, 104.

26. Bukharin also understood chance in this way. See Bukharin, *Historical Materialism*, 43–44.

27. Yakhot, *Suppression of Philosophy*, 115.

28. Plekhanov, "On the Question," 305.

29. According to Josef Révai, this shift was already evident in Engels and Plekhanov (as well as in Heinrich Cunow) with their "naturalization" of dialectics. See Révai, "Lukács Georg."

30. Lenin, "Materialism and Empiriocriticism," 190 (and on practice as a criterion for the success of a theory and the truthfulness of ideas, see 110, 138–39, 142–43).

31. On the separation of the subjectivity of cognition, see Merleau-Ponty, *Adventures of the Dialectic*, 60, 67.

32. Merleau-Ponty, *Adventures of the Dialectic*, 64.

33. Sviták, "Little Base," 57–58.

34. Zelený, *O historickém materialismu*, 62.

35. Zelený, *O historickém materialismu*, 61.

36. Klofáč et al., *Problémy determinismu a pokroku*, 66.

37. Klofáč et al., *Problémy determinismu a pokroku*, 65.

38. Klofáč et al., *Problémy determinismu a pokroku*, 69–70.

39. Zelený, *O historickém materialismu*, 67.

40. On Stalin's "stages," see Stalin, "Dialectical and Historical Materialism," 266–69. For its problematization, see Klofáč et al., *Problémy determinismu a pokroku*, 285–86.

41. See Voříšek, *Reform Generation*, 127–84, esp. 181–83. Voříšek shows how the same debate eventually led to the emergence of sociology as an empirical science by gradually splitting away from historical materialism. However, while he mainly traces institutional impacts (the establishment of a new discipline), we are primarily interested here in the epistemic issues.

42. This designation is not arbitrary or created by us. It was Josef Cibulka who coined the name for this group, and he was probably the only one who consciously used it. Its extrapolation to other authors is a choice we made.

43. According to his own words, Josef Cibulka had already begun working on his conception of dialectical laws in 1953. He presented this work in textual form for the first time in the article "Marxovo pojetí." He then detailed it in an independent publication: *Přínos Marxova Kapitálu*, which he finished writing in 1958, and in numerous articles published throughout the 1960s, especially in the Czech and Slovak journals *Filosofický časopis* and *Otázky marxistickej filozofie*. Later, he presented a complex ontology of dialectical determinism in the compendious *Dialektika a ontologie*.

44. Besides Karel Kosík and Radovan Richta, Jindřich Zelený is also among the most prominent and most translated Czech Marxists who have received attention in recent times. From his publications in the 1960s, we highlight Zelený, *Logic of Marx*; and Zelený, "Kant, Marx and the Modern Rationality."

45. Černík, *Dialektický vedecký zákon*, 112.

46. Černík, *Dialektický vedecký zákon*, 113.

47. Cibulka, *Dialektika a ontologie*, 147, 149–50.

48. Cibulka, *Dialektika a ontologie*, 148.

49. Cibulka, "Marxovo pojetí," 889; and Cibulka, *Přínos Marxova Kapitálu*, 65.

50. Cibulka, "Marxovo pojetí," 881.

51. For criticism of this conception, see also Slejška, *Dialektika výrobních sil*, 28. Here, the author directly states: "Their difference [i.e., the forces of production and relations of production] cannot be given by any special location, but by specific features of dialectical mediation, that is, the conflicting unity of polarities in the inner structure of the forces of production, and in economic relations."

52. This definition does not apply universally, and it is undoubtedly true that the post-Stalinists were also interested in various forms of transition from one formation to another. Nevertheless, it is necessary to emphasize once again that the direction of development was not unambiguous for them, or, more precisely, that they began to question this unambiguity and givenness in the name of a "truly" scientific and "truly" dialectical understanding of development itself. Nor is it true that orthodox thinking about dialectics utterly precludes the question of something new emerging. But what is important for us is that they never formulated this problem in the same terms as the dialectical determinists (and the post-Stalinists in general), which is to say in terms of the genesis of something new. The phrase "genesis of the new" is not meant to be only a unidirectional change of quality (i.e., a transition from one quality to another), but also a differentiation of development into multiple directions and the logical nondeducibility of this development from its previous stages.

53. In this respect, they aligned with Egon Bondy's ontology ("Egon Bondy" was the pen name of Zbyněk Fišer). See Fišer, *Útěcha z ontologie*. For a more detailed analysis of Bondy's early ontology, see Kužel, "Nesubstanční ontologie."

54. As Cibulka writes, we "mustn't understand" this contradiction as a driving force for movement "in the sense of a metaphysical idea about an impulse to movement that isn't identical with this movement. Then it wouldn't be internal self-development. Inconsistency is not a structural-morphological given property of objects; it is the structural aspect of the essential movement itself." See Cibulka, *Přínos Marxova Kapitálu*, 15. It is important to note, however, that Cibulka warned against the assumption—advanced by Engels, his intellectual successors, and also figures such as Evald Ilyenkov—that contradiction must be sought immediately within any form of movement, including those that are merely local or mechanical. In Cibulka's view, such movements (or "motions" to be precise) are not inherently contradictory; contradiction emerges only in those forms of movement that give rise to qualitative change. These transformative movements, he argues, are related to local or cyclical motion only through

some form of mediation. This is precisely why movement is the "most basic" and "most essential" element for the dialectical determinists: because it explains qualitative development in society and in nature. On Engels's and Ilyenkov's conceptions of contradiction as immediately present in every type of movement, see Engels, "Anti-Dühring," 111–12; and Ilyenkov, *Dialectics of the Abstract*, 94–97.

55. Cibulka, *Přínos Marxova Kapitálu*, 44.

56. Cibulka, *Přínos Marxova Kapitálu*, 45 (emphasis added).

57. Cibulka, *Přínos Marxova Kapitálu*, 45.

58. Hegel directly terms this form of thinking "dialectical," and he distinguishes it from reasoning that fixes things in their differences. It should be added, however, that—just like Hegel—the dialectical determinists are ultimately aiming toward speculative thinking, in which these contradictions are understood in their unity (i.e., as the post-Stalinist Marxists would say, in their totality). However, the notion of the speculative was probably entirely taboo in their vocabulary thanks to its idealistic tinge. See Hegel, *Encyclopedia of the Philosophical Sciences*, § 79–81.

59. Cibulka, *Dialektika a ontologie*, 142.

60. When criticizing formalizing approaches, Cibulka makes frequent references to two works: Bertalanffy, *Das biologische Weltbild*; and Klaus, *Kybernetik*. He also does not neglect to mention that for Bertalanffy the analogies themselves only represent the lower degree of formalization. Still, no matter how primitive they are, they form a kind of foundation from which it is possible to progress to more complex formalizations such as logical homology and scientific laws. Cibulka adds, the principle of formalization itself and therefore also a certain homogenization remain unproblematized in their works. See Cibulka, *Dialektika a ontologie*, 145–46.

61. Cibulka, *Dialektika a ontologie*, 145.

62. Cibulka, "K otázce exaktnosti," 299.

63. Cibulka, "Jde o otázku zrodu," 292.

64. Cibulka, "Jde o otázku zrodu," 292.

65. For Marx's own formulation of this problem, see Marx, *Capital, Vol. III*, 232–33.

66. Cibulka, *Přínos Marxova Kapitálu*, 83.

67. Cibulka, *Dialektika a ontologie*, 235. See also Slejška, *Dialektika výrobních sil*, 56.

68. Here, Cibulka analyzes Stalinism, which replaces the contradictory system with a teleological one. See Cibulka, *Dialektika a ontologie*, 71.

69. For Cibulka, in this case it meant the removal of "the progressive core of capitalism's self-regulation levers," and its incorporation into socialist social relations. See Cibulka, *Dialektika a ontologie*, 273.

70. Cibulka, *Dialektika a ontologie*, 267.

71. Cibulka, *Dialektika a ontologie*, 267. At the same time, Cibulka does not deny the need to introduce a centrally directed system in certain situations, but he understands it as an exceptional state of emergency, from which the bureaucratic deformation for the first time in history created a "permanent system." See Cibulka, *Dialektika a ontologie*, 268.

72. Cibulka, *Dialektika a ontologie*, 286.

73. Cibulka, *Dialektika a ontologie*, 131.

74. According to Zelený, "All their critiques of the existing world and their programmes for its alteration remain within the bounds of bourgeois forms of life; they are only platitudes, different interpretations of what already is" (*Logic of Marx*, 212).

75. Zelený, *Logic of Marx*, 212.

76. Zelený, *Logic of Marx*, 211–12.

77. Sobotka, *Člověk, práce a sebevědomí*.

78. Cibulka, "Rehabilitovat Marxe!" 377.

79. According to Sochor, "Whereas the English political economy dealt with the sphere of material necessity in social life and made man into the object of this necessity, German idealistic dialectics, conceiving of man as a spiritual being, examined the human conditions of freedom and the free activity of the subject. Marx, on the other hand, found that the human practice was the basis of this social necessity and freedom, and he proved that only revolutionary human practice subordinates the sphere of economic necessity to the 'realm of true freedom.'" Sochor, *Filosofie a ekonomie*, 72.

80. Nový, "Filosofie a politika," 188n. Nový was well aware of this affiliation and he also shifted the meaning of Gramsci's expression, thus emphasizing the novelty of the philosophical perspective. By contrast, Ivan Landa is more of the opinion that expressions such as the philosophy of practice, Marxist sociology, or perhaps techno-optimistic reformulation of the forces of production are just an elaboration of one and the same discipline—historical materialism. However, in our view, this loses the unifying and innovative aspect that Nový (and all the Marxist humanists) had wanted to give it. See Landa, "Technology and Politics."

81. See also Růžička, "Formování historického materialismu."

82. Kosík, *Dialectics of the Concrete*, 70.

83. Marx, "Theses on Feuerbach," 4.

84. It is, of course, extremely likely that the humanists would have understood Kant's antinomies (particularly the solution of the antinomies of judgment in *Critique of Judgment*) precisely as a product of bourgeois capitalist society.

85. According to Sochor, "[Marx] discovered that in practical activities there is a unity of subject and objects, that practice is simultaneously objective and subjective, that the practical man as a social being mediates the unity of

'created' society (social circumstances, conditions of social life, social 'institutions and relations'), and societies 'forming' (conscious or spontaneous human activity)." Sochor, *Filosofie a ekonomie*, 72.

86. Kosík, *Dialectics of the Concrete*, 71. In the *Critique of Judgment*, Kant speaks of the organization of nature according to mechanical and teleological causes, where the former is the subject of determining judgment with objective validity, and the latter is the subject of reflecting judgment and has only subjective validity. See Kant, *Critique of Judgment*, § 69–72.

87. For more details on this subject, see Landa, "Marxova filosofická antropologie."

88. Marx, "Economic and Philosophic Manuscripts," 276–77.

89. Marx states, "A spider conducts operations that resemble those of a weaver, and a bee puts to shame many an architect in the construction of her cells. But what distinguishes the worst architect from the best of bees is this, that the architect raises his structure in imagination before he erects it in reality." Marx, *Capital, Vol. I*, 188. Taking the last sentence into account, the philosophers of praxis went even beyond Marx (at least in the case cited). At the end of the process mentioned here, we do not usually encounter what was present in ideal form in the beginning. That would still be a purely Hegelian, idealist view. On the other hand, as a Czech philosopher, Milan Průcha, points out, Marx already criticized this concept of objectification in *Economic and Philosophical Manuscripts*. See Průcha, "Filosofické problémy."

90. This is mainly true for Plekhanov. See Plekhanov, *Materialist Understanding of History*, 619.

91. Kosík, *Dialectics of the Concrete*, 136.

92. Nový, "Marxova filosofie," 129.

93. Průcha, "Filosofické problémy," 54.

94. See Průcha, "Filosofické problémy," 48n220.

95. In his 1947 text, Lucien Goldmann characterizes the difference between Hegel and Marxism regarding the role of conceptual knowledge in the following sense: While for Hegel the conceptual knowledge is the goal and practical activity is the intermediary, for Marxism it is the other way around—conceptual knowledge is the intermediary whereas practice (transformation of the world through practical activity) is the goal. See Goldmann, "Le matérialisme dialectique," 15–18. The same goes for the Czechoslovak Marxists. To this it is only necessary to add that, for Marxists, such transformative activity should always be emancipatory in its essence.

96. For both citations, see Kosík, "Hašek a Kafka," 128. For the English version of this text, see "Hašek and Kafka." Josef Švejk is the main character of Jaroslav Hašek's novel *The Good Soldier* Švejk (1921–1923), which Kosík appraised as the mirror of modern society and which he compared with works of Franz Kafka.

97. Here, we are thinking of Husserl's early conception of consciousness, which is determined precisely and only by its intentionality (i.e., focusing on the object). We are aware that the late Husserl and post-Husserl phenomenology further elaborated the non-intentional moments of consciousness (horizons, sensations) that act together with or condition the activity of consciousness. However, we are dealing here still with the constitution of an object in consciousness, and not with the genesis of a real object outside of consciousness. Genesis in phenomenology and genesis in the Marxist philosophy of praxis thus refer to different levels of reality (of objects of consciousness on the one hand, and of material objects on the other). On the non-intentional dimension in phenomenology and on the phenomenological current that developed out of this perspective, see Welton, *The Other Husserl*.

98. We are aware that Heidegger replaced his early determination of the human individual through the concept of care with the later concept of "shepherd of being." It may be an important shift in his philosophy, but from the Marxist perspective it is a negligible difference. The shepherd certainly does not treat being as a "disposable" and "extractable" existence; however, for Marxists (or, more broadly, philosophers of praxis) this position is still too passive. There is no denying that it suited Heidegger this way, but for the Marxists it still did not explain the fact of the genesis and development of human society and civilization in general.

99. For more details on this, see Landa, "Labour and Time."

100. In his famous lecture on modern technology, Heidegger determines its nature through the expressions *Ge-stellen* (meaning an en-framing or gathering-together) and *Herausfordern* (to challenge forth, to enforce), which should evoke the historical originality of this technique—its attempt to create a thing out of nature, which will be available as an extractable source. See Heidegger, "Question Concerning Technology."

101. Kosík, *Dialectics of the Concrete*, 40–41. This is also a way in which the Marxist philosophy of praxis fundamentally differs from all hermeneutically or linguistically oriented philosophical approaches that understand language or speech as the fundamental structural moment of the human essence.

102. Nový, "Marxova filosofie dějin," 128. A similar conclusion was reached by Jiří Bednář, who, in this regard, was following Lukács's interpretation of young Hegel. See Bednář, "Hegelova kritika," 530.

103. Richta, "Ekonomika jako civilizační dimenze," 20.

104. However, it should be noted that the late Stalinist engineering and architectural projects already contained the idea and elements of the new technology. See Gestwa, *Die stalinistische Großbauten*; and Olšáková and Janáč, *Cult of Unity*. We are grateful to Jiří Janáč for drawing our attention to these sources.

105. See Stalin's proclamation in the Report to the Seventeenth Party

Congress on the Work of the Central Committee of the C.P.S.U.(B.), 331, cited in Richta, *Ekonomika jako civilizační dimenze*, 11.

106. Dubská, *Objevování Ameriky*, 156.

107. Klein, "Vědeckotechnická revoluce," 58–59. This was originally published as "Révolution scientifique et technique et style de vie," in *L'homme et la societé*, no. 9 (1968) and as "Die Wissenschaftlich-technische Revolution und die Gestaltung des Lebenstils," in *Futurum*, no. 2 (1968). The German version is a working paper.

108. Richta is probably referring here to passages from *Dialectics of the Concrete*, in which Kosík speaks of the subject of the capitalist economy without making a significant distinction between commodity and value. At the same time, Kosík considers the commodity to be a mystifying subject. See Kosík, *Dialectics of the Concrete*, 109–110.

109. Richta, "Ekonomika jako civilizační dimenze," 17. For Richta, Marxist-humanist criticism thus seems not to be based on Marx, but on Ricardo!

110. Richta, "Ekonomika jako civilizační dimenze," 30–31.

111. Richta, "Ekonomika jako civilizační dimenze," 32, 34. "The great problem of bourgeois industrial civilization is not found in the inverting tendency of commodity production, but in the subjectivity of capital."

112. Richta, "Ekonomika jako civilizační dimenze," 39.

113. Auerhan, *Technika, kvalifikace, vzdělání*, 126–27.

114. Auerhan, *Technika, kvalifikace, vzdělání*, 127.

115. Richta, "Ekonomika jako civilizační dimenze," 46–47.

116. Auerhan, *Technika, kvalifikace, vzdělání*, 110.

117. Auerhan, *Technika, kvalifikace, vzdělání*, 41.

118. Auerhan, *Technika, kvalifikace, vzdělání*, 138–39. Here, Jan Auerhan is directly citing Marx's *Grundrisse*: "The saving of labour time is equivalent to the increase of free time, i.e. time for the full development of the individual, which itself, as the greatest productive force, in turn reacts upon the productive power of labour." Marx, "Economic Manuscripts," 97.

119. Klein, "Vědeckotechnická revoluce," 51.

120. Marx, "Economic Manuscripts," 97.

121. Dubská, *Objevování Ameriky*, 153.

122. On the nodal line, see Klein, "Hledání lidské varianty," 117. In the original: "Pour un modèle humain d'une civilisation technicienne," in *Démocratie nouvelle*, numéro spécial, nos. 9–10 (1966), 105; Richta, "Ekonomika jako civilizační dimenze," 26.

123. Auerhan, *Technika, kvalifikace, vzdělání*, 134.

124. Auerhan, *Technika, kvalifikace, vzdělání*, 134.

125. Auerhan, *Technika, kvalifikace, vzdělání*, 135, 137.

126. Auerhan, *Technika, kvalifikace, vzdělání*, 139.

127. Klein, "Hledání lidské varianty," 117.
128. Ree, *Political Thought of Joseph Stalin*, 262.
129. Kopeček, *Hledání ztraceného smyslu revoluce*.
130. Engels, "Anti-Dühring," 110–32; and "Dialectics of Nature," 492–98.
131. Other fundamental problems in dialectics are the relationship between necessity and chance and the essence of phenomena. However, these do not *immediately* touch upon the question that is fundamental for orthodox Marxism, that of development and change.
132. Stalin, "Dialectical and Historical Materialism," 249–50. It is necessary to add that in this text, dialectics (in contrast to metaphysics) is understood more broadly. The two above-mentioned laws are preceded by two features that are essential for dialectics: (a) the fact that dialectics does not examine nature as "an accidental agglomeration of things, of phenomena," but as "a connected and integral whole, in which things, phenomena, are organically connected with, dependent on, and determined by, each other"; (b) "dialectics holds that nature is not a state of rest and immobility, stagnation and immutability, but a state of continuous movement and change, of continuous renewal and development." See Stalin, "Dialectical and Historical Materialism," 249–50.
133. Authorial collective, *Základy marxistické filosofie*, 250 (originally published in Moscow, 1959).
134. Marx, Preface to *A Contribution to the Critique of Political Economy*, 263.
135. Plekhanov, "Development of the Monist View," 581, 613.
136. Oittinen, "Which Kind of Dialectician Was Lenin?" 72–74.
137. Lenin, "On the Significance of Militant Materialism," 233.
138. Lenin, "Conspectus."
139. It seems that Kosík had a certain reserved attitude toward this appeal by Lenin (Kosík, *Dialectics of the Concrete*, 107–8); however, he still did not escape the necessity of citing the above-mentioned passage (Kosík, "Hegel a naše doba," 39).
140. Plekhanov, "Development of the Monist View," 493.
141. Cibulka, *Dialektika a ontologie*, 48. For Lenin's note that was mentioned in the text, see Lenin, "Conspectus," 154.
142. According to Cibulka, in the thirteenth chapter of the third volume of *Capital*, Marx determines it as a diminishing share of living labor (variable capital) in the total share of capital as a result of increasing productivity of labor (technological advancement), which also reduces the share of unpaid living labor that makes up surplus value and therefore also profit. However, in the fourteenth chapter, he immediately describes the phenomena that work against it. These consist in the intensification of labor (increasing the degree of exploitation, pushing wages below the value of the labor force, reducing the

elements of constant capital, relative overpopulation, foreign trade, and growth of share capital). Cibulka, *Přínos Marxova Kapitálu*, 21, 77–85; and *Dialektika a ontologie*, 201.

143. Merleau-Ponty, *Adventures of the Dialectic*, 62.

144. Horkheimer, *Eclipse of Reason*, 3–39 (originally published in 1947). Kosík's and Horkheimer's analyses of rationality share striking similarities. The difference between them is probably that for Horkheimer, the main "culprit" is John Locke, and for Kosík it is Descartes.

145. Kosík, *Dialectics of the Concrete*, 57–58.

146. Kosík, *Dialectics of the Concrete*, 60 (emphasis in the original).

147. "Dialectical reason is negativity, which historically situates the achieved degrees of knowledge and realization of human freedom and theoretically and practically exceeds every achieved degree of its inclusion in the totality of development." Kosík, *Dialectics of the Concrete*, 74.

148. Cibulka, "K otázce exaktnosti," 299.

149. Cibulka, "K otázce exaktnosti," 299.

150. This debate took place on the pages of *Filosofický časopis*. It is difficult to identify its starting point, but its first stimulus was probably an article by Cibulka ("O metodě poznání společenských jevů"), where the author criticized the insufficiency of formal logic and also mentioned Materna's work. Materna responded with a polemical gloss ("O 'formalismu'"). Both Cibulka ("Na obranu dialektiky"), and Javůrek ("Dialektika a metafory") replied to this. The debate was closed with Pavel Materna's answer ("Odpověď na kritiku").

151. Materna, "O 'formalismu.'" 375.

152. Cibulka, "Na obranu dialektiky," 285.

153. As in other cases, it is not our intention to judge who was right in these discussions. It would be all the more complicated, because the debate was ultimately oriented toward the struggle to interpret one of the passages in Ilyenkov's *Dialectics of the Abstract*. Both sides, but particularly Materna, eventually admitted that they were speaking (or that they should have been speaking) about somewhat different things. Cibulka and Javůrek were speaking about knowledge, or about reality, and Materna was speaking about logic and by extension about language. While Materna only wanted to speak about "the structure of our expression" and formulating "the laws that this structure is subject to" without speaking about things (because, in his view, no "formally logical approach to things" exists), Cibulka and Javůrek did want to speak about the mode of cognition of things. Of course, it is quite possible that both dialectical theorists had been provoked by Materna's original intention of speaking about the method, which they interpreted as a method of cognition of the things in the world.

154. Tenzer, *Abstrakcia*.

155. "With D. Ricardo, the relationship between specific individual labor and labor as such is a formal relationship between the individual and general, while in Marx the relationship between specific labor and abstract labor is a relationship between the two opposite sides of all labor, and the antinomy between their natural and social sides." Tenzer, *Abstrakcia*, 125 (emphasis in the original).

156. See, for example, Arab-Ogly et al., *Kybernetika*; Král, *Věda a řízení společnosti*; and Sommer et al., *Řídit socialismus jako firmu*, 38–44. For a broader context, see Gerovitch, *From Newspeak*.

157. On principles of automation, see Richta, *Civilization at the Crossroads*, 28–32; on regulators, see 238–39. And, more generally, on the broader applicability of cybernetics outside the area of purely mechanical or perhaps automated applications, see Kolman, "Nové filosofické spory." On cybernetics as higher rationality, see Richta, *Civilization at the Crossroads*, 234.

158. Among the Marxists, Roger Garaudy expresses this hope quite explicitly. See Garaudy, *Marxismus 20. století*, 58. Within the milieu of Czechoslovak Marxist thought, one thinker who explicitly professed it was Jiří Zeman, in *Poznání a informace*, 95–96; and another was Juraj Bober, in "O kybernetickom prístupe," 212–13. Václav Černík provides a good overview of attempts to link cybernetics with dialectics in "Kybernetické modelovanie."

159. This is evident, for example, in the statement in Zeman's book *Poznání a informace*, 101.

160. Bober, "O kybernetickom prístupe," 206–7.

161. Zeman, *Poznání a informace*, 99, 101. On a more general level, it can be said that in this conception of the system the main focus was not some "better clarity and controllability of the world," which would seem to be "closed" into it, but, on the contrary, it was on respecting the complexity of the external world that the system had to constantly cope with. Vítězslav Sommer, by contrast, employs a constraining concept of the system. See Sommer et al., *Řídit socialismus jako firmu*, 23. However we have to agree that the main idea in this conception was about more effective management of society.

162. Zeman, *Poznání a informace*, 101.

163. Zeman, *Poznání a informace*, 26.

164. Bober, "O kybernetickom prístupe," 212.

165. Bober, *Stroj, člověk, spoločnosť*, 94.

166. Cibulka, "O dialektické pojetí kvality"; and Cibulka, "Jde o otázku zrodu."

167. Zeman writes: "The necessary existence of a difference between the subject and the object does not represent a boundary, but a condition of knowledge. It is a guarantee of the continual existence of something that was previously unknown, though of course not unknowable. Abolishing the difference between the subject and object would mean the end of knowability, the end of

knowledge; the question of the knowability or unknowability of something ceases to make sense where these is no sense in talking about knowledge." Zeman, *Poznání a informace*, 49.

168. Zeman, *Poznání a informace*, 39.

169. This is paradoxical, especially with regard to Zeman's persistent criticism of Kant, which, however, pertained to the problem of thing-in-itself (i.e., in Zeman's vocabulary, and also the vocabulary of orthodox Marxism, the problem of inaccessibility of objective reality to knowledge.

170. According to Zeman, "The uncertainty, incompleteness, and unsaturatedness of the concept leads to the state of affairs that the development of knowledge with the contents of concepts is continually enriched and refined. The concept is based on the hypertrophy of certain aspects, on the intensification of some contrast, on the creation of some difference, imbalance, contradiction." Zeman, *Poznání a informace*, 32. From this perspective, dialectical philosophers would claim that the development of knowledge cannot bring about any qualitative changes.

171. Kosík, *Dialectics of the Concrete*, 1–8.

172. Deleuze and Guattari, *What Is Philosophy?* 37.

173. Deleuze and Guattari, *What Is Philosophy?* 38.

174. Plekhanov, "Materialist Understanding of History," 619.

175. A passage in Kosík's *Dialectics of the Concrete* beautifully illustrates this Deleuzian pre-philosophical presupposition of philosophy: "The process of forming a (socio-human) reality is a *prerequisite* for disclosing and comprehending reality in general. Praxis as the process of forming human reality is also a process of uncovering the universe and reality in their being. Praxis is not man's being walled in the idol of socialness and of social subjectivity, but his openness toward reality and being." (Kosík, *Dialectics of the Concrete*, 139, emphasis added). Praxis, now understood as prephilosophical presupposition, makes possible any understanding and conceptualizing of a reality. Praxis thus plays for Marxist humanists (and one is tempted to say, for all post-Stalinist Marxism) exactly the same role as the "preontological understanding of Being" in Heidegger. See Deleuze and Guattari, *What Is Philosophy?* 40.

176. The fact that simultaneous thinking of the totality of reality and of the multiplicity of lines of development can and did (at least within the framework of post-Stalinist Marxism) produce serious inconsistencies and dead-ends with crucial and disastrous implications for concrete political practice will be addressed in chapter 6.

CHAPTER 3. SEEKING A NEW SUBJECTIVITY

Epigraph: From the opening speech at the Slovak Historical Society conference held in Martin in 1968. Lipták, "Úloha a postavenie historiografie," 101–2.

Epigraph: Ilya Ehrenburg, cited in Bartošek, "Naše nynější krize," 63.

1. It is also a banal but true statement that we find similar philosophical or ideological activities in all political and social regimes and groups. At this point we can perhaps only speculate to what extent and in what historical constellations these forms of subjectivization are independent of the given power relations or supraindividual structures and processes, and to what extent they support, maintain, or oppose them. These questions are doubtlessly important for research; however, they significantly exceed the limits of our interest here and they would require not only a somewhat different approach but also a much wider selection of sources.

2. Lenin, "Imperialism, What Is to Be Done," esp. 384–85, 453.

3. It can, of course, be argued that Russian social democracy lost its "elitist" and professional character fairly early. The 1905 revolution, when the number of members rose quickly to as many as 160,000, had been decisive in setting the stage for this development. See Krausz, *Reconstructing Lenin*, 118.

4. Hellbeck, *Revolution on My Mind*; see also the literary generalization from the pen of Arthur Koestler. (*Darkness at Noon*).

5. Quoted by Ree in *Political Thought of Joseph Stalin*, 132.

6. Ree, *Political Thought of Joseph Stalin*, 128; and Rockmore, "Introduction," 13.

7. For example: "Will our state remain in the period of Communism also? Yes, it will, unless the capitalist encirclement is liquidated, and unless the danger of foreign military attack has disappeared. [. . .] No, it will not remain and will atrophy if the capitalist encirclement is liquidated and a Socialist encirclement takes its place." Stalin, "Report on the Work," 422. We are grateful to Kristina Andělová for this reference.

8. Ree, *Political Thought of Joseph Stalin*, 134.

9. Hellbeck, *Revolution on My Mind*, 6–14, 19; and Pinsky, "Origins of Post-Stalin Individuality." Jaroslav Šabata's correspondence with his wife, Anna Šabatová, is more than illustrative in this sense. In a letter of March 31, 1950, he states: "I don't want to go back to that old crap, Hanka. I am firmly convinced that what cut the ground under our feet was the inconsistency in the practical implementation of communist principles: about the relation to work in my case, and in your case the apparently individualistic principles (in other things also bourgeois views and practices)." Archiv Moravského zemského muzea, fond "Anna Šabatová."

10. By this, we certainly do not mean to say that the transition took place without conflicts and certain forms of repression. The party's interventions within the famous campaign against revisionists, and, later, the difficulties encountered by the editors of critically oriented (mainly literary) magazines in the first half of the 1960s were especially notable examples. For more on this, see Mervart, *Naděje a iluze*.

11. Nečasová, *Nový socialistický člověk*, 68.

12. Fritzsche and Hellbeck, "New Man," 302–3.

13. See, for example, Vertov, *Kino-eye*, 7–8. See also Fritzsche and Hellbeck, "New Man," 316. On Bogdanov's conceptions of man as an immediate part of the indivisible collective unity, see White, *Red Hamlet*, 95–97, 397–98.

14. Fritzsche and Hellbeck, "New Man," 317.

15. On Nietzsche's unacknowledged or unconscious influence on Stalinism, see Rosenthal, *New Myth*.

16. Fritzsche and Hellbeck, "New Man," 319–20; and Nečasová, *Nový socialistický člověk*, esp. 8–110.

17. Nečasová, *Nový socialistický člověk*, 100–103.

18. Hellbeck, *Revolution on My Mind*.

19. Foucault, *Birth of Biopolitics*, 39–41, 317–19. Foucault's view on liberalism is, of course, much more varied, because within it he distinguishes among various approaches to analyzing relations between the government/state and the governed/civil society (e.g., the French "legal" and English "utilitarian" schools).

20. As Collier emphasizes, this is not a totalitarian principle of governing the society with the state; instead, it is a principle of planning, whose norms are projective and society is irrelevant as a concept for it. Collier, *Post-Soviet Social*, 63.

21. Hoffmann, *Stalinist Values*, 155.

22. Cibulka, "Rehabilitovat Marxe!" 373–74

23. Černík, *Dialektický vedecký zákon*, 283.

24. According to Černík, "It is necessary to seek the specificity of controlling the social laws under socialism deeper than just in their simple use and in guiding the forms of their manifestation. It consists in the direct social management of production, the focus of which is on the scientific prediction and control of the movement and development of the internal contradictions of the socialist social processes." Černík, *Dialektický vedecký zákon*, 289.

25. Černík, *Dialektický vedecký zákon*, 288.

26. Cibulka writes, "If objective laws are internally contradictory, nascent, and conflicting tendencies, then the enforcement of one tendency that is subject to a law against another such tendency requires the historically progressive social class to decide for a certain tendency in order to recognize that this tendency—by contrast with other tendencies—better expresses the current mutual incorporation of contradictory self-developments, so that it can therefore consciously choose this tendency over other acting tendencies and so that it can incorporate this tendency into more substantial contradictory movements." Cibulka, *Dialektika a ontologie*, 317.

27. Cibulka, *Dialektika a ontologie*, 315.

28. Cibulka, *Dialektika a ontologie*, 318.

29. Let us add, that the problem of Stalinism does not stem from using abstract laws that are constructed through reason, as most conservative, liberal, and critical theoretical thinkers had accused Stalinism (and by extension Marxism) of doing. Besides the usual suspects here such as Friedrich von Hayek and Karl R. Popper (as well as Theodor Adorno), Rio Preisner can be identified as part of the Czech intellectual milieu sharing this perspective. See, for example, Preissner, "K hegeliánským principům marxismu," 730–736; and Preissner, *Kritika totalitarismu*. Especially for the first two thinkers, the main culprit is ultimately Hegel and his dialectics.

30. Cibulka, *Dialektika a ontologie*, 328.

31. Cibulka, *Dialektika a ontologie*, 317.

32. Karel Kosík objected to the one-sided "philosophy of man," which distorts the image of the human individual because "he understands it as fragmented again, and not as a whole." See Kosík, "Odpověď v anketě," 101; in a similar vein see Kusý, "Zinštitucionalizovaný človek," 260–63.

33. Kusý, *Filozofia politiky*, 78. See also the following passage of Jan Smíšek: "*The most productive force of socialism is man*, and the task of socialism is not to develop material production as the prioritized factor, but man as the goal, the sense, but also a means in freeing up space for all of his dimensions." Smíšek, *Pojednání o člověku*, 156.

34. See Mlynář, *K teorii socialistické demokracie*; on the legal theorists' contribution to the drafting of the constitution, see Sommer, "Experti," 131–35.

35. Catalano, "Zdeněk Mlynář"; and Hoppe, Škodová, Suk, and Caccamo, "*O nový československý model socialism.*"

36. Kieran Williams and James Krapfl, "For Civic Socialism and the Rule of Law"; Kopeček, "Vládnout právem," 45–50; and Feinberg, "Občan alebo človek?"

37. The interests of people and social groups were put back into play by period sociology, led by Pavel Machonin. See Machonin, *Československá společnost*. For more, see Andělová, "Intelektuální dějiny reformního komunismu"; and Voříšek, *Reform Generation*, 208–36.

38. Kusý, *Filozofia politiky*, 110; and Šamalík, *Člověk a instituce*, 199.

39. Lakatoš, *Občan, právo a demokracie*, 19.

40. Mlynář, *Stát a člověk*, 28.

41. Mlynář, *Stát a člověk*, 27–31. This was also published along with an excerpt from Kusý as an attempt at a socialist solution for relations between the citizen and the state in Mlynář and Kusý, "Pokus o socialistické řešení."

42. Lakatoš, *Občan, právo a demokracie*, 18.

43. Kusý, "Člověk a inštitúcia," 33. An uncensored version of the chapter was included in Kusý's book *Filozofia politiky*.

44. Kusý, "Člověk a inštitúcia," 39.

45. Šamalík, *Člověk a instituce*, 21.
46. Kusý, *Filozofia politiky*, 125.
47. Most frequently, there was discussion of "socialist legality." Michal Lakatoš, referring to the fact that laws in the strict sense of the world can also mean compliance with unconstitutional laws, changed this expression to "legal certainty." Lakatoš, *Úvahy o hodnotách demokracie*, 172–85. See also Kopeček, "Vládnout právem," 45–50; and Kopeček, "Socialist Conception," 268–71.
48. Mlynář, *Stát a člověk*, 29.
49. Lakatoš, *Občan, právo a demokracie*, 21; Kusý, *Filozofia politiky*, 126–27; and Fibich, "Institucionální odcizení."
50. Lakatoš, *Občan, právo a demokracie*.
51. Kusý, "Člověk a inštitúcia," 46–47.
52. Šamalík, *Člověk a instituce*, 311–12.
53. Lakatoš, *Úvahy o hodnotách demokracie*. For more, see Feinberg, "Občan alebo človek?"
54. Kusý, "Zinštitucionalizovaný človek." Here, Kusý probably has in mind mainly the period journalism in *Kultúrny život*; this is also the spirit behind Mlynář's critique of Karel Kosík's *Dialectics of the Concrete*, which reproaches the author for implicitly placing politics and political institutions in the sphere of pseudo-concretenost, which was supposed to be changed through revolutionary practice. See Mlynář, "Filosofie aktivity."
55. Kosík, "Přeludy a socialismus," 59.
56. Gardavský, *Naděje ze skepse*, 66.
57. The most well-known works on existentialism include Václav Černý's reflections and considerations. See V. Černý, *První a druhý sešit*. A book by the Brno-based philosopher Josef Šafařík, which he managed to publish in 1948, is also indispensable in grasping the reception of existentialism: Šafařík, *Sedm listů Melinovi*. The period polemics by the future Marxist historian František Červinka with Gustav Bareš's condemnation of existentialism in *Nová mysl* also deserves mention. See Červinka, "Existencialismus a kritika" (originally published in 1947–1948).
58. Musilová, *Na okraj jedné návštěvy*. See also, Srp, *Ti druzí*.
59. One philosopher in particular devoted himself to a deeper and more insightful analysis of Merleau-Ponty's work: Milan Průcha, especially in two texts, "Existencializmus M. Merleau-Pontyho," and *Kult člověka*.
60. Lukács, "Existentialism." For the Czech edition of Lukács's texts on existentialism, see Lukács, *Existencialismus či marxismus?*
61. Similarly to the Christian-Marxist dialogue, this experience also demonstrates that there was not only a unidirectional movement where non-Marxist impulses were absorbed, but contemporary Marxism also reached outside its own circles.

62. Bodnár, "Úvod," 19–20.

63. Dubský, "Domov a bezdomoví"; F. Cigánek, *Spor o návrat člověka*; Hermach, *Uskutečnění současného člověka*; Dubská, "Filosofii pro každý den"; Michňák, *Metafyzika subjektivity*; and Michňák, *Ke kritice antropologismu*. However, this circumstance did not lead Hermach and Dubská to cease considering themselves Marxists.

64. For a detailed analysis of this trend, see Tucker, *Philosophy and Politics*.

65. At this point, we do not want to provide a detailed report on the period reception of existentialism; we are more interested in the moment in which this direction was reflected in the definition of post-Stalinist subjectivity. At the same time, we believe that the critique of existentialism illustrates the breadth and internal diversity of post-Stalinist thought. For more detailed analysis of the relationship between existentialism and Czechoslovak post–Stalinist Marxism, see Růžička and Mervart, "Marxism and Existentialism."

66. Bodnár, "Úvod," 19.

67. Cibulka, *Dialektika a ontologie*, 328.

68. Kusý, *Filozofia politiky*, 76–77.

69. Here, we have in mind especially the first and third theses as well as Marx's famous reflections on man as a "species being" from the fragment on "estranged labour" in the "Economic and Philosophic Manuscripts." See Marx, "Theses on Feuerbach"; and Marx, "Economic and Philosophic Manuscripts," 275–77. Incidentally, we are not evaluating the justifiability of this connection. It is of course problematic mainly because even for the early Marx, consciousness is a product of sensory activity, and not its driving force.

70. Kalivoda, "Marxismus a libertinismus," 148 (originally published in 1967). See also the most recent edition of this work, Kalivoda, *Moderní duchovní skutečnost*.

71. Kalivoda, "Marxismus a libertinismus," 136.

72. It should be noted that post-Stalinist Marxists based their reception, evaluation, and critique of Sartre's existentialism particularly on their reading of *Being and Nothingness: The Critique of Dialectical Reason*, and its methodological introduction, which was translated into Czech in 1966 (*Marxismus a existencialismus*), was perceived as a step toward Marxism, albeit written on a platform that was essentially based on the main premises of *Being and Nothingness*. As Průcha put it: "*Being and Nothingness* still represents a magnetic pole from which Sartre is perhaps moving away, but which, through its force curves, continues to influence the structure of Sartre's philosophical field" (Průcha, "Doslov," 159–60). One of the few authors who have studied the *Critique* in depth and have been able to adequately capture the differences and shifts between Sartre's two main philosophical works was the Brno aesthetician and philosopher Oleg Sus. Sus notes precisely how the "late" Sartre retreats from his overly abstract and

solitary conception of existence and introduces various degrees of mediation (between it and the world) and sociologizing and psychologizing determinants. Sus, "Burňák stočený do láhve," 56–89 (this text is the result of merging and reworking two texts published by Oleg Sus in the journal *Slovenský filozofický časopis*: "Pokus o reform existencialismu," and "Burňák stočený do láhve," which was published in the magazine *Host do domu*).

73. Bodnár, "Fenomenologická ontológia," 122–23; and Bodnár, "Fundamentálna ontológia," 567–68.

74. Bodnár, "Fenomenologická ontológia"; Kosík, "Človek a filozofia," 46–47; and Kusý, *Filozofia politiky*, 76–77.

75. Kalivoda, "Marxismus a libertinismus," 148n44. See also Šíma, *Člověk a svět*, 141.

76. Kosík, "Človek a filozofia," 47. This lecture was given at the World Congress of Philosophy held in Mexico City in 1963, where Kosík presented some of the theses from *Dialectics of the Concrete*.

77. A few of these translated works include Marcuse, *Psychoanalýza a politika* [Psychoanalysis, Politics, and Utopia]; Fromm, *Umění milovat* [The Art of Loving]; Fromm, *Člověk a psychoanalýza* [Man for Himself: An Inquiry Into the Psychology of Ethics], and a volume edited by Milena Tlustá, *Antologie textů soudobé západní filosofie*. This anthology mainly comprised translated texts written by Erich Fromm, but also included some written by his associates, such as Karen Horney.

78. See Hudis, "Karel Kosík."

79. Schaff, *Marxizmus a ľudské indivíduum*; Kopčok, *Človek a odcudzenie*. During the 1960s, original contributions and translations by members of *Praxis*, Milan Kangrga, Gajo Petrović, Mihajlo Mihajlović, and Predrag Vranicki, were also regularly reprinted, mainly in the Slovak philosophical magazine *Otázky marxistickej filozofie* (published since 1966 under the name *Filozofia*).

80. Garaudy, "Kafka."

81. On translations into Czech, see, for example, Garaudy, *Realismus bez břehů*; Garaudy, *Perspektivy člověka*; Garaudy, *Od klatby k dialogu*; and Garaudy, *Marxismus 20. století*. See also Garaudy, *Questions à Jean-Paul Sartre*. Garaudy was reacting to the first volume of Sartre's *Critique of Dialectical Reason* (English translation first published in 1976). For a Czech translation of selected parts, see Sartre, *Marxismus a existencialismus*.

82. See Althusser, "Humanist Controversy."

83. Besides the political connotations associated with the overvaluing of the human individual, Ilyenkov mainly reproached Schaff for excessive abstraction in his concept of the human being, which abstracts him from social relations—and it is interesting to note that he labeled the humanist tendencies as neopositivist. On this subject, see Woźniak, "Marksizm a abstrakcja."

84. See, for example, Jan Cigánek's heavily Heideggerean-influenced book *Spor o návrat člověka*, and the collection of essays written by one member of Richta's team, Jiří Hermach, *Uskutečnění současného člověka*.

85. Kalivoda's explanatory passage is more than eloquent: "It is an attempt at a critical interpretation of psychoanalysis from the perspective of the Marxist philosophy of man, which is of course also an attempt at a critical integration of psychoanalysis into the Marxist philosophy of man, [and] at a certain development of the problems of this philosophy, realized through this critical integration." Kalivoda, "Marx a Freud," 48.

86. Kosík, "Odpověď v anketě" (originally published in 1964). In this context, Johann P. Árnason states that when addressing the ontological question of "who is man," Kosík rejected the anthropologism of the Polish Marxists Adam Schaff and Leszek Kołakowski. See Árnason, "Perspectives and Problems," nos. 5–6, 219.

87. Kusý, "Spor o východisko," 275, quoted in Raisa Kopsová, "Miesto Miroslava Kuseho," 721.

88. Kalivoda, "Marx a Freud," 46.

89. Průcha, "Filosofické problémy," 39.

90. Průcha, *Kult člověka*, passim.

91. Sommer, "Experti," 130.

92. Kalivoda, "Marx a Freud," 51–52.

93. Sviták, "Vlna pravdy," 73.

94. Kosík, *Dialectics of the Concrete*, 138; and Šíma, *Člověk a svět*, 51–56. Šíma would add to this list the moment of the existentially vital activities of man (the bodily and self-regulating dimension of praxis), "which ensure a continuous balance and metabolism between man and the environment" (51). It is noteworthy that Šíma understood this dimension of praxis as the privileged object of inquiry of systems and behavioral theories, which are primarily concerned with the relationship between the system, its environment, and the establishment of their mutual balance. The validity of cybernetic theory, which represented for techno-optimists a general method of analyzing and managing (not only) society, would therefore be limited to this area of yet unreflected, more or less instinctive reactions. On the philosophical development of Rudolf Šíma, see Holub, "Za šestým smyslem."

95. Kosík, *Dialectics of the Concrete*, 125. For in-depth analysis of the relation between praxis and labor and labor and culture, see Angus, "Inception of Culture." For a more elaborated version of this article, see Angus, *Groundwork of Phenomenological Marxism*, 177–230.

96. Kosík never ceases to emphasize that the realm of freedom can in no way be understood as leisure that exists alongside labor. Kosík, *Dialectics of the Concrete*, 125, 131n52).

97. Sviták, "Vlna pravdy," 57. This is an unpublished manuscript that Sviták worked on after his expulsion from the KSČ and his sacking from the Institute of Philosophy at the ČSAV while he was at the Film Institute in Prague. Kosík, *Dialectics of the Concrete*.

98. See, for example, Fibich, "Institucionální odcizení"; Kusý, "Človek a inštitúcia," 24–38; Kusý, "Boj proti odcudzeniu," esp. 81–89; Šamalík, *Člověk a instituce*, 314–49; and Lakatoš, *Úvahy o hodnotách demokracie*, 122–29. Here we will also mention Dominik Tatarka's statement: "Philosophers, writers in the West began to talk about alienation. The capitalist state alienated everything from the citizen. When we began to think about it in our socialist establishment, we soon found out that this degree of alienation had taken place in our country at a higher, more perfect, and even perfect degree in our very establishment." Tatarka, "Obec božia," 24.

99. Sviták, "Vlna pravdy," 39–40, 73.

100. See Kosík, *Dialectics of the Concrete*, 50–56.

101. Kosík, "Hašek and Kafka," 86 (originally published in 1963).

102. See Landa, "Marxova filosofická antropologie."

103. Kosík, *Dialectics of the Concrete*, 46.

104. Kosík, *Dialectics of the Concrete*, 54.

105. Kosík, "Švejk and Bugulma," 92, 94 (originally published in 1969).

106. Sviták, "Vlna pravdy," 71. See also "Hrdinové odcizení," for a magazine publication.

107. Kosík, "Hašek a Kafka," 83–84.

108. Sviták, "Vlna pravdy," 71.

109. Sviták, "Vlna pravdy," 41.

110. In this regard, it should be added that (whether it is admitted or not) they were drawing upon non-Marxist philosophical-anthropological literature, namely, the works of Max Scheler, which explicitly speak about science as a certain type of fragmentary grasp of the human being.

111. Kosík, *Dialectics of the Concrete*, 20.

112. Kosík, *Dialectics of the Concrete*, 48.

113. Sviták, "Vlna pravdy," 95. See also Sviták, *Windmills of Humanity*, 36.

114. Marx, "Theses on Feuerbach," 3.

115. Kosík, *Dialectics of the Concrete*, 136.

116. Similarly, the writer and editor in chief of the literary magazine *Orientace*, Jaroslav Putík, said: "I'm not opposed to science, but it is essential to recognize its limits. Humor, wit, and irony, can serve as antidotes. But what's needed, above all, is a nonstereotyped, authentic expression of life." In Liehm, *Politics of Culture*, 250 (originally published in 1967). The Czech original also includes the following sentence: "The hero of our time is the one who preserves the most humanity. It also includes a wonderful ability to behave illogically." See Liehm, *Generace*, 146.

117. Sviták, "Člověk a poezie," 180 (originally published in 1963); and Sviták, "Surrealistický obraz člověka," published in English as "The Surrealist Image of Humankind."

118. Šamalík, *Člověk a instituce*, 313.

119. Chvatík, *Smysl moderního umění*, 101.

120. Kosík, "Hašek a Kafka," 79, emphasis added.

121. Kosík, "Švejk and Bugulma," 92. It should be noted that in this and other later essays written in 1968–1969, Kosík is slowly moving away from the notion of human subjectivity as an inherently active entity and is increasingly emphasizing its original passivity, or even resistance to change. This can be seen especially in those passages where Kosík emphasizes the "fatefulness" of Švejk's character, who, although he constantly experiences new and unique encounters on his adventures, does not change or undergo any kind of catharsis or change of heart. This moment also brings him very close to the late Heidegger and, on the contrary, distances him from Lukács, who according to him is a philosopher who dynamizes seemingly fixed and eternal essences. Kosík argues, however, that this in itself is nothing new and precisely represents the essential characteristic of all modern philosophy, which dissolves all stability into an ever-changing flux. Nevertheless, the manipulability of modern society is thus, according to him, not transcended at all but rather confirmed. For different aspects of the concept of praxis and the role of passivity within it in Kosík's thought, see Tava, "Praxis in Progress"; and on Kosík's "turn" to more Heideggerian themes, see especially J. Černý, "Karel Kosík and Martin Heidegger."

122. We saw in chapter 2 that Lubomír Nový is basically moving in a very similar direction when he speaks about a "discrepancy between the project and the result" and about history as a "field of undecided possibilities" or "events without guarantees." Nový, "Marxova filosofie dějin," 129.

123. Sviták, "Člověk a poezie," 180; and Kosík, "Hašek a Kafka," 135.

124. This phenomenon appears in the cinematography of the West just as in Eastern Europe (for example, the American film *Rebel Without a Cause* by Nicholas Ray from 1955 and French New Wave films, especially *The 400 Blows* by François Truffaut [1959] and *Breathless* [1960] by Jean-Luc Godard), but in both cases we find a disruption of the commonplace everyday life of the modern world in Sviták's and Kosík's sense. For period reception of the antiheroes of Western culture, we use František Červinka as an example. In connection with films by Federico Fellini, Pier Paolo Pasolini, and Antonio Pietrangeli and books by Vercors (Jean Bruller), Červinka noted that "it is the street girl who becomes practically a positive and central figure in artists' works, whose consistent search for the moral principles of contemporary humanism cannot be doubted in the slightest." Červinka, "Nana a její družky," 78. It should be noted that in Eastern Europe to all the above must be added the disruption of the

Stalinist interpretation of recent history (see, for example, the figure of Maciej from Wajda's famous *Popel a démant* [Ashes and Diamonds, 1956] or the figure of the German captive in Stanislav Barabáš's film *Zvony pre bosých* [The Bells Toll for the Barefooted, 1965] and Krista in Kachyňa's *Kočár do Vídně* [Carriage to Vienna, 1966]. On this subject, see Jan Bárta, "At' žije republika"; and Bárta, "Klos, Kadár, and Wajda." On the Soviet enthusiasm for Ernest Hemingway, see Genis and Vail, *60. Léta*, 56–67.

125. Sviták, "Vlna pravdy," 80.

126. Sviták, "Vlna pravdy," 37.

127. Here, we are referring to Gardavský's reflections in *Naděje ze skepse*.

128. Kosík, "Modernost, Lidovost a socialismus," 96.

129. Kalivoda, "Marx a Freud," 52.

130. Kalivoda, "Marx a Freud," 53. Kalivoda attributes this tendency to the Lukácsean-phenomenological current in Marxism, which ontologizes categories such as alienation, objectification, and the like, without—by contrast with structuralism—performing a real historical analysis. See Kalivoda, "O struktuře a strukturalismu."

131. Kalivoda, "Marx a Freud," 70.

132. Kalivoda, "Marx a Freud," 81.

133. This way of thinking is also close to Josef Zumr's. See Landa and Mervart, "Formy pod napětím"; see also Erazim Kohák's ideas, which in many ways intersected with the Marxist humanists' (Trnka, *Filosof Erazim Kohák*). In connection with chapter 4 in this book, we cannot help remarking that this principle had already been suggested by Zdeněk Nejedlý: "There is an evil hatred if a man hates another man for gross personal reasons. And there is holy hatred, hatred for evil and for those who sow and bring forth evil." Nejedlý, "Komunisté, dědici velkých tradic," 291.

134. Kalivoda, "Marx a Freud," 84. In the essay "Marxismus a libertinismus," Kalivoda gives a different concrete example: "While social-political anarchism seeks a *material* act that is bound to fail or has no hope of lasting results, an act of 'accursed [maudit] poetry' is an act that is *dematerialized, sublimated, and spiritual*. It simply creates a utopianism of a new type, a utopianism of the 'poetic solution.'" Kalivoda, "Marxismus a libertinismus," 128.

135. Engels, "Dialectics of Nature," 498–501.

136. Kalivoda, "Marxismus a libertinismus," 123.

137. Kalivoda contrasts this libertinism with another historical trend that calls for the emancipatory ideals of equality and freedom—bourgeois liberalism. In the latter, the ideal of freedom is entirely "emptied" and only functions as a "form of expressing the life situation and life goals of the saturated social group that has power in its hands." For Kalivoda, bourgeois liberalism and Jacobin libertinism are two parallel trends of thinking about freedom and equality and

thus one cannot be deduced from the other. Kalivoda, "Marxismus a libertinismus," 104–5.

138. Kalivoda, "Marxismus a libertinismus," 137.

139. Kalivoda, "Marxismus a libertinismus," 137.

140. Kalivoda, "Marxismus a libertinismus," 138.

141. "We should not overestimate, but also not underestimate, the last ten years. We find ourselves at the beginning of socialist libertinism, and there is growing differentiation [of opinions]." "Marienbader protokolle," 473.

142. Sviták, "Vlna pravdy," 76; Sviták, "Umění v průmyslové společnosti"; Sviták, "Člověk a poezie," 172; and Kosík, "Modernost, lidovost a socialismus," 96–97 (originally published in 1958). For a similar take, see Průcha, "Vědeckotechnická revoluce."

143. Sviták, "Umění v průmyslové společnosti," 3.

144. Sviták, "Vlna pravdy," 76. See also Sviták, *Windmills of Humanity*, 111–12.

145. Kosík, "Modernost, lidovost a socialismus," 96. Kosík illustrates this as follows: "Not only Shostakovich's symphonies but also the human ear, which is able to perceive its own modern problems is part of modern culture. Not only Picasso's pictures but also the human eye, which is historically (socially and artistically) adapted to see them as expressions of heroic effort at expressing the problems and beauty of the modern world. Not only Mayakovsky's poems but also the human intellect and human emotion, human imagination, which is able to experience them as the reality of the modern socialist man." Kosík, "Modernost, lidovost a socialismus," 96–97.

146. Kosík, "Modernost, lidovost a socialismus," 96–97. Similarly, the art historian Luděk Novák claimed that "modern art, and namely painting, cannot be understood by the senses with which we understand the beauty of nature or of classic art. To understand modern art requires a modern sensibility, a new manner of artistic perception." Luděk Novák, *Století moderního malířství* (Prague: Orbis, 1968), cited in Bartlová, *Dějiny českých dějin umění*, 328.

147. See Landa, "Struktury významu."

148. Kalivoda directly refers to Karel Teige, whom he defends against the accusation of utopianism in favor of an asymptomatic approach to the ideal through human creativity. See Kalivoda, "Marxismus a libertinismus," 147–48. In this connection, he quotes Teige: "A poem, realizing desire, desires to be realized in earthly life so that man, the slave of reality, may become the ruler of reality. *A goal that cannot be approached asymptomatically, but which will never be reached*, no matter what kind of social organization there is: therefore, the poet is the eternal revolutionary, to whom changes in his living circumstances are only steps on an infinitely rising staircase" (133).

149. Gardavský, *Naděje ze skepse*, 66.

150. Here, one of the things on our minds is the concept of the publishing project of *Lidové noviny*. See Mervart, "Radical Democrats."

151. For a general take on this topic, see Landa and Mervart, *Proměny Marxist-Křesťanského dialogu*. For a broader context of East-West dialogue in philosophy, see Ferenc-Flatz and Takács. "From Polemics to Dialogue."

152. See Machovec, *O tak zvané "dialektické" teologii*; Machovec, *Novotomismus*; Machovec, *O teológii súčasného protestantizmu*; and Gardavský, *Fenomén Německo*. At the same time, Machovec considered religiosity as a "reactionary" aspect in a book he coauthored with Markéta Machovcová (*Utopie blouznivců a sektářů* [Prague: Nakladatelství Československé akademie věd, 1960]), and he also operated with it in a debate on Kalivoda's *Husitská ideologie*. See Machovec, "K zápasu"; and Machovec, "Diskuse o metodologických otázkách." The entire debate was originally published in *Filosofický časopis* 9, no. 5 (1962): 790–824.

153. Gardavský, *God Is Not Yet Dead*, 149–57. For the original Czech edition, see *Bůh není zcela* mrtev. Machovec, *Smysl lidského života*, 220.

154. Gardavský, *God Is Not Yet Dead*, 151.

155. Gardavský, *God Is Not Yet Dead*, 154.

156. Gardavský, *God Is Not Yet Dead*, 172. Gardavský's assumption is based on the author's reading of Marx's *On the Jewish Question* but is clearly also based in contemporary empirical findings (esp. Kadlecová, *Sociologický výzkum religiozity*), which indicate that the struggle against religion and for atheistic child-rearing certainly did not result in a reduction of religiosity.

157. Gardavský, *God Is Not Yet Dead*, 157.

158. Gardavský, *God Is Not Yet Dead*, 154.

159. Machovec, *Smysl lidského života*, 244.

160. Gardavský, *God Is Not Yet Dead*, 149.

161. Gardavský, *God Is Not Yet Dead*, 203.

162. Gardavský, *God Is Not Yet Dead*, 149.

163. Gardavský, *God Is Not Yet Dead*, 205. For an interpretation of this quote, see Bartoš, "K předpokladům," 241–42.

164. Gardavský, *God Is Not Yet Dead*, 205.

165. Machovec, *Smysl lidského života*, 246.

166. For both quotes, see Gardavský, *God Is Not Yet Dead*, 212.

167. Gardavský, *God Is Not Yet Dead*, 215.

168. Gardavský, *God Is Not Yet Dead*, 216. For a general take, see Gardavský, *God Is Not Yet Dead*, 215–18. The example of the development of thought is more than obvious at this point. Whereas in 1967 Gardavský spoke of the concept of a love that does not exclude the class struggle and can mean the death penalty as well as putting his own life at stake (Gardavský, *God Is Not Yet Dead*, 216), two years later, he concluded his reflections with the maximal extent of dialogue, "dialogical creationism" (Gardavský, *Naděje ze skepse*, 66).

169. Machovec, *Smysl lidského života*, 219.
170. Machovec, *Smysl lidského života*, 220.
171. Gardavský draws attention to this moment in *God Is Not Yet Dead*, 200–201.
172. Bartoš, "K předpokladům," 242.
173. Červinka, "Nana a její družky," 81. For a similar take, see also Gardavský: "The Marxist theory of subjective identity and transcendence is materialist and dialectic. Both the individual and mankind in general as they enter history are subjective. The individual, the 'ego,' refuses to be reduced to a mere sum of social relationships come together and alter; society in its turn is a subjective identity, not merely as the sum of its individuals, but as an everlasting fire in which new flames are constantly blazing up to replace the old ones which have burnt themselves out." Gardavský, *God Is Not Yet Dead*, 210.
174. See Liehm and Kosík, "A. J. Liehm's Interview with Karel Kosík," 411–12.
175. Selucký, *Ekonomika*, 47–49; and Richta, *Civilization at the Crossroads*, 87, 173.
176. Evidence is provided not only in separate passages dedicated to this issue in Richta's famous *Civilization at the Crossroads*, but above all in Radoslav Selucký's analysis in *Ekonomika, morálka, život* as well as in Blanka Filipcová's *Člověk, práce, volný čas*. In the latter two publications mentioned here, the subject of leisure time is discussed from a broader sociological and economic perspective, which offers a more complex view of the issue. We were mainly concerned with capturing the philosophical issue from the perspective of creating a new subjectivity. For more, see Franc and Knapík, "Volný čas." For broader context, see Sommer, "Last Battlefield."
177. Richta, "Ekonomika jako civilizační dimenze," 44.
178. Richta, "Ekonomika jako civilizační dimenze," 60.
179. On the function and position of tools in industrial civilization, see Richta, *Civilization at the Crossroads*; and Richta, *Technika a situace člověka*, 19.
180. Richta, *Technika a situace člověka*, 14.
181. Selucký, *Ekonomika*, 51.
182. See Klein, *Životní styl*, 28–31, esp. 29.
183. Richta, *Člověk a technika*, 74 (emphasis added).
184. Richta, *Člověk a technika*, 68.
185. Klein, "Ke krizi emocionality," 88.
186. Richta, *Civilization at the Crossroads*, 152.
187. Klein, "Ke krizi emocionality"; Kotásek and Pařízek, "Vědeckotechnická revoluce"; J. Havelka, "Vědeckotechnická revoluce"; Havlínová, "Nová povaha vzdělání v technicky"; and Hrouda, "Vysoké školy."
188. Richta, "Ekonomika jako civilizační dimenze," 25.

189. Richta, "Ekonomika jako civilizační dimenze," 24n. Richta notes here that this imperative of self-transformation and overcoming one's own limits is already implied in Marx's texts, which he sets into contrast with Engels's texts in which this subjectively revolutionary moment is missing.

190. Dubská, *Objevování Ameriky*, 153, 163–64. It should be noted that unlike the other techno-optimists Dubská considered the transformation of the nature of work to be extremely important, although she also referred to the leading role of the party, initiative in production, in culture, in managing the state, and in the development of mechanisms for socialist democracy.

191. Klein, "Ke krizi emocionality," 85.

CHAPTER 4. BETWEEN FOLKNESS AND THE NATION

Epigraph: Kundera, "Český úděl," 1.

1. Lenin, "Imperialism, What Is to Be Done?"
2. See, for example, Slezkine, "USSR as a Communal Apartment."
3. See Mervart, "Czechoslovakism and the Party Theory." However, the term "turn" is relative in the sense that while in the center we can observe the national tendencies of the dominant ethnic group, at the periphery the exact opposite is true within the framework of the "struggle against bourgeois nationalism." This was no different in Czechoslovakia: for example, Ľubomír Lipták spoke of Stalinism as a turn to the class perspective that replaced the nationally oriented historiography of the previous era. See Lipták, "Úloha a postavenie historiografie."
4. For an overview of the Stalinist conception of the disciplines that focus on people, see Skalník, "Czechoslovakia," 58–63.
5. See Ducháček, "Německá inspirace zakladatelů," 48; and Brenner, "Zwischen Ost und West," 94–112.
6. Nejedlý, "Odkaz našich národních dějin," 231. This is a text from 1948, which is included in the anthology mentioned here in the section titled "Communists, the Heirs of the Great Traditions of the Czech Nation."
7. On the original pan-Slavism, see Maxwell, "Effacing Panslavism"; see also the essay by Nahodil and Kramařík, "Práce J. V. Stalina."
8. Nejedlý, "Odkaz našich národních dějin," 229.
9. See Lenin, "Critical Remarks." On this subject, see also Andělová and Mareš, "Hledání české radikální demokracie," 187–88.
10. Górny, *Mezi Marxem a Palackým*.
11. Nejedlý, "Komunisté, dědici velkých tradic," 259.
12. See Nejedlý, "Slovo o české filosofii" (originally published in 1946); and Křesťan, "Nejedlého projev," 307–19. In another postwar lecture Nejedlý formulated this trait as follows: "The man of the people thinks far more simply, and therefore also far more correctly than sometimes an intellectual does." Nejedlý, "Komunisté, dědici velkých tradic," 269.

13. For more details, see Kopeček, "Czech Communist Intellectuals," 356–67.

14. See Mukařovský, "Lidovost jako základní činitel." In connection with Mukařovský, Roman Kanda mentions the influence of Stalin's *Economic Problems of Socialism in the USSR* (1952); however, above all else, in relation to the subject of this present work, he also draws attention to another important aspect. Even though the principle of "folkness" was "sociologically distinguished very vaguely," it allowed Mukařovský that which structuralism did not, either artistically or socially: "[connecting] the individual psychologically and through values with the 'folk' collectivity." See Kanda, "Strukturalisté dělají marxismus." Nejedlý was one of the promoters of the folkness in Alois Jirásek's novels. See, for example, Nejedlý, "Komunisté, dědici velkých tradic," 263–64, 287–88. On folkness as a Nejedlean category in the history of the fine arts, see Bartlová, *Dějiny českých dějin umění*, 437–43.

15. On Nejedlý, see especially Křesťan, *Zdeněk Nejedlý*.

16. Kopeček, "Czech Communist Intellectuals," 356–67. In this respect, the author consciously builds upon previous works by Alexej Kusák and Miloš Havelka: Kusák, *Kultura a politika*; and M. Havelka, *Dějiny a smysl*. See also Górny, *Mezi Marxem a Palackým*.

17. Červinka, *Zdeněk Nejedlý*, 354–55.

18. On Herbartism, see Galmiche et al., *Herbartovi dědicové*. On Smetana, see St. Pierre, *Bedřich Smetana*, 101–7.

19. Górny, *Przedewszystkim ma być naród*; and Zaremba, *Komunizm, legitymizacja, nacjonalizm*.

20. Kusák, *Kultura a politika*, 261–305; the influence of this interpretation is perceptible, for example, on Miloš Havelka (*Spor o smysl*) and Marci Shore ("Engineering in the Age of Innocence"). For a discussion of the first Czech publications that are critical, see Andělová and Mareš, "Hledání české radikální demokracie"; and Feinberg, "People as Philosopher?"

21. Šámal, "'Česká otázka'"; and Kopeček, "Czech Communist Intellectuals."

22. See Knapík, *V zajetí moci*.

23. Kopeček, "Czech Communist Intellectuals," 356–67, esp. 367.

24. The seductive paradox of Kusák's thesis consists in attributing an ultraleftist angle to the critique of Stalinism articulated by the generation entering politics after 1945, and it claims that radical Stalinism is what later enabled this generation to defend a thorough de-Stalinization. However, in reality, this claim lacks convincing substantiation. Its analytical weakness appears in the moment when it is applied to a longer span of time. Thus, Kopeček shows that in an article about Masarykism, Kosík tactically "demolished Nejedlý's interpretation of Masaryk" through criticism of his own contemporary, the philosopher Milan

Machovec (Kopeček, "Czech Communist Intellectuals," 372). The attack on Masaryk's writings was motivated by his belief that they were undialectical and essentially idealistic. In the following interpretation, however, Kopeček comes to the statement that "with the approaching midpoint of the nineteen-fifties the times have started to change and the generation of 'blue shirts,' which Kosík was also a member of, was hit by a wave of disillusionment with the unfolding de-Stalinization" (Kopeček, "Czech Communist Intellectuals," 103). But at the same time, the question of the relationship between "radical Stalinism," based on which Kosík had so scathingly dealt with Nejedlý, with the critique of Stalinism remains unanswered. Kosík's positive evaluation of the originally "reactionary bourgeoisie" (Palacký), but also of Masaryk, which contrasts with his early work, expressed in the 1960s is recorded—though not sufficiently explained—by Kopeček.

25. Górny, *Mezi Marxem a Palackým*, 252.

26. Křesťan, *Zdeněk Nejedlý*, 422; for more details, see 421–26.

27. Even this statement cannot be taken literally. See Kosík, "Třídy a reálná struktura společnosti." The English version was published as "Classes and the Real Structure of Society." However, if we remain with the example of Kosík, we cannot find a similar text dedicated to this concept in the 1960s, though a reformulated concept of the nation as well as the people will be among his permanent intellectual interests.

28. Kopeček analyzes the revival of interest in the nation in the 1960s in Kopeček, "Czech Communist Intellectuals," esp. 380–89.

29. Feinberg, "Lid jako filosof," 236. Feinberg deals with the tension between the masses and the avant-garde in connection with Slovak folklore in the subchapter of his monograph titled "Between the People and the Vanguard (Contradictions of Communist Folklorism)." See Feinberg, *Paradox of Authenticity*, 43–56, and then in another text, with reference to Robert Bird, he introduces the Soviet debate from the 1920s and presents folklore festivals as an officially supported activity in which the masses were given the possibility of participating in a project created by the avant-garde (the party) through spontaneous expression. See Feinberg, "Between Vanguard and Mass."

30. For example, František Červinka concluded one of his essays with the words: "The issue of the social order is becoming more complex. In socialist society this kind of atmosphere of tolerance is a prerequisite for clearing up controversies that only historians will be writing tomorrow and the day after. We have no doubt that in particulars, one of them will justify a lack of faith in today's unique attempts and experiments. However, we have no doubts at all that most of the 'folk' objections to the overall trend of our contemporary art will dissipate and this art will be proudly shown as an advanced part of the world culture of the 20th century." Červinka, "O 19. století," 64 (originally published in 1964).

31. Feinberg, "Lid jako filosof," 232.

32. Elsewhere, Kosík drew lines against Mukařovský's folkness and Felix Vodička's concept of "community tasks." See Kosík, "Filosofie a dějiny literatury" (originally published in 1961). We are grateful to Milan Ducháček for explicating the passages about folklore as a part of socialist realism.

33. Kosík, "Modernost, lidovost a socialismus," 94 (originally published in 1958). We entirely agree with Michal Kopeček that here, the assertion of the dialectical principle represents a fundamental act of delimitation against Nejedlý. See Kopeček, "Czech Communist Intellectuals," 368.

34. Kosík, "Modernost, lidovost a socialismus," 94.

35. See Ducháček, "Německá inspirace zakladatelů," esp. 50; Teige, "Nové umění"; and Teige, "Foto, kino, film."

36. Kosík, "Modernost, lidovost a socialismus," 92.

37. Červinka, "O 19. století," 59.

38. Kosík, "Our Current Crisis," 27.

39. Kosík, "Our Current Crisis," 26.

40. Kosík, "Our Current Crisis," 26.

41. Liehm and Kosík, "A. J. Liehm's Interview with Karel Kosík," 411–12.

42. Liehm and Kosík, "A. J. Liehm's Interview with Karel Kosík," 411–12.

43. "Folk satire went hand in hand with enlightened critique, plebian laughter helped tear down the walls of the old society just as much as progressive philosophy." Kosík, "Modernost, lidovost a socialismus," 92.

44. Kosík, "Modernost, lidovost a socialismus," 93.

45. Landa, "Historical Bloc and Revolution."

46. Kosík, "Jediná záchrana." For an English version, see Kosík "The Only Chance."

47. Kosík, "Our Current Crisis," 28.

48. Kosík, "Váha slov," 17. This was a polemic with Havel's text "Český úděl?" [The Czech Destiny?], which was reacting to Kundera's article "Český úděl" [The Czech Destiny] in which Havel evaluated the year 1968 as a period of words and gestures. The English version of Kosík's article was published as "The Weight of Words."

49. Kundera, "Český úděl," 5; for a similar take, see also Tatarka, "Kultúra ako obcovanie," 54.

50. Kundera, "Český úděl," 1.

51. See Mervart, *Kultura v karanténě*, esp. 100–105.

52. Kosík, "Zdeněk Nejedlý a pokrokové," 3.

53. Kopeček, "Czech Communist Intellectuals," 376. To the genealogy of the concept of concrete totality, see Hermann, "Karel Kosík."

54. The connection between post-Stalinists and Nejedlý was elaborated in an unpublished manuscript written by J. G. Feinberg (see Feinberg, "People as Philosopher?").

55. Kopeček also draws attention to this moment. We would like to add that the study of progressive, ergo "folk," traditions in Czech thought was one task in the basic set of research goals in the 1950s for the Cabinet for Philosophy, and that in addition to Kosík's *Česká radikální demokracie*, Kalivoda's *Husitská ideologie* and Josef Zumr's work on Czech Herbartianism also emerged. See Mervart, "Filozofický ústav ČSAV," 596–600.

56. Kosík, *Česká radikální demokracie*, 197–200.

57. Let us take this entire passage as an illustration: "However, what appears to Nejedlý as a parallelism in the development of Czech literature and music in reality is the fundamental problem in *all* components of the social consciousness of the epoch of the Czech bourgeois democratic revolution. Therefore, Nejedlý also can only state the parallelism in the development of music and literature (and this 'mere' statement, expressed in the beginning of the 20th century is of course a great discovery), but he does not inquire into its origins. Within the framework of *this* parallelism the question of causes is not even possible. . . . Of course, Nejedlý, who always held the knowledge of specific truths, and not the articulation of dogma, in his heart, in an exceptional analysis does clarify within one of these spheres—Smetana's music—some of the fundamental problems of social consciousness as a whole." Kosík, *Česká radikální demokracie*, 197–98. Here, Kosík is referring to Zdeněk Nejedlý's, *Zpěvohry Smetanovy* from 1954 (originally published in 1908).

58. Sviták, "Některé příčiny zaostávání teorie," 5.

59. See, for example, František Červinka's articles dedicated to Nejedlý's thought in the interwar era, through which the author returned not only to Masaryk, Šalda, and Čapek but also to Nejedlý as an intellectual giant whose legacy deserves to be reckoned with: Červinka, "O 19. století"; Červinka, "F. X. Šalda a Zdeněk Nejedlý" (originally published in 1967); Červinka, "Vztah Zdeňka Nejedlého" (originally published in 1968); Červinka, "Zdeněk Nejedlý o demokracii" (originally published in 1968); and Červinka, *Spor o smysl*, (originally published in 1969). Most of these texts have been incorporated into the monograph *Zdeněk Nejedlý* published in 1969, which Červinka introduces with the words: "I'm going to disappoint readers who expect a rehabilitation of the awareness of Nejedlý, who was celebrated in the nineteen-fifties. However, I'm also going to disappoint those readers who assume that the period of encomium has been replaced with a period of sweeping criticism and an affected reaction to the previous period." Červinka, *Zdeněk Nejedlý*, 8.

60. Kalivoda "K Machovcovu 'Zápasu,'" 211 (originally published in 1963). In our judgment, Kalivoda's appreciation of Nejedlý does not contradict Martin Nodl's assessment. Nodl considers Kalivoda's *Husitská ideologie* [Hussite Ideology] (1961), which is what the above-mentioned debate was about, to be a paradigmatic breakthrough in Marxist research on the Hussites, which was only

exceeded by František Šmahel at the end of the 1980s. See Nodl, "Kontinuita a diskontinuita," 115–22.

61. "Although Machovec was able to dedicate his *Hus* [*Husovo učení a význam v tradici českého národa* (Prague: Nakladatelství Československé Akademie věd, 1953)] to Nejedlý, he clearly has been unable to honestly intellectually reckon with Nejedlý." See Kalivoda "K Machovcovu 'Zápasu,'" 184.

62. Červinka, "F. X. Šalda a Zdeněk Nejedlý," 100; the same passage is also found in Červinka's monograph *Zdeněk Nejedlý*, 71.

63. Kopeček, "Czech Communist Intellectuals," 370.

64. Kopeček, "Czech Communist Intellectuals," 369.

65. Kalivoda, "K Machovcovu 'Zápasu,'" 209. Kalivoda is referring to Zdeněk Nejedlý's work *Hus a naše doba*.

66. See Kosík, *Česká radikální demokracie*; and Kosík, "O Havlíčkově demokratismu" (originally published in 1969). An English version was published as "Havlíček's Principles of Democracy."

67. Červinka, *Spor o smysl*, 213.

68. "Diskuse o metodologických otázkách," 142 (the author of the statement is Josef Zumr). This was a debate of various philosophers and historians organized by the Institute of Philosophy and published in *Filosofický časopis*. As one example that can represent all the others, let us mention the ideas of historical connection that were related to the progressive interpretation founded by Masaryk in a more than obvious way: "With his earthly philosophy of earthly human enjoyment incorporated into a Chiliastic framework, [Comenius] is also a direct heir to Tábor radicalism. However, he enriches its legacy—and the entire Hussite idea—with the results of Renaissance thought and hands it over in this form to the next, 'enlightened' century." Kalivoda and Zumr, "Úvod," 27. At the same time, it should be noted that in the treatises by Josef Zumr and Robert Kalivoda there are lines of Czech history and their contact with the world that are continually influenced by the universalist dimension of human emancipation: thus, Zumr classifies Ladislav Klíma's oeuvre as a "cosmic probe into eternal humanity," and Kalivoda characterizes the era of Comenius, the interwar avant-garde, and to a certain degree also the 1960s, as a natural form of "Czech universalism." See Zumr, "Filosof hrdé lidskosti," 22; and Kalivoda, "České kulturní vědomí."

69. On this subject, see Galmiche, "Paradoxy odkazu."

70. See especially Kalivoda and Zumr, *Antologie z dějin*; Kalivoda, *Moderní duchovní skutečnost*; and Zumr, "Filosof hrdé lidskosti." For more details on Zumr, see also Mervart, "Zumrova 'emancipace člověka'"; and Mervart, "Czechoslovak Marxist Humanism."

71. According to Jiří Křesťan, Nejedlý's relationship to the avant-garde underwent changes. Before the war it was more like a mutually shared sym-

pathy and coexistence, and after 1945 a reserved and even negative attitude prevailed. Křesťan, "'Poslední husita' odchází," 25–27.

72. Xavier Galmiche highlights a certain connection between the aesthetic normativism of Herbartianism, which was Nejedlý's original background, and the normativity of socialist realism; he also points out that the critique of structuralism enabled Nejedlý, in a certain concordance with fathers of Herbartism Josef Durdík and Otakar Hostinský, to create a national historical anthropology of a populist and militant nature that socialist realism enjoyed. See Galmiche, "Paradoxy odkazu," 77–78. František Červinka wrote one of the most significant polemics concerning Nejedlý's national revivalist progressivism, which led to a rejection of the avant-garde in the 1960s. See Červinka, *Spor o smysl*, esp. 207–9.

73. Bartošek's quote ends with "it was left vacant." See Bartošek, "Český 'smysl dějin,'" 27–28 (originally published in 1969).

74. By contrast with Zumr's and Kalivoda's concepts of emancipation, Kosík's democratism of course did not introduce any suprahistorical principle, but a daily "struggle" for the character of the national society (the similarity with Masaryk's "small works" is more than evident).

75. Górny, *Mezi Marxem a Palackým*, 252–53.

76. Červinka, "Článek o TGM," 127 (originally published in 1968).

77. This connection is also accepted by Miloš Havelka. See M. Havelka, *Spor o smysl*, 31–37; and M. Havelka, *Dějiny a smysl*, 61.

78. See, for example, Trencsényi et al., *History of Modern Political Thought*, vol. 2, part I, 453–69.

79. See Mervart, "Czechoslovakism and the Party Theory."

80. Kárník, *Socialisté na rozcestí*. Bohumír Šmeral (1880–1941) was a leading Czech theoretician of Austromarxism and a leading figure of the Czech Social Democratic Party. In May 1921, he cofounded the Communist Party of Czechoslovakia, of which he was the most important representative before its Stalinization.

81. Nejedlý, "Komunisté, dědici velkých tradic," 262.

82. However, by contrast with Nicolae Ceaușescu's Romania, neither the party led by Antonín Novotný (and certainly not the president himself) nor the party's theoreticians who worked on the "national question" participated in the development of a national path to socialism. And although later normalization campaigns against the reform wing in the party lacked the anti-German elements present in the 1950s, the renewal of order would be built upon the rejection of a Czechoslovak path to socialism (which is labeled as a manifestation of nationalism) and it would consistently adhere to Soviet internationalism, which is a superordinate socialist model, and one that is lacking any kind of Czechoslovak exceptionalism.

83. On the renaissance of the category of the nation in historiography,

see Michal Kopeček, "Historical Studies of Nation-Building"; and Kopeček, "Czech Communist Intellectuals," On the Slovak question, see Brown, "Socialism with a Slovak Face."

84. Střítecký, "Úděl proměny," 19.

85. The thinking of the Czech radical democrats, such as Emanuel Arnold, Karel Sabina, and Jan Knedlhans Liblínský, is set into the context of the thinking and political activities of figures such as Vissarion Grigoryevich Belinsky, Alexander Ivanovich Herzen, Nikolai Gavrilovich Chernyshevsky, the Polish revolutionary Tadeusz Krępowiecki, Giuseppe Garibaldi, and Marx's collaborator Arnold Ruge.

86. Kosík, *Česká radikální demokracie*, 197.

87. Kosík, "Neruda myslitel," 3.

88. See especially Nejedlý, *Zpěvohry Smetanovy*, 124–31 (originally published in 1908). However, Nejedlý also repeated this motif in 1946: "When *Neruda* presented his poems. Even in the eyes of the dull and uncomprehending, he was a 'cosmopolitan,' a non-patriot, who was betraying his homeland and his nation, because he dared to follow in Mácha's footsteps [to] take Czech poetry farther and higher. . . . However, perhaps the most terrible wave of this ignominy was then unleashed on *Smetana*." Nejedlý, "Komunisté, dědici velkých tradic," 294–95. The heretical question is then whether one can spot a structural similarity between Nejedlý's defense of Smetana and Kundera's later defense of Leoš Janáček. See Kundera, *Můj Janáček*.

89. In *Zpěvohry Smetanovy*, Nejedlý commonly makes statements such as: "Smetana, an artist with a worldview who could not give up his great artistic plans, even though he longed for a truly national art" (21). In his earlier writing, worldliness is marginalized (see Nejedlý's Preface to the book written in 1954: "So let this book be a lesson, even today . . ., on what it means to be a national artist. That it is not playing with art, but merging entirely with the nation" (11–12). Eventually, this is implicitly replaced by Sovietism. Even before the war, Nejedlý left no one in any doubt that the center of historical progress is the Soviet Union (on the role of the Soviets as an instrument of real democracy, see Dalberg, "Demokratie als Entwicklungsmodell"; on the role of the USSR in the 1930s, see Křesťan, "Společnost pro hospodářské"; and Křesťan, *Zdeněk Nejedlý*, 186–93, 242–49. On the same question after 1945, see Nejedlý, *30 let Sovětského svazu*. In a lecture dated January 9, 1948, in connection with the importance of progressive traditions of Czech history, Nejedlý directly declared: "However, we also have another and especially beautiful example of how history can be used today. And that's the Soviet Union . . . so Soviet science teaches us how we should revise fixed opinions and not let ourselves be mistaken." Nejedlý, "Odkaz našich národních dějin," 230–31.

90. Kundera, "Nesamozřejmost národa." See a polemical text by Robert

Kalivoda, in which the way of inquiring about worldliness is considered as an unjustified underestimation and an overestimation of Czech intellectual development. From the perspective of our interest, though, it is possible to classify this text in the same series as Kundera's; even when the author rejects the overestimation of the development of that time, and spells out its limits in the form of an underestimation of structuralism, psychoanalysis, and existentialism, he still considers the 1960s to be the third period during which a universalistic dimension in Czech culture manifested itself (after Comenius and the interwar avant-garde). See Kalivoda, "České kulturní vědomí."

91. Kundera, "Český úděl," 5. Here, we will not engage with the debate that ensued. For more on that, see, for example, West, "Destiny as Alibi," 401–28.

92. Zumr, "Konfrontace Marxismu," 10; and Kalivoda, "Demokratizace a kritické myšlení," 6. A year later, Emanuel Mandler ("Naše světové stíny") called to mind the fact that Jan Patočka had also considered 1968 to be the peak of Czech history (see especially Patočka, "Dilema v našem národním programu.").

93. For example, "Our desire for a specific path to socialist democracy has its historical background. How much we would rather not be an exception," was Červinka's reflection on Masaryk's legacy. See Červinka, "Článek o TGM," 127–28. See also Nový, *Filosofie T. G. Masaryka*.

94. Bartošek, "Naše nynější krize a revoluce," 59. On this subject, Milan Kundera said: "The events we have lived through in the last thirty years were no milk and honey, but they gave us a tremendous working capital for artistic exploitation. Our experience with democracy, fascism, Stalinism and socialism contains everything essential that makes the twentieth century what it is. Our experience may thus enable us to ask more basic questions and create more meaningful myths than those who have not lived through this whole political anabasis." In Liehm, *Politics of Culture*, 63 (originally published in 1967).

95. Liehm and Kosík, "A. J. Liehm's Interview with Karel Kosík," 404–5.

96. Nový, "Metakritika krize," 17.

97. Liehm, "Diktát moci a trhu," 11.

98. Kosík, "Rozum a svědomí," 1; also, [Fourth] *IV. sjezd svazu československých spisovatelů*, 107–9. The English version was published as "Reason and Conscience."

99. "Reason without conscience becomes a utilitarian and technical reason of calculation, counting, and a civilization based upon this is a civilization without reason, in which man is subordinated to things and to their technical logic." Kosík, "Rozum a svědomí," 1.

100. Kosík, "Our Current Crisis," 31. Again, we cannot miss the connection to Zdeněk Nejedlý. This sentence appears in a passage in *Zpěvohry Smetanovy*: "Smetana's starting point in art was his progressiveness; i.e., the

truthfulness of each work of art, and from this truthfulness flowed its Czechness." Nejedlý, *Zpěvohry Smetanovy*, 121.

101. Kosík, "Our Current Crisis," 31.

102. "We lag behind the revivalists who thought about culture in the sense of national existence. For us, the 'Czech question' no longer exists. By detaching reflections on culture from thinking about a 'philosophy of Czech history,' we have given up the most essential *justification* of culture and its *privileged* role in national life." Kosík, "Irreplaceable Nature of Modern Culture," 102 (originally published in 1967). And, Kosík, "Our Current Crisis," 30.

103. Kosík, "Irreplaceable Nature," 102.

104. Kosík, "Our Current Crisis," 30.

105. Nový, "Metakritika krize," 18.

106. Kosík, "Our Current Crisis," 31; and Nový's statement in "Metakritika krize": "The Czech question is important insofar as it is a world question, and generally a human question" (18).

107. Kalivoda, "Zoči-voči," 100–101. "To realistically politically ensure true freedom for both of our nations is the only *possible* and, at the same time, the only *dignified* realism, that both of our nations and the federalized Czechoslovakia can afford." Kalivoda, "Zoči-voči," 103; and Bartošek, "Naše nynější krize," 61.

108. See Kopeček, "Czech Communist Intellectuals," 386. Kosík returned to the topic a year later in a text that discussed Central Europe: "And so the Czechs may find themselves in a situation where they repeat the limitations of their previous adversaries and play the ridiculous role of moralizers who understand nothing and indoctrinators in relation to the new, awakening historical subject—to the Slovaks." Kosík, "What Is Central Europe?" 167 (originally published in 1969).

109. Kosík, "Illusions and Realism," 112 (originally published in 1969).

110. Kosík, *Crisis of Modernity*, 101. Kosík returned to the subject of Central Europe in an independent essay. See Kosík, "What Is Central Europe?" 167–68. See also Dalberg, "Die verschwundene Mitte Europas." Kosík also mentioned the need to create a political nation; that is, a historical entity and not a subject created through external circumstances, in a debate in March 1969. See Kosík, "Příspěvek v diskusi," 9. (Besides Kosík, Vladimír Blažek, Jiří Brabec, and Felix Vodička also participated in a debate with the same name). The English version was published as "On the Czech Question."

111. Kosík, "What Is Central Europe?" 151.

112. On this subject, see Mervart, *Naděje a iluze*.

113. "The Slovak nation was to lose the historical awareness of its uniqueness. It was to Czechify, it was to merge into the Czechoslovak people even in terms of language, according to the Generalissimo's theses on linguistics into a

zonal language; finally it is understood to fall apart, in the way all kinds of ethnic groups melt into the United States." Tatarka, "Kultúra ako obcovanie," 51.

114. See esp. Benko and Hudek, "Slovak Communists"; and Doskočil, "Czechoslovakism and Ludakness."

115. Mináč et al., "Náš rozhovor s Vladimírem Mináčem."

116. At a practical level, debates concerning the national and democratic character or sometimes about how to guide it were mainly conducted in connection with the weekly published by the Union of Slovak Writers, *Kultúrny život*. See Doskočil, "Czechoslovakism and Ludakness." Dominik Tatarka expressed this moment in a period interview in these words: "And yet I consider such a situation [orientation to the nation] to be a fairly normal one; it is not necessarily harmful or dangerous, providing of course that it is coupled with a vigorous and steadily expanding democracy. If these two national egoisms . . . found democratic means to continually ventilate, and critically evaluate one another, and analytically investigate in democratic conditions, absolutely positive forces could develop." Liehm, *Politics of Culture*, 161. The last sentence is translated from the original (*Generace*, 161).

117. The inspiration of national liberation struggles in the Third World almost never appears in these types of reflections.

118. Tatarka, "Púť po Slovensku," 159.

119. For an overview of the subject, see Tatarka, *Hovory o kultúre*, especially the texts "Obec božia" (esp. 20), "Kultúra ako obcovanie," "Povedomie kultúry" (esp. 47), and "Otázky pre Dominika Tatarku" (esp. 76–77) on the subject of the conscience as a general human topic.

120. Mináč et al., "Náš rozhovor s Vladimírem Mináčem."

121. "We could dissolve as nations, in the name of reason give up our national individuality." Tatarka, "Obrana tvorby," 84–85.

122. Tatarka, "Obrana tvorby—obrana národnej kultúry," 85.

123. Tatarka, "Obec božia," 28.

124. Galmiche, "Paradoxy odkazu," 77.

125. Nejedlý, "Komunisté, dědici velkých tradic," 263.

126. Bartošek, "Český 'smysl dějin,'" 28; and Bartošek, "Naše nynější krize," 62.

127. Klein, "Ke krizi emocionality."

CHAPTER 5. THINKING REVOLUTION

Epigraph: Šulc, *Ideály, iluze a skutečnost*, 63.

1. Let us emphasize that the reform proposals coming from post-Stalinist thought, mainly those concerning the political order and economic restructuring, are not so significant for our aims here. Instead, we are concerned with the categories through which change is thought out. We are not looking at

questions of change through a reformist lens. This perspective was derived from empirical data, especially in the period's sociological and economic analyses. Nor are we much interested in a return to empirical reality as represented by the sociology of the time—which the sociologist Hana Havelková in her research about the 1960s termed the "epistemological reform" (Havelková, "[De]centralizovaná genderová politika," 141).

2. In a chapter of *Crossing Borders* titled "The Intelligentsia, the Masses, and the West," Michael David-Fox speaks about a "neo-revolutionary revival that superseded the dark Stalinist imagery of masked enemies lurking everywhere" in the Soviet context (69).

3. For example, one of these contradictions was the unresolved contradiction between the effort to resolve the collectivization of agriculture and the pressure to shift labor power out of rural areas and into industrial production that accompanied the Czechoslovak collectivization drive. See Boštík, *Venkov bez mezí*.

4. An understanding for the need for violent, discontinuous change in the period in which the capitalist system was transforming into a socialist one can be found, for instance, in Radovan Richta's works, and to a lesser extent in Josef Cibulka's. However, it is necessary to add that in the post-Stalinist era the concept of a "New Democratic Revolution," which would differ from a classic bourgeois democratic revolution as well as from a full-fledged socialist revolution, was under consideration. Its specificity lay in its creating conditions for a gradual takeover of power by the proletariat, even if it was still going to accomplish this through bourgeois democratic means. This concept, therefore, represented a kind of precursor to the socialist revolution that did not take place based on abrupt and violent changes, but through a smooth process where the one flows into the other. On the concept of the New Democratic Revolution, see Houška, "Charakter a význam."

5. The only significant exception was Egon Bondy, who advocated a Maoist concept of cultural revolution among Czech students in Prague. See Mervart, "Envisioning Socialist Utopia."

6. These are the famous notes: "Leaps, Leaps, Leaps!" that Lenin wrote into the margins of his excerpts from Hegel's *Logic*. See Lenin, "Conspectus," 123.

7. In this regard, Lenin's ferocity in defending himself as well as in refuting all the accusations of artificially "introducing" socialism in Russia, of "skipping" the stage of "bourgeois democratic revolution," or of "immediately transforming the revolution into a socialist one" are utterly typical. See Lenin, "Tasks of the Proletariat"; and Lenin, "Letters on Tactics."

8. On the theory of the intensification of the class struggle, see Stalin, "Right Deviation," 37–41.

9. Priestland, *Stalinism*, 37.

10. Cibulka, *Dialektika a ontologie*, 60, 72.

11. See, for example, this quote taken from a period document by Ivan Sviták: "Instead of a dialectical conception of development in all its complexity, a kind of evolutionist conception either of a straight path toward improvement, in the case of socialism, or of a straight path to degeneration, in the case of capitalism." National Archives, Prague, fond Ivan Sviták, box 60, "O projevech a překonávání takzvaného kultu osobnosti ve filozofii," 7.

12. Cibulka, *Spory o dialektiku*, 106–7.

13. Kalivoda, *Husitská ideologie*, 39.

14. Cibulka, *Dialektika a ontologie*, 87–90.

15. This is also attested to by Kalivoda's remarks about the "feudalization" of commercial capital in the case of Florence, a process that is unthinkable in the case of industrial capital. Kalivoda, *Husitská ideologie*, 72.

16. Kalivoda, *Husitská ideologie*, 71.

17. Kalivoda, *Husitská ideologie*, 45–46. With these reformulations of the concept of dialectical development, Kalivoda also managed to methodologically rework a somewhat one-dimensional pattern of the origin and development of capitalism that had been paradigmatically based in the case of England. And while the island's "journey" may have been the first, it certainly was not the only one. Kalivoda demonstrated this fact particularly through the phenomenon of "refeudalization"—the emergence of serfdom anew in the seventeenth century. In his view, reversal did not represent a regression *back* to feudalism, but the "nobility succumbing to a new mode of production: precapitalist commodity production." The second serfdom was thus not a renewal of the first, but a "function of commodity production [that] with its content and purpose [was] an antifeudal manifestation." The origin of these "one-dimensional" conceptualizations of the development (not only) of capitalism can doubtlessly be traced back to the Preface to the first volume of *Capital*, where Marx often regaled potentially naive German readers who comforted themselves with the thought that conditions were not nearly so bad in Germany with the expression "De te fabula narratur" [about you the tale is told] (Marx, *Capital, Vol. I*, 8.). We already find a reference to different forms of development (though in this case it would perhaps be more appropriate to speak of modifications to a particular one) of capitalism in Lenin; see Krausz, *Reconstructing Lenin*, 89–92, 107–8. Karl Korsch was one of the first Western Marxists to criticize the one-dimensional model of capitalism. See Korsch, "Zehn Thesen" (originally published in 1950).

18. In his historical analysis of the Hussite revolution (1419–1434), Kalivoda emphasized the early years of commune in the newly established city of Tábor (1420) where, in his view, the truly emancipatory revolutionary ideas came into existence.

19. Kalivoda, "Marxismus a libertinismus," 111.

20. Kalivoda, "Demokratizace a kritické myšlení," 6; and Kalivoda, "O perspektivách."

21. It is necessary to add that Jaroslav Klofáč, Vojtěch Tlustý, and Miloš Svoboda, who were also targets of Cibulka's criticism, also worked with conceptions of inner and outer dialectics that were very similar: "We are convinced of the dialectical connection of external conditions and internal contradictions by the fact that in the same (similar) conditions and under the same (similar) external action various phenomena develop in various ways in connection to the particularities of their inner structures, their own internal contradictions, and in connection with the internal movement of the given phenomenon. This means the same external movement is transformed in various ways into internal movement and therefore the movement and development of the given thing cannot be explained merely by external movement and external action." Klofáč, Tlustý, and Svoboda, *Problémy determinismu a pokroku*, 10. Cibulka believed their shortcoming was that they failed to elaborate a truly dialectical concept of determination.

22. Here, Cibulka is mainly referring to the essay by Evald Ilyenkov, "Logicheskoe i istoricheskoe"; and Cibulka, *Dialektika a ontologie*, 52.

23. Cibulka, *Dialektika a ontologie*, 74 (emphasis added).

24. Cibulka, *Spory o dialektiku*, 61. Naturally, the cybernetic approaches of the period considered systems (or rather states of systems) as systems that were not aiming toward equilibrium. In their view, they have very short durations unless, of course, the example was not the universe as a whole (if it is indeed a whole), which—at least according to Josiah W. Gibbs's ideas cited by Wiener—"shows a tendency toward extinction." See Wiener, *Kybernetika a společnost*, 29, 49.

25. Cibulka, *Dialektika a ontologie*, 98.

26. Javůrek, *Dialektika obecného*, 94–100, 114, 172.

27. Despite his classification of Kosík in the category of "Heideggerian Marxism," this moment was convincingly elaborated by Ivan Landa in an essay on Kosík's concept of labor and time. See Landa, "Labour and Time."

28. Kosík, *Dialectics of the Concrete*, 42 (translation changed).

29. Kosík, "Zítřek je v našich rukou," 74.

30. Kosík, *Dialectics of the Concrete*, 85.

31. Kalivoda, "Marxismus a libertinismus," 106.

32. Kalivoda, "Marxismus a libertinismus," 131.

33. Kalivoda, "Marxismus a libertinismus," 132.

34. Kalivoda, "Marxismus a libertinismus," 132.

35. Gardavský, *God Is Not Yet Dead*, 208.

36. Gardavský, *God Is Not Yet Dead*, 211 (translation changed).

37. Machovec, *Smysl lidského* života, 201.
38. Machovec, *Smysl lidského* života, 203.
39. Richta, *Civilization at the Crossroads*, 267–73.
40. Richta, *Civilization at the Crossroads*, 269.
41. Richta, *Civilization at the Crossroads*, 268.
42. Richta, *Civilization at the Crossroads*, 268, 54.
43. Kusý, *Filozofia politiky*. The authors of the book on Soviet man attribute a similar penchant for the present time to the writers clustered around Aleksandr Tvardovskii's magazine *Novy Mir*: "Even though this camp of writers theoretically shares the goals of October, they practically built an ideal society in the real present, and not in a utopian future." Genis and Vail, *60. léta*, 143.
44. Sommer, "'Are We Still Behaving as Revolutionaries?'"; Sommer, "Scientists of the World, Unite!" For the most recent take, see Sommer et al., *Řídit socialismus jako firmu*, esp. 52–67.
45. Richta, *Vědeckotechnická revoluce a alternativy*, 24.
46. Richta defines integral productivity as a "the relationship between output and total inputs of living and materialized labour." See Richta, *Vědeckotechnická revoluce*, 38.
47. Richta, *Vědeckotechnická revoluce*, 38.
48. Richta, *Vědeckotechnická revoluce*, 37–38.
49. Šulc, *Ideály, iluze a skutečnost*, 22–23.
50. For a general take on these aspects of cybernetics from the philosophical perspective, see Bober, *Stroj, človek, spoločnosť*, 63–68.
51. Bober, *Stroj, človek, spoločnosť*, 81.
52. Richta, *Člověk a technika*, 12.
53. Šulc, *Ideály, iluze a skutečnost*, 26.
54. Richta, *Civilization at the Crossroads*, 18.
55. Richta, *Civilization at the Crossroads*, 42.
56. By the expression "art produced as art" we mean the fact that the creators truly intended to create art as a higher form of culture with a social-critical reach, and not just as artifacts for entertainment and enjoyment.
57. Šamalík, *Člověk a instituce*, 348.
58. Alexander Genis and Petr Vail attribute the character of poetry to post-Stalinism and speak of the unmistakable role of spiritual culture in Soviet intellectual life. See Genis and Vail, *60. léta*.
59. "The plot of the novel became the *self-clarification of the author in the process of writing*; that is, seeking himself through words, pictures, [and] testimonies about himself, not about the world. This structural change has its classical expression in the modern disintegration of the traditional form of the novel and in its transformation *into a means for self-expression, one's own efforts at de-alienization, in the breakdown of the homogeneity of the empirical world with its*

disjunction of facts. The same was proclaimed in the New Wave of the 1960s as the breakdown of film conventions created by commercial production." Sviták, "Vlna pravdy," 48. Emphasis added.

60. Sviták, "Umění filosofie," 18 (originally published in 1956).

61. Sychra, *Hudba očima vědy*, 147. Ludvík Vaculík had similar thoughts: "If literature, art, is to liberate people, then it has to be by leading them to actions. And the deed is for the good health in the areas of politics and society. What's bad about that?" Liehm, *Politics of Culture*, 185 (translation changed).

62. This is true both for supporters of the magazine *Tvář* (see Špirit, *Tvář*) and, for example, for the surrealist Vratislav Effenberger. See Svěrák, "Strukturalistická inspirace."

63. Sviták, "Umění filosofie," 12.

64. Šotola, "Příspěvek v debatě," 3. Josef Zumr and Jiřina Zumrová expressed similar ideas in an unpublished paper: "Art as well as science—regardless of their necessary class conditionality—develop within individual cultural circles and eras as a whole organism, in which it isn't possible to forcibly isolate one part and develop it at the expense of the others. The internal law [governing] the development of art forces the essentially even development of all its constituent parts and creates a suitable tension among them, which is a necessary condition of artistic progress." Zumr and Zumrová, "Některé otázky diskuse," 24.

65. The current research of one of the coauthors of this study supports this finding. See Mervart, *Kultura v karanténě*.

66. J. Cigánek, "Kritik věčného hledačství," 6.

67. Liehm, "Diktát moci a trhu," 11. Of course, not everyone accepted this idea uncritically: Karel Kosík, for instance, in reference to the discussion on ideology, emphasized that it is not possible to simply remove art from social processes and set it entirely outside of politics and ideology. See Kosík, "Slepá ulička" (originally published in 1957).

68. Sviták, "Umění filosofie," 32. This is an original text that was prepared in 1956 for *Literární noviny*, from which only some parts could be published. The passage cited in the chapter was first published in the book just mentioned.

69. Kalivoda, "Dialektika strukturalismu," 40 (originally published in 1966).

70. Otčenášek, "Diskusně o současných problémech," 3.

71. Kosík, "Hašek and Kafka," 86 (translation changed), (originally published in 1963).

72. See the editorial note on the texts "Stav a perspektivy našeho umění," "Diskusně o diskusi," "Diskusně o současných problémech literatury," and "nezastupitelnost národní kultury" in Kosík, *Dialektika, kultura a politika*, 260–62.

73. The magazines included *Plamen, Host do domu, Literární noviny, Kultúrny život, Kulturní tvorba, Světová literatura*, and *Orientace*.

74. Debates over whether the new socialist art should orient itself in an entirely new direction and reject bourgeois art (as an expression of the bourgeoisie's repression of the proletariat) or build on the foundations created by bourgeois art had been raging since the beginning of the 1920s. At the time the avant-garde (including Lukács) was facing off with the theorists, such as Lenin, Lunacharsky, and Trotsky. As we can see, in the 1960s the relevance of this question waned. On the debates about proletarian art in the 1920s, see Komanická, "Zrod proletárskej kultúry."

75. Luděk Novák, *Století moderního malířství* (Prague: Orbis, 1968), cited in Bartlová, *Dějiny českých dějin umění*, 326–27.

76. See, for example, Liehm, *Rozhovor*.

77. Cf. Sartre, "Projev na moskevském kongresu"; and Sartre, "Myšlenky proti myšlenkám," 6.

78. "J.-P. Sartre a ti druzí," 2–3.

79. Janoušek, *3 a 1/2*, 150.

80. Chvatík, *Smysl moderního umění*, 113. This book was compiled from lectures and texts composed between 1960 and 1964.

81. In Czechoslovakia in the 1960s, these were typical theater forms in which satiric improvisation was combined with music. These forms were consciously or unconsciously related to interwar avant-garde theater productions. For the citation, see Sviták, "Filozofie malých forem," 60 (originally published in 1963).

82. See Kellner, *Schöpfertum und Freiheit*.

83. Chvatík, *Smysl moderního umění*, 28.

84. Fischer, "Franz Kafka"; Fischer, "Kafkovská konference"; Sviták, "Kafka—filosof," 95; and Kusák, "Poznámky,"174. At this place in the text Alexej Kusák refers to Kosík's passage in *Dialectics of the Concrete* on the role of modern art in the destruction of the pseudoconcrete (168).

85. Goldstücker, "Shrnutí diskuse," 269. The furore in the GDR was caused by a conference participant who was one of the leaders of the SED (the Socialist Unity Party, also sometimes referred to as the East German Communist Party in English), Alfred Kurella. See Kaplan, *Kořeny československé reformy 1968*, 1:122–25.

86. Chvatík, *Smysl moderního umění*, 113; and Kalivoda, "Marx a Freud," 86.

87. Sviták, "Antropologické předpoklady," 96 (originally published in 1964).

88. Sviták, "Antropologické předpoklady," 95; and Kalivoda, "Dialektika strukturalismu," 38. "In fact, the knowledge of a particular person (and hence his transformation and self-actualization) is the content of our humanism." Draft opinion by the Central Committee of the SČSS (Union of Czechoslovak

Writers) on certain questions in Czechoslovak literature, in [Fourth] *IV. sjezd Svazu československých spisovatelů*, 11.

89. Chvatík, *Smysl moderního umění*, 29.

90. Naturally, Marxist humanism was not a monolithic block of opinion. For example, Karel Kosík inclined toward a rather Lukácsean approach to this question and treated artistic avant-gardes in an overly simplified manner. In his eyes, a work of art had to fulfill the conditions of timelessness and a relationship to the complexity of the world. In the Preface to a Czech edition of Hemingway's *For Whom the Bell Tolls*, Kosík evaluated the author's view of the world positively because it was not flattened to only human beings as individuals, but endeavored to create a holistic concept of the world that connects "killing, love, death, awareness of time and age, overcoming nothingness, and a relationship to nature." In other words, for Kosík, Hemingway is exactly the type of author whose claim to complexly capturing reality corresponds to his concept of a Marxist humanism that deals with man in the totality of his relations and not only in selected aspects. See Kosík, "Smrt a láska," 123.

91. Sviták, "Antropologické předpoklady," 109, 92.

92. Sviták, "Antropologické předpoklady," 89.

93. Kalivoda, "Dialektika strukturalismu," 38. For a detailed analysis of Kalivoda's reception of structuralism, see Kanda, "K estetickému myšlení."

94. See Sviták, "Vlna pravdy." On alienation interpreted as a Marxist category, see Hudec, "Marx, nejenom Kafka."

95. Chvatík, *Smysl moderního umění*, 29.

96. Kopeček, *Hledání ztraceného smyslu revoluce*.

97. Kalivoda, "Marx a Freud," 86.

98. Kalivoda, "Marx a Freud," 81.

99. Kalivoda, "Marxismus a libertinismus," 137.

100. Chvatík, *Strukturalismus a avantgarda*, 98. This book was based on texts written in 1966–1968.

101. Kalivoda, "Dialektika strukturalismu," 38.

102. Chvatík, *Strukturalismus a avantgarda*, 103.

103. Kalivoda, "Marxismus a libertinismus," 128.

104. Kalivoda, "Marxismus a libertinismus," 132–33.

105. Kosík, "Modernost, lidovost a socialismus," 93.

106. Marx, "Theses on Feuerbach," 5.

107. Sviták, "Umění filosofie," 35.

108. Kosík, *Dialectics of the Concrete*, 8.

109. Kosík, *Dialectics of the Concrete*, 8–9.

110. In the text "Všední život a dějiny" [Everyday Life and History], Kosík demonstrates how Bertolt Brecht's approach to everyday life is critical in a revolutionary way, and how it alienates people from their everyday relations. In

Kosík's view, in *Mother Courage*, Brecht accomplishes a "destruction of pseudo-concreteness" by means of "alienation, as existential modification and as revolution transformation." Kosík, "Všední život a dějiny," 117. See also Šamalík, *Člověk a instituce*, 348.

111. The power of art as an actor in revolutionary praxis, which Kosík suggests in *Dialectics of the Concrete*, also appears in György Lukács's work, and—even more powerfully—in Antonio Gramsci's. Although Kosík did not devote any significant independent text to Gramsci, the influence of the Italian thinker on Kosík's oeuvre is striking. Gramsci's own analysis of the hegemony of civil society, which exercises social control along with the state and its institutions, led him to the conception of creating a cultural hegemony based on a socialist and not a bourgeois foundation. In a review of one of the first Czech editions of Gramsci's works, Kosík wrote that, in the Italian author's view, "in the struggle against Catholicism and religion as forces that subjugated the *entire* man, not just his intellect, but also feelings, imagination, and acts, only a *new* culture that will create a new man can win." Kosík, "Gramsci o kultuře," 106. This thesis cannot be read literally as an opposition between socialist and bourgeois: for Kosík it probably had a metaphorical meaning in the sense of a contrast between the official party culture and the actual socialist one. Cultural hegemony is understood here as a hegemony of modern socialist art, which is free of ideological pressures and which, freely and in the spirit of Kosík's understanding of Marxist humanism, shapes and develops ("constitutes") socialist reality.

112. Kosík's political approach to culture consciously differed from the manifestos issued by artists and avant-garde groups. In his estimation, just like the reduced philosophy of man they do not make it possible to capture the world in its entirety; revolutionary ethos is therefore fragmentary and necessarily illusory. Kosík, "Gramsci o kultuře," 106. By contrast, Růžena Grebeníčková grants avant-garde art a right to fragmentation, because it is itself formed by the atomized nature of the modern world. Its inability to capture the world in its entirety is not only understandable, but the requirement itself is practically impossible to fulfill. See Grebeníčková, "Cesty Marxistické literární teorie," 101. However, in contrast to Robert Kalivoda and Josef Zumr, Grebeníčková and Kosík share a critical view of Czech structuralism, and, moreover, she comments in the same article on Karel Teige as an eclectic. We are grateful to Roman Kanda for drawing our attention to this text. Kanda discusses the Marxist aspects of Grebeníčková's work in Kanda, "Reprezentativní výbor."

113. See Liehm and Kosík, "A. J. Liehm's Interview with Karel Kosík," 398–99 (translation changed).

114. Kusý, "Zinštitucionalizovaný človek," 264. The nature of human change in the context of the scientific-technical revolution was evaluated with similar caution by Milan Průcha, who was close to the humanists to a certain extent

while also criticizing their unresolved ontology of the human being. He was one of the collaborators on Richta's team. See Průcha, "Vědeckotechnická revoluce." At the same time, this was not just a philosophical critique of the optimism associated with the civilizational transformation. Psychiatry was also issuing warnings about the impacts of mechanization and automation in this period. Sarah Marks refers to this perspective in connection with Oldřich Starý's "Humanist Manifesto," published in the journal *Československá psychiatrie* [Czechoslovak Psychiatry] in 1962. See Marks, "Ecology, Humanism and Mental Health," 140–41.

115. Sviták, "Vlna pravdy," 3.

116. Kosík, "Our Current Crisis."

117. Zumr, "Plastiky Vladimíra Preclíka," 21. If we are speaking about art, let us recall Jiří Trnka's short film that was shot according to a short story originally written by Ivan Klíma titled *Kybernetická babička* [Cybernetic Grandma] (Jiří Trnka, *Kybernetická babička*, Czechoslovakia 1962, 29 min.), which seemed to anticipate the solution proposed several years later by Ota Klein for the changed (replaced) role of mothers in child-rearing. See Klein, "Ke krizi emocionality."

118. Draft opinion by the Central Committee of the Union of Czechoslovak Writers [SČSS] on certain questions in Czechoslovak literature, in [Fourth] *IV. sjezd Svazu československých spisovatelů*, 12.

119. Kosík, "What Is Central Europe?" 179 (originally published in 1969). Here is a more extensive quote for comparison: "But isn't the danger of *Gleichschaltung*, uniformity, and greyness hidden in the 'new measure' that determines the aspect of the modern age? And the unstoppable progress of 'electricity and steam'; i.e., the grouping of technology, science, and industry into a new *symbiosis*, that will enslave people and nature, history and culture, in a manner even more drastic than the imperfect historical symbioses; i.e., Prussian, Austrian, and tsarist, were capable of?" Kosík, "What Is Central Europe?" 179 (translation changed).

120. Klein, "Ke krizi emocionality," 88–91.

121. Selucký, *Ekonomika*, 91.

122. Selucký, *Ekonomika*, 57; and Kosík, *Dialectics of the Concrete*, 48 (translation changed).

123. Kolář, *Der Poststalinismus*, 239.

124. Kolář, *Der Poststalinismus*, 10, 138, 258, 274.

CHAPTER 6. BEYOND THE HORIZONS OF POST-STALINISM

Epigraph: Kalivoda, "V lidských dějinách," 23 (R. Kalivoda to J. Válka, September 21, 1982).

1. Mikhail N. Epstein characteristically speaks of "totalism" as the main principle in Russian philosophy. See Epstein, "Main Configurations of Russian Thought," 37.

2. Miroslav Petříček follows this whole transformation of philosophical thinking, especially through the examples of Emmanuel Lévinas, Jacques Derrida, and Theodor Adorno. See Petříček, *Filosofie en noir*. On the rejection of the universalist concept of dialectics, see Ciccariello-Maher, *Decolonizing Dialectics*.

3. See Bondy, *Pracovní analýza*; and Kužel, "Marxist Criticism."

4. See an unauthorized document, "O přípravě a základních rysech," in Pelikán, *Tanky proti sjezdu*, 143–65.

5. On the content of communist reformists' political thought, see Andělová, "Intelektuální dějiny reformního komunismu."

6. See Voříšek, *Reform Generation*, 231.

7. Nový, "Filosofie a politika," 111.

8. Kosík, "Přeludy a socialismus," 56.

9. This was one of the party meetings that took place within the campaign against revisionism. See the personal archive of Josef Zumr, "Minutes of the Meeting of the Party Group of the Department of Historical Materialism in the Institute of Philosophy, ČSAV, held on May 18, 1959."

10. Kosík, "Přeludy a socialismus," 56.

11. By contrast with the Soviet proclamations, the Chinese references to Lenin seemed more genuine, for it was the dialectical law of the "unity and struggle of opposites" developed by Lenin on which Mao Zedong built a campaign using the motto "let a hundred flowers bloom, let a hundred schools of thought contend." See, for example, Zedong, "On Correctly Handling Contradictions." For references to the Chinese documents, see, for example, Kosík, "Hegel a naše doba" and "Slepá ulička," and Zumrová and Zumr, "Některé otázky diskuse."

12. See Sommer et al., *Řídit socialismus jako firmu*; and Kosík, *Dialektika, kultura a politika*. See also the selection of texts from the 1960s by Ivan Sviták, *Lidský smysl kultury*; and Chvatík, *Smysl moderního umění*.

13. Mlynář, *Stát a člověk*, 25.

14. Šamalík, *Člověk a instituce*, 335. Šamalík was referring to the Russian edition of the *Prison Notebooks*.

15. If Lenin was read philosophically, his post-Stalinist evaluation was based on an emphasis on his *Philosophical Notebooks* over Stalin's preferred *Materialism and Empirio-criticism*. Sochor and Šabata did the same, ten years earlier than Kosík ("Hegel a naše doba"). Sochor compares Lenin's contributions to the development of Marxism with those of Korsch and Lukács, and especially of Gramsci, highlighting the latter's orientation toward praxis, derived within the framework of historical materialism from a greater sense of historicism and setting it in contrast to Lenin's emphasis on materialism. Sochor, "Lenin a Gramsci jako filosofové," 3. For the citations, see Šabata, "Lenin a Gramsci," 3; and Sochor, "Lenin a Gramsci," 3.

16. Šabata, "Lenin a Gramsci," 3.
17. Mlynář, *Stát a člověk*, 113; and Šamalík, *Člověk a instituce*, 90.
18. See Gramsci, *Poznámky o Machiavellim*.
19. Mlynář, "Filosofie aktivity." However, František Šamalík gave the same passage of *Dialectics of the Concrete* a much more sympathetic reading; in it he saw the basis for a conception of science "which gives *society* the possibility of orienting itself in the set of conditions determining and conditioning its state and development, the possibility to recognize and thus also to control the institutions that govern society, a concept that 'excludes' the transformation of science into apologetics, into an instrument for emotional influence and one-sided manipulation, and which thus 'doesn't allow" a contradiction to be created from within science between its 'manipulative' and 'rationalizing' functions." Šamalík, *Člověk a instituce*, 110–11.
20. Kosík, *Dialectics of the Concrete*, 136.
21. Kosík, "Irreplaceable Nature."
22. Landa, "Historical Bloc and Revolution."
23. See Kalivoda, "Demokratizace a kritické myšlení" (1968), 1 and 13; (1968), 6. Karel Bartošek's text, which was explicitly aiming for a positive definition of politics gave the most programmatic impression. See Bartošek, "Naše nynější krize."
24. Bartošek, *Češi nemocní dějinami*.
25. Landa puts the Leninist conception of politics in connection with the techno-optimistic vision of the scientific-technical revolution and argues that Mlynář's conception, including the KSČ action program of April 1968, is founded on a technocratic idea of impulses coming from above. For an extensive analysis of this, see Landa, "Technology and Politics." On the historical bloc, see also Landa, "Historical Bloc and Revolution."
26. We do not want to argue with the interpretive concept of radical democracy; however, we do examine the limits of its period elaboration. See Mervart, "Radical Democrats."
27. On the topic of proclaimed solidarity that did not lead to a true political alliance, see Mervart, *Kultura v karanténě*.
28. Kosík, "Three Observations," 106. This was originally heard at the roundtable debate at the magazine *Plamen* in 1969, where, besides Kosík, other participants included Lubomír Sochor, Petr Pithart, Josef Macek, and František Šamalík.
29. Kosík, "Three Observations," 106. Lubomír Sochor expressed himself similarly in the same debate and proclaimed this moment as Machiavelli's greatest contribution: "Machiavelli socialized the knowledge that Machiavellianism has to be defeated by Machiavellianism." Sochor, "Machiavelli a machiavellismus," 10.

30. Andělová, "Reformní komunismus."

31. Bartošek, "Naše nynější krize," 60.

32. Liehm and Kosík, "A. J. Liehm's Interview with Karel Kosík," 400. In 1992 Kosík returned to this motif: "Palacký and Masaryk justified the political program philosophically. Political action was rooted in the questions of who is man, what is truth, and what is history. Measured at this level, today's 'political scene' in this country seems like a deterioration." Kosík, "Third Munich?" 147. We are grateful to Ivan Landa for drawing our attention to this connection. Kosík saw a challenge to reevaluate politics in this way in his observations on Machiavelli: "Machiavelli's conception is therefore a challenge, whether or not a different and new conception of politics, based on a new and original understanding of man and the world, of history and nature, is possible." Kosík, "Three Observations," 106.

33. Nový, "Masarykova idea."

34. Kopeček, "Čeští komunističtí intelektuálové," 109. The paper is an elaborated version of Kopeček's previously published paper titled "Czech Communist Intellectuals," and the cited passage is not part of the original English version.

35. "I'm not in favor of [what is said today . . .], that the only thing left for us is 'spirit,' cultural survival, etc. . . . precisely owing to the culture of experience that it has, our national collective doesn't only need to 'live spiritually,' but also to act politically autonomously. Politics, political thinking, in my opinion, belongs to national culture." Bartošek, "Česká otázka," 51 (originally published in 1969).

36. Bartošek, "Naše nynější krize."

37. For more on this subject, see Andělová, "'Labutí píseň.'"

38. Kalivoda, "V lidských dějinách," 23.

39. Besides Richta himself, who, according to Zdeněk Mlynář, had coined the phrase "socialism with a human face," it was mainly economists such as Ota Šik who had supported democratization. See, for example, Zdislav Šulc's vehement call for a change of the political elites: Šulc, *Ideály, iluze a skutečnost*, 64–65.

40. According to Vítězslav Sommer, the term "sociotechnics" was used in the sociology of the late 1980s in criticisms of technocratic types of analysis. See Sommer et al., *Řídit socialismus jako firmu*, 112. It is also used by Michal Kopeček, "Expertní kořeny postsocialismu, esp. 32–33; see also Sommer, "Are We Still Behaving as Revolutionaries?"

41. Stříteský, "Úděl proměny," 20.

42. Feinberg, "And the 'Thing Itself.'" He also refers to Kosík's essay "Our Current Crisis," 30.

43. Adamczak, *Beziehungsweise Revolution*, 200–201, cited in Ort, "Dát řeč touze," 221.

44. Valiavicharska, *Restless History*, 101.

45. Bartošek, "Naše nynější krize," 55–56; Kosík, "Hašek and Kafka"; Kosík, "What Is Central Europe?"; and Kosík, "Illusions and Realism," 109–12. This topic, along with the Czech question, appears in nearly all Kosík's texts from 1969.

46. Kosík, "Illusions and Realism," 110–11.

47. See, for example, Jan Tesař's work, which was divided into separate articles and published as "Vlastenci a bojovníci," 16. For the complete version of the text, see Tesař, *Mnichovský komplex*. It is significant that, for instance, Karel Kosík was still thinking along the same lines in the 1990s. Although in an interview with Raúl Fornet-Betancourt and Martin Traine, he still spoke about the Germans as important philosophers but also mentioned their absolute lack of a democratic sense and put them de facto in contrast to the Czechoslovaks (or perhaps only Czechs) as born democrats. See Fornet-Betancourt et al., "Dass die Bürger es sind."

48. Pažout, *Mocným navzdory*, esp. 145–241; and Havel et al., "Trialog o radikalismu." See Uhl, *Za svobodu*.

49. Kopeček, "Czech Communist Intellectuals," 386.

50. Mináč et al., "Náš rozhovor," 4. We are thinking here about Vladimír Mináč, who complained that there are very few voices like Kosík's on the Czech intellectual scene. Kosík, "What Is Central Europe?" 167.

51. In 2004 Milan Kundera spoke about a monograph on Max Brod: "Remember this: the first monograph written about Janáček—about that sincere patriot—is not Czech, but German." Milan Kundera, "Nepravděpodobný osud," 76. See Kosík, *Předpotopní úvahy*; Kosík, *Poslední eseje*; and Sviták, *Sametová normalizace*.

52. Kosík, "Third Munich."

53. Sviták, "Odrození nebo obrození," 55; Sviták, "Třetí Mnichov," unpublished typed manuscript.

54. Sviták, "Restaurační scéna," 25.

55. Kosík, "Third Munich."

56. Sviták, "Prolog."

57. Tesař, *Sme autentickí dediča*. Here, see, for instance "Bráňme si dedovizeň."

58. Feinberg, "And the 'Thing Itself.'"

59. Genis and Vail, *60. Léta*, 211.

60. Karkov, "Decolonizing *Praxis*"; Valiavicharska, *Restless History*, esp. chapter 3, "In the Darkness of Humanism."

61. Profant compares Kosík's and Patočka's reflections on this topic and even though he is much more inclined toward Kosík's view, his "doesn't necessarily have to" indicates an awareness of the openness of various outcomes,

and he does not consider either thinker's treatment of the relationship between the nation and politics to be unproblematic. See Profant, "O jednom vyústění," 67, 79.

62. On the relationship of the Serbian intelligentsia to nationalism, see Dragović-Soso, "*Saviours of the Nation.*" See also Bešlin et al., "Aporias and Contradictions."

63. Jaroslav Střítecký commented on this aspect with the apt remark that the post-Stalinists "apply Lenin's words about Russia's second-class status after the victory of socialism in a more advanced country to themselves." Střítecký, "Úděl proměny," 22. Michal Voříšek notes the same moment, and refers to Radoslav Selucký, Jiří Cvekl, Miroslav Jodl, and Michal Reiman in Voříšek, *Reform Generation*, 290.

64. Recently, many researchers have been examining the Czechoslovak topic from this point of view. See, for example, Buzássyová, "Back to Africa?"

65. Cibulka, *Dialektika a ontologie*, 298.

66. Cibulka, *Dialektika a ontologie*, 277.

67. Cibulka, "Rehabilitovat Marxe!" 377.

68. Dubská, *Objevování Ameriky*, 159.

69. Karkov, "Decolonizing *Praxis*," 196.

70. Mňačko, "Mňačko protestiert," 6.

71. "Spisovatelé o středním východě," an interview with Arnošt Lustig, Ivan Klíma, Oldřich Daňek, and Jan Procházka in *Literární noviny*, which was banned by the period censors. National Archives, Prague fond KSČ—Ústřední výbor 1945–1989, f. 02/1 (presidium ÚV KSČ 1962–1966), vol. 38, a. j. 38, b. 12. We are grateful to Zdeněk Doskočil for making this document available to us.

72. See Karkov, "Decolonizing *Praxis*," 192.

73. See Klein, "Vědeckotechnická revoluce a tvorba," 48 (version of the paper written in 1968).

74. Simonsohn, "Der Nahostkonflikt," 44.

75. "'Spisovatelé o středním východě,' cenzurou pozastavený rozhovor Arnošta Lustiga, Ivana Klímy, Oldřicha Daňka a Jana Procházky v *Literárních novinách*," Fond KSČ—Ústřední výbor 1945–1989, f. 02/1 (předsednictvo ÚV KSČ 1962–1966), sv. 38, a. See also, for example, Mňačko, "Mňačko protestiert"; and I. Klíma, "Jeden projekt," 5.

76. See, for example, "Debate by the Central Committee of the KSČ's Cabinet for Philosophy of the Czechoslovak Academy of Sciences on the Current State and Tasks for the Dialectical Material Division from 1955." (Personal archive of Josef Zumr.)

77. Sviták, *Ekonomické legendy*; and Sviták, "Změny hodnotových orientací," 29.

78. At this point, Karkov refers to Maria Todorova's work, "The Balkans: From Discovery to Invention," *Slavic Review* 53, no. 2 (1994): 453–82. See Karkov, "Decolonizing *Praxis*," 197. According to Karkov, a strong affinity for the West led Polish and Hungarian Marxist humanists to move away from Marxism, which they felt was exhausted, to liberalism. This was unproblematic for them because, among other reasons, it was a product of Western thought.

79. "Marienbader Protokolle," 473.

80. Kundera, "Tragedy of Central Europe"; and Kundera, "Kidnapped West." On the persistence of this manner of thinking, see Donskis, *Yet Another Europe*.

81. See also Ivan Sviták's statement, according to which the "Sovietization of a Western European state, a democratic nation, and Christian-democratic culture" had taken place in Czechoslovakia in the years 1938–1948. Sviták, "Filosofie dějin," 142. Kundera's attitude is not unusual within this geographical area. Moreover, it is possible to track parallels in the pan-Hungarian concept of Central Europe from Sándor Márai, a native of Košice, since the 1940s, and Kundera's position is also close to Czesław Miłosz's perception of Central Europe. See Labov, *Transantlantic Europe*, 55–79.

82. See also the inspiring text written by Ondřej Slačálek, in which Kundera's essay is set in a postcommunist perspective. Slačálek, "Postcolonial Hypothesis," esp. 36–38. It is also important to note that meanings of Central Europe could have changed and still can change in relation to points of view. For example, in 1988, the magazine *Cross Currents* organized a writers' debate in Lisbon. And there, certain Russian authors shared a colonial perception of the area, which prompted a vigorous response and postcolonial critique by authors from the American and Caribbean regions. See Labov, *Transantlantic Europe*, 79–89.

83. Sabatos, "Shifting Contexts," 31.

84. Australian Left Review, "Interview with Lukacs," 70.

85. For a detailed analysis of changes in the attitudes of the French intellectual left and along with it the Czechoslovak exile milieu, see Schmidt, *Lettre Internationale*, 177–214.

86. Zdislav Šulc even introduced the perspective that by removing people from the sphere of production, the scientific-technical revolution would be able to overcome the division in society between those who are in control and those who are controlled. See Šulc, *Ideály, iluze a skutečnost*, 19.

87. Voříšek, *Reform Generation*, 289–94.

88. Voříšek refers to John Connelly's work, *Captive University*; and Blaive, *Promarněná příležitost*; see also Voříšek, *Reform Generation*, 289–90.

89. Milena Bartlová arrives at the same finding for the field of art history. Bartlová, *Dějiny českých dějin umění*, 54.

90. One of the Prague salons was also convened in the apartment of the grandparents of Jiří Růžička, a coauthor of this book. Regular participants included Ivan Sviták and František Červinka. However, despite the continuity with the interwar intelligentsia that we have indicated, certain social phenomena essentially no longer appear in the post-Stalinist intelligentsia. For instance, many households of the avant-garde elite were still paying for the services of a maid, even in the Stalinist era. Jana Černá, the daughter of Milena Jesenská, has spoken critically about this moment. See Militzová, *Ani víru, ani ctnosti*, 76–77.

91. Voříšek, *Reform Generation*, 231.

92. Šamalík, *Člověk a instituce*, 335.

93. Kosík of course deals with everyday life at some length in *Dialectics of the Concrete* and warns against ripping it away from the larger scale of history. However, at the same time, this is not an attempt to valorize it, as Pavel Kolář has claimed (see Kolář, *Der Poststalinismus*, 239). For Kosík, everyday life remains an element of pseudo-concreteness, at a merely phenomenal level that certainly is not a site of truth. On this, see especially Kosík, *Dialectics of the Concrete*, 48.

94. Kosík, "What Is Central Europe?" 151.

95. Entries from June 13, 1970, Neratovice, and June 14, 1970, Prague. In Putík, *Odchod ze Zámku*, 144.

96. Page, *Czechoslovak Reform Movement*, 100.

97. Bondy, "Báseň literárním novinám."

98. We are grateful to Holly Case for this metaphor, which she used as a comparison with American democracy. Seminar at the Imre Kertész Kolleg on February 17, 2020, Jena.

99. Bartošek, "Naše nynější krize," 58.

100. Fornet-Betancourt et al., "Dass die Bürger es sind," 19.

101. Voříšek, *Reform Generation*, 292.

102. National Archives, Prague, fond KSČ—Ústřední výbor 1945–1989, fond Antonín Novotný, box 25, Stanovisko ov KSČ v Domažlicích k informaci ÚV KSČ o průběhu a výsledcích IV. sjezdu Svazu čs. spisovatelů, 19.7.1967.

103. Stříteckÿ, "Úděl proměny," 21.

104. Vaculík, "A co dělníci," 5.

105. Možný, *Proč tak snadno*, 52.

106. Oates-Indruchová, "Unraveling a Tradition," esp. 922–28. We are grateful to Marianna Placáková for drawing our attention to this study. This part of the chapter was published as Mervart, "'Dissatisfied Breadwinners.'"

107. See, for example, Klímová, *Nechte maličkých přijíti*.

108. Placáková, "On the Czech Translation"; and Jechová, "Cesta k emancipaci."

109. Hanáková, "Feminist Style."

110. Placáková, "Československá zkušenost," 33.

111. H. Havelková, "(De)centralizovaná genderová politika." Let us also mention Kateřina Lišková's research on the discussion of sexuality both among experts and among the public. See Lišková, *Sexual Liberation*, 137–46.

112. See, for example, Selucký, *Člověk a jeho volný čas*, 86. On the debates about the disproportionate quantity of household chores done by women and men, see Franc and Knapík, "Volný čas," 56–60.

113. Klein, "Ke krizi emocionality." According to the lead paragraph written by Jan Šindelář, who prepared the study for publication, this was a fragment from a more extensive manuscript in Klein's estate. This text was also published under the title Klein, "Krize emocionality," 129–49.

114. Klein, "Ke krizi emocionality," 62. A year later, *Sociologický časopis* published a study by Libuše Háková which clearly represents the best-elaborated period reflections on the role of women in socialist—and by extension, all advanced industrial societies. At the same time, Háková directly drew from Klein in her openness to future developments. See Háková, "Úvaha a podněty." We are grateful to Denisa Nečasová for the reference to this text.

115. Slejška, "Problémy aktivity žen."

116. Cited from Blagojević, "Praxis Journal and Women Intellectuals," 59.

117. Feinberg, "And the 'Thing Itself.'"

118. Střítecký, "Úděl proměny," 19.

119. Sviták, "Člověk," 61. These were notes he took during the "practice" at the district committee of the KSČ in Kyjov, where he was sent as part of the campaign against revisionism.

120. Kosík, "Božena Němcová," 46.

121. For the Stalinist image of women, see Nečasová, *Nový socialistický člověk*, 125–68. On the essentialist understanding of femininity in Irena Dubská and Helena Klímová, see Placáková, "On the Czech Translation," 155–68.

122. Kosík, "Havlíček's Principles of Democracy."

123. Dana Musilová states that in his interview with Simone de Beauvoir, A. J. Liehm paid more attention to the author's literary activities and said that readers of the interview, which was published in the magazine *Kultúrny život*, "did not have a chance to learn something more about her philosophical views, let alone reflections on the relations between men and women (24)." According to the Musilová, in Bratislava all the male members of the editorial staff merely treated de Beauvoir as Sartre's partner. See Musilová, *Na okraj jedné návštěvy*, 22–25.

124. Musilová, *Na okraj jedné návštěvy*, 24; Placáková, "On the Czech Translation."

125. Sviták, "Human Being or Sexus?" Along with his comments on *The*

Second Sex, Sviták also expressed his opinions on Betty Friedan's *The Feminine Mystique* (1963). Sviták's second text was published later (see Sviták, "Response from Ivan Sviták") in response to reactions by Jan Patočka and Irena Dubská. For more, see Placáková, "On the Czech Translation."

126. Sviták, "Response from Ivan Sviták," 184.

127. Marianna Placáková reads Sviták in a more sympathetic light, as an expression of Marxist criticism. See Placáková, "On the Czech Translation," 163.

128. Sviták, *Lidský smysl kultury*; and Sviták, "Surrealistický obraz člověka"; and Sviták, *Windmills of Humanity*. See also chapter 3 in this book.

129. Sviták, "Human Being or Sexus?" 174.

130. "What should a woman do to achieve full emancipation? First, of course, the social problem needs to be solved in society, and then that 'male' contradiction between a woman's biological mission and the full application of her intellect and abilities will disappear." Liehm, *Rozhovor*, 77, cited in Musilová, *Na okraj jedné návštěvy*, 45.

131. Sviták, "Human Being or Sexus?"175.

132. Placáková, "On the Czech Translation," 155–68.

133. Placáková, "On the Czech Translation," 155–68; Hana Havelková points out that it is actually their "return to biologism" by contrast with the "social construction of gender" that is necessary to take as "part of a resistance to the official approach," which in her view was represented by, for example, the state population commission. See H. Havelková, "(De)centralizovaná genderová politika," 158.

134. See, for example, B. Havelková, "Three Stages of Gender," 31–56; and B. Havelková, "Genderová rovnost."

135. Klein, "Ke krizi emocionality," 86–87.

136. Cited in Hanáková, "Feminist Style," 213. Translated by Melinda Reidinger from the Czech version of the article: Hanáková, "Feministický styl," 431.

137. Blagojević, "Praxis Journal and Women Intellectuals." In addition to writing reviews and reports, Blagojević mainly mentions the translating work that the women engaged in at *Praxis*. The genre distribution of female authors is clearly closely connected to the role of women within philosophy itself. If we take a cursory look at Czechoslovak periodicals (*Filosofický časopis*, *Otázky marxistickej filozofie*, and *Filozofia*) through this lens, we see that women (such as Irena Dubská, Evelína Bodnárová, and Vlasta Černíková) were usually the authors of works in the same genres that Una Blagojević mentions. They also occasionally contributed to discussions, but their authorial share in the category of "studies" is incomparable with the numbers of contributions written by men. Moreover, not even one female author is represented in the jubilee anthology

60 let Filosofického časopisu [60 Years of the *Philosophical Journal*]. One of the few female professors in Czech philosophy was Jiřina Popelová Otáhalová (1904–1985), whose interests included the history of philosophy, ethics, and the study of Comenius. Her role and her intergenerational contacts are undoubtedly a worthy challenge for further research.

138. This impression is underlined in the concluding passage of Dubská's book *Objevování Ameriky* [Discovering America], in which she discusses the negative aspect of the "mediated moment" that enters personal relationships. Mediating interventions from outside can lead to an "absolute affirmation or absolute submission of the other's personality," which is a more primitive form of interpersonal relationships, especially in contrast to a critical and equal relationship between two individualities. The paradox consists in the spontaneity of "confirmation" or "submission" and gives them apparent (phenomenal) persuasiveness or "fullness," which Dubská claims is also true for historical changes in the relations between men and women. See Dubská, *Objevování Ameriky*, 167–68.

139. See Blaženka Despot's unique text, "Women and Self-Management" (originally published in 1981). Despot, "Women and Self-Management." For more on this subject, see Loránd, *Feminist Challenge*, 42–83.

140. Matonoha, "Dispositives of Silence." On the incorrect images of femininity and women in the cinematography of the 1960s, see Hanáková, "Od zednice Mařky." We are grateful to Marianna Placáková for drawing our attention to this text.

141. Sviták, "Paradoxy lásky," 94.

142. Sviták, *Devět životů*, 231.

143. Sviták, "Vlna pravdy," 36.

144. In addition to their social origin, which was already mentioned, it is impossible to overlook the strikingly traditionalist relationship to the tool of the Marxist humanists: art. Although Karel Kosík speaks about modern art as one of the instruments for destroying pseudo-concreteness in *Dialectics of the Concrete*, aesthetically it is close to Lukács, and despite considering a work of art that only becomes such when it exceeds the "topicality" of its time, it also endorses the idea that art reveals the truth (i.e., it requires a relationship between art and reality). This is the perspective through which he looks at Hemingway, Kafka, and Hašek. We can see a similar relationship to art in Sviták (see his praise for Menzel's "objectivity"), which he—along with a conservative thinker, Rio Preisner—contrasts with the "degeneracy" and "vulgarity" of the novel. See Pelc, ...*A bude hůř*; Sviták, "Šmejd z andrgraundu"; the originally exile publication *Právo lidu*, no. 4, (1985): 5. Michaela Kašičková is correct when she claims that Sviták was not primarily interested in Pelc's text, but in settling scores with the values and aesthetics of Czechoslovak underground culture as such. See Kašičková, "Přijetí románu," 24–25.

145. Oates-Indruchová, "Unraveling a Tradition," 941.

146. In his analysis of Kosík's shift in thinking, Jan Černý interprets traditionalism as a result of a turn away from Marxism toward Heidegger. However, even though we agree with Černý's conclusions, when it is measured by these criteria it seems to be an organic development. See J. Černý, "Karel Kosík and Martin Heidegger."

147. "Stenografický protokol," 9. We are grateful to Zdeněk Doskočil for drawing our attention to Ladislav Novomeský's critique of the uncritically pro-Israeli attitudes, as well as for making the document available to us.

148. Mináč et al., "Náš rozhovor," 4.

149. Ilyenkov, *Dialectics of the Abstract*; and Althusser, *Reading Capital*.

150. See Patočka, "Česká filosofie," 326.

151. See Kosík, *Předpotopní úvahy*; Kosík, *Poslední eseje*; and Fornet-Betancourtet al., "Dass die Bürger es sind," 18.

152. Sviták, *Epochální iluze*; and Sviták, *Třetí Mnichov*, 7. See also Holubec, "Ivan Sviták"; and Andělová, "Česká nekomunistická levice."

153. Likavčan, "Civilizace na rozcestí."

154. Liehm and Kosík, "A. J. Liehm's Interview with Karel Kosík," 401.

155. Fornet-Betancourt et al., "Dass die Bürger es sind," 20.

156. Postone, *Time, Labor, and Social Domination*.

157. Fornet-Betancourt et al., "Dass die Bürger es sind," 21.

158. Machovec, *Filosofie tváří*.

159. These earlier hints can be seen especially in the television show *Šest naléhavých disputací*. On the understanding of the ecological crisis, see Likavčan, "Civilizace na rozcestí." This trend is also confirmed by Matěj Spurný under the subheading "Proměna sensitivity" [A Transformation of Sensitivity], which describes changes in attitudes toward the technocratically conceived urban reconstruction projects in Most and Bratislava. See Spurný, "Nehostinnost spočitatelného světa," esp. 176–83.

160. Klaučo and Duda, *Fenomén techniky*.

161. In its most apparent form this antinomy is formulated by Rudolf Šíma, in *Člověk a svět*, 182.

BIBLIOGRAPHY

ARCHIVAL SOURCES

Archiv Moravského zemského muzea, Brno
    fond Anna Šabatová
Literární archiv Památníku národního písemnictví, Prague
    fond Karel Kosík
Lukács Archive, Budapest
National Archives, Prague
    fond Ivan Sviták
    fond Zdeněk Mlynář
    fond KSČ–Ústřední výbor 1945–1989, f. 02/1 (předsednictvo ÚV KSČ 1962–1966)
    fond Antonín Novotný
Personal Archive of Josef Zumr

PERIODICALS

Concordia
Filosofický časopis
Filozofia
Host do domu
Kultúrny život
Listy
Literární listy
Literární noviny
Neues Forum
Orientace
Otázky marxistickej filozofie
Plamen
Rudé právo
Sociologický časopis
Tvář

BIBLIOGRAPHY

LITERATURE

Allen, Robert C. *Farm to Factory: A Reinterpretation of the Soviet Industrial Revolution.* Princeton University Press, 2003.

Althusser, Louis. "The Humanist Controversy." In *The Humanist Controversy and Other Writings*, edited by François Matheron, 221–305. Translated by G. M. Goshgarian. Verso, 2003.

Althusser, Louis, ed. *Reading Capital: The Complete Edition*, edited by Étienne Balibar et al. Translated by Ben Brewster and David Fernbach. Verso, 2016.

Andělová, Kristina. "Česká nekomunistická levice po roce 1989 a myšlení alternativ." Master's thesis, Charles University, 2013.

Andělová, Kristina. "Intelektuální dějiny českého reformního komunismu 1968–1990." PhD diss., Charles University, 2021.

Andělová, Kristina. "'Labutí píseň pražského jara': Politické perspektivy opoziční skupiny kolem časopisu Listy po roce 1971." In *Šest kapitol o disentu*, edited by Jiří Suk, Michal Kopeček, Kristina Andělová, Tomáš Vilímek, Tomáš Hermann, and Tomáš Zahradníček, 49–78. Ústav pro soudobé dějiny AV ČR, v. v. i, 2017.

Andělová, Kristina, and Jan Mareš. "Hledání české radikální demokracie: Karel Kosík a filozofie (českých) dějin." In *Dějiny—teorie—kritika* 11, no. 2 (2014): 183–211.

Angus, Ian. *Groundwork of Phenomenological Marxism: Crisis, Body, World.* Lexington Books, 2021.

Angus, Ian. "Inception of Culture from the Ontology of Labour: The Original Contribution of Karel Kosík to a Marxian Theory of Culture." In Feinberg, Landa, and Mervart, *Karel Kosík*, 107–28.

Arab-Ogly, Eduard, Arnošt Kolman, and Jiří Zeman, eds. *Kybernetika ve společenských vědách.* Nakladatelství Československé akademie věd, 1965.

Árnason, Johann P. "Communism and Modernity." In *Multiple Modernities*, edited by Shmuel N. Eisenstadt, 61–90. Routledge, 2002.

Árnason, Johann P. "Perspectives and Problems of Critical Marxism in Eastern Europe." *Thesis Eleven* 3, no. 4 (1982): 68–95; nos. 5–6 (1982): 215–45.

Aronova, Elena, and Simone Turchetti, eds. *Science Studies During the Cold War and Beyond: Paradigms Defected.* Palgrave Macmillan, 2016.

Auerhan, Jan. *Technika, kvalifikace, vzdělání.* Prague: Nakladatelství politické literatury, 1965.

Australian Left Review. "An Interview with Lukacs." *Australian Left Review* 3, no. 3 (1968): 66–71.

Authorial collective. "Diskuse o metodologických otázkách zpracování středověké myšlenkové látky." In Dvořák, *60 let Filosofického časopisu*, 127–74.

Authorial collective. *Inspirace Pražské jaro 1968: Literární noviny—sborník statí.* Sumbalon, 2014.

BIBLIOGRAPHY

Authorial collective. *Základy marxistické filosofie: Učební pomůcka*. Státní nakladatelství politické literatury, 1960.

Baer, Brian James, ed. *Contexts, Subtexts, and Pretexts: Literary Translation in Eastern Europe and Russia*. John Benjamins, 2011.

Bairoch, Paul. *Révolution industrielle et sous-développement*. S.E.D.E.S, 1984.

Bakhurst, David. "On Lenin's Materialism and Empirio-criticism." *Studies in East European Thought* 70, no. 3 (2018): 107–19.

Bárta, Jan. "Ať žije republika: Kočár do Vídně; Dvojice reinterpretací konce války v kontextu širší diskuse 60. Let." In Pažout and Portmann, *Ve stínu války*, 398–417.

Bárta, Jan. "Klos, Kadár, and Wajda. "Pokus o srovnání válečné demytizace v československé a polské kinematografii 50. a 60. Let." In Pažout and Portmann, *Ve stínu války*, 418–31.

Bartlová Milena, *Dějiny českých dějin umění 1945–1969: Věda o umění slouží vědě o člověku*. UMPRUM, 2020.

Bartoš, Vít. "K předpokladům marxistického univerzalismu v díle Vítězslava Gardavského." In Landa and Mervart, *Proměny marxisticko-křesťanského dialogu*, 231–44.

Bartošek, Karel. *Češi nemocní dějinami: Eseje, studie, záznamy z let 1968–1993*. Paseka, 2003.

Bartošek, Karel. "Česká otázka." In Bartošek, *Češi nemocní dějinami*, 49–51.

Bartošek, Karel. "Český 'smysl dějin.'" In Bartošek, *Češi nemocní dějinami*, 10–33.

Bartošek, Karel. "Naše nynější krize a revoluce." In Bartošek, *Češi nemocní dějinami*, 52–64.

Bazarov, Vladimir A. "Methodology of Perspective Plans." In Spulber, *Foundations of Soviet Strategy for Economic Growth*, 365–77.

Bednář, Jiří. "Hegelova kritika 'bürgerliche Gesellschaft' ve Fenomenologii ducha a Filosofii práva." *Filosofický časopis* 12, no. 4 (1964): 529–38.

Benjamin, Walter. "On the Concept of History." In Benjamin, *Selected Writings I*, 389–400.

Benjamin, Walter. *The Origin of German Tragic Drama*. Translated by John Osborne. Verso, 2003.

Benjamin, Walter. *Selected Writings I*, edited by Howard Eiland and Michael W. Jennings. Belknap Press of Harvard University Press, 2003

Benko, Juraj, and Adam Hudek. "Slovak Communists and the Ideology of Czechoslovakism." In Hudek, Kopeček, and Mervart, *Czechoslovakism*, 313–42.

Beránková, Jana Ndiaye, Michael Hauser, and Nick Nesbitt, eds. *Revolutions for the Future: May '68 and Prague Spring*. Suture Press, 2020.

Berman, Marshall. *All That Is Solid Melts into Air: The Experience of Modernity*. Penguin USA, 1988.

BIBLIOGRAPHY

Bertalanffy, Ludwig von. *Das biologische Weltbild*. Francke, 1949.

Bešlin, Milivoj, Gazela Pudar Draško, and Balša Delibašić. "Aporias and Contradictions of the (Post-)Yugoslav Left: Orthodoxy in a Praxis Way." *Contradictions: A Journal for Critical Thought* 5, no. 2 (2021): 107–20.

Bílý, Matěj. "Debata o XX. sjezdu KSSS a proměny legitimizace diktatury KSČ." In Bílý, Lóži, and Šlouf, *Nervová vlákna diktatury*, 223–80.

Bílý, Matěj, Marián Lóži, and Jakub Šlouf. *Nervová vlákna diktatury: Regionální elity a komunikace uvnitř KSČ v letech 1946–1956*. Karolinum, 2019.

Blagojević, Una. "The Praxis Journal and Women Intellectuals." *Contradictions: A Journal for Critical Thought* 4, no. 2 (2020): 47–69.

Blaive, Muriel. *Promarněná příležitost: Československo a rok 1956*. Prostor, 2001.

Bober, Juraj. "O kybernetickom prístupe ku skúmaniu skutočnosti." In *Problémy dialektiky*, edited by Juraj Bober, 191–219. Vydavateľstvo Slovenskej akadémia vied, 1968.

Bober, Juraj. *Stroj, človek, spoločnosť: Kybernetika*. Osveta, 1967.

Bodnár, Ján, ed. *Existencializmus a fenomenológia*. Obzor, 1967.

Bodnár, Ján. "Fenomenologická ontológia Jean-Paul Sartra." *Otázky marxistickej filozofie* 20, no. 2 (1965): 113–24.

Bodnár, Ján. "Fundamentálna ontológia Martina Heideggera." *Otázky marxistickej filozofie* 20, no. 6 (1965): 557–69.

Bodnár, Ján. "Úvod." In *Existencializmus a fenomenológia*, edited by Ján Bodnár, 5–25. Obzor, 1967.

Bondy, Egon. "Báseň Literárním novinám." In *Egon Bondy, Básnické spisy II. 1962–1975*, edited by Martin Machovec, 147–48. Argo, 2015.

Bondy, Egon. *Pracovní analýza a jiné texty*, edited by Petr Kužel. Filosofia, 2017.

Boštík, Pavel. *Venkov bez mezí: kolektivizace zemědělství v Pardubickém kraji v letech 1949–1960*. Národní zemědělské muzeum, s.p.o., 2020.

Brenner, Christiane. *"Zwischen Ost und West": Tschechische politische Diskurse 1945–1948*. R. Oldenbourg, 2009.

Brown, Scott. "Socialism with a Slovak Face: Federalization, Democratization, and the Prague Spring." *East European Politics and Societies* 22, no. 3 (2008): 467–95.

Brzeźinski, Dariusz. "Human Praxis, Alternative Thinking, and Heterogeneous Culture—Zygmunt Bauman's Revisionist Thought." *Hybris* 37, no. 2 (special issue on Polish Philosophical Revisionists in Marxism, edited by B. Tuchańska and M. M. Bogusławski, 2017): 61–80.

Bukharin, Nikolai, N. *Historical Materialism: A System of Sociology*. International, 1925.

Buzássyová, Barbora. "Back to Africa Speaking Slovak? 'Third World' Students at the Preparatory Language Centre in the City of Senec During the 1960s." *Práce z dějin Akademie věd* 10, no. 2 (2018): 1–19.

BIBLIOGRAPHY

Bykova, Marina F. "Lenin and the Crisis of Russian Marxism." *Studies in East European Thought* 70, no. 4 (2018): 235–47.

Catalano, Alessandro. "Zdeněk Mlynář a hledání socialistické opozice: Od aktivní politiky přes disent k ediční činnosti v exilu." *Soudobé dějiny* 20, nos. 1–2 (2003): 277–344.

Černík, Václav. "Dialektika a ontológia Jozefa Cibulku." *Filozofia* 24, no. 4 (1969): 455–59.

Černík, Václav. *Dialektický vedecký zákon*. Vydavateľstvo politickej literatúry, 1964.

Černík, Václav. "Kybernetické modelovanie vývinových procesov a dialektika." *Filozofia* 24, no. 5 (1969): 497–507.

Černý, Jan. "Karel Kosík and Martin Heidegger: From Marxism to Traditionalism." In Feinberg, Landa, and Mervart, *Karel Kosík*, 281–303.

Černý, Václav. *První a druhý sešit o existencialismu*, edited by Jarmila Víšková. Mladá fronta, 1992.

Červinka, František. "Článek o TGM si napište sami." In Červinka, *Studie, eseje, polemiky*, 117–28.

Červinka, František. "Existencialismus a kritika." In Červinka, *Studie, eseje, polemiky*, 235–40.

Červinka, František. "F. X. Šalda a Zdeněk Nejedlý: O jejich vzájemné úctě i o některých sporech." In Červinka, *Studie, eseje, polemiky*, 95–115.

Červinka, František. "Nana a její družky v literatuře, ve filmu a v životě." In Červinka, *Studie, eseje, polemiky*, 77–94.

Červinka, František. "O 19. století, lidu a umění." In Červinka, *Studie, eseje, polemiky*, 57–64.

Červinka, František. "Spor o smysl český dějin 1912." In Červinka, *Studie, eseje, polemiky*, 191–213.

Červinka, František. *Studie, eseje, polemiky*, edited by Martin Kučera. Sumbalon, 2017.

Červinka, František. "Vztah Zdeňka Nejedlého k marxismu a T. G. Masarykovi po roce 1918." In Červinka, *Studie, eseje, polemiky*, 153–76.

Červinka, František. *Zdeněk Nejedlý*. Melantrich, 1969.

Červinka, František. "Zdeněk Nejedlý o demokracii a myšlení Karla Čapka v letech dva-cátých." In Červinka, *Studie, eseje, polemiky*, 177–90.

Chew, Sing C., and Pat Lauderdale, eds. *Theory and Methodology of World Development: The Writings of Andre Gunder Frank*. Springer, 2010.

Chrobák, Ondřej, Pavel Kappel, and Jana Písaříková. *1968: computer.art—levá hemisféra vs. pravá hemisféra* [exhibition catalog]. Moravská galerie v Brně, 2018.

Chvatík, Květoslav. *Smysl moderního umění*. Československý spisovatel, 1965.

Chvatík, Květoslav. *Strukturalismus a avantgarda*. Československý spisovatel, 1970.

BIBLIOGRAPHY

Cibulka, Josef. *Dialektika a ontologie*. Vydavateľstvo Slovenskej akadémie vied, 1968.

Cibulka, Josef. "Jde o otázku zrodu nových kvalit, ne o kybernetiku." *Otázky marxistickej filozofie* 20, no. 3 (1965): 290–92.

Cibulka, Josef. "K otázce exaktnosti ve filosofii." *Filozofia* 22, no. 3 (1967): 297–301.

Cibulka, Josef. "Marxovo pojetí vnitřní rozpornosti společenských zákonů." *Filosofický časopis* 6, no. 6 (1958): 872–902.

Cibulka, Josef. "Na obranu dialektiky." *Filosofický časopis* 13, no. 2 (1965): 285–90.

Cibulka, Josef. "O dialektické pojetí kvality a kvalitativních změn." *Otázky marxistickej filozofie* 19, no. 4 (1964): 327–42.

Cibulka, Josef. "O metodě poznání společenských jevů." *Filosofický časopis* 11, no. 6 (1963): 765–78.

Cibulka, Josef. *Přínos Marxova Kapitálu k poznání společenských zákonů*. Nakladatelství Československé akademie věd, 1962.

Cibulka, Josef. "Rehabilitovat Marxe!" *Filozofia* 22, no. 4 (1967): 371–78.

Cibulka, Josef. *Spory o dialektiku: Formalizácia poznania, existencializmus a marxistická dialektika*. Vydavateľstvo politickej literatúry, 1968.

Ciccariello-Maher, George. *Decolonizing Dialectics*. Duke University Press, 2017.

Cigánek, Jan. "Kritik věčného hledačství." *Literární noviny* 6, no. 14 (1957): 6.

Cigánek, Jan. *Spor o návrat člověka*. Mladé letá, 1968.

Collier, Stephen J. *Post-Soviet Social: Neoliberalism, Social Modernity, Biopolitics*. Princeton University Press, 2011.

Connelly, John. *Captive University: The Sovietization of East Germany, Czech, and Polish Higher Education, 1945–1956*. University of North Carolina Press, 2000.

Cvekl, Jiří. *Lid a osobnost v dějinách: Studie z materialistické teorie dějin*. Státní nakladatelství politické literatury, 1961.

Cvekl, Jiří, ed. *Sedmkrát o smyslu filosofie*. Státní nakladatelství politické literatury, 1964.

Dalberg, Dirk Mathias. "Demokratie als Entwicklungsmodell: Zdeněk Nejedlýs Demokratietheorie in den Zwanzigerjahren des 20. Jahrhunderts." *Práce z dějin Akademie věd* 6, no. 1 (2014): 1–19.

Dalberg, Dirk Mathias. "Die verschwundene Mitte Europas: Zur Mitteleuropavorstellung des tschechischen Philosophen Karel Kosík." *Forum für osteuropäische Ideen- und Zeit-geschichte* 19, no. 1 (2015): 119–44.

David-Fox, Michael. *Crossing Borders: Modernity, Ideology, and Culture in Russia and the Soviet Union*. University of Pittsburgh Press, 2015.

David-Fox, Michael. "The Intelligentsia, the Masses, and the West." In David-Fox, *Crossing Borders*, 48–71.

BIBLIOGRAPHY

Deleuze, Gilles. *Proust and Signs: The Complete Text.* Translated by Richard Howard. University of Minnesota Press, 2000.

Deleuze, Gilles, and Felix Guattari. *What Is Philosophy?* Translated by Hugh Tomlinson and Graham Burchell. Columbia University Press, 1994.

Despot, Blaženka. "Women and Self-Management" (introduction by Zsófia Lóránd). *Contradictions: A Journal for Critical Thought* 4, no. 2 (2020): 141–51.

Donskis, Leonidas, ed. *Yet Another Europe after 1984: Rethinking Milan Kundera and the Idea of Central Europe.* Rodopi, 2012.

Doskočil, Zdeněk. "Czechoslovakism and Ludakness in the 1960s Reform Period." In Hudek, Kopeček, and Mervart, *Czechoslovakism*, 343–70.

Dragović-Soso, Jasna. *"Saviours of the Nation": Serbia's Intellectual Opposition and the Revival of Nationalism.* McGill-Queen's University Press, 2002.

Dubská, Irena. *Auguste Comte a vytvoření sociologie.* Československá akademia věd, 1963.

Dubská, Irena. "Filosofii pro každý den." In Cvekl, *Sedmkrát o smile filosofie*, 23–38.

Dubská, Irena. *K problematice stranickosti a vědeckosti Marxisticko-leninské filosofie.* Československá akademia věd, 1960.

Dubská, Irena. *Objevování Ameriky: Příspěvek k otázkám "moderního člověka."* Československý spisovatel, 1964.

Dubský, Ivan. "Domov a bezdomoví." *Filosofický časopis* 14, no. 2 (1966): 181–208.

Ducháček, Milan. "Německá inspirace zakladatelů Českého lidu: Čeněk Zíbrt a Lubor Niederle v tavícím kotlíku rodících se věd o člověku, 'lidu' a společnosti." In *Zrození lidu v české kultuře 19. století*, edited by Pavla Machalíková, Taťána Petrasová, and Tomáš Winter, 40–54. Academia, 2020,

Dvořák, Petr, ed. *60 let Filosofického časopisu.* Filosofia, 2013.

Engels, Friedrich. "Anti-Dühring: Herr Eugen Dühring's Revolution in Science." In Karl Marx and Friedrich Engels, *Collected Works*, vol. 25, 5–309. International, 1987.

Engels, Friedrich. "Dialectics of Nature." In Karl Marx and Friedrich Engels, *Collected Works*, vol. 25, 313–588. International, 1987.

Epstein, Mikhail N. "Main Configurations of Russian Thought in the Post-Stalin Epoch." In *Philosophical Thought in Russia in the Second Half of the Twentieth Century: A Contemporary View from Russia and Abroad*, edited by Vladislav A. Lektorsky and Marina F. Bykova, 35–52. Cambridge University Press, 2019.

Feinberg, Joseph Grim. "And the 'Thing Itself' Is Man: Radical Democracy and the Roots of Humanity." In Feinberg, Landa, and Mervart, *Karel Kosík*, 187–204.

Feinberg, Joseph Grim. "Between Vanguard and Mass: On the Socialist Content of Communist Folkloristics." In *Folklore and Ethnography in the Soviet Western Borderlands: Socialist in Form, National in Content*, edited by Toms Ķencis, Simon J. Bronner, and Elo-Hanna Seljamaa, 59–82. Lexington Books, 2023.

BIBLIOGRAPHY

Feinberg, Joseph Grim. "Lid jako filosof: Folklór a masový intelektualismus v socialistickém hnutí." In Landa and Mervart, *Imaginace a forma*, 231–38.

Feinberg, Joseph Grim. "Občan alebo človek? Alebo, či v reformnom procese šlo vôbec o občiansku spoločnost'..." In Tížik and Kmet', *Príliš ľudská tvár socializmu?* 64–89.

Feinberg, Joseph Grim. *The Paradox of Authenticity: Folklore Performance in Post-Communist Slovakia*. University of Wisconsin Press, 2018.

Feinberg, Joseph Grim. "The People as Philosopher? The Concept of 'the People' in Postwar Czech Thought." Unpublished manuscript.

Feinberg, Joseph Grim. *Vrátit' folklór ľudom*. AKAmedia and Sociologický ústav SAV, 2018.

Feinberg, Joseph Grim, Ivan Landa, and Jan Mervart, eds. *Karel Kosík and the Dialectics of the Concrete*. Brill, 2020.

Fibich, Jindřich. "Institucionální odcizení a svoboda člověka." *Filozofia* 22, no. 6 (1967): 607–17.

Filipcová, Blanka. *Člověk, práce, volný čas*. Svoboda, 1967.

Fischer, Ernst. "Franz Kafka." *Světová literatura* 8, no. 4 (1963): 56–91.

Fischer, Ernst. "Kafkovská konference." In *Franz Kafka*, 151–60.

Fišer, Zbyněk. *Útěcha z ontologie*. Academia, 1967.

Fitzpatrick, Sheila. *On Stalin's Team: The Years of Living Dangerously in Soviet Politics*. Princeton University Press, 2015.

Ferenc-Flatz, Christian, and Ádam Takács. "From Polemics to Dialogue: Redrawing Genre Boundaries in Eastern European Philosophy During State Socialism." *Studies in East European Thought* (2025). https://doi.org/10.1007/s11212-025-09717-x.

Fornet-Betancourt, Raúl, Martin Traine, and Karel Kosík. "Dass die Bürger es sind, die eine freie Welt gründen." *Concordia: Internationale Zeitschrift für Philosophie* 44 (1993): 13–23.

Foucault, Michel. *Birth of Biopolitics*, François Ewald et al. Translated by Graham Burchell Palgrave Macmillan, 2009.

Foucault, Michel. *The Order of Things: An Archaeology of the Human Sciences*. Pantheon Books, 1970.

Foucault, Michel. "Polemics, Politics and Problematizations": Interview by P. Rabinow, May 1984." In *The Essential Works of Michel Foucault, 1954–1984*. Vol. 1, *Ethics: Subjectivity and Truth*, edited by Paul Rabinow, 111–19. Translated by Robert Hurley. New Press, 1998.

[Fourth] *IV. sjezd Svazu československých spisovatelů*. Praha 27.–29. června 1967. Prague: Československý spisovatel, 1968.

Franc, Martin, and Věra Dvořáčková, eds. *Dějiny Československé akademie věd I. 1952–1962*. Academia, 2020.

BIBLIOGRAPHY

Franc, Martin, and Jiří Knapík. "Volný čas 1957–1967. Dobové diskuse a vymezení." *Dějiny—teorie—kritika* 9, no. 1 (2012): 33–68.

Franz Kafka: Liblická konference 1963. Nakladatelství Československé akademie věd, 1963.

Fritzsche, Peter, and Jochen Hellbeck. "The New Man in Stalinist Russia and Nazi Germany." In *Beyond Totalitarianism Stalinism and Nazism Compared*, edited by Michael Geyer and Sheila Fitzpatrick, 302–42. Cambridge University Press, 2009.

Fromm, Erich. *Člověk a psychoanalýza*. Translated by Irena Petřinová and Marta Hubscherová. Aurora, 1967.

Fromm, Erich. *To Have or to Be?* Abacus Classic Library, 1967.

Fromm, Erich. *Umění milovat*. Translated by Jan Vinař. Portál, 1966.

Galmiche, Xavier. "Paradoxy odkazu: Případ Zdeňka Nejedlého." In Landa and Mervart, *Imaginace a forma*, 69–82.

Galmiche, Xavier, Jan Svoboda, and Josef Zumr, eds. *Herbartovi dědicové*. Filosofia, 2024.

Garaudy, Roger. "Kafka, moderní umění a my." In *Franz Kafka*, 195–201.

Garaudy, Roger. *Marxismus 20. Století*. Translated from the French by J. A. Pechar and Vladimír Mikeš. Svoboda, 1968.

Garaudy, Roger. *Od klatby k dialogu*. Translated from the French by M. Prucha. Svoboda, 1967.

Garaudy, Roger. *Perspektivy člověka*. Translated from the French by Milan Průcha et al. Nakladatelství politické literatury, 1964.

Garaudy, Roger. *Questions à Jean-Paul Sartre: Précédées d'une lettre ouverte*. Clarte, 1960.

Garaudy, Roger. *Realismus bez břehů: Picasso, Saint-John Perse, Kafka*. Translated from the French by Eva Janovcová et al. Československý spisovatel, 1964.

Gardavský, Vítězslav. *Bůh není zcela mrtev: Úvaha o Křesťanském teismu a marxistickém ateismu*. Československý spisovatel, 1967.

Gardavský, Vítězslav. *Fenomén Německo: Studie ke konkrétní dialektice univerzalismu a partikularismu*. Svoboda, 1967.

Gardavský, Vítězslav. *God Is Not Yet Dead*. Translated from the German by Vivienne Menkes. Penguin Books, 1973.

Gardavský, Vítězslav. *Naděje ze skepse*. Svoboda, 1969.

Genis, Alexander, and Petr Vail. *60. léta: Svět sovětského člověka*. Translated from the Russian by Linda Lenz. Volvox Globator, 2019.

Gerovitch, Slava. *From Newspeak to Cyberspeak: A History of Soviet Cybernetics*. MIT Press, 2004.

Gestwa, Klaus. *Die stalinistische Großbauten des Kommunismus: Sowjetische Technik- und Umweltgeschichte, 1948–1967*. Oldenbourg Wissenschaftsverlag, 2010.

BIBLIOGRAPHY

Golan, Galia. *The Czechoslovak Reform Movement: Communism in Crisis 1962–1968*. Cambridge University Press, 1971.
Golan, Galia. *Reform Rule in Czechoslovakia: The Dubček Era 1968–1969*. Cambridge University Press, 1973.
Goldmann, Lucien. "Le matérialisme dialectique est-il une philosophie?" In Goldmann, *Recherches dialectiques*, 11–25.
Goldmann, Lucien. *Recherches dialectiques*. Gallimard, 1959.
Goldstücker, Eduard. "Shrnutí diskuse." In *Franz Kafka*, 265–74.
Górny, Maciej. *Mezi Marxem a Palackým: Historiografie v komunistickém Československu*. Volvox Globator, 2018.
Gramsci, Antonio. *Poznámky o Machiavellim, politice a moderním státu*. Translated and edited by Lubomír Sochor. Svoboda, 1970.
Grebeníčková, Růžena. "Cesty marxistické literární teorie a léta třicátá." *Československá rusistika* 6, no. 2 (1961): 88–101.
Guth, Stefan. "One Future Only: The Soviet Union in the Age of the Scientific-Technical Revolution." *Journal of Modern European History* 13, no. 3 (2015): 355–76.
Hájek, Miloš. *Paměť české levice*. Ústav pro soudobé dějiny AV ČR, 2011.
Háková, Libuše. "Úvaha a podněty k chápání společenských funkcí ženy." *Sociologický časopis* 6, no. 5 (1970): 436–48.
Halas, Juraj. "Intelektuálne dejiny československého poststalinismu." *Kontradikce: Časopis pro kritické myšlení* 5, no. 1 (2021): 154–57.
Hanáková, Petra. "Feministický styl v československé kinematografii: Ženský manuscript filmů Věry Chytilové a Ester Krumbachové." In *Vyvlastněný hlas: Proměny genderové kultury české společnosti 1948–1989*, edited by Hana Havelková and Libora Oates-Indruchová, 427–53. Sociologické nakladatelství, 2015.
Hanáková, Petra. "The Feminist Style in Czechoslovak Cinema: The Feminine Imprint in the Films of Věra Chytilová and Ester Krumbachová." In Havelková and Oates-Indruchová, *Politics of Gender Culture*, 211–33.
Hanáková, Petra. "Od zednice Mařky k černobílé Sylvě: Obrazy žen v české vizuální kultuře a východoevropský vizuální paradox." In Petra Hanáková, Libuše Heczková, Eva Kalivodová, and Kateřina Svatoňová, *Volání rodu*, 126–41. Akropolis, 2013.
Hann, Chris, Mihaly Sarkany, and Peter Skalnik, eds. *Studying Peoples in the People's Democracies: Socialist Era Anthropology in East-Central Europe*. Lit-Verlag, 2005.
Harding, Neil. *Leninism*. Duke University Press, 1996.
Hašek, Jaroslav. *The Good Soldier Švejk*. Translated by Cecil Parrott. Penguin Books, 2016.

BIBLIOGRAPHY

Havel, Václav, Jaroslav Střítecký, and Milan Uhde. "Trialog o radikalismu." *Host do domu* 15, no. 6 (1969): 32–36.

Havelka, Jaroslav. "Vědeckotechnická revoluce a změny ve struktuře práce, v kvalifikaci pracujících a v úrovni vzdělání." *Sociologický časopis* 2, no. 2 (1966): 196–204.

Havelka, Miloš. "Česká kultura a politika před různými horizonty generační zkušenosti." In Miloš Havelka, *Ideje, dějiny, společnost: Studie k historické sociologii vědění*, 336–61. Centrum pro studium demokracie a kultury (CDK), 2010.

Havelka, Miloš. *Dějiny a smysl: Obsahy, akcenty a posuny "české otázky," 1895–1989*. Lidové noviny, 2001.

Havelka, Miloš. "Ideologická kritika ideologické kritiky normalizace." *Soudobé dějiny* 25, nos. 1–2 (2018): 229–43.

Havelka, Miloš. *Spor o smysl českých dějin, 1938–1989: Posuny a akcenty české otázky*. Torst, 2006.

Havelková, Barbara. "Genderová rovnost v období socialismu." In *Komunistické právo v Československu: Kapitoly z dějin bezpráví*, edited by Michal Bobek, Pavel Molek, and Vojtěch Šimíček, 179–207. Mezinárodní ústav politologie Masarykovy univerzity (IIPS), 2009.

Havelková, Barbara. "The Three Stages of Gender in Law." In Havelková and Oates-Indruchová, *Politics of Gender*, 31–56.

Havelková, Hana. "(De)centralizovaná genderová politika: Role Státní populační komise." In *Vyvlastněný hlas: Proměny genderové kultury české společnosti 1948–1989*, edited by Hana Havelková and Libora Oates-Indruchová, 125–68. Sociologické nakladatelství, 2015.

Havelková, Hana, and Libora Oates-Indruchová, eds. *The Politics of Gender Culture under State Socialism: An Expropriated Voice*. Routledge, 2014.

Havlínová, Miluše. "Nová povaha vzdělání v technicky vyspělé civilizaci." *Sociologický časopis* 2, no. 2 (1966): 218–22.

Hegel, Georg Wilhelm Friedrich. *Encyclopedia of the Philosophical Sciences in Basic Outline. Part I: Science of Logic*. Cambridge University Press, 2010.

Heidegger, Martin. "The Question Concerning Technology." In *The Question Concerning Technology and Other Essays*. Translated by William Lovitt, 3–35. Garland, 1977.

Hellbeck, Jochen. *Revolution on My Mind: Writing a Diary Under Stalin*. Cambridge University Press, 2006.

Hermach, Jiří. *Uskutečnění současného člověka: Několik otázek, které autor považuje za podstatné*. Symposium, 1969.

Hermann, Tomáš. "Biologický ústav ČSAV a biologické vědy." In Franc and Dvořáčková, *Dějiny Československé akademie věd I*, 543–69.

Hermann, Tomáš. "Karel Kosík and His 'Radical Democrats': The Janus Face of Dialectics of the Concrete." In Feinberg, Landa, and Mervart, *Karel Kosík*, 39–54.

Heumos, Peter. *"Vyhrňme si rukávy, než se kola zastaví!" Dělníci a státní socialismus v Československu 1945–1968*. Ústav pro soudobé dějiny AV ČR, 2006.

Hočevar, Marko. "Art as Praxis: Danko Grlić's Conception of Art Beyond Technological Determinism." *Thesis Eleven* 159, no. 1 (2020): 96–109.

Hoffmann, David Lloyd. *Stalinist Values: The Cultural Norms of Soviet Modernity, 1917–1941*. Cornell University Press, 2003.

Holub, Ondřej. "Za šestým smyslem marxistické filosofie: Ideový vývoj Rudolfa Šímy jako reflexe perspektiv a mantinelů československé marxistické filosofické antropologie 60. let." *Kontradikce: Časopis pro kritické myšlení* 5, no. 1 (2021): 45–68.

Holubec, Stanislav. "Ivan Sviták v letech 1990–1994: K dějinám polistopadové levice." *Časopis Národního muzea: Řada historická* 170, nos. 1–2 (2001): 89–113.

Hoppe, Jiří. *Opozice '68. Sociální demokracie, KAN a K 231 v období pražského jara*. Historický ústav AV ČR, 2009.

Hoppe, Jiří, Markéta Škodová, Jiří Suk, and Francesco Caccamo. *"O nový československý model socialismu": Čtyři interdisciplinární vědecké týmy při ČSAV a UK v 60. letech*. Historický ústav AV ČR, 2015.

Horkheimer, Max. *Eclipse of Reason*. Bloomsbury Academic, 2004.

Horvath, Julius, and Vítězslav Sommer. "From Nationalization to Privatization: Understanding the Concept of Ownership in Czechoslovakia, 1948–1990." In *Populating No Man's Land*, edited by János Mátyás Kovács, 87–111. Rowman and Littlefield, 2019.

Houška, Jiří. "Charakter a význam demokratických přístupů k socialistické revoluci v soudobé epoše." In *Základní teoretické otázky výstavby socialismu a komunismu ve světle výsledků společenských věd*, edited by Jiří Houška, 74–94. Nakladatelství Československé akademie věd, 1962.

Hříbek, Tomáš. "Kosík's Notion of 'Positivism.'" In Feinberg, Landa, and Mervart, *Karel Kosík*, 229–47.

Hrouda, Milan. "Vysoké školy a vědeckotechnická revoluce." *Sociologický časopis* 2, no. 2 (1966): 205–12.

Hrubý, Karel. *Cesty komunistickou diktaturou: Kritické studie a eseje*. Argo and Ústav pro soudobé dějiny AV ČR, 2018.

Hudek, Adam, Michal Kopeček, and Jan Mervart, eds. *Czechoslovakism*. Routledge, 2021.

Hudec, Zdeněk. "Marx, nejenom Kafka: Odcizení v Postavě k podpírání." In Hudec, Schnapková, *Postava k podpírání*, 78–95.

Hudec, Zdeněk, and Andrea Schnapková. *Postava k podpírání: Kritické a analytické studie*. Casablanca, 2017.

Hudis, Peter. "Karel Kosík and U.S. Marxist Humanism." In Feinberg, Landa, and Mervart, *Karel Kosík*, 325–42.
Ilyenkov, Evald. *The Dialectics of the Abstract and the Concrete in Marx's Capital*. Translated by Sergei Kuzyakov. Progress, 1982.
Ilyenkov, Evald. "Logicheskoe i istoricheskoe." In *Voprosy dialekticheskogo materializma: Elementy dialektiki*, edited by P. V. Tavanec, 310–43. Izdatel'stvo Akademii nauk SSSR, 1960.
Janoušek, Jiří, ed. *3 a 1/2*. Prague: Orbis, 1965.
Javůrek, Zdeněk. "Dialektika a metafory." *Filosofický časopis* 13, no. 2 (1965): 291–97.
Javůrek, Zdeněk. *Dialektika obecného a zvláštního*. Nakladatelství Československé akademie věd, 1962.
Jechová, Květa. "Cesta k emancipaci: Postavení ženy v české společnosti 20. století: Pokus o vymezení problému." In *Pět studií k dějinám české společnosti po roce 1945*, edited by Oldřich Tůma and Tomáš Vilímek, 113–16. Ústav pro soudobé dějiny AV ČR, 2008.
"J.-P. Sartre a ti druzí: Mírová koexistence a boj idejí" (debate among multiple participants). *Plamen* 6, no. 1 (1964): 1–7.
Kadlecová, Erika. *Sociologický výzkum religiozity Severomoravského kraje*. Academia, 1967.
Kadlecová, Erika. *Úloha Křesťanství v historii třídních bojů*. Filozofická fakulta UK, 1950.
Kalivoda, Robert. "České kulturní vědomí, svět a současnost." *Orientace* 3, no. 1 (1968): 44–48.
Kalivoda, Robert. "Demokratizace a kritické myšlení." *Literární listy* 1, no. 10 (1968): 1 and 13; no. 11 (1968): 6.
Kalivoda, Robert. "Dialektika strukturalismu a dialektika estetiky." In Kalivoda, *Moderní duchovní skutečnost*, 9–44.
Kalivoda, Robert. *Husitská ideologie*. Nakladatelství Československé akademie věd, 1961.
Kalivoda, Robert. "K Machovcovu 'Zápasu o náročnější metodologický přístup k středověké myšlenkové látce.'" In Dvořák, *60 let Filosofického časopisu*, 175–215.
Kalivoda, Robert. "Marx a Freud." In Kalivoda, *Moderní duchovní skutečnost*, 45–102.
Kalivoda, Robert. "Marxismus a libertinismus." In Kalivoda, *Moderní duchovní skutečnost*, 103–48.
Kalivoda, Robert. *Moderní duchovní skutečnost a marxismus*. Československý spisovatel, 1968.
Kalivoda, Robert. *Moderní duchovní skutečnost a marxismus*, edited by Roman Kanda. Academia, 2021.

Kalivoda, Robert. "O perspektivách socialistické demokracie." *Rudé právo*, May 3, 1968, 3.

Kalivoda, Robert. "O struktuře a strukturalismu." *Filosofický časopis* 17, no. 1 (1969): 114–18.

Kalivoda, Robert. "Od nadstavby k dialektice a od dialektiky k nadstavbě." *Filosofický časopis* 4, no. 2 (1956): 239–55.

Kalivoda, Robert. "Revolučně romantický charakter Marxova učení." *Filosofický časopis* 15, no. 6 (1967): 788–802.

Kalivoda, Robert. "Tikal a český surrealismus (Projev na zahájení posmrtné výstavy V. Tikala v domě pánů z Kunštátu v Brně)." *Host do domu* 13, no. 7 (1966): 65–67.

Kalivoda, Robert. "V lidských dějinách není nic fatální: Z korespondence Roberta Kalivody a Josefa Války," edited by Miloš Caňko. *A2* 16, no. 1 (2020): 22–23.

Kalivoda, Robert. "Zoči-voči." *Slovenské pohľady* 84, no. 11 (1968): 99–102.

Kalivoda, Robert, and Josef Zumr, eds. *Antologie z dějin československé filosofie*. Nakladatelství Československé akademie věd, 1963.

Kalivoda, Robert, and Josef Zumr. "Úvod." In Kalivoda and Zumr, *Antologie*, 9–27.

Kanda, Roman. *Český literárněvědný marxismus*. Host, 2021.

Kanda, Roman. "K estetickému myšlení Roberta Kalivody." *Česká literatura* 62, no. 4 (2014): 527–48.

Kanda, Roman. "Reprezentativní výbor z díla Růženy Grebeníčkové?" *Svět literatury* 27, no. 56 (2017): 149–54.

Kanda, Roman. "Strukturalisté dělají marxismus." *Česká literatura* 67, no. 5 (2019): 711–36.

Kant, Immanuel. *Critique of Judgment*. Translated by Werner S. Pluhar. Hackett, 1987.

Kaplan, Karel. *Kořeny československé reformy 1968. Díl I–II*. Doplněk, 2000.

Kaplan, Karel. *Kořeny československé reformy 1968. Díl III–IV*. Doplněk, 2002.

Karkov, Nikolay. "Decolonizing *Praxis* in Eastern Europe: Toward a South-to-South Dialogue." *Comparative and Continental Philosophy* 7, no. 2 (2015): 180–200.

Karkov, Nikolay, and Zhivka Valiavicharska. "Rethinking East-European Socialism: Notes Toward an Anti-Capitalist Decolonial Methodology." *International Journal of Postcolonial Studies* 20, no. 6 (2018): 785–813.

Kárník, Zdeněk. *Socialisté na rozcestí: Habsburk, Masaryk či Šmeral?* Svoboda, 1968.

Kašičková, Michaela. "Přijetí románu Jana Pelce . . . a bude hůř v proměnách politického režimu." Bachelor's thesis, Charles University, 2013.

Kellner, Erich, ed. *Schöpfertum und Freiheit in einer humanen Gesellschaft: Marienbader Protokolle*. Europa Verlag, 1969.

Klaučo, Jaromír, and Emil Duda. *Fenomén techniky: K otázkam vedecko-technickej revolúcie*. Vydavateľstvo politickej literatúry, 1967.

BIBLIOGRAPHY

Klaus, Georg. *Kybernetik in philosophischer Sicht*. Dietz, 1961.
Klein, Ota. "Ke krizi emocionality." In Dubská and Richta, *Ota Klein*, 61–94.
Klein, Ota. "Vědeckotechnická revoluce a tvorba životního stylu." In Dubská and Richta, *Ota Klein*, 37–60.
Klein, Ota. *Životní styl a moderní civilizace*. Edited by Irena Dubská, Jan Orlický and Radovan Richta. Symposium, 1969.
Klein, Ota. "Hledání lidské varianty technické civilizace." In Klein, *Životní styl a moderní civilizace*, 95–119.
Klíma, Ivan. "Jeden projekt a jedna strana." *Literární listy* 1, no. 9 (1968): 5.
Klíma, Ladislav. *Vteřiny věčnosti*. Mat'a, 2009.
Klímová, Helena. *Nechte maličkých přijíti aneb civilizace versus děti?* Československý spisovatel, 1966.
Klofáč, Jaroslav. *Materialistické pojetí dějin: Základní problémy*. Státní nakladatelství politické literatury, 1962.
Klofáč, Jaroslav, Vojtěch Tlustý, and Miloš Svoboda. *Problémy determinismu a pokroku: Studie z historického materialismu*. Nakladatelství Československé akademie věd, 1963.
Knapík, Jiří. *V zajetí moci: Kulturní politika, její systém a aktéři 1948–1956*. Libri, 2006.
Koestler, Arthur. *Darkness at Noon*. Translated by Daphne Hardy. Scribner, 2019.
Kohák, Erazim. "Filosofický smysl Československého jara 1968." Unpublished manuscript, 1981.
Kolář, Pavel. *Der Poststalinismus: Ideologie und Utopie einer Epoche*. Böhlau, 2016.
Kolář, Pavel. *Soudruzi a jejich svět: Sociálně myšlenková tvář komunismu*. Nakladatelství Lidové noviny, 2020.
Kolman, Arnošt. "Nové filosofické spory kolem kybernetiky." In Kolman, *Výhledy do budoucna*, 116–25. Československý spisovatel, 1962.
Komanická, Ivana. "Zrod proletárskej kultúry v Košiciach." *Kontradikce: Časopis pro kritické myšlení* 2, no. 1 (2018): 41–51.
Kondratiev, Nikolaj D. "Critical Remarks on the Plan for the Development of the National Economy." In Spulber, *Foundations of Soviet Strategy for Economic Growth*, 438–51.
Konrád, George, and Ivan Szelényi. *The Intellectuals on the Road to Class Power*. Translated from the Hungarian by Andrew Arato and Richard E. Allen. Harcourt Brace Jovanovich, 1979.
Kopčok, Andrej, ed. *Človek a odcudzenie (štúdie juhoslovanských autorov)*. Vydavateľstvo Slovenskej akadémie vied, 1967.
Kopeček, Michal, ed. *Architekti dlouhé změny: Expertní kořeny postsocialismu v Československu*. Argo and Univerzita Karlova, Filozofická fakulta, Ústav pro soudobé dějiny AV ČR, v.v.i, 2019.

Kopeček, Michal. "Čeští komunističtí intelektuálové a 'národní cesta k socialismu': Zdeněk Nejedlý a Karel Kosík, 1945–1968." *Soudobé dějiny* 23, nos. 1–2 (2016): 77–117.

Kopeček, Michal. "Czech Communist Intellectuals and the 'National Road to Socialism': Zdeněk Nejedlý and Karel Kosík, 1945–1968." In *Ideological Storms: Intellectuals, Dictators, and the Totalitarian Temptation*, edited by Vladimir Tismaneanu and Bogdan C. Iacob, 345–89. CEU Press, 2019.

Kopeček, Michal. "Expertní kořeny postsocialismu: Výzkumné perspektivy a metodologické nástroje." In Kopeček, *Architekti dlouhé změny*, 9–40.

Kopeček, Michal. "Historical Studies of Nation-Building and the Concept of Socialist Patriotism in East Central Europe 1956–1970." In *Historische Nationsforschung im geteilten Europa 1945–1989*, edited by Pavel Kolář and Miloš Řezník, 121–36. SH-Verlag, 2012.

Kopeček, Michal. *Hledání ztraceného smyslu revoluce: Zrod a počátky marxistického revizionismu ve střední Evropě 1953–1960*. Argo, 2009.

Kopeček, Michal. "Polemika Milan Kundera—Václav Havel: Spory o českou otázku v letech 1967–1969 a jejich historický obraz." In *Pražské jaro 1968. Literatura—Film—Média. Materiály z mezinárodní konference pořádané Literární akademií za spolupráce s Městskou knihovnou: Praha 20.–22. května 2008*, 129–38. Literární akademie, 2009.

Kopeček, Michal. "The Socialist Conception of Human Rights and Its Dissident Critique Hungary and Czechoslovakia, 1960s–1980s." *East Central Europe* 46 (2019): 261–89.

Kopeček, Michal. "Vládnout právem: Česká právní věda od 'represivní legality' k právnímu státu, 1969–1994." In Kopeček, *Architekti dlouhé změny*, 41–101.

Kopsová, Raisa. "Miesto Miroslava Kuseho v slovenskej filozofii 60-tych rokov." *Filozofia* 57, no. 10 (2002): 713–24.

Korsch, Karl. "The Present State of the Problem 'Marxism and Philosophy': An Anti-Critic." In *Marxism and Philosophy*. Translated by Fred Halliday, 98–144. Verso, 2019.

Korsch, Karl. "Zehn Thesen über Marxismus heute." In Karl Korsch, *Politische Texte*, edited by Erich Gerlach and Jürgen Seifert, 385–87. Europäische Verlagsanstalt, 1974.

Kosík, Karel. "Božena Němcová 4. 2. 1820–21. 1. 1862." In *Kulturně politický kalendář 1962*, 46–48. Orbis, 1961.

Kosík, Karel. *Česká radikální demokracie: Příspěvek k dějinám názorových sporů v české společnosti 19. Století*. Státní nakladatelství politické literatury, 1958.

Kosík, Karel. "Classes and the Real Structure of Society." *Contradictions: A Journal for Critical Thought* 1, no. 2 (2017): 187–204.

Kosík, Karel. "Člověk a filozofia." In *Člověk, kto si?* edited by Ján Bodnár, 40–50. Obzor, 1965.

BIBLIOGRAPHY

Kosík, Karel. "Co je střední Evropa." In Kosík, *Krize moderní doby*, 271–312.

Kosík, Karel. *The Crisis of Modernity: Essays and Observations from the 1968 Era*, edited by James H. Satterwhite. Translated by Julianne Clarke et al. Rowman and Littlefield, 1995.

Kosík, Karel. *Dialectics of the Concrete: A Study on Problems of Man and World*. Translated by Karel Kovanda and James Schmidt. Reidel, 1976.

Kosík, Karel. *Dialektika konkrétního: Studie o problematice člověka a světa*. Academia, 1963.

Kosík, Karel. *Dialektika, kultura a politika: Eseje a články z let 1955–1969, Sebrané spisy Karla Kosíka, vol. 4*, edited by Jan Mervart. Filosofia, 2019.

Kosík, Karel. "Filosofie a dějiny literatury." In Kosík, *Dialektika, kultura a politika*, 152–63.

Kosík, Karel. "Gramsci o kultuře." In Kosík, *Dialektika, kultura a politika*, 105–6.

Kosík, Karel. "Hašek a Kafka neboli groteskní svět." In Kosík, *Dialektika, kultura a politika*, 126–37.

Kosík, Karel. "Hašek and Kafka, or, the World of the Grotesque." In Kosík, *Crisis of Modernity*, 77–86.

Kosík, Karel. "Havlicek's Principles of Democracy." In Kosík, *Crisis of Modernity*, 199–202.

Kosík, Karel. "Hegel a naše doba." In Kosík, *Dialektika, kultura a politika*, 39–46.

Kosík, Karel. "Illusions and Realism." In Kosík, *Crisis of Modernity*, 109–12.

Kosík, Karel. "Iluze a realismus." In Kosík, *Krize moderní doby*, 143–48.

Kosík, Karel. "The Irreplaceable Nature of Modern Culture." In Kosík, *Crisis of Modernity*, 101–2.

Kosík, Karel. "Jediná záchrana—spojenectví s lidem: Vystoupení na zasedání ÚV KSČ 15. listopadu 1968." In Kosík, *Krize moderní doby*, 187–92.

Kosík, Karel. *Krize modern doby: Články, projevy a rozhovory o československém roce 1968 a střední Evropě, Sebrané spisy Karla Kosíka, vol. 5*. Edited by Ivan Landa, Roman Kanda, and Jan Mervart. Filosofia, 2024.

Kosík, Karel. "Machiavelli a machiavellismus." In Kosík, *Krize modern doby*, 149–52.

Kosík, Karel. "Modernost, lidovost a socialismus." In Kosík, *Dialektika, kultura a politika*, 90–97.

Kosík, Karel. "Naše nynější krize." In Kosík, *Krize moderní doby*, 91–130.

Kosík, Karel. "The Nation and Humanism." In Kosík, *Crisis of Modernity*, 137–42.

Kosík, Karel. "Neruda myslitel." *Literární noviny* 3, no. 39 (1954): 3.

Kosík, Karel. "Nezastupitelnost národní kultury." In Kosík, *Dialektika, kultura a politika*, 171–72.

Kosík, Karel. "O dělnických řadách—kriticky." In Kosík, *Krize moderní doby*, 175–77.

Kosík, Karel. "O Havlíčkově demokratismu." In Kosík, *Století Markéty Samsové*, 146–49.

Kosík, Karel. "Odpověď v anketě 'Mírová koexistence a boj idejí.'" In Kosík, *Dialektika, kultura a politika*, 100–101.

Kosík, Karel. "On the Czech Question." In Kosík, *Crisis of Modernity*, 135–36.

Kosík, Karel. "The Only Chance—An Alliance with the People." In Kosík, *Crisis of Modernity*, 211–15.

Kosík, Karel. "Our Current Crisis." In Kosík, *Crisis of Modernity*, 17–51.

Kosík, Karel. *Poslední eseje*. Filosofia, 2004.

Kosík, Karel. *Předpotopní úvahy*. Torst, 1997.

Kosík, Karel. "Přeludy a socialismus." In Kosík, *Dialektika, kultura a politika*, 47–60.

Kosík, Karel. "Příspěvek v diskusi 'Česká otázka.'" In Kosík, *Krize moderní doby*, 269–70.

Kosík, Karel. "Reason and Conscience." In Kosík, *Crisis of Modernity*, 13–15.

Kosík, Karel. "Rozhovor Mileny Mášové s Karlem Kosíkem: O literatuře a filosofii." In Kosík, *Dialektika, kultura a politika*, 185–89.

Kosík, Karel. "Rozum a svědomí." In Kosík, *Krize moderní doby*, 159–62.

Kosík, Karel. "Slepá ulička neplodného myšlení." In Kosík, *Dialektika, kultura a politika*, 61–67.

Kosík, Karel. "Smrt a láska v Hemingwayově románu Komu zvoní hrana." In Kosík, *Dialektika, kultura a politika*, 118–25. Filosofia, 2019.

Kosík, Karel. *Století Markéty Samsové*. Český spisovatel, 1993.

Kosík, Karel. "Švejk a Bugulma neboli zrození velkého humoru." In Kosík, *Dialektika, kultura a politika*, 138–51.

Kosík, Karel. "Švejk and Bugulma or the Birth of Great Humor." In Kosík, *Crisis of Modernity*, 87–99.

Kosík, Karel. "The Third Munich." *Telos*, no. 94 (1992–1993): 145–54.

Kosík, Karel. "Three Observations on Machiavelli." In Kosík, *Crisis of Modernity*, 105–7.

Kosík, Karel. "Třetí Mnichov?" In Kosík, *Století Markéty Samsové*, 156–71.

Kosík, Karel. "Třídy a reálná struktura společnosti." *Filosofický časopis* 6, no. 5 (1958): 721–33.

Kosík, Karel. "Váha slov." In Kosík, *Krize moderní doby*, 211–14.

Kosík, Karel. "Všední život a dějiny." In Kosík, *Dialektika, kultura a politika*, 114–17.

Kosík, Karel. "The Weight of Words." In Kosík, *Crisis of Modernity*, 113–16.

Kosík, Karel. "What Is Central Europe?" In Kosík, *Crisis of Modernity*, 147–79.

Kosík, Karel. "A Word of Caution on Workers' Councils." In Kosík, *Crisis of Modernity*, 209–10.

Kosík, Karel. "Zdeněk Nejedlý a pokrokové české myšlení." *Literární noviny* 2, no. 5 (1953): 3.

BIBLIOGRAPHY

Kosík, Karel. "Zítřek je v našich rukou." In Kosík, *Dialektika, kultura a politika*, 72–76.

Kosík, Karel, Josef Macek, Petr Pithart, Lubomír Sochor, and František Šamalík. "Machiavelli a machiavellismus." *Plamen* 11, no. 2 (1969): 2–10; no. 3 (1969): 7–13.

Kotásek, Vlastimil, and Jiří Pařízek. "Vědeckotechnická revoluce a vzdělávací systém." *Sociologický časopis* 2, no. 2 (1966): 213–17.

Kotkin, Stephen. *Magnetic Mountain: Stalinism as a Civilization*. University of California Press, 1995.

Kovanda, Karel. "Labor in Management, Czechoslovakia 1968–69: A Study in Radical Democracy." PhD diss., Massachusetts Institute of Technology, 1974.

Kowalski, Józef. *Ruští revoluční demokraté a polské lednové povstání*. Rovnost, 1951.

Kozlov, Denis, and Eleonory Gilburd, eds. *The Thaw: Soviet Society and Culture During the 1950s and 1960s*. University of Toronto Press, 2013.

Kozlov, Denis, and Eleonory Gilburd. "The Thaw as an Event in Russian History." In Kozlov and Gilburd, *Thaw*, 18–81.

Král, Miloslav, ed. *Věda a řízení společnosti*. Svoboda, 1967.

Krausz, Tamás. *Reconstructing Lenin: An Intellectual Biography*. Monthly Review Press, 2015.

Křesťan, Jiří. "Nejedlého projev 'Slovo o české filosofii' v historickém kontextu." In *Věda v Československu v letech 1945–1953*, edited by Blanka Zilynská and Petr Svobodný, 307–19. Karolinum, 1999.

Křesťan, Jiří. "'Poslední husita' odchází: Zdeněk Nejedlý v osidlech kulturní politiky KSČ po roce 1945." *Soudobé dějiny* 12, no. 1 (2005): 9–44.

Křesťan, Jiří. "Společnost pro hospodářské a kulturní styky s SSSR a obraz Sovětského svazu v prostředí české levicové inteligence (1925–1939)." In *Bolševismus, komunismus a radikální socialismus v Československu*, vol. 2, edited by Zdeněk Kárník and Michal Kopeček, 84–109. Dokořán, 2004.

Křesťan, Jiří. *Zdeněk Nejedlý: Politik a vědec v osamění*. Národní archiv, 2012.

Krylova, Anna. "Soviet Modernity: Stephen Kotkin and the Bolshevik Predicament." *Contemporary European History* 23, no. 2 (2014): 167–92.

Kundera, Milan. "Český úděl." *Listy* 1, nos. 7–8 (1965): 1, 5.

Kundera, Milan. "A Kidnapped West or Culture Bows Out." *Granta* 11 (1984): 95–118.

Kundera, Milan. *Můj Janáček*. Edited by Jitka Uhdeová. Atlantis, 2014.

Kundera, Milan. "Nepravděpodobný osud (interview s Tomášem Sedláčkem)." In Milan Kundera, *Můj Janáček*, 57–79. Atlantis, 2004.

Kundera, Milan. "Nesamozřejmost národa." In [Fourth] *IV. sjezd Svazu československých spisovatelů*, 22–28.

Kundera, Milan. "The Tragedy of Central Europe." *New York Review of Books* 31, no. 7 (1984): 33–38.
Kundera, Milan. Žert. Československý spisovatel, 1967.
Kusák, Alexej. *Kultura a politika v Československu 1945–1956*. Torst, 1998.
Kusák, Alexej. "Poznámky k marxistické interpretaci Kafky." In *Franz Kafka*, 161–75.
Kusin, Vladimir V. *The Intellectual Origins of the Prague Spring: The Development of Reformist Ideas in Czechoslovakia 1956–1967*. Cambridge University Press, 1971.
Kusin, Vladimir V. *Political Grouping in the Czechoslovak Reform Movement*. Palgrave Macmillan, 1972.
Kusý, Miroslav. "Boj proti odcudzeniu v oblasti riadenia." In Kusý, *Politika a inštitúcie*, 81–111.
Kusý, Miroslav. "Človek a inštitúcia." In Kusý, *Politika a inštitúcie*, 31–54.
Kusý, Miroslav. *Filozofia politiky: K niektorým filozofickým otázkam politického riadenia spoločnosti*. Vydavateľstvo politickej literatúry, 1966.
Kusý, Miroslav. *Politika a inštitúcie*, edited by Dagmar Kusá and Jozef Bátora. Kalligram, 2013.
Kusý, Miroslav. "Spor o východisko, zmysel a charakter marxistickej filozofie." *Filozofia* 22, no. 3 (1967): 275.
Kusý, Miroslav. "Systém a štruktúra marxistickej filozofie." *Filozofia* 22, no. 4 (1967): 425–31.
Kusý, Miroslav. "Zinštitucionalizovaný človek." In Kusý, *Politika a inštitúcie*, 249–74.
Kužel, Petr. "Marxist Criticism of Soviet-Type Society in Czechoslovakia: The Political Thought of Egon Bondy after 1968." *Thesis Eleven* 159, no. 1 (2020): 78–95.
Kužel, Petr, ed. *Myšlení a tvorba Egona Bondyho*. Filosofia, 2018.
Kužel, Petr. "Nesubstanční ontologie v raných filozofických pracích Egona Bondyho." In Kužel, *Myšlení a tvorba Egona Bondyho*, 27–54.
Labov, Jessie. *Transatlantic Europe: Contesting Geography and Redefining Culture Beyond the Nation*. Central European University Press, 2018.
Lakatoš, Michal. *Občan, právo a demokracie*. Svobodné slovo, 1966.
Lakatoš, Michal. *Úvahy o hodnotách demokracie*. Melantrich, 1968.
Landa, Ivan. "Historical Bloc and Revolution: The Radical Democratic Interpretation of the Prague Spring of 1968." In *The Prague Spring as a Laboratory: Proceedings of the Annual Conference of Collegium Carolinum*, edited by Martin Schulze, 117–41. Vandenhoeck & Ruprecht, 2019.
Landa, Ivan. "Labour and Time: Karel Kosík's Temporal Materialism." In Feinberg, Landa, and Mervart, *Karel Kosík*, 75–106.

Landa, Ivan. "Marxova filosofická antropologie." *Filosofický časopis* 63, no. 3 (2015): 339–55.

Landa, Ivan. "Struktury významu: Karel Kosík a problém kultury." *Dějiny—teorie—kritika* 14, no. 1 (2018): 7–42.

Landa, Ivan. "Technology and Politics: A Philosophical Lesson from the Prague Spring 1968." In Beránková, Hauser, and Nesbitt, *Revolutions for the Future*, 216–56.

Landa, Ivan, and Jan Mervart. "Formy pod napětím: Josef Zumr a dějiny české filosofie." In Landa and Mervart, *Imaginace a forma*, 11–23.

Landa, Ivan, and Jan Mervart, eds. *Imaginace a forma: Mezi estetickým formalismem a filosofií emancipace*. Filosofia, 2018.

Landa, Ivan, and Jan Mervart, eds. *Proměny marxisticko-křesťanského dialogu v Československu*. Filosofia, 2017.

Lenin Vladimir I. "Conspectus of Hegel's Book the Science of Logic." In *Collected Works, vol. 38*, 85–237. Progress, 1976.

Lenin Vladimir I. "Critical Remarks on The National Question." In *Collected Works, vol. 20*, 17–51. Progress, 1977.

Lenin, Vladimir I. "Imperialism, the Highest Stage of Capitalism." In *Collected Works, vol. 22*, 185–304. Progress, 1974.

Lenin, Vladimir I. "Imperialism, What Is to Be Done." In *Collected Works, vol. 5*, 347–520. Progress, 1977.

Lenin, Vladimir I. "Letters on Tactics." In *Collected Works, vol. 24*, 42–54. Progress, 1964.

Lenin, Vladimir I. "Materialism and Empiriocriticism." In *Collected Works, vol. 14*, 17–358. Progress, 1962.

Lenin Vladimir I. "On the Significance of Militant Materialism." In *Collected Works, vol. 33*, 227–36. Progress, 1973.

Lenin, Vladimir I. "The Tasks of the Proletariat in the Present Revolution." In *Collected Works, vol. 24*, 19–26. Progress, 1964.

Liehm, Antonín J, "Diktát moci a trhu." *Literární listy* 1, no. 3 (1968): 11.

Liehm, Antonín J. *Generace*. Československý spisovatel, 1990.

Liehm, Antonín J. *Politics of Culture*. Translated by Peter Kussi. Grove Press, 1970.

Liehm, Antonín J. *Rozhovor*. Československý spisovatel, 1966.

Liehm, A. J., and Karel Kosík. "A. J. Liehm's Interview with Karel Kosík." In Liehm, *Politics of Culture*, 397–412.

Likavčan, Lukáš. "Civilizace na rozcestí po padesáti letech." Unpublished manuscript, n.d.

Linhart, Lubomír, ed. "Lenin o kultuře a umění." *Plamen* 7, no. 4 (1965): 29–34.

BIBLIOGRAPHY

Lipták, Ľubomír. "Úloha a postavenie historiografie v našej spoločnosti." *Historický časopis* 17, no. 1 (1969): 98–118.

Lišková, Kateřina. *Sexual Liberation, Socialist Style: Communist Czechoslovakia and the Science of Desire, 1945–1989*. Cambridge University Press, 2018.

Loránd, Zsófia. *The Feminist Challenge to the Socialist State in Yugoslavia*. Palgrave Macmillan, 2018.

Losurdo, Domenico. *Staline: Histoire et critique d'une légende noire*. Aden, 2011.

Lukács, Georg. "Existentialism." In *Marxism and Human Liberation: Essays on History, Culture and Revolution*, 243–66. Dell, 1973.

Lukács, Georg. *History and Class Consciousness: Studies in Marxist Dialectics*. Translated from the German by Rodney Livingstone. MIT Press, 1972.

Lukács, György. *Dějiny a třídní vědomí: Studie o marxistické dialektice*. Edited by Ivan Landa. Translated from the German by Lubomír Sochor. Academia, 2020.

Lukács, György. *Existencialismus či marxismus*. Nová osvěta, 1949.

Machonin, Pavel, ed. *Československá společnost: Sociologická analýza sociální stratifikace*. Institut sociálních vztahů, 1969.

Machovec, Milan. *Filosofie tváří v tvář zániku*. Akropolis, 1998.

Machovec, Milan. "K zápasu o náročnější metodologický přístup k středověké myšlenkové látce." In Dvořák, *60 let Filosofického časopisu*, 97–126.

Machovec, Milan. *Marxismus und dialektische Theologie: Barth, Bonhoeffer und Hromádka in atheistisch-kommunistischer Sicht*. Translated from the Czech by Dorothea Neumärker. EVZ, 1965.

Machovec, Milan. *Novotomismus: O teologii a filosofii současného katolicismu*. Nakladatelství politické literatury, 1962.

Machovec, Milan. *O tak zvané "dialektické" teologii současného protestantismu*. Nakladatelství Československé akademie věd, 1962.

Machovec, Milan. *O teológii súčasného protestanzimu*. Vydavateľstvo politickej literatúry, 1964.

Machovec, Milan. *Smysl lidského života: Studie k filosofii člověka*. Nakladatelství politické literatury, 1965.

Mandler, Emanuel. "Naše světové stíny." *Tvář* 4, no. 6 (1969): 6–11.

Marcuse, Herbert. *Psychoanalýza a politika*. Translated by Lubomír Sochor. Svoboda, 1969.

"Marienbader Protokolle." *Neues Forum* 14, nos. 162–63 (1967): 469–83.

Marks, Sarah. "Ecology, Humanism and Mental Health." In *Psychiatry in Communist Europe (Mental Health in Historical Perspective)*, edited by Mat Savelli and Sarah Marks, 134–52. Palgrave Macmillan, 2015.

Marušiak, Juraj. "Kultúrny život a reformný proces roku 1968." In Tížik and Kmeť, *Príliš ľudská tvár socializmu?* 430–61.

BIBLIOGRAPHY

Marx, Karl. *Capital, Volume I.* In *Karl Marx and Friedrich Engels, Collected Works,* vol. 35, 1–761. International, 1996.

Marx, Karl. *Capital, Volume III.* In *Karl Marx and Friedrich Engels, Collected Works,* vol. 37, 1–897. International, 1998.

Marx, Karl. "Economic and Philosophic Manuscripts of 1844." In *Karl Marx and Friedrich Engels, Collected Works,* vol. 3, 229–346. Lawrence and Wishart, 1975.

Marx, Karl. "Economic Manuscripts of 1857–58." In *Karl Marx and Friedrich Engels, Collected Works,* vol. 29, 3–417. Progress, 1987.

Marx, Karl. "German Ideology." In *Karl Marx and Friedrich Engels, Collected Works,* vol. 5, 19–539. International, 1976.

Marx, Karl. "Grundrisse: Outlines of the Critique of Political Economy." In *Karl Marx and Friedrich Engels Collected Works,* vol. 28, 49–537. Progress, 1986.

Marx, Karl. Preface to *A Contribution to the Critique of Political Economy.* In *Karl Marx and Friedrich Engels, Collected Works,* vol. 29, 261–65. Progress, 1987.

Marx, Karl. "Theses on Feuerbach." In *Karl Marx and Friedrich Engels, Collected Works,* vol. 5, 3–5. Lawrence and Wishart, 1976.

Materna, Pavel. "O 'formalismu' a metaforickém vyjadřování dialektiky." *Filosofický časopis* 12, no. 3 (1964): 375–78.

Materna, Pavel. "Odpověd' na kritiku." *Filosofický časopis* 13 (1965): 298–300.

Matonoha, Jan. "Dispositives of Silence: Gender, feminism and Czech Literature Between 1948 and 1989." In Havelková and Oates-Indruchová, *Politics of Gender Culture,* 162–87.

Maxwell, Alexander. "Effacing Panslavism: Linguistic Classification and Historiographic Misrepresentation." *Nationalities Papers* 46, no. 4 (2018): 633–53.

Merleau-Ponty, Maurice. *Adventures of the Dialectic.* Translated from the French by Joseph Bien. Northwestern University Press, 1973.

Mervart, Jan. "Czechoslovak Marxist Humanism and the Revolution." *Studies in East European Thought* 69, no. 1 (2017): 111–26.

Mervart, Jan. "Czechoslovakism and the Party Theory of the 'Nationality Question.'" In Hudek, Kopeček, and Mervart, *Czechoslovakism,* 371–95.

Mervart, Jan. "'Dissatisfied Breadwinners' in Search of the Human Being: How Gender Inequality Was Seen—and Not Seen—in Czechoslovak Marxist Humanism." *Contradictions: A Journal for Critical Thought* 4, no. 2 (2020): 71–85.

Mervart, Jan. "Envisioning Socialist Utopia: The Czechoslovak Program of Self-Governing Socialism." In Beránková, Hauser, and Nesbitt, *Revolutions for the Future,* 260–79.

Mervart, Jan. "Filozofický ústav ČSAV." In Franc and Dvořáčková, *Dějiny Československé akademie věd I,* 602–13.

BIBLIOGRAPHY

Mervart, Jan. *Kultura v karanténě: Umělecké svazy a jejich konsolidace za rané normalizace.* Nakladatelství Lidové noviny, 2015.

Mervart, Jan. *Naděje a iluze: Čeští a slovenští spisovatelé v reformním hnutí šedesátých let.* Host, 2010.

Mervart, Jan. "Radical Democrats Between Reform and Revolution." In *The Prague Spring as a Laboratory*, edited by Martin Schulze Wessel, 99–116. Vandenhoeck & Ruprecht, 2019.

Mervart, Jan. "Zumrova 'emancipace člověka' a smysl českých dějin." In Landa and Mervart, *Imaginace a forma*, 297–321.

Mervart, Jan, and Jiří Růžička. "Czechoslovak Post-Stalinism: A Distinct Field of Socialist Visions." *East Central Europe* 48, nos. 2–3 (2021): 220–49.

Michňák, Karel. *Ke kritice antropologismu ve filosofii a teologii.* Svoboda, 1969.

Michňák, Karel. *Metafyzika subjektivity a její pojetí člověka jako animal rational.* Univerzita Karlova, 1968.

Militzová, Anna. *Ani víru, ani ctnosti člověk nepotřebuje ke své spáse: Příběh Jany Černé.* Burián a Tichák, 2015.

Mináč, Vladimír, Pavol Števček, and Štěpán Šugár. "Náš rozhovor s Vladimírem Mináčem a Pavolem Števčekem: Ke sporům o tvář naší budoucnosti." *Rudé právo*, May 19, 1968, 4.

Mlynář, Zdeněk. "Filosofie aktivity—aktivita filosofie." *Kulturní tvorba* 3, no. 30 (1965): 4–5.

Mlynář, Zdeněk. *K teorii socialistické demokracie.* Státní nakladatelství politické literatury, 1961.

Mlynář, Zdeněk. *Stát a člověk: Úvahy o politickém řízení za socialismu.* Státní nakladatelství politické literatury, 1964.

Mlynář, Zdeněk, and Miroslav Kusý. "Pokus o socialistické řešení vztahů mezi občanem a státem," edited by Joseph Grim Feinberg and Jan Mervart. *Kontradikce: Časopis pro kritické myšlení* 3, no. 1 (2019): 1–9.

Mňačko, Ladislav. "Mňačko protestiert: Ich reise nach Israel." *Frankfurter Allgemeine Zeitung*, August 11, 1967, 6.

Mňačko, Ladislav. *Oneskorené reportáže.* Vydavateľstvo politickej literatúry, 1963.

Možný, Ivo. *Proč tak snadno . . . Některé rodinné důvody sametové revoluce: Sociologický esej.* Slon, 2009.

Mukařovský, Jan. "Lidovost jako základní činitel literárního vývoje." *Česká literatura* 2, no. 3 (1954): 193–219.

Musilová, Dana. *Na okraj jedné návštěvy: Simone de Beauvoir v Československu.* Oftis, 2007.

Nahodil, Otakar, and Jaroslav Kramařík. "Práce J. V. Stalina o jazykovědě a některé otázky české ethnografie." *Český lid* 38 (1951) nos. 1–2 (1951): 6–17.

Nečasová, Denisa. *Nový socialistický člověk: Československo 1948–1956.* Brno: Host, 2018.

BIBLIOGRAPHY

Nejedlý, Zdeněk. *Hus a naše doba.* Svoboda, 1952.

Nejedlý, Zdeněk. "Komunisté, dědici velkých tradic českého národa." In Nejedlý, *O smyslu českých dějin*, 242–98.

Nejedlý, Zdeněk. "Odkaz našich národních dějin." In Nejedlý, *O smyslu českých dějin*, 227–41.

Nejedlý, Zdeněk. *O smyslu českých dějin.* Svoboda, 1952.

Nejedlý, Zdeněk. "Slovo o české filosofii." *Filosofický časopis* 36, no. 3 (1978): 441–52.

Nejedlý, Zdeněk. *30 let Sovětského svazu.* Orbis, Svaz přátel SSSR, 1948.

Nejedlý, Zdeněk. *Zpěvohry Smetanovy.* Státní nakladatelství politické literatury, 1954.

Němec, Jiří. *Zápisníky I (1960–1964).* Edited by Robert Krumphanzl. Triáda, 2018.

Němec, Jiří. *Zápisníky II (1965–1969).* Edited by Robert Krumphanzl. Triáda, 2020.

Nesbitt, Nick. "The Grundrisse (1858)." In *The Bloomsbury Companion to Marx*, edited by Jeff Diamanti, Andrew Pendakis, and Imre Szeman, 40–55. Bloomsbury Academic, 2018.

Nešpor, Zdeněk. *Ne/náboženské naděje intelektuálů: Vývoj české sociologie náboženství v mezinárodním a interdisciplinárním kontextu.* Scriptorium, 2008.

Nešpor, Zdeněk. "Význam Eriky Kadlecové a sociologie náboženství v marxisticko-křesťanském dialogu šedesátých let." In Landa and Mervart, *Proměny marxisticko-křesťanského dialogu*, 87–103.

Nodl, Martin. *Dějepisectví mezi vědou a politikou: Úvahy o historiografii 19. a 20. Století.* Centrum Pro Studium Demokracie a Kultury, 2007.

Nodl, Martin. "Kontinuita a diskontinuita husitologického bádání 50. a počátků 60. let 20. Století." In Nodl, *Dějepisectví mezi vědou a politikou*, 105–22.

Nový, Lubomír. "Filosofie a politika." In Cvekl, *Sedmkrát o smyslu filosofie*, 101–27, 188–90.

Nový, Lubomír. *Filosofie T. G. Masaryka.* Státní pedagogické nakladatelství, 1962.

Nový, Lubomír. "Marxova filosofie dějin v otevřených dějinách." In *Marx a dnešek*, edited by Eduard Urbánek, 17–143. Svoboda, 1968.

Nový, Lubomír. "Masarykova idea Čs. Republiky." *Listy* 1, no. 3 (1968): 1, 9.

Nový, Lubomír. "Metakritika krize." *Host do domu* 15, no. 9 (1969): 15–19.

Oates-Indruchová, Libora. "Unraveling a Tradition, or Spinning a Myth? Gender Critique in Czech Society and Culture." *Slavic Review* 75, no. 4 (2016): 919–43.

Oittinen, Vesa. "Which Kind of Dialectician Was Lenin?" In Rockmore and Levine, *Palgrave Handbook*, 63–87.

Olšáková, Doubravka, and Jiří Janáč. *The Cult of Unity: The Stalin Plan for the Transformation of Nature in Czechoslovakia, 1948–1964.* Academia, 2021.

BIBLIOGRAPHY

Ort, Jakub. "Dát řeč touze po solidaritě." *Kontradikce: Časopis pro kritické myšlení* 3, no. 1 (2019): 213–23.

Otčenášek, Jan. "Diskusně o současných problémech literatury." *Literární noviny* 14, no. 23 (1965): 3.

Page, Benjamin B. *The Czechoslovak Reform Movement, 1963–1968: A Study in the Theory of Socialism*. Grüner, 1973.

Památce Radovana Richty (1924–1983). Ústav pro filozofii a sociologii ČSAV, 1983.

Patočka, Jan. "Česká filosofie a její soudobá faze." In *Češi I*, 306–27. Edited by Karel Palek and Ivan Chvatík. OIKOYMENH, 2006.

Patočka, Jan. "Dilema v našem národním programu: Jugmann a Bolzano." *Divadlo* 20, no. 1 (1969): 1–8.

Pažout, Jaroslav. *Mocným navzdory: Studentské hnutí v šedesátých letech 20. století.* Prostor, 2008.

Pažout, Jaroslav, and Kateřina Portmann, eds. *Ve stínu války: Protektorát Čechy a Morava, Slovenská republika, Říšská župa Sudety a další odtržená československá území v letech 1938/39–1945*. Technická univerzita v Liberci–ÚSTR, 2019.

Pelc, Jan. *A bude hůř*. Mat'a, 2007.

Pelikán, Jiří. *Tanky proti sjezdu: Protokol a dokumenty XIV. (vysočanského) sjezdu KSČ*. Novela Bohemica, 2018.

Petříček, Miroslav. *Filosofie en noir*. Karolinum, 2018.

Pinsky, Anatoly. "The Origins of Post-Stalin Individuality: Aleksandr Tvardovskii and the Evolution of 1930s Soviet Romanticism." *Russian Review* 76, no. 3 (2017): 458–83.

Placáková, Marianna. "Československá zkušenost jako východisko: Feministické umění v období státního socialismu." *Sešit pro umění, teorii a příbuzné zóny* 13, no. 27 (2019): 26–63.

Placáková, Marianna. "On the Czech Translation of Simone de Beauvoir's *The Second Sex*." *Contradictions: A Journal for Critical Thought* 4, no. 2 (2020): 155–86.

Plekhanov, Georgi V. "The Development of the Monist View of History." In *Selected Philosophical Works, vol. 1*, 486–703. Progress, 1977.

Plekhanov, Georgi V. "Essays on the History of Materialism." In *Selected Philosophical Works, vol. 2*, 31–182 Progress, 1976.

Plekhanov, Georgi V. "The Materialist Understanding of History." In *Selected Philosophical Works, vol. 2*, 596–627. Progress, 1976.

Plekhanov, Georgi V. "On the Question of the Individual's Role in History." In *Selected Philosophical Works, vol. 2*, 283–315. Progress, 1976.

Postone, Moishe. *Time, Labor, and Social Domination: A Reinterpretation of Marx's Critical Theory*. Cambridge University Press, 1993.

BIBLIOGRAPHY

Prebisch, Raúl. *The Economic Development of Latin America and Its Principal Problems.* United Nations Department of Economic Affairs, 1950.

Preisner, Rio. "K hegeliánským principům marxismu." In Preisner, *Když myslím na Evropu,* 2:730–36.

Preisner, Rio. *Když myslím na Evropu,* vol. 2, edited by Jan Šulc. Torst, 2004.

Preisner, Rio. *Kritika totalitarismu: Fragmenty.* Křesťánská akademie, 1973.

Priestland, David. *Stalinism and Politics of Mobilization: Ideas, Power, and Terror in Inter-War Russia.* Oxford University Press, 2007.

Profant, Martin. "O jednom vyústění české otázky neboli Švejk a duchovní člověk." In *Dějiny, smysl a modernita: K 75. narozeninám Miloše Havelky,* edited by Milan Hanyš and Tomáš W. Pavlíček, 63–79. Masarykův ústav a Archiv AV ČR, 2019.

Průcha, Milan. "Doslov." In *Jean-Paul Sartre, Marxismus a Existencialismus,* 157–67. Svoboda, 1966.

Průcha, Milan. "Existencializmus M. Merleau-Pontyho." In Bodnár, *Existencializmus a fenomenológia,* 139–80.

Průcha, Milan. "Filosofické problémy existence člověka." In Cvekl, *Sedmkrát o smyslu filosofie,* 39–69.

Průcha, Milan. *Kult člověka.* Svoboda, 1966.

Průcha, Milan. "Marxism and the Existential Problems of Man." In *Socialist Humanism: An International Symposium,* edited by Erich Fromm, 151–61. Doubleday, 1965.

Průcha, Milan. "Vědeckotechnická revoluce a problémy tzv. 'filosofické antropologie.'" *Sociologický časopis* 2, no. 2 (1966): 253–54.

Putík Jaroslav. *Odchod ze Zámku: Deníkové záznamy z let 1968–1989.* Hynek, 1998.

Rákosník, Jakub. *Sovětizace sociálního státu: Lidově demokratický režim a sociální práva občanů v Československu 1945–1960.* Filozofický fakulta UK, 2010.

Ree, Erik van. *The Political Thought of Joseph Stalin: A Study in Twentieth-Century Revolutionary Patriotism.* London: Routledge, 2002.

Ree, Erik van. "Stalin as a Marxist Philosopher." *Studies in East European Thought* 52, no. 4 (2000): 259–308.

Révai, Josef. "Lukács Georg: Geschichte und Klassenbewusstsein" [book review]. *Archiv für die Geschichte des Sozialismus und der Arbeiterbewegung* 11, edited by Carl Grünberg, (1925): 227–29.

Richta, Radovan. *Civilizace na rozcestí: Společenské a lidské souvislosti vědeckotechnické revoluce.* Svoboda, 1969.

Richta, Radovan. *Civilization at the Crossroads: Social and Human Implications of the Scientific and Technological Revolution.* Translated from the Czech by Marian Šlingová. International Arts and Sciences Press, 1969.

BIBLIOGRAPHY

Richta, Radovan. *Člověk a technika v revoluci našich dnů*. Československá společnost politických a vědeckých znalostí, 1963.

Richta, Radovan. "Ekonomika jako civilizační dimenze." In *Úvahy o socialistické ekonomice*, edited by Karel Kouba, 11–64. Svoboda, 1968.

Richta, Radovan. *Technika a situace člověka: K fenomenologii problému*. Filosofický ústav ČSAV, 1968.

Richta, Radovan. *Vědeckotechnická revoluce a alternativy moderní civilizace*. Filosofický ústav, 1968.

Rindzeviciute, Egle. *The Power of Systems: How Policy Sciences Opened Up the Cold War World*. Cornell University Press, 2016.

Rockmore, Tom. "Introduction." In Rockmore and Levine, *Palgrave Handbook*, 1–59.

Rockmore, Tom. "Marx, Marxism, and Philosophical Modernity." *Studies in Soviet Thought* 25, no. 3 (1983): 165–84.

Rockmore, Tom, and Norman Levine, eds. *The Palgrave Handbook of Leninist Political Philosophy*. Palgrave Macmillan, 2018.

Rosenthal, Bernice Glatzer. *New Myth, New World: From Nietzsche to Stalinism*. Pennsylvania State University Press, 2002.

Rowley, David G. "Bogdanov and Lenin: Epistemology and Revolution." *Studies in East European Thought* 48, no. 1 (1996): 1–19.

Růžička, Jiří. "Formování historického materialismu: Několik poznámek k debatě o historickém materialismu ve Filosofickém časopise v druhé polovině 50. a začátkem 60. Let." In Storchová and Horský, *Paralely, průsečíky, mimoběžky*, 95–121.

Růžička, Jiří. "Poststalinismus jako (ne)stalinský projekt modernity? Možnosti konceptuálního uchopení intelektuálních 'reformních' diskurzů v období 1956–1968." *Soudobé dějiny* 26, nos. 1–2 (2018): 208–28.

Růžička, Jiří, and Jan Mervart. "Marxism and Existentialism in State Socialist Czechoslovakia." *Studies in East European Thought* 75, no. 3 (2023): 399–416.

Šabata, Jaroslav. "Lenin a Gramsci jako revoluční myslitelé." *Kulturní tvorba* 5, no. 25 (1967): 1, 3.

Sabatos, Charles. "Shifting Contexts: The Boundaries of Milan Kundera's Central Europe." In Baer, *Contexts, Subtexts, and Pretexts*, 19–31.

Šafařík, Josef. *Sedm listů Melinovi: Z dopisů příteli přírodovědci*. Edited by Jitka Uhdeová. Atlantis, 1948.

Šámal, Petr. "'Česká otázka' ve světle stalinismu: Karel Kosík a koncept levicového radikalismu." *Soudobé dějiny* 12, no. 1 (2005): 45–61.

Šamalík, František. *Člověk a instituce: Antinomie moderní demokracie*. Svoboda, 1967.

Sartre, Jean-Paul. *Being and Nothingness: An Essay on Phenomenological Ontology*. Translated by Hazel E. Barnes. Routledge, 2003

BIBLIOGRAPHY

Sartre, Jean-Paul. *Critique de la raison dialectique: Précédé de question de méthode.* Gallimard, 1960.

Sartre, Jean-Paul. *Critique of Dialectical Reason: Vols. 1–2.* Translated by Quintin Hoare. Verso, 2004–2006.

Sartre, Jean-Paul. *Marxismus a existencialismus.* Translated from the French by Oldřich Kuba. Svoboda, 1966.

Sartre, Jean-Paul. "Myšlenky proti myšlenkám." *Literární noviny* 12, no. 38 (1963): 6.

Sartre, Jean-Paul. "Projev na moskevském kongresu pro odzbrojení." *Plamen* 5, no. 1 (1963): 54–59.

Satterwhite, James H. *Varieties of Marxist Humanism: Philosophical Revision in Postwar Eastern Europe.* University of Pittsburgh Press, 1992.

Schaff, Adam. *Marxizmus a l'udské indivíduum: Príspevok k marxistickej filozofii človeka.* Translated by Andrej Kopčok and Róbert Roško. Vydavatel'stvo politickej literatúry, 1966.

Schapiro, Leonard, ed. *Political Opposition in One-Party States.* Wiley, 1972.

Schmarc, Vít. *Země lyr a ocele: Subjekty, ideologie, modely, mýty a rituály v kultuře českého stalinismu.* Academia, 2017.

Schmidt, Roman Léandre. *Lettre Internationale: Geschichte einer europäischen Zeitschrift.* Wilhelm Fink Verlag, 2017.

Selucký, Radoslav. *Člověk a jeho volný čas: Pokus o ekonomickou formulaci problému.* Československý spisovatel, 1966.

Selucký, Radoslav. *Ekonomika, morálka, život.* Česlkoslovenský spisovatel, 1963.

Sharov, S. "Goal of Plan and Tasks of Economy." In Spulber, *Foundations of Soviet Strategy for Economic Growth*, 378–92.

Shore, Marci. "Engineering in the Age of Innocence: A Genealogy of Discourse Inside the Czechoslovak Writers' Union, 1949–67." *East European Politics and Societies* 12, no. 3 (1998): 397–441.

Siermiński, Michał. *Dekada Przełomu: Polska Lewica opozycyjna 1968–1980.* Instytut Wydawniczy Książka i Prasa Język wydania, 2016.

Šíma, Rudolf. *Člověk a svět.* Bratislava: Epocha, 1969.

Simonsohn, Bertold. "Der Nahostkonflikt und die Verwirrung der Linken." In Berthold Simonsohn, *Ausgewählte Schrifften 1934–1977*, edited by Wilma Aden-Grossmann, 44–61. Kassel University Press, 2012.

Skalník, Peter. "Czechoslovakia: From Národopis to Etnografie and Back." In *Studying Peoples in the People's Democracies: Socialist Era Anthropology in East-Central Europe*, edited by Chris Hann, Mihaly Sarkany, and Peter Skalnik, 56–86. Lit-Verlag, 2005.

Skilling, H. Gordon. "Background to the Study of Opposition." In Schapiro, *Political Opposition in One-Party States*, 72–103.

Skilling, H. Gordon. *Czechoslovakia's Interrupted Revolution.* Princeton University Press, 1976.

Slačálek, Ondřej. "The Postcolonial Hypothesis: Notes on the Czech 'Central European' Identity." *Annual of Language & Politics and Politics of Identity* 10 (2016): 27–44.

Slejška, Dragoslav. *Dialektika výrobních sil a socialistických ekonomických vztahů (ve všelidovém sektoru).* Nakladatelství Československé akademie věd, 1962.

Slejška, Dragoslav. "Problémy aktivity žen při účasti na řízení v průmyslovém závodě." *Sociologický časopis* 1, no. 5 (1965): 509–23.

Slezkine, Yuri. "The USSR as a Communal Apartment, or How a Socialist State Promoted Ethnic Particularism." *Slavic Review* 53, no. 2 (1994): 414–52.

Smíšek, Jan. *Pojednání o člověku.* Melantrich, 1969.

Sobotka, Milan. *Člověk, práce a sebevědomí: Problém praxe v Německé klasické filosofii.* Svoboda, 1969.

Sochor, Lubomír. "Filozofie a ekonomie." In Cvekl, *Sedmkrát o smyslu filosofie,* 71–99.

Sochor, Lubomír. "Lenin a Gramsci jako filosofové." *Literární noviny* 16, no. 17 (1967): 1, 3.

Sochor, Lubomír. "Machiavelli a machiavellismus." *Plamen* 11, no. 2 (1969): 10.

Sommer, Vítězslav. *Angažované dějepisectví: Stranická historiografie mezi stalinismem a reformním komunismem (1950–1970).* Nakladatelství Lidové noviny, 2011.

Sommer, Vítězslav. "'Are We Still Behaving as Revolutionaries?' Radovan Richta, Theory of Revolution and Dilemmas of Reform Communism in Czechoslovakia." *Studies in East European Thought* 69, no. 1 (2017): 93–110.

Sommer, Vítězslav. "Experti, právo a socialistický stát: Právní věda v ČSAV a její činnost v letech 1952–1960." *Soudobé dějiny* 23, nos. 1–2 (2016): 118–36.

Sommer, Vítězslav. "The Last Battlefield of the Cold War: From Reform-Oriented Leisure Studies to Sociological Research on the 'Socialist Lifestyle' in Czechoslovakia, 1950s–1989. In *Cold War Social Science: Transnational Entanglements,* edited by Mark Solovey and Christian Dayé, 225–54. Palgrave Macmillan, 2021.

Sommer, Vítězslav. "Scientists of the World, Unite! Radovan Richta's Theory of Scientific and Technological Revolution." In Aronova and Turchetti, *Science Studies During the Cold War,* 177–204.

Sommer, Vítězslav. "Zkoumání budoucnosti socialismu: 'vědeckotechnická revoluce' a reforma v reformě a 'konsolidaci.'" In Sommer, Mrňka, and Spurný, *Řídit socialismus jako firmu,* 52–82.

Sommer, Vítězslav, Jaromír Mrňka, and Matěj Spurný. *Řídit socialismus jako firmu: Technokratické vládnutí v Československu, 1956–1989.* Nakladatelství Lidové noviny, 2019.

BIBLIOGRAPHY

Šotola, Jiří. "Příspěvek v debatě Stav a perspektivy našeho umění." *Literární noviny* 13, no. 20 (1964): 1, 3.

Špirit, Michael, ed. *Tvář: Výbor z časopisu*. Prague: Torst, 1995.

Spulber, Nicolas, ed. *Foundations of Soviet Strategy for Economic Growth: Selected Soviet Essays, 1924–1930*. Indiana University Press, 1965.

Spurný, Matěj, "Nehostinnost spočitatelného světa: Proměna představ o domově jako jeden z kořenů krize technokratického socialismu." In Sommer, Mrňka, and Spurný, *Řídit socialismus jako firmu*, 175–90.

Srp, Karel. *Ti druzí: Jean-Paul Sartre a Československo 1934–1970*. Arbor vitae, 2023.

St. Pierre, Kelly. *Bedřich Smetana: Myth, Music and Propaganda*. University of Rochester Press, 2017.

Stalin, Josef V. "Concerning Questions of Agrarian Policy in the U.S.S.R" [speech delivered at a conference of Marxist students of agrarian questions December 27, 1929]. In *Works: Vol. 12*, 147–78. Foreign Languages Publishing House, 1954.

Stalin, Josef V. "Dialectical and Historical Materialism." In *Stalin's Master Narrative: A Critical Edition of the History of the Communist Party of the Soviet Union (Bolsheviks): Short Course*, edited by David Brandenberger and Mikhail Zelenov, 248–73. Yale University Press, 2019.

Stalin, Josef V. *Economic Problems of Socialism in the U.S.S.R*. Foreign Languages Press, 1972.

Stalin, Josef V. "Industrialisation of the Country and the Right Deviation in the C.P.S.U.(B.)" [speech delivered at the plenum of the C.P.S.U.(B.), November 19, 1928]. In *Works, vol. 11*, 255–302. Foreign Languages Publishing House, 1954.

Stalin, Josef V. "Report on the Work of the Central Committee to the Eighteenth Congress of the C.P.S.U.(B.)." In *Works, vol. 14*, 355–429. Red Star Press, 1978.

Stalin, Josef V. "To the Seventeenth Party Congress on the Work of the Central Committee of the C.P.S.U.(B.)." In *Works, vol. 13*, 288–388. Foreign Languages Publishing House, 1954.

Stalin, Josef V. "The Right Deviation in the C.P.S.U.(B.)*. Speech Delivered at the Plenum of the Central Committee and the Central Control Commission of the C.P.S.U.(B.) in April 1929. " In *Works, vol. 12*, 1–113. Foreign Languages Publishing Houses, 1954.

Steila, Daniela. "Lenin's Philosophy in Intellectual Context." In Rockmore and Levine, *Palgrave Handbook*, 89–120.

"Stenografický protokol z konferencie Zväzu slovenských spisovateľov" [Stenographic Protocol from the Conference of the Union of Slovak Writers]. *Kultúrny život* 23, no. 19 (1968): 3–9.

BIBLIOGRAPHY

Storchová, Lucie and Jan Horský, eds. *Paralely, průsečíky, mimoběžky: Teorie, koncepty a pojmy v české a světové historiografii 20. století*. Albis International, 2009.

Střítecký, Jaroslav. "Úděl proměny a tvář sebeklamu." *Host do domu* 15, no. 5 (1969): 16–22.

Strumilin, Stanislav G. "Perspective Guidelines." In Spulber, *Foundations of Soviet Strategy for Economic Growth*, 426–37.

Suk, Jiří. *Veřejné záchodky ze zlata: Konflikt mezi komunistickým utopismem a ekonomickou racionalitou v předsrpnovém Československu*. Prostor, 2016.

Suk, Jiří, Michal Kopeček, Kristina Andělová, Tomáš Vilímek, Tomáš Hermann, and Tomáš Zahradníček. *Šest kapitol o disentu*. Ústav pro soudobé dějiny AV ČR, v. v. i, 2017.

Šulc, Zdislav. *Ideály, iluze a skutečnost: Eseje o socialismu*. Svoboda, 1968.

Sus, Oleg. "Burňák stočený do láhve." *Host do domu* 13, no. 11 (1968): 20–28.

Sus, Oleg. "Burňák stočený do láhve." In *Bez bohů geneze?* 56–89. Vetus Via, 1996.

Sus, Oleg. "Pokus o reformu existencialismu: Poznámky k nové přeměně Sartrovy teorie." *Slovenský filozofický časopis* 15, no. 3 (1960): 296–313.

Svěrák, Šimon. "Strukturalistická inspirace v surrealistické (psycho)ideologii Vratislava Effenbergera." In Landa and Mervart, *Imaginace a forma*, 131–50.

Sviták, Ivan. "Antropologické předpoklady moderní kultury." In Sviták, *Lidský smysl kultury*, 66–109.

Sviták, Ivan. "Člověk." In *Nevědecká anthropologie: Dialectica modo bohemico demonstrata*, 59–66. Self-published manuscript, 1984.

Sviták, Ivan. "Člověk a poezie." In Sviták, *Lidský smysl kultury*, 169–89.

Sviták, Ivan. "Člověk nebo sexus?" *Literární noviny* 16, no. 9 (1967): 1, 6.

Sviták, Ivan. *The Czechoslovak Experiment 1968–1969*. Columbia University Press, 1971.

Sviták, Ivan. *Devět životů: Konkrétní dialektika*. Sakko, 1992.

Sviták, Ivan. *Ekonomické legendy aneb Tobogan do Bolívie?* Borgis, 1991.

Sviták, Ivan. *Epochální iluze*. Nadácia Vladimíra Clementisa, 1992.

Sviták, Ivan. "Filosofie dějin." In *Velký skluz: Dobrovolná sovětizace 1938–1948*, 141–48. Orbis, 1990.

Sviták, Ivan. "Filozofie malých forem." In Sviták, *Lidský smysl kultury*, 47–65.

Sviták, Ivan. "Hrdinové odcizení (Obraz člověka v současné československé kinematografii mladé vlny)." *Film a doba* 13, no. 2 (1967): 60–67.

Sviták, Ivan. "Human Being or Sexus?" *Contradictions: A Journal for Critical Thought* 4, no. 2 (2020): 169–75.

Sviták, Ivan. "Kafka—filosof, Franz Kafka." In *Franz Kafka*, 85–96.

Sviták, Ivan. *Kulatý čtverec: Dialektika demokratizace*. Naše vojsko, 1990.

Sviták, Ivan. *Lidský smysl kultury*. Československý spisovatel, 1968.

BIBLIOGRAPHY

Sviták, Ivan. "Little Base and Little Superstructure." In Sviták, *Windmills of Humanity*, 57–58.

Sviták, Ivan. "Některé příčiny zaostávání theorie." *Literární noviny* 5, no. 16 (1956): 5.

Sviták, Ivan. "Odrození nebo obrození: Projev na schůzi bývalých poslanců Federálního shromáždění, 10. června 1993." In *Sametová normalizace*, 54–55.

Sviták, Ivan [Vasil Katyn]. "Paradoxy lásky: Instruktáž stárnoucímu muži." In *Nevědecká antropologie: Dialectica modo bohemico demonstrata. II*, 94–98. Self-published, n.d.

Sviták, Ivan. "Prolog." In "Třetí Mnichov," 5.

Sviták, Ivan. "Response from Ivan Sviták." *Contradictions: A Journal for Critical Thought* 4, no. 2 (2020): 181–84.

Sviták, Ivan. "Restaurační scéna, Chomutov 20. dubna 1993." In "Třetí Mnichov," 21–26.

Sviták, Ivan. *Sametová normalizace: Výroční zpráva o České republice za rok 1993*. Self-published manuscript, 1993.

Sviták, Ivan. "Šmejd z andrgraundu." In *Ivan Jirous, Magorův zápisník*, edited by Michael Špirit, 644–51. Torst, 1997.

Sviták, Ivan. "The Surrealist Image of Humankind." In Sviták, *Windmills of Humanity*, 111–17.

Sviták, Ivan. "Surrealistický obraz člověka." In Dvořák, *60 let Filosofického časopisu*, 281–91.

Sviták, Ivan. "Třetí Mnichov." Unpublished typed manuscript, 1993.

Sviták, Ivan. "Umění filosofie." In Sviták, *Lidský smysl kultury*, 7–46.

Sviták, Ivan. "Umění v průmyslové společnosti." *Výtvarná práce* 16, no. 11 (June 25, 1968): 3.

Sviták, Ivan. "Vlna pravdy ve filmu." Self-published manuscript, n.d.

Sviták, Ivan. *Windmills of Humanity: On Culture and Surrealism in the Manipulated World*, edited and translated by Joseph Grim Feinberg. Kerr, 2014.

Sviták, Ivan. "Změny hodnotových orientací: Projev na semináři klubu sociologů v Kutné Hoře 14.–15. května 1993." In "Třetí Mnichov," 26–33.

Sychra, Antonín. *Hudba očima vědy: Pět kapitol o hudební estetice pro hudebníky i ne-hudebníky*. Československý spisovatel, 1965.

Tatarka, Dominik. *Démon súhlasu*. Slovenský spisovateľ, 1963.

Tatarka, Dominik. *Hovory o kultúre a obcovaní*. Edited by Ján Mlynárik. Ipeľ, 1995.

Tatarka, Dominik. "Kultúra ako obcovanie." In Tatarka, *Hovory o kultúre*, 48–73.

Tatarka, Dominik. "Obec božia." In Tatarka, *Hovory o kultúre*, 18–37.

Tatarka, Dominik. "Obrana tvorby—obrana národnej kultúry." In Tatarka, *Hovory o kultúre*, 84–85.

Tatarka, Dominik. "Otázky pre Dominika Tatarku do relácie Stretnutie s umením." In Tatarka, *Hovory o kultúre*, 74–82.

Tatarka, Dominik. "Povedomie kultúry." In Tatarka, *Hovory o kultúre*, 38–48.
Tatarka, Dominik. "Púť po Slovensku." In Tatarka, *Hovory o kultúre*, 123–60.
Tava, Francesco. "Praxis in Progress: On the Transformations of Kosík's Thought." In Feinberg, Landa, and Mervart, *Karel Kosík*, 57–74.
Teige, Karel. "Foto, kino, film." In Teige, *Výbor z díla*, 64–82.
Teige, Karel. "Nové umění a lidová tvorba." In Vlašín, *Avantgarda známá*, 150–54.
Teige, Karel. *Výbor z díla I. Svět stavby a básně: Studie z dvacátých let*. Edited by Jiří Brabec, Vratislav Effenberger, Robert Kalivoda, and Květoslav Chvatík. Československý spisovatel, 1966.
Tenzer, Oliver. *Abstrakcia: O modeloch abstrahovania*. Vydavateľstvo politickej literatúry, 1966.
Tesař, Jan. "Bráňme si dedovizeň proti euromolochovi: Príhovor na seminári Slovenská republika v procese demokratických premien a integrácie Európy v Bratislave v júni 1995." In Tesař, *Sme autentickí dediča*, 117–23.
Tesař, Jan. *Sme autentickí dediča*. Stála konferencia slovenskej inteligencie Slovakia Plus, 1995.
Tesař, Jan. "Vlastenci a bojovníci." In *Mnichovský komplex: Jeho příčiny a důsledky*, 147–48. Prostor, 2014.
Tesař, Jan. "Vlastenci a bojovníci 1–9." *Listy* 2, nos. 11–19 (1969): 16.
Tismaneanu, Vladimir, and Bogdan C. Iacob, eds. *Ideological Storms: Intellectuals, Dictators, and the Totalitarian Temptation*. CEU Press, 2019.
Tížik, Miroslav, and Norbert Kmeť, eds. *Príliš ľudská tvár socializmu? Reforma zdola a okolnosti reformného procesu v Československu* 1968. Sociologický ústav Slovenskej akadémie vied, 2016.
Tlustá, Milena, ed. *Antologie textů soudobé západní filosofie*. Státní pedagogické nakladatelství, 1965.
Tlustá, Milena, ed. *Antologie textů soudobé západní filosofie: Výběr z díla Herberta Marcuse*. Státní pedagogické nakladatelství, 1969.
Touraine, Alain. *The Self-Production of Society*. Translated by Derek Coltman. University of Chicago Press, 1977.
Trávníček, Jiří, ed. *V kleštích dějin: Střední Evropa jako pojem a problém*. Host, 2009.
Trencsényi, Balász, Michal Kopeček, Luka Lisjak Gabrijelčič et al. *A History of Modern Political Thought in East Central Europe: Vol. 1: Negotiating Modernity in the "Long Nineteenth Century."* Oxford University Press, 2016.
Trencsényi, Balász, Michal Kopeček, Luka Lisjak Gabrijelčič, Maria Falina, Mónika Baár, and Maciej Janowski. *A History of Modern Political Thought in East Central Europe: Vol 2: Negotiating Modernity in the "Short Twentieth Century" and Beyond, Part I: 1918–1968*. Oxford University Press, 2018.
Trnka, Jakub. *Filosof Erazim Kohák*. Filosofia, 2020.

BIBLIOGRAPHY

Tucker, Aviezer. *The Philosophy and Politics of Czech Dissidence from Patočka to Havel.* University of Pittsburgh Press, 2001.

Uhl, Petr. *Za svobodu je třeba neustále bojovat: Vybrané texty 1968–1989,* edited by Matěj Metelec. Neklid, 2021.

Urbánek, Eduard, ed. *Marx a dnešek.* Svoboda, 1968.

Vaculík, Ludvík. "A co dělníci." *Literární listy* 1, no. 6 (1968): 5.

Valiavicharska, Zhivka. *Restless History: Political Imaginaries and Their Discontents in Post-Stalinist Bulgaria.* McGill-Queen's University Press, 2021.

Vertov, Dziga. *Kino-eye: The Writings of Dziga Vertov.* Edited by Annette Michelson. University of California Press, 1984.

Vlašín, Štěpán, ed. *Avantgarda známá a neznámá I: Od proletářského umění k poetismu.* Svoboda, 1971.

Voříšek, Michael. *The Reform Generation: 1960s Czechoslovak Sociology from a Comparative Perspective.* Kalich, 2012.

Wagner, Peter. *Modernity as Experience and Interpretation.* Polity Press, 2008.

Wagner, Peter. *A Sociology of Modernity: Liberty and Discipline.* Routledge, 1994.

Wagnerová, Alena. "Ještě o Karlu Kosíkovi." *Listy* 36, no. 5 (2006): 11–13.

Welton, Donn. *The Other Husserl: The Horizons of Transcendental Phenomenology.* Indiana University Press, 2000.

West, Tim. "Destiny as Alibi: Milan Kundera, Václav Havel and the 'Czech Question' After 1968." *Slavonic and East European Review* 87, no. 3 (2009): 401–28.

White, James D. *Red Hamlet: The Life and Ideas of Alexander Bogdanov.* Brill, 2019.

Wiener, Norbert. *Kybernetika a společnost.* Translated from the English by Karel Berka. Nakladatelství Československé akademie věd, 1963.

Williams, Kieran, and James Krapfl. "For Civic Socialism and the Rule of Law: The Interplay of Jurisprudence, Public Opinion and Dissent in Czechoslovakia, 1960s–1980s." In *Eastern Europe in 1968: Responses to the Prague Spring and Warsaw Pact Invasion,* edited by Kevin McDermott and Matthew Stibbe, 23–43. Springer, 2018.

Woźniak, Monika. "Marksizm a abstrakcja jednostki ludzkiej: Adam Schaff oczami Ewalda Iljenkowa." *Annales Universitas Paedagogicae Cracoviensis, Studia politologica* 17 (2016): 24–32.

Yakhot, Yehoshua. *The Suppression of Philosophy in the USSR (The 1920s and 1930s).* Translated from the Russian by Frederick S. Choate. Mehring Books, 2012.

Yurchak, Alexei. *Everything Was Forever Until It Was No More: The Last Soviet Generation.* Princeton University Press, 2006.

Zaremba, Marcin. *Komunizm, legitymizacja, nacjonalizm: Nacjonalistyczna legitymizacja komunistycznej władzy w Polsce.* Trio, 2005.

Zedong, Mao. "On Correctly Handling Contradictions Among the People (February 27, 1957)." In *The Writings of Mao Zedong, 1949–1976: Volume II: January 1956–December 1957*, edited by John K. Leung and Michael Y. M. Kau, 308–51. M. E. Sharpe, 1992.

Zelený, Jindřich. "Kant, Marx and the Modern Rationality." In *Methodological and Historical Essays in the Natural and Social Sciences*, vol. 14, edited by Robert S. Cohen and Marx W. Wartofsky, 362–75. Dordrecht, 1974.

Zelený, Jindřich. *The Logic of Marx*. Translated and edited by Terrell Carver. Basil Blackwell, 1980.

Zelený, Jindřich. *O historickém materialismu*. Státní nakladatelství politické literatury, 1960.

Zelený, Jindřich. *Praxe a rozum: Pojetí racionality a překonání tradiční ontologie v Marxově kritice Hegela*. Academia, 1968.

Zeman, Jiří. *Poznání a informace*. Nakladatelství Československé akademie věd, 1962.

Zumr, Josef. "Filosof hrdé lidskosti." In Klíma, *Vteřiny věčnost*, 7–33. Odeon, 1967.

Zumr, Josef. "Konfrontace marxismu a dnešního duchovního světa." *Listy* 2 (1968): 10.

Zumr, Josef. "Plastiky Vladimíra Preclíka." *Host do domu* 15, no. 6 (1964): 21.

Zumr, Josef, Roman Kanda, and Jan Mervart. "Rozhovor s Josefem Zumrem." In Landa and Mervart, *Imaginace a forma*, 325–69.

Zumr, Josef, and Jiřina Zumrová. "Některé otázky diskuse o socialistickém umění po XX. sjezdu KSSS." Unpublished manuscript, 1957.

INDEX

Note: References following "n" refer notes.

Adamczak, Bini, 243
Adorno, Theodor W., 227, 228, 300, 331
alienation, 85, 214; modern culture and, 215; of man in modern society, 31, 34, 77, 81, 84, 118, 131–38, 212–15, 243, 246, 249, 281n86, 305n98, 307n130, 328n94; manipulation and, 37, 84; as result of scientific-technical revolution, 37, 221
Allen, Robert C., 274
Althusser, Louis, 48, 127–29, 145, 267, 283, 384
Andělová, Kristina, 238, 240
Aristotle, 150
Árnason, Johann P., 10, 11, 43, 282, 304
Arnold, Emanuel, 171, 318
Auerhan, Jan, 293
automation, 88, 151–52, 155, 205–6, 222–23, 259, 272, 296n157, 330n114
Bakhurst, David, 277
Barabáš, Stanislav, 307
Bareš, Gustav, 163, 301
Barthes, Roland, 227

Bartlová, Milena, 336
Bartoš, Vit, 148
Bartošek, Karel, 173, 177, 181, 182, 238, 239, 244, 256, 317, 332
Bauman, Zygmunt, 283
Bazarov, Vladimir A., 50
Beauvoir, Simone de, 261–64, 338
Beck, Ulrich, 275
Bednář, Jiří, 292
Belinsky, Vissarion G., 162, 318
Benjamin, Walter, 45, 285
Berdyaev, Nikolai A., 277
Berman, Marshall, 9
Bernal, John D., 34
Bernstein, Eduard, 44
Bertalanffy, Ludwig von, 289
Bílý, Matěj, 280
Bird, Robert, 313
Blagojević, Una, 260, 264, 339
Blažek, Vladimír, 320
Bober, Juraj, 99, 296
Bodnárová, Evelína, 339
Bogdanov, Alexander A., 108, 277, 299
Bondy, Egon, 45, 244, 255–57, 268, 288, 322
Brabec, Jiří, 320

INDEX

Bratislava, 120, 268, 338n123, 341n159
Brecht, Bertolt, 219, 328, 329
Brezhnev, Leonid I., 30
Brno, 176, 233, 239–40, 301n57, 302n72
Brod, Max, 334
Brouk, Bohuslav, 138, 139
Bukharin, Nikolai N., 50, 286
Bykova, Marina F., 277
Camus, Albert, 120
Čapek, Karel, 315
capitalism, 9, 60, 71–72, 84–87, 98, 132, 189, 323n11; critique of, 193, 268; contradictions of, 73, 194; as economic formation, 189; origin of, 190–91, 193, 323n11; progressive core of, 289n69; restoration of, 246, 268; selfnegation of, 200; socialism and, 55, 60, 129–30, 186, 188–99, 192, 194–95, 212, 252, 268, 323n11; Stalinism and, 73, 132, 144; supercapital and, 268; transition from feudalism to, 71, 283n97; state, 228, 268
Case, Holly, 337
Castoriadis, Cornelius, 10
Ceaușescu, Nicolae, 317
Černá, Jana, 337
Černík, Václav, 38, 62, 112–15, 129, 296, 299
Černíková, Vlasta, 339
Černý, Jan, 341
Černý, Václav, 301
Červinka, František, 148, 162, 166, 170–73, 274, 301, 306, 313, 315–17, 319, 337
Chelčický, Jan, 171
Chernyshevsky, Nikolai G., 158, 318
Chvatík, Květoslav, 126, 136, 213, 214, 215, 217, 220, 224

Chytilová, Věra, 133, 258, 264
Cibulka, Josef, 38, 46, 62, 63, 65–73, 76, 93–96, 100, 101, 112, 114, 115, 123–25, 129, 190, 192–96, 225, 241, 248, 251, 287–89, 290, 294, 295, 299, 322, 324
Cigánek, Jan, 211, 304
citizen, 9, 305n98; socialist, 28, 117–19, 144, 166, 181, 233, 257–58, 300n41
civil society, 111, 119; Gramsci and, 329n111; Foucault and, 299n19; socialist, 117, 119, 144, 240
civilization, 84, 104, 120, 149, 152, 155, 205, 207, 212, 215, 220, 223, 247, 249–50, 259, 269, 272, 319n99; industrial, 4, 83, 84, 87, 89, 149–50, 155, 201, 202, 222, 225, 227, 229, 272, 273n4, 293n111, 310n179; modern, 31, 35, 37, 210, 214; postindustrial, 34, 151; premodern, 81; scientific and technological, 120, 151, 153; socialist, 104, 111, 204; Soviet union as center of, 8
class, 27–28, 119, 138, 158–60, 164, 167, 182, 187, 243, 247, 262, 278n50, 326n64; alliance between, 166–67; analysis, 127, 137, 158, 169, 243, 311n3; category of, 164, 182; conditions, 130; consciousness, 257; crisis of, 166; differences, 253; enemy, 137, 187–88, 194; institutions, 272; party intelligentsia and, 30, 254–56, 260; nation and, 159–60; popular, 160; as position, 9; progressive, 160, 299n26; roots, 144; ruling, 110; struggle, 23, 27, 119, 144, 147, 159, 187, 189, 210, 309n168, 322n8; working, 14, 167, 171, 217, 219, 230, 257, 260

INDEX

Cohen, Gerald, 48
Collier, Stephen J., 285, 299
communism, 3, 147–48, 167, 268; establishment of, 88; as the future state 203; goal of, 34; humanistic project of, 141; postwar, 173; reform, 174; scientific 26; scientific-technical revolution and, 207; Stalinist idea of, 201; transition from socialism to, 50, 55, 60, 185, 195, 223
Comte, August, 28
Connelly, John, 336
Contradiction, 55; antagonistic and nonantagonistic, 72–73; between ideal and reality, 143, 167; capitalism and, 60, 73, 77, 186; cybernetics and, 100–102, 297n170; dialectical determinism and, 65–66, 70, 74, 93, 97, 103, 113–14, 192–94, 267, 288n54, 289n58, 299n24, 324n21; formal logic and, 96–97, 135; human subjectivity and, 247; Marxist humanism and, 95, 102, 125, 332n19; orthodox Marxism and, 55, 64–65, 73, 91–93; post-Stalinism and, 229, 266, 271, 275n20; socialism and, 24, 185; Stalinism and, 71–72, 185; technooptimism and, 86, 88–89
convergence, theory of, 27, 130
culture, 104, 177, 212, 218, 220, 239, 251, 262, 282n88, 304n95, 308n145, 311n190, 313n30, 323n56, 323n58; bourgeois, 204, 210, 260; as community of God, 179; consumer of, 164; Czech question and, 320n102; European, 244, 251, 260; as free sphere, 211; human, 130; as human activity, 184; as human creative potential, 151; intellectual salons of, 254; Leninist conception of, 36, 160; Marxist humanism and, 33, 165, 217, 220, 232, 283n102, 229n111; modern, 142; modern civilization and, 214, 222, 330n119; modern Czech, 33, 163, 172, 174, 177, 220, 232, 244; modern Czechoslovak, 120; modern socialist, 165, 168, 210, 215, 229n111; nation and, 162, 165, 172, 179, 181, 244, 319n90, 333n35; peaceful coexistence and, 213; replacement with politics, 220, 235; as revolutionary act, 169, 186, 218; Stalinism and, 216, 274n11; Stalinist model of, 211; technology and, 223–24; underground, 340, Western, 212, 306n124. *See also* alienation: modern culture and
Cunow, Heinrich, 287
Cvekl, Jiří, 23, 335
Czech question, 176–78, 244, 334n45; Central Europe and, 178. *See also* culture: Czech question and
Czech Radical Democracy (Česká *radikální demokracie*), 169, 171, 174
Daněk, Oldřich, 335
David-Fox, Michael, 273, 322
Debray, Régis, 239
Deleuze, Gilles, 79, 103, 227, 228, 297
democracy, 252, 261, 319n94, 321n116; integral, 166; interwar, 173, 185, 252; parliamentary, 9, 176; people's, 28, 159, 228; radical, 242, 283n102, 332n26;

INDEX

socialist, 117–79, 179, 265, 266, 311n190, 319n93; Soviet, 318n89
Derrida, Jacques, 227, 228, 331
Descartes, René, 295
Despot, Blaženka, 264
determinism, 62, 112; dialectical, 5, 38, 56, 62, 93, 101, 114, 266, 271, 287n43; Hegelian, 155; historical, 124, 243; mechanical, 60, 189; Stalinist, 134, 191, 243
Dialectics of the Concrete (*Dialektika konkrétního*), 94, 101–2, 138, 219, 234–35, 255, 257, 293n108; critique of, 234, 301n54; Lukács and, 329n111; Patočka and, 267
dialectics, 4, 17, 27, 36, 38, 40, 46–47, 59, 80, 90, 294n131; cybernetics and, 98–99, 101, 296n158; decolonization and, 331n2; Engels and, 91; existentialism and, 124; formal logic and, 96; Hegelian (Hegel's), 90, 92, 186, 193, 227–28, 241, 290n79, 300n29; Lenin and, 92; Marx's, 76, 193, 206; materialist, 63, 93, 103, 227; nature of, 27; negative, 227; post-Stalinist, 59, 92–94, 102, 324n21; Stalinist, 53, 189, 294n132
dialogue, 27, 143, 148, 156, 168, 309n151, 309n168; internal, 146–48; Marxist-Christian, 18, 126–27, 143, 156, 201, 213, 252, 279n54, 301n61; self-reflection and, 156
Doskočil, Zdeněk, 335, 341
Dubská, Irena, 28, 152, 229, 249, 254, 261–64, 279, 302, 311, 338–40
Ducháček, Milan, 314
Duda, Emil, 270
Dunayevskaya, Raya, 127
Durdík, Josef, 317

Effenberger, Vratislav, 326
Ehrenburg, Ilya G., 106
Engels, Friedrich, 20, 32, 48, 53, 54, 56, 91, 93, 102, 141, 287, 288, 289, 311
Epstein, Mikhail N., 330
existentialism, 20, 32, 40, 45, 79, 80, 84, 120, 126, 196, 301n57, 302n65, 319n90; dialectical determinism and, 123; Kosík's criticism of, 81; Marxist humanism and, 124–26, 128, 135, 212, 261, 285n119; Sartre's, 81, 127, 302n72; success of, 121–23; temporality and, 196–7
Feinberg, Joseph Grim, 117, 164, 242, 243, 246, 260, 313, 314
Fellini, Federico, 306
fetishism, 85. *See also* alienation: of man in modern society
feudalism, 189–90, 192, 265, 276n35, 323n11; as economic formation, 189. *See also* capitalism: transition from feudalism to
Feuerbach, Ludwig, 77, 218
Fichte, Johann G., 75
field of thought, 5, 266, 271–72
Filipcová, Blanka, 310
Fischer, Ernst, 33, 212–214
Fišer, Zbyněk (*see* Bondy, Egon), 244, 288
Fitzpatrick, Sheila, 7
Forman, Miloš, 133
Fornet-Betancourt, Raúl, 334
Foucault, Michel, 145, 156, 227, 284, 299
freedom, 9, 119, 131, 141–42, 155, 191, 198, 224, 233, 256, 257, 264, 290n79, 307n137, 320n107; association of, 179; creative, 211; choice of, 129, 142, 154; the hu-

INDEX

man being (human) of, 76, 82, 95, 113, 130, 200, 218, 241, 260, 268, 295n147; existentialist, 124–25; expression of, 18; the individual of, 28, 124, 218; information of, 167; Marxism as philosophy of, 131; necessity and, 141; temporality (present, future) and, 200; spirit of, 75; realm of, 31, 119, 131, 151, 290n79, 304n96; Stalinist, 123

Freud, Sigmund, 138, 140
Frič, Josef Václav, 171, 173, 177
Friedan, Betty, 338
Fritzsche, Peter, 110
Fromm, Erich, 33, 126, 127, 138, 303
Galmiche, Xavier, 181, 317
Garaudy, Roger, 33, 127, 128, 296, 303
Gardavský, Vítězslav, 119, 127, 138, 143–48, 156, 200, 201, 254, 279, 307, 309, 310
Garibaldi, Giuseppe, 318
Genis, Alexander, 325
Gibbs, Josiah W., 324
Gilburd, Eleonory, 4, 274
Godard, Jean-Luc, 306
Goldmann, Lucien, 79, 264, 279, 291
Goldstücker, Eduard, 281
Górny, Maciej, 160, 163, 173
Gottwald, Klement, 29, 30, 188
Gramsci, Antonio, 32, 46, 76, 118, 167, 233–36, 238–40, 290, 329, 331
Graus, František, 283
Grebeníčková, Růžena, 220, 278, 279, 329
Grlić, Danko, 283
Groman, Vladimir G., 50
Guth, Stefan, 275, 278
Háková, Libuše, 338

Halas, Juraj, 285
Hanáková, Petra, 258, 263
Harding, Neil, 29
Hašek, Jaroslav, 79, 133, 136, 212, 244, 251, 291, 340
Havel, Václav, 174, 242, 246, 314
Havelka, Miloš, 284, 312, 317
Havelková, Hana, 258, 322, 339
Havlíček Borovský, Karel, 161, 171, 244, 261
Hayek, Friedrich von, 300
Hegel, Georg W. F., 32, 36, 54, 75, 79, 92–94, 97, 104, 124, 141, 186, 193, 227, 228, 232, 241, 262, 271, 289, 291, 292, 300, 322
Heidegger, Martin, 40, 81, 94, 120, 121, 123–25, 196, 197, 201, 221, 271, 292, 297, 306, 341
Helge, Ladislav, 276
Hellbeck, Jochen, 110
Heller, Ágnes, 283
Hemingway, Ernest, 137, 307, 328, 340
Herbart, Johann F., 162
Herder, Johann G., 164, 246
Hermach, Jiří, 223, 302, 304
Herzen, Alexander I., 158, 162, 318
historical bloc, 167–68, 234–36, 332n25
historical subject, 114, 178, 256, 242, 245, 255; Slovakia and, 320n108
Hochfeld, Julian, 281
Holbach, Paul H. D. von, 32
Horkheimer, Max, 94, 95, 295
Horney, Karen, 303
Hostinský, Otakar, 317
Hrabal, Bohumil, 265
Hrubý, Karel, 283
Hudek, Adam, 276
humanism, 118, 164, 216, 250–51, 256, 265, 268, 306n124, 327n88;

383

INDEX

abstract, 263; antihumanism and, 138; Marxist, 5, 31, 33, 37–38, 43, 84, 119, 123, 128, 130, 134, 143–44, 165, 171, 198, 215, 217, 233, 241, 243, 246–47, 251, 264–66, 271, 274n13, 328n90, 329n111; Masaryk (Masaryk's) and, 170; socialist, 127–28; Stalinist, 110; techno-optimism and, 184, 220, 225

Hus, Jan, 171

Husák, Gustáv, 30, 178, 236

Husserl, Edmund, 267, 292

ideology, 11, 30–31, 44, 140, 210; knowledge and, 145–46; official (party's), 21, 140, 281n86; politics and, 16, 326n67; post-Stalinist, 30; reform communism and, 174; Stalinist, 21; theory and, 210

Ilyenkov, Evald V., 128, 193, 195, 267, 288, 289, 295, 303, 324

inequality, 61, 265; gender, 233, 258, 263, 265; socialism in, 88; social, 233, 263, 265

intelligentsia, 253–54, 2580, 282n82, 337n90; alliance with, 148–49, 167–68, 235; nonparty, 244; party, 6, 18, 20–21, 25, 27, 29–31, 33, 39, 46–47, 59, 143, 168, 174, 185–86, 189, 215, 225, 228, 230–32, 236, 237, 241–42, 249, 251, 253–59, 264–67, 276nn27–28, 278n50, 283n105, 337n90; radical young Stalinist, 165, 169; Russian, 246, 282n82; Serbian, 335n62; Soviet, 251

Janáč, Jiří, 292

Janáček, Leoš, 318, 334

Javůrek, Zdeněk, 38, 39, 62, 96, 195, 196, 229, 295

Jechová, Květa, 258

Jesenská, Milena, 337

Jesenská, Zora, 179

Jirásek, Alois, 172, 312

Jireš, Jaromil, 213

Jodl, Miroslav, 335

Kachyňa, Karel, 307

Kadlecová, Erika, 23, 279

Kafka, Franz, 127, 133, 136, 212, 214, 219, 244, 251, 291, 340

Kalandra, Záviš, 138

Kalivoda, Robert, 13, 32, 124–26, 128, 130, 138–43, 151, 155, 170–73, 176, 177, 181, 190–92, 196, 198–200, 202, 211, 215–18, 220, 224–26, 229, 240, 251, 254, 275, 283, 304, 307–9, 315–17, 319, 323, 328, 329

Kanda, Roman, 23, 278, 280, 312, 329

Kangrga, Milan, 303

Kant, Immanuel, 62, 75–77, 290, 291, 297

Karkov, Nikolay, 246, 249, 251, 336

Kašičková, Michaela, 340

Kautsky, Karl, 44

Khrushchev, Nikita S., 25, 27, 30, 231, 246

Klaučo, Jaromír, 270

Klein, Ota, 155, 156, 182, 229, 259, 263, 330, 338

Klíma, Ivan, 330, 335

Klíma, Ladislav, 172, 316

Klímová, Helena, 261, 263, 264, 338

Klofáč, Jaroslav, 23, 60, 62, 324

Knedlhans Liblínský, Jan, 318

Koestler, Arthur, 298

Kohák, Erazim, 37, 43, 270, 307

Kołakowski, Leszek, 304

Kolář, Pavel, 4, 10, 25, 26, 47, 184, 225, 337

Kolářová, Běla, 258

Kollontai, Alexandra, 108

INDEX

Kolman, Arnošt, 19, 163
Komenský, Jan Amos (Comenius), 171, 316, 319, 340
Kondratiev, Nikolai D., 50, 51
Konrad, Kurt, 177
Kopeček, Michal, 117, 162, 163, 169, 170, 216, 239, 245, 280, 284, 312–15, 333
Korsch, Karl, 32, 44, 53, 90, 233, 323, 331
Kosík, Karel, 32, 35, 40, 43, 45, 46, 77–79, 81, 94–96, 101, 102, 116, 119, 125–28, 131–38, 141–43, 148, 156, 163, 165–71, 173–77, 181, 196–98, 200–202, 209, 210, 212, 218–23, 225, 229, 231, 234–37, 239–42, 244–46, 251, 254, 255, 257, 261, 262, 267–69, 275, 283–85, 287, 291, 293–95, 300, 301, 303, 304, 306, 308, 312–15, 317, 320, 324, 326–29, 331–34, 337, 340, 341
Kotkin, Stephen, 4, 273
Kovanda, Karel, 43
Kozlov, Denis, 4, 273
Kožušník, Čestmír, 285
Krapfl, James, 117
Krępowiecki, Tadeusz, 318
Křesťan, Jiří, 163, 316
Krumbachová, Ester, 258, 263
Krylova, Anna, 29
Krzhizhanovsky, Gleb M., 50
Kundera, Milan, 158, 168, 174–77, 181, 209, 242, 251, 252, 254, 264, 276, 314, 318, 319, 334, 336
Kurella, Alfred, 327
Kuroń, Jacek, 268
Kusák, Alexej, 162, 163, 312, 327
Kusý, Miroslav, 37, 39, 116, 118, 119, 124, 128, 203, 220, 229, 232, 277, 278, 300, 301

labor, 35–36, 85, 88, 97–98, 111, 150–52, 196, 205, 207; abstract, 98, 202, 296n155; division of, 55, 86–87, 98, 118, 152, 217, 224, 243; force (power), 86, 88, 149–50, 204, 206, 214, 294n142, 322n3; industrial society and, 126, 149–50, 152, 201–3, 214; intellectual (mental), 88; time, 35, 66, 89, 98, 151; liberation of, 268; living, 86, 294n142; manual (physical), 87; objectified, 86; praxis and, 130–32, 304n95; private, 66, 73; process, 151; social, 66, 73, 207; specialization, 89; temporality and, 201–3, 324n27; value and, 98, 294n142
Lacan, Jacques, 227, 228
Lakatoš, Michal, 39, 118, 119, 144, 232, 301
Landa, Ivan, 43, 167, 235, 236, 283, 290, 324, 332, 333
law, 49, 56, 59–60, 65, 73, 74, 96, 114, 149, 153, 158, 164, 326n64; causal, 64–65, 103; dialectical, 43, 46–47, 49, 59, 61–62, 65, 66, 70, 74, 76, 92–93, 95, 103, 112–13, 119–20, 123, 137, 187, 267, 287n43, 299n26, 331n11; economic, 50, 52; historical, 26, 28, 31, 38, 51, 69, 74, 82, 83, 92, 106, 111–12, 114–46, 147, 153–54, 156, 166, 192, 195, 198, 253; legal, 24, 28, 54, 98, 118, 182, 232, 278n49, 301n47; logical, 135, 295n153; Marxist (Stalinist) orthodoxy and , 52, 55, 56, 82, 91–92, 112, 103, 123, 194, 294n132, 300n29; natural, 50, 52, 56, 113, 122, 148, 153, 187, 195; necessity and, 60–61, 74, 123;

INDEX

objective reality of, 123; randomness and, 60–61, 123; scientific, 289; social, 56, 129, 107, 122, 137, 148, 154, 187, 210, 299n24; tendency of the rate of profit to fall of, 70, 93; thermodynamics of, 206; uneven development of, 61; value of, 66

leisure time, 35–6, 88–90, 103, 149–52, 155, 182, 222, 224

Lenin, Vladimir I., 14, 15, 20, 21, 44, 56, 57, 83, 92, 93, 107, 108, 129, 158, 160, 162, 167, 174, 186, 187, 219, 230–33, 248, 252, 277, 294, 322, 323, 327, 331, 335

Leninism, 20–21, 29, 39, 43, 187, 230–21; as political theory, 230–32, 235–36, 240; renaissance of, 21, 232

Lévinas, Emmanuel, 331

Liehm, Antonín J., 209, 211, 239, 254, 268, 284, 338

Likavčan, Lukáš, 268, 270

Lipták, Ľubomír, 106, 179, 276, 311

Lišková, Kateřina, 338

Locke, John, 85, 97, 295

Losurdo, Domenico, 6

Lukács, György, 32, 44, 49, 90, 102, 120, 158, 215, 233, 252, 271, 279, 285, 292, 301, 306, 327–29, 331, 340

Lukeš, Klement, 254

Lunacharsky, Anatoly V., 327

Lustig, Arnošt, 264, 335

Luxemburg, Rosa, 167

Macek, Josef, 332

Mácha, Karel, 279

Mácha, Karel Hynek, 171, 318

Machiavelli, Niccolò, 234, 235, 239, 332, 333

Machonin, Pavel, 230, 281, 300

Machovcová, Markéta, 309

Machovec, Milan, 32, 127, 143–48, 156, 170, 171, 201, 269, 270, 279, 309, 313, 316

Man (man, human individual, human being), 36, 52, 77–78, 88, 121–23, 130, 136, 158, 198, 210, 220–21, 242, 255–56, 158, 164, 197, 247, 249, 260, 290n79, 292n98, 297n175, 299n13, 303n83; activity (practical, revolutionary) and, 95, 114, 219, 273n2; as a set of social relations, 133; as active subject, 81, 85, 115–17, 120, 124, 129, 131–32, 134–35, 137, 155, 219; as creator, 78, 80, 81, 149, 154, 179, 212, 219, 290–81n85; as mortal being, 147; as irreducible being (not calculable), 132, 137, 148, 212; as species being, 77–78, 302n69; as the citizen, 117, 119; as the object, 118–19; as the producer, 54, 56, 152, 254; as the subject of, 120; become to, 36; cybernetics and, 134, 207; determination of, 133; distinctive to animals, 77–78; fragmented, 260, 305n110; freedom and, 28, 124, 130, 141, 220; humanization of, 104, 219; individuality of, 85, 117; instinctive nature of, 138–43; institution and, 119, 129, 156, 232; labor activity, 130, 132; labor power and, 152; liberation and, 36–37, 82, 131, 176, 179, 191, 200, 218, 223–24, 233, 247, 300n33; mediation and, 78; modern society and, 26; modern, 81, 138, 263, 308n145; nature and, 36, 76, 130, 195, 268–70, 304n94; nature of, 132, 142; new post-Stalinist, 142,

INDEX

329n111; new socialist (Stalinist, Soviet), 107, 110, 112–13, 254, 325n43; onto-creativity and, 75, 78, 81, 198, 267; ontology of, 126, 329–30n114; philosophy of, 128–29, 300n32, 304n85, 329n112; production and, 86, 88, 151, 153; reduction of, 132, 138; self-realization and, 90, 148, 207; self-transformation (self-education), 152, 155, 254; society and, 89; Stalinism and, 116, 154, 201; things and, 77, 319n99; time and, 196; totality of, 126, 133, 328n90; transcendence and, 146–47, 200; transformation (development) of, 90, 103–4, 110, 133; truly, 135; types of, 142, 215; unity with dialectics, history and, 77; universal definition (abstract) of, 246, 265–66; well-rounded (fully developed, fully realized, total), 31, 128, 141, 149, 183, 216–17, 243, 246–47, 260, 267; women and, 258–62, 264–65; world, 76, 81, 122, 125, 135–37, 213, 333n32. *See also* alienation: of man in modern society

Maňák, Vladimír, 277

Mandler, Emanuel, 319

manipulation, 74–75, 121, 102, 121, 133, 145, 306n121, 332n19; non-manipulation and, 235, 332n19; object of, 135, 138, 255; people of, 74, 131, 235; political (and institutional), 119, 234, 238; ready-made thing of, 221; Stalinist, 118; subject of, 133; technology and, 222, 268, 270; world of, 75, 81. *See also* alienation: manipulation and

Mao Zedong, 331

Márai, Sándor, 336

Marcuse, Herbert, 84, 126, 132, 138–40, 214, 264, 303

Marković, Mihailo, 247, 249, 250

Marks, Sarah, 330

Marx, Karl, 9, 20, 32, 34, 36, 46, 48, 54, 70, 72, 75–78, 88, 91, 96, 97, 102, 113, 123, 130, 138, 141, 158, 160, 214, 257, 269, 270, 290, 291, 293, 294, 296, 302, 309, 311, 318, 323

Marxist-Leninism, 17–18, 26, 43, 91; orthodox, 48, 91; Soviet, 158; Stalinist, 4, 30, 44, 53, 90, 93, 122

Masaryk, Tomáš Garrigue, 167, 170–73, 176, 177, 239, 242, 244, 312, 313, 315–17, 319, 333

Materna, Pavel, 96, 295

Matonoha, Jan, 264

Mayakovsky, Vladimir V., 308

mediation, 31, 98, 289n54, 303n72; dialectical, 93, 102, 153, 288n51; Lenin and, 92; Marxist orthodoxy (mechanical) and, 58–59, 78, 104; post-Stalinist Marxism and, 59, 93, 102, 153, 228, 271; as praxis, 78, 79

Menzel, Jiří, 264, 265, 340

Merleau-Ponty, Maurice, 59, 93, 120, 279, 301

Michňáková, Irena, 262

Mihajlović, Mihajlo, 303

Milošević, Slobodan, 247

Miłosz, Czesław, 336

Mináč, Vladimír, 178, 179, 265, 334

Mlynář, Zdeněk, 30, 39, 117–19, 144, 229, 232, 233–35, 239, 301, 332, 333

Mňačko, Ladislav, 250, 276, 277

INDEX

modernity, 9, 28, 30, 41, 110, 129, 175, 181, 214, 218, 225, 248, 272; capitalist, 183; European, 37, 173, 247, 249; industrial, 205; organized, 4–5, 9, 10–12, 28, 129, 225, 271–72; periodization of, 9; postindustrial, 270; post-Stalinist, 5, 9, 37, 43, 46, 59, 62, 173, 185, 266; reflexive, 275n26; restricted, 9; socialist, 3–5, 9, 11, 18, 20, 31, 69, 73, 106, 185; Soviet, 7–8, 174, 251, 274n9, 275n14; Stalinist, 8, 10, 17, 31, 34, 159, 187, 189, 205, 272; Western, 251
Modzelewski, Karol, 268
Montaigne, Michel de, 32
Možný, Ivo, 258
Mukařovský, Jan, 161, 216, 217, 280, 312, 314
Musilová, Dana, 261, 338
nation, 47, 92, 249–50, 256; as collective subjectivity, 166, 182; folkness and, 164, 226; modern Czech national identity and, 208; nationalism and, 181, 246–47, 335n62; Nejedlý's concept of the Czech nation and, 160, 181, 282n87; the people and, 38, 43, 160, 177, 182–83, 244, 247, 313n27, 318nn88–89; political, 178, 235–36, 255; post-Stalinist, 168, 173–79, 181, 242–46, 253, 257, 265, 313nn27–28; Slovak, 174, 178–79, 320n113; Stalinism and, 159, 164
Nečasová, Denisa, 110, 111, 338
necessity, 52, 60, 75, 89, 107, 130, 152, 155, 176, 182, 185, 200, 206, 215, 222, 239; chance and, 59–61, 141, 191, 294n131; freedom and, 125, 131, 141, 177, 290n79; historical, 116, 121, 200, 202; law and, 60, 74, 113, 123; natural, 75–76; praxis and, 155; realm of, 131, 151; social, 185, 290n79; teleological, 166, 189
Nejedlý, Zdeněk, 33, 42, 49, 159–75, 177, 181, 244, 275, 280, 307, 311–19
Němcová, Božena, 171, 261
Němec, Jiří, 279
neopositivism, 45, 285n119
Neruda, Jan, 169, 171, 174, 175, 318
Nesbitt, Nick, 283
new left, 186, 234, 242, 244
Nezval, Vítězslav, 163
Niederle, Lubor, 159
Nietzsche, Friedrich, 110, 162, 299
Nodl, Martin, 315
Novák, Luděk, 212, 308
Novomeský, Ladislav, 178, 265, 341
Novotný, Antonín, 30, 175, 317
Nový, Lubomír, 3, 27, 78, 82, 176, 230, 239, 290, 306
Oates-Indruchová, Libora, 258, 265
Oittinen, Vesa, 92
Our Current Crisis (Naše nynější krize), 166–67, 176, 235, 239, 242, 245, 269, 319n100
Page, Benjamin, 255
Palacký, František, 160, 171, 173, 177, 244, 313, 333
Pasolini, Pier Paolo, 306
Passer, Ivan, 133
Pasternak, Boris, 47
Patočka, Jan, 261, 262, 267, 319, 334, 339
Pekař, Josef, 177
Pelc, Jan, 340
Petříček, Miroslav, 331
Petrović, Gajo, 303
Picasso, Pablo, 308

INDEX

Pietrangeli, Antonio, 306
Pinsky, Anatoly, 15, 16
Pisarev, Dmitri I., 162
Pithart, Petr, 332
Placáková, Marianna, 258, 261, 263, 337–40
Plekhanov, Georgi V., 53, 54, 56, 91–93, 103, 286, 287, 291
Plíšková, Naděžda, 258
political thought, 229, Central and Eastern Europe in, 162; Czech, 174; Leninism and, 230–31, 236, 238; Masaryk and, 242; reform communism and, 230, 238, 240–41, 331n5
politics, 54, 92, 146; 1968 of, 229, 236–38, 255, 332n6; art and, 211; autonomous, 239; cultural, 120, 165; ideology and, 16, 326n67; Leninism and, 15–16, 230, 232, 235–36, 238, 277n40, 283n102; manipulative techniques and, 234–35, 301n54; modern Czech and, 160; party, 117, 219, 278n50; post-Stalinist party intelligentsia and, 16; post-Stalinist, 118–19, 166, 176–77, 232, 241; as power struggle, 238–39; science and, 210–11; social democratic, 100; Stalinist, 15, 159, 312; technology and, 221; techno-optimism and, 240. *See also* culture: replacement with politics; nation: political
Popelová Otáhalová, Jiřina, 340
Popper, Karl R., 300
positivism, 56, 80, 228
Postone, Moishe, 269
post-Stalinism, 3, 5–9, 11, 16, 25, 245–46, 325n58; "actually existing socialism" and, 24; antinomy of, 271–72; Central and Eastern Europe in, 7; collective subjectivity and, 162, 164–65; Czechoslovak, 5, 11, 21–23, 37, 41, 47, 138, 169, 175, 181, 185, 217, 220, 225, 236, 252, 267; difference to Stalinism, 15–18, 22, 24, 29, 49, 59, 83, 104, 117, 120, 134, 143–45, 154, 156, 164, 170, 186–88, 218, 231, 253–54, 263; as epistemic field, 38, 41, 266, 271; gender and, 258; historicity and, 14; internal plurality and, 31; leisure time and, 149; Leninism and, 232; as modernizing project, 166, 184, 266, 272; nation and, 182; organized modernity and, 5, 10; as overcoming of Stalinism, 29, 62, 153, 174, 216, 219, 228, 234, 267; party intelligentsia and, 241; scientific knowledge and, 15; as self-reflexivity, 12
Prague, 127, 162, 268, 304n97, 322n5, 337n90; centric, 283
praxis, 5, 35–36, 43, 47, 49, 74, 76–79, 81–82, 94, 129, 135–38, 142, 166, 271, 304n94, 306n121; creation and, 131, 135, 148, 267, 271; emancipation and, 216; fetishized, 234; freedom and, 131; genetic side of, 79; and Hegel, 79; history and, 198; Marx and, 123; mediation and, 78; labor (production) and, 130–31, 304n95; as objectifying activity, 94, 135, 137, 198; philosophy of, 76, 80, 138, 141, 155, 198, 291n89, 292nn97–98, 292n101, 331n15; practice and, 273n2; as preontological understanding of being, 297n175; as realization of human being, 198; revolutionary, 219, 233, 234,

INDEX

329n111; subjectivity and, 147, 177; Švejk and, 79, 137
Preisner, Rio, 300, 340
Preobrazhensky, Yevgeni A., 50
Priestland, David, 188
Procházka, Jan, 335
production, 71, 72, 74, 78, 79, 85, 87–89, 104, 115, 149–50, 152, 154, 203, 300n33, 311n90, 336n86; automated, 155, 206–7; capitalist, 70; commercial, 326n59; commodity, 98, 293n111, 323n17; craft, 34; forces of, 27, 34, 38, 49, 54–55, 59, 63–64, 67, 83–84, 86, 88, 90–91, 93, 98, 103, 149, 152, 155, 166, 205, 207, 228, 233, 272, 286n20, 288n51, 290n80; industrial (machine), 71, 86, 152–53, 165, 190, 201–5, 214, 322n3; intellectual, 22–23, 39, 41, 237–38, 253, 256; management of, 115, 299n24; Marxist orthodoxy and, 103; mass, 72; means of, 14, 22, 31, 47, 49, 52, 54–55, 66, 86–87, 119, 150, 158, 166, 186, 188, 191, 193, 214, 217, 243; mode(s) of, 54–55, 64, 72, 84, 98, 151, 186, 188, 190, 323n17; praxis (practice) and, 57, 78, 130; relations (relationships) of, 49, 54–55, 60, 63–65, 71, 83, 91, 248, 286n51; reproduction and, 12, 24, 49, 149–50, 198; socialist, 118; Stalinist planning, 51, 52
Profant, Martin, 247
Průcha, Milan, 43, 79, 127, 128, 155, 229, 291, 301, 302, 329
pseudo-concreteness, 102, 143, 197, 219, 234–36, 255, 301n54, 329n110, 337n93; destruction of, 219, 235, 239
Putík, Jaroslav, 255, 305

Ray, Nicholas, 306
reason (rationality), 10, 28, 75, 94, 122, 145, 152, 167, 176, 200, 300n29, 319n99, 321n121, 295n144; contemplative, 167; cybernetics and, 98, 296n157; dialectical, 94–95, 241, 249, 295n147; European, 269; history of, 95; human, 77, 135; objective, 95; practical, 75; rational, 94–95; Stalinist, 10; subjective, 94; technical, 176, 319n99
reflexivity, 11, 135, 233; late socialist, 24; modernity, 275n26; post-Stalinist, 11–12, 14, 21–22, 24, 230, 245; organized modernity and, 225
Reiman, Michal, 335
Reiman, Pavel, 163, 280
Révai, Josef, 287
revolution, 22, 43, 47, 88, 164, 174, 183–85, 230, 233; bourgeois democratic, 170, 315n57, 322n4, 322n7; French, 9, 191; Hussite, 191, 323n18; cultural, 186, 224; (dis)continuous, 184, 188, 205, 207, 322n4; existential, 239, 329n110; industrial, 34, 130, 132; institutional, 118; political, 87; post-Stalinist, 91, 186; Russian, 44, 298n3; scientific-technical, 27, 34–35, 37, 43, 83–84, 88–89, 149, 151–53, 182–83, 202–3, 205–7, 220–22, 224, 230, 232, 240, 248, 254, 259, 268, 275n26, 329n114, 332n25, 336n86; social, 210, 217, 219, 322n4; socialist, 84, 184, 194; Stalinist, 7–8, 26, 185, 189, 228
Ricardo, David, 66, 85, 95, 97, 293, 296

INDEX

Richta, Radovan, 9, 35, 37, 38, 42, 43, 85–87, 125, 150, 152, 201–7, 222, 225, 229, 240, 254, 259, 268, 276, 282, 284, 287, 293, 304, 310, 311, 322, 325, 330, 333
Rockmore, Tom, 15, 277
Rosenthal, Bernice, 110
Rowley, David G., 14, 15, 277
Ruge, Arnold, 318
Růžička, Jiří, 337
Šabata, Jaroslav, 233, 234, 240, 298, 331
Šabatová, Anna, 298
Sabina, Karel, 171, 318
Šafařík, Josef, 301
Ságlová, Zorka, 258
Saint-Simon, Henri de, 201
Šalda, František X., 315
Šámal, Petr, 163, 169
Šamalík, František, 39, 118, 119, 136, 144, 208, 232–34, 254, 331, 332
Sartre, Jean-Paul, 81, 120, 123–27, 209, 212, 213, 302, 303, 338
Satterwhite, James H., 5, 274
Schaff, Adam, 127, 128, 303, 304
Schauer, Hubert Gordon, 175
Scheler, Max, 305
Schelling, Friedrich W., 75
Schmarc, Vít, 22
science 10, 36, 54, 87, 109, 128, 147, 77, 182, 202, 204, 213, 217, 222, 257, 259; art and, 16, 326n64; autonomy of, 278n52; civilizational role of, 270; cybernetics and, 99; bourgeois, 204, 248; as force of production, 27, 31, 34, 88, 90, 103, 206–7, 241, 254; as human activity (creative potentiality), 151, 184; ideology and, 145; Leninism and, 187; limits of, 133–35, 220–21, 224, 269–70; 305n110, 305n116; manipulation and, 270, 330n119, 332n19; modern, 79–80, 84, 94, 122, 150–51; party's position on, 15; politics and, 210, 229; production and, 88, 149; social 42–43; Stalinism and, 15, 187; technology and, 5, 35, 74, 76, 84, 89, 203; revolution (change) and, 33, 35, 208, 221–23
Second International, 4, 36, 44, 48, 59, 100, 112, 129, 194, 259; orthodox Marxism of, 44, 53, 64, 266; Soviet Marxism and, 44
Selucký, Radoslav, 36, 43, 222, 223, 229, 254, 310, 335
Shore, Marci, 312
Shostakovich, Dmitri D., 308
Šik, Ota, 45, 285, 333
Šíma, Rudolf, 304, 341
Šindelář, Jan, 338
Skilling, H. Gordon, 3, 21
Skinner, Quentin, 25
Škvorecký, Josef, 264
Slačálek, Ondřej, 336
Slánský, Rudolf, 163
Slejška, Dragoslav, 43, 259, 260
Šmahel, František, 316
Šmeral, Bohumír, 174, 239, 317
Smetana, Bedřich, 162, 169, 170, 174, 175, 312, 315, 318, 319
Smíšek, Jan, 300
Smith, Adam, 85
Sobotka, Milan, 74, 76
Sochor, Lubomír, 233, 236, 239, 286, 290, 331, 332
socialism, 14, 17, 21, 24, 28, 36, 86–88, 218; "actually existing," 3, 11–12, 22–24, 232, 238–41, 248, 252, 258, 265–66, 268; art and, 210; building of, 3, 17, 57, 71, 73, 107, 116, 144, 154, 160,

186–88, 254; class struggle under, 187, 189; cybernetic system and, 206; Czechoslovak, 129, 176, 220, 243, 263; democratic, 33, 168–69, 175, 181, 192, 235, 239, 243, 268; deformation of, 71–73, 275n14; destructive tendencies within, 215, 217; development of, 3–4, 31, 99, 117, 185, 220, 224; as economic formation, 189, 191, 248; establishment (establishing) of 50–51, 117, 146, 186; goal of, 34, 204, 243; history of, 165; human face with, 21, 120, 239, 333n39; humanization of, 118, 155; late, 10, 24; liberation and, 221; modeling of, 20; as modern social form (modern), 166, 171, 182, 249; nation and, 178, 239; national (Czechoslovak) path to, 17, 174, 249, 252, 274n9, 317n82; nonantagonistic contradictions of, 72, 194–95; party and, 16; present state of (post-Stalinist), 27, 33, 153, 200, 203, 214, 218, 228, 247; proclamation of, 10, 12, 25, 27–28, 40, 129, 182, 228; realization of, 154; Soviet, 10, 173; Stalinist, 70, 73, 83, 185, 191, 247; state, 7, 9, 11–12, 14, 24, 30, 208, 229, 233, 258, 264, 267–68; superiority of, 248, 253; technocratic, 37; transition from capitalism to, 60, 195; transition from people's democracy to, 159; varieties of, 228; visions (new interpretations) of, 45, 140, 155, 191, 208, 228. *See also* capitalism and socialism
socialist (Marxist) libertinism, 141–43, 151, 155, 198, 200, 307–8n137

Sommer, Vítězslav, 5, 23, 24, 129, 203, 240, 280, 296, 333
Spurný, Matěj, 341
Stalin, Joseph, V. 3, 6, 10, 12, 15–17, 20, 21, 23, 26, 29, 30, 40, 52, 53, 59, 61, 87, 90, 91, 107, 108, 111, 118, 160–62, 174, 186–89, 216, 251, 253, 285, 287, 292, 312, 331
Stalinism 4, 9–10, 14–18, 22–3, 25–26, 38, 49–50, 52, 59, 61, 69, 74, 100, 106, 109–11, 115, 132, 144–46, 159, 185, 198; as abrupt change, 188, 205, 302n4; capitalism and, 73, 132, 144, 186; Central and Eastern Europe in, 7–8, 17, 42; Christianity and, 156; crisis of, 4; critique of, 38, 42, 44, 72, 84, 86, 112, 117, 127, 144, 178, 189, 193–94, 196–97, 201, 250–51, 275n14, 276n35, 312n24; demise of, 3, 33, 59; Czechoslovak, 22, 41, 49, 159–60, 162, 253, 280n63, 283n105; experience with, 176; folkness and, 33; historical continuity and, 252; as ideology of modernization, 4; as ideological formation, 109; institutions and, 20, 22; intelligentsia and, 30; late, 7, 111, 273n6; legacy of, 36; liberal critique of, 300n29; Marxism and, 43; modernity and, 8, 110, 205, 272, 275n4; as organized modernity, 10, 272; orthodoxy (Marxist orthodoxy), 44, 72, 102, 114, 130, 137, 208, 226, 266, 277n40; party and, 124; Soviet, 7, 10, 162; thaw and, 10; women's emancipation and, 258. *See also* post-Stalinism: as overcoming of Stalinism; post-Stalinism: difference to Stalinism

Starý, Oldřich, 330
Steila, Daniela, 14
Števček, Pavol, 179
Štoll, Ladislav 163
Strinka, Július, 179, 229
Střítecký, Jaroslav, 174, 242, 257, 260, 335
Strumilin, Stanislav G., 50–52
subject (subjectivity), 41, 43, 47, 65, 76, 85, 88, 94, 101, 105, 112, 114, 116, 120, 123, 125–26, 135, 142, 144, 146, 148, 151, 153, 156, 187, 217, 264, 310n176; abstract, 148, 150–51; active (engaged), 57, 115, 145–46, 148, 156, 179, 210, 290n79; artistic, 217; atheist conception of, 147; autonomous, 85, 117, 232; capital of, 85, 293n108, 293n111; choice of, 129; collective (as nation), 156, 158–59, 162, 164, 166, 170, 173, 177–79, 182–83, 242–43, 245, 247, 276n35, 320n110; creation of, 168; decision of, 115, 154; dialogue and, 146; education of, 152, 155; epistemological (of knowledge, of cognition), 15, 56–57, 107, 112, 120, 115, 151, 253–24, 287n31; existentialist, 123, 125; historical, 114, 148, 155–56, 178, 236, 242, 245, 255, 276n35, 320n108, 320n110; human, 22, 31, 35, 47, 85, 106, 112–13, 116, 119, 121, 124–26, 129, 131–32, 134, 137, 143, 149–55, 153, 164, 203, 247, 256, 306n121; individual, 23, 147, 156, 158, 164, 177, 243; judgement (Kant) of, 291n86; legal, 152; leisure time of, 310n176; Leninist, 28; manipulable, 133; mediation and, 153; modern, 132, 142; object and, 76–77, 79, 84–85, 101, 104, 148, 150–51, 203, 270, 290n85, 296n167; ontology and, 129; political, 113, 119, 168; post-Stalinist, 4, 49, 115, 130, 144, 149, 153–54, 156–57, 164, 210, 226, 302n65; revolutionary, 12, 33, 114–15, 123, 203, 206, 217, 221, 257; socialist, 113, 154, 112, 119; as sociological factor, 270, 297n175; Stalinist, 107, 109, 111–12, 116, 124, 133

Šulc, Zdislav, 184, 204, 333, 336
Sus, Oleg, 302, 303
Švankmajerová, Eva, 258
Švecová, Soňa, 258
Sviták, Ivan, 26, 27, 32, 57, 58, 104, 125, 127, 130–35, 137, 138, 142, 155, 170, 172, 210, 211, 213, 215, 216, 218, 220, 221, 229, 231, 239, 245, 251, 254, 260–65, 268, 275, 278, 281, 305, 306, 323, 336, 337, 339, 340
Svoboda, Miloš, 23, 60, 324
Sychra, Antonín, 210
Tatarka, Dominik, 179–81, 276, 305, 321
Teige, Karel, 138, 166, 172, 200, 308, 329
temporality, 185, 196; humanist conception of, 201; labor and, 196, 202; post-Stalinism and, 6, 196; revolutionary forms of, 198; Stalinist conception of, 101
Tenzer, Oliver, 97
Tesař, Jan, 334
the people (*lid*), 159–60, 164–68, 236, 244, 311n4 and 12; democratism and, 174; folkness (*lidovost*) and, 158–59, 164, 169, 173; revolutionary, 235; urban proletariat

and, 166. *See also* nation: the
people and
thing, 197; manipulative, 58, 74;
ready-made, 78, 80–81, 197
Tlustý, Vojtěch, 23, 60, 62, 324
Todorova, Marie N., 336
Togliatti, Palmiro, 234
totality (as a concept), 43, 47, 49, 59,
63, 70, 92, 95, 104, 132, 221, 241,
289n58, 295n147, 297n176; concrete, 102, 169, 195, 219, 314n53;
dialectical, 192–93; human being
(Man) and, 35, 48, 126, 128, 133,
200, 260, 328n90; interaction
and, 63; national life of, 176;
reason (rationality) and, 94–95,
200; as social and historical formation, 66, 71, 98, 192, 193; and
Stalinist orthodoxy, 72; system
and, 70, 101, 193
Touraine, Alain, 10, 12, 14, 18, 29,
42, 144, 225
Traine, Martin, 334
Trnka, Jiří, 330
Trotsky, Leon D., 327
Truffaut, François, 306
Tvardovskii, Alexandr T., 15, 16, 325

Vaculík, Ludvík, 264, 326
Vail, Petr, 246
Valiavicharska, Zhivka, 243, 246
Vercors (Bruller, Jean), 306
Vodička, Felix, 280, 320, 314, 320
Voříšek, Michael, 41, 230, 253, 254,
257, 281, 284, 287, 335, 336
Vranicki, Predrag, 260, 303
Wagner, Peter, 4, 9, 10, 11, 12, 109,
129, 216, 225, 271
Wagner, Richard, 162
Wagnerová, Alena, 41
Wajda, Andrzej, 307
Weber, Max, 10
Western Marxism, 33, 37, 84
Wiener, Norbert, 34, 324
Williams, Kieran, 117
Yadov, Vladimir, A. 281
Zelený, Jindřich, 23, 38, 60–62,
74–76, 286, 287, 290
Zeman, Jiří, 99, 101, 296, 297
Zíbrt, Čeněk, 159
Žižka, Jan, 168, 173
Zumr, Josef, 32, 126, 171–73, 176,
220, 229, 254, 307, 315–17, 326,
329
Zumrová, Jiřina, 326